FOUNDING GENERATIONS

Democracy's Origins and Parallels
in America and India

SIDDHARTH

Copyright©2021 Siddharth Siddharth

ISBN: 978-1-62249-594-8

Published by
Biblio Publishing
Columbus, Ohio
BiblioPublishing.com

To
Babaji
who is no more

EVENTS TIMELINE – AMERICA

Year	Key Event	Benjamin Franklin	George Washington
1754	French and Indian War begins	Publishes "*Join, or Die*" cartoon and appeals for unity between the colonies	Inadvertently starts the war
1765	British Parliament passes the Stamp Act	Campaigns in London to get the Stamp Act repealed	
1773	Boston Tea Party	Converts to the American cause	Enraged at the turn of events
1775	Second Continental Congress convenes	Fiercely advocates to declare Independence	Named Commander-in-chief of the Continental Army
1776	Congress declares Independence on July 4	Serves on various committees	
1778	Treaty of Alliance with France	Plays key diplomatic role	Leads the American forces on the battlefield
1783	Treaty of Paris acknowledges American Independence	Plays key diplomatic role	
1786	Virginia Statute for Religious Freedom		
1787	Constitutional Convention	Delegate to the Convention	Presides over the Convention
1789	Government under the U.S. Constitution begins		Elected the first president
1796-97	First peaceful transition of power		Publishes the Farewell Address and goes into retirement
1800-01	Second peaceful transition of power, first between rival political parties		
1803	The Louisiana Purchase		

John Adams	Thomas Jefferson	James Madison	Alexander Hamilton
Enraged at the turn of events			
Fiercely advocates to declare Independence			
Serves on various committees	Writes the Declaration of Independence		
Plays key diplomatic role			
	Was drafted by him in 1777	Plays key role in getting it enacted	
Ambassador to Great Britain	Ambassador to France	Central role in making the Convention a success	Collaborates with Madison on *The Federalist Papers* to gather support for Constitution's ratification
Elected the first vice president	First Secretary of State	A very powerful member of Congress	First Secretary of the Treasury
Elected the second president	Elected the second vice president. Discreetly also the key Opposition leader	Jefferson's key collaborator in the Opposition	Opposes both Adams and Jefferson
Averts a war with France	Elected the third president	Secretary of State to Jefferson	Politically downhill by now
	Uses his authority to see the purchase through	Plays key role	

EVENTS TIMELINE – INDIA

Year	Key Event	Mohandas Gandhi	Vallabhbhai Patel
1915		Returns to India from South Africa	
1920-22	Non-Cooperation Movement	Emerges as the leader of the freedom struggle	Becomes Gandhi's trusted aide
1930	Purna Swaraj/Declaration of Independence	Launches the Civil Disobedience Movement with the Salt March	Emerges as Gandhi's chief lieutenant
1932	Poona Pact	Goes on fast unto death in prison over the issue of separate electorate for the Untouchables	Incarcerated by the British
1937	Provincial Elections held under the British auspices	Focused mostly on social issues rather than active politics during this period	Emerges as a very powerful leader of the Congress Party
1942	Quit India Movement	Incarcerated until 1944 by the British	Incarcerated by the British
1947	India gets Independence on August 15 but is also partitioned		First Home Minister of Independent India. Plays key role in the territorial integration of India
1947-49	Important Debates in the Constituent Assembly	Assassinated in 1948	Plays key role in various debates around Fundamental Rights, Abolition of Zamindaris, Reservation, etc.
1954-56	Hindu Code Bills are passed in the Parliament		
1956	Creation of linguistic states		
1959	Swatantra Party is formed		

C. Rajagopalachari	Jawaharlal Nehru	B. R. Ambedkar	Subhas Bose
Already in awe of Gandhi			
Leads the movement in South India	Emerges as a young leader		
	Hoists the national flag as Congress Party's president		Emerges as a young leader
Plays key role in bringing Gandhi and Ambedkar on the same page	Incarcerated by the British	Opposes Gandhi and emerges as the leader of the Untouchables	Incarcerated by the British
	Emerges as a popular leader with a pan-Indian appeal	Fights the elections against the Congress Party	Elected the president of the Congress the next year to be ousted from the presidency in 1939
Proposes the Rajaji Formula to start discussions with the Muslim League but is rebuffed	Incarcerated by the British		Establishes the Indian National Army and fights against the Allied Forces with support from the Axis powers
First Governor of West Bengal	First Prime Minister of Independent India	First Law Minister of Independent India	
	Plays key role in various debates around National Language, Linguistic Provinces, Hindu Code, etc.	Chief draftsman of the Constitution	
	Plays key role in the passage of the bills	Had earlier drafted the Hindu Code Bills	
	Accedes to the demand		
Chief force behind the Swatantra Party	Pursues centralization and socialist policies		

CONTENTS

Preface	1
1. Minorities	29
2. Power	89
3. Opposition	145
4. Equality	203
5. Nationalism	259
6. Compromises	317
Epilogue	373
Acknowledgments	383
About the Author	385

PREFACE

2021 started with a bang when the United States Capitol was stormed by a violent mob in the first week of the new year. What unfolded on January 6 in Washington, D.C. shocked the entire world. As armed protestors violently stormed the Capitol to demand the overturning of the presidential election results, legislators had to be evacuated for saving their lives. American democracy thus suffered an irreparable blow to its integrity and esteem. The American democracy had always justly prided itself for its more than two-centuries-old record of the peaceful transition of power. But, the events of January 6, 2021, shook the foundation of this fundamental feature of American democracy.

Two months later, the non-profit organization Freedom House released its annual report which downgraded India's democracy from free to partly free. This happened for the first time in more than thirty years. Otherwise, a glowing exception in Asia for its robust and healthy democratic practices, India's score on the freedom index has steadily and swiftly decreased from 77 in 2018 to 67 in 2021. Similarly, Sweden's V-Dem's Institute also listed India among the top ten nations most quickly sliding toward becoming autocracies. The chief factors leading to this decline have been the unprecedented number of people charged with the colonial-era sedition law by the incumbent government and its treatment of the Muslim minority. Many political observers today believe that the pluralistic spirit of the Indian democracy is under multiple attacks spearheaded by the government's stringent crackdown on the freedom of expression and dissent.

We are thus living in a turbulent era in which the rise of an authoritarian China and the ongoing COVID-19 pandemic have further accelerated multiple social, economic, and political processes. Nobody knows where all this will lead to. It may well be that this tempestuous period may prove to be the harbinger of a major transition in the world and for the fate of democracy as an institution of governance. It is thus natural to look back to the past, specifically to the origin of democracy in the world's oldest democratic nation, the United States of America, and the world's largest democratic nation, India, in the hope of gaining a guiding light as we embark toward an uncertain future. This book is a quest in the above direction.

The Oxford English Dictionary defines the noun *Nation* as *A community of people of mainly common descent, history, language, etc., forming a state or inhabiting a territory.*[1] The definition appears to be cogent and yet on a closer inspection stands falsified when applied to the world's oldest democratic nation (the United States of America) and to the world's largest democratic nation (India). This is because neither of these nations was founded on the European model of nationalism which is based on affiliation with a particular language, religion, culture, or common descent. Both of these nations are highly diverse along many axes such as geography, ethnicity, religion, language (India, more so), culture, cuisine, and political ideology. In the case of both these nations, the enormous diversity under one nation's dwelling can be attributed to the peculiar circumstances during the birth of the nation as a republic. This is because the institutions of governance of the nation were founded with the creation of a republic. These institutions fashioned by the nation's founding fathers played a major role in sustaining and flourishing the nation's diversity. Furthermore, in addition to diversity, there are four obvious historical parallels that set these two nations apart from most other democracies.

First, in both nations, birth as a republic was a clear break from the past. In America, before the Revolutionary War (American War of Independence), the thirteen colonies were more or less dependent on their mother country Britain for everything from trade to governance. The inhabitants of these colonies were loyal subjects of the British monarch. The swift victory in the Revolutionary War heralded a new beginning for the colonies. The establishment of a republican government by these states (former colonies) was a pivotal moment in human history since the American republic was unprecedented in scale compared to any other republic in the history of the world. This republican experiment ushered new ideas about self-rule on the world stage. Since this political revolution happened at a time when the world was saturated with monarchies and despotism, the significance of the American Revolution can never be underestimated.

In India too, the rapid culmination of the freedom struggle meant that the political elite procured a clean slate to inscribe their ideas. For centuries, India had been a most unequal society, plagued with inequalities along caste and religion. In the eighteenth century, from the lap of fratricidal Mughal emperors, India had fallen into the arms of equally brutish European colonialists. Across centuries, India had maintained a distinct cultural identity. But, it was the British under whom the whole of the Indian subcontinent became a single administrative unit. However, the British form of governance was, well, British. It was the most extractive form of colonial administration whose primary interest in India was economic. In multiple social and economic aspects, the British left India in much the same condition as they had found her. Thus, after independence, the arrival of the republican government in India with the universal adult franchise (a first for just born nation) was not conducive to the socio-economic conditions of the nation. 'Democracy in India is only a top-dressing on an Indian soil, which is essentially undemocratic,' remarked B. R. Ambedkar, one of the Indian founding fathers, while introducing the draft constitution.[2] The policy of one-person one-vote was antithetical to the deeply rooted caste and creed prejudices. This meant that the founders played a bet on India's future by trusting a population that had no experience of self-rule. Hence, in both nations, it was as if history halted for a brief moment around the founding to put a period, before resuming again. Though this can also be said for some other former European colonies, most of them had to undergo iterations of dictatorship, civil war, or monarchy before they transformed into stable democracies—and none were as large and diverse as India or the United States.

Second, both nations were born amidst highly adverse circumstances. Americans fought the war against the most powerful empire of the world. Without the benefit of hindsight, American victory in the war was by no means certain. Thousands of American revolutionaries died fighting in the war (while even more were claimed by smallpox). The American forces were no match for the battle-hardened British troops and neither could the thirteen colonies, loosely aligned together by the Articles of Confederation (a weak constitution instituted after the war had begun), raise economic and warfare resources commensurate with the British empire. The newly born nation had no professional army or navy and no financial institutions such as banks or a Department of Treasury to establish credit. Thus, when the war ended, the nation found itself not only bankrupt but also under huge foreign debt. After the peace was established, in the absence of a common sense of purpose or history of common governance, the thirteen states started drifting apart and becoming entangled in disputes over trade and territory. There was no executive authority that could govern the whole nation and pay back the war debt. Later, with the creation of a republic, the nation stepped towards an uncharted territory surrounded by the colonies of wily European monarchies. Finally, soon after the French Revolution, Britain and France were again at war. With fraternal and ideological ties to both Britain and France, the newly forged American Republic found itself spiraling towards the European conflict.

The Republic of India was born amidst the tremors of partition which triggered the largest human migration in the history of mankind and unleashed violence in which more than a million perished. The displacement of over 14 million people created a refugee crisis that imposed a heavy burden on the state. The newly established upstart nation was one of the most impoverished and poor countries in the world with a mostly illiterate population. The nation was dependent on foreign aid for basic provisions such as food and security. Its administration contained stains of the abusive colonial police-state and the armed forces bequeathed to the infant nation by the British had a long history of being employed against the population.[3] Furthermore, the nation's territory was dotted with more than 560 political units (some as large as European nations—both in size and population) which had their own administrations during the British era. Many of these so-called princely states were now flirting with the notion of their own independence. The nation had no history of republican government. It had tens of linguistic groups (with many languages having their own script) and millions of people belonging to different ethnicities, divided along caste hierarchy, and following all the major religions of the world. Finally, the newborn nation was under attack from its neighbor Pakistan while it was confronting the anti-democratic forces from the extreme right (Hindu communalism) and the extreme left (communism). Shortly after Independence, the Communist Party of India had declared war against the infant Indian state.[4]

Third, it is striking that the nationalism fostered in both nations under such perilous circumstances averted the most probable outcome—anarchy. Instead of chaos, these tumultuous times gave way to the founding of political institutions that united the nation. American historians widely believe that America was founded twice. Historian Joseph Ellis writes, 'There were really two founding moments: the first in 1776, which declared American independence, and the second in 1787-88, which declared American nationhood.'[5] The second founding refers to the ratification of the constitution drafted by the Constitutional Convention in Philadelphia. This constitution united the states under a federal government and thus brought them together. It is a fact of utmost wonder that even after 230 years of the ratification, the basic structure of the American constitution and governance remains the same. However, in 1788, the survival of the new government was far from certain. The Constitutional Convention is a story of multiple compromises between the states and of the expression of opinions about governance which ranged from adopting a British-style monarchy to pursuing no changes in the Articles of Confederation.[6] The constitution finally drafted through compromises over power-sharing between the federal and state governments became an inspiration for many constitutions around the world. In a first, the constitution directed the separation of state and religion, and clearly defined separation of powers between the three arms of government—executive, legislature, and judiciary. It was the political institutions established by this constitution that paved the way to unite the nation, install financial institutions to bind the colonies together and establish credit, pay the foreign debt, and most importantly, the success of the republican experiment. To scupper the possibility of descent towards monarchy, or even worse—anarchy, the founders later interpreted the constitution in a flexible manner to bolster the institutions of governance, as we shall see in the following chapters.

Granville Austin, historian of the Indian constitution writes about its framing that it 'was perhaps the greatest political venture since that originated in Philadelphia in 1787 [referring to the drafting of the American Constitution].'[7] The constitution of India, after many compromises between the delegates, bound the whole nation to form a Union while making provisions for all minorities—across religion, caste, language, and tribe. In a highly unequal society dependent mostly on agriculture, the constitution made provisions for land redistribution. Furthermore, it made India the first nation to provide universal adult franchise to all its inhabitants right from the republic's creation. In fact, every adult Indian citizen received the right to vote more than a decade before the civil rights movement forced the American administration to provide the same to African Americans by removing the system of disenfranchisement targeted toward them. Thus, the constitution paved the way for a social revolution simultaneously with a political one. A major achievement of the constitution was that it facilitated for each citizen the flexibility to cultivate multiple identities—based on loyalty to their own linguistic group, religion, and community—while being identified as an Indian. The political integration of India i.e. assimilating the 562 princely states of British India to the Union of India was the other significant step that was successfully executed to forestall the plummet into pandemonium. The process of Indianization of the British Army with definitive civilian control and the commitment of the constitution to secular values were other factors that helped in establishing the legitimacy of the national government in India. Finally, one personality, that of Jawaharlal Nehru, played a major role in holding India together during the crucial years after independence (a role similarly played by George Washington as president of the newly born United States of America).

Fourth, in both nations, amidst such tempestuous circumstances, there came forward a generation of leaders who nurtured their fledgling republic in many ways. In fact, it can be argued persuasively that, but for these leaders, the two nations would not have come into being in their present form. No single leader in either nation can be addressed as the sole founder of the nation. In America, the historical positioning allowed the founding generation to show unrestrained creativity in establishing the republic. This is because everything from establishing republican traditions to setting up a secular state was a novel venture. In the words of one of the founding fathers John Adams

> It has been the will of Heaven that we should be thrown into existence at a period when the greatest philosophers and law-givers of antiquity would have wished to live. A period when a coincidence of circumstances without example, has afforded to thirteen Colonies, at once, an opportunity of beginning government anew from the foundation, and building as they choose.[8]

No founding father could have done everything alone. The founding fathers played crucial roles in all the major events (sometimes alone, sometimes in collaboration with each other, and sometimes in opposition to each other) from the time of the Revolutionary War to the formation of political parties.

In India, the founding generation (especially Mohandas Gandhi) devised methods of non-violent struggle towards achieving Independence from Britain and then utilized its unique position of leadership to create a framework for political and social revolution. It is notable that though both nations have a single founding father positioned above the rest (George Washington in America and Mohandas Gandhi in India), it was only due to the collective effort by the founding generation that history came into being. This was unlike many other nations such as China, Russia, or Turkey where autocracy dominated the modern nation's founding era. Just like the American founding generation, each Indian founding father had his own methods to achieve the shared goals (as we shall see later in the book). The Indian founding fathers often worked in tandem but sometimes positioned themselves against each other, leading to healthy debates between their competing ideas of nationhood. In both nations, as a consequence of the extensive roles played by the two founding generations, we can trace the origin of the current political and social institutions to a specific and short period of time. This is unlike nations such as the United Kingdom, France, Germany, and Italy where multiple iterations of political and social changes across generations brought about the present institutions of governance.

Taken together the above four parallels in history are scarcely true for any other nation. Furthermore, for both nations, during the founding era, foreigners painted a grim view of the future by predicting the impossibility of the republic's survival. Fortunately, both the United States of America and India successfully emerged as outliers in being able to achieve the confluence of all sorts of diversities with nationhood within a republican establishment.

The founding generation of each nation was composed of astute leaders who were men of letters as well as men of action. They expressed their thoughts and ideas in the form of books, essays, and orations. But, they were not content with the vocal expression only. They worked hard towards realizing their political ideas. Yet, they were thinkers first and politicians second. Politics came to them as a means of attaining their objectives. In both nations, as we shall see in this book, the founders not only gave expression to their thoughts but used all means of politics and compromises to sculpt the republic of their conception.

It is an oft-asked question in America that how a population of less than 3 million (equivalent to that of Chicago today) residing in a political backwater compared to Europe, produced an extraordinary array of leaders who ushered a political revolution that changed the form of governance across the world. This question touches on the debate around the "great man theory," which hypothesizes if history can be largely explained by the impact of great men. With self-reflection on this question in the Indian context, Nehru wrote, 'We are little men serving great causes, but because the cause is great, something of that greatness falls upon us also.'[9] We may not be able to answer the question but we can surely say that the role played by the founding generation (whether that of India or of America) remains distinct and above that of all succeeding generations because of its positioning as being the first. In both nations, a constant process of debate and dissension underwent between the founding fathers. These debates shaped their views which in turn shaped the two nations. As historian Paul Johnson writes about the American founding fathers, '[W]hat was particularly providential was the way in which their strengths and weaknesses compensated each other, so that the group as a whole was infinitely more formidable than the sum of its parts.'[10]

The world's largest and its oldest democracy have never been so intimately connected in every respect as they are now. A decade ago, former American President Barack Obama proclaimed India and the United States as "natural allies" in the 21st century.[11] However, as we saw above, in ways more than one, the historical trajectory of these democracies already had many parallels. There is much for both nations to learn from each other's history, especially from the two founding generations.

Both nations have a keen sense of their history which they tend to ruminate, understand, absorb, debate, evaluate, re-evaluate, and re-re-evaluate through an ever-growing amount of literature. The interest in their own founding fathers has been ever-increasing in both nations. The founding fathers are often eulogized, sometimes denounced, but are never forgotten. They have become heroes in the national pantheon. Every year, in both nations, many works are published about their own founding fathers. The motives of these works vary from venerating these historical figures to debating their political ideas to excoriating their actions to vilifying their personal lives. In addition to the scholarly research, the largest contributing factor which drives this tendency is that every single political debate in each nation still invokes arguments from the founding era. Since the present institutions of government trace their ancestry to the times when their seeds were sowed and watered by the founding generation, the lawmakers in each nation still debate the political actions and intentions of the founding fathers.

In America, the founding generation has been mythologized like in no other nation. The founding fathers have become wise superhumans so much so that no other political elite in the world is thought to come close to them. In a way, this is natural since the founding fathers of America are characters from a very distant past—from the times which we can only imagine and endeavor to comprehend but never fully interpret. Millions of Americans flock to the Washington Monument on the National Mall and the Jefferson Memorial every year to pay homage to these figures. There are television series, movies, and musicals that bring alive the founders for the present generation while books on the founding fathers trend at the top on bestseller lists. Furthermore, based on its policies, the ruling government adopts and discards the founders as per its need (for example, Alexander Hamilton was adopted by Theodore Roosevelt and discarded for Thomas Jefferson by Franklin Roosevelt). The founding fathers pervade every aspect of American life—from the means of entertainment to banknotes and governance.

In India, the founding fathers are not so chronologically distant as to be so much mythologized as in America. After all, there still exists a generation that has seen them in person. The members of the founding generation have been selectively adopted by different political and social groups for their own agendas. Still, from the debates in the national parliament to the roadside discussions over tea in a village, the founding fathers and their actions are often invoked. Their birthdays are celebrated with pomp by their admirers with governments across the nation honoring them. Unfortunately, since the haze of wonder and mythology has not fully subsumed the founding generation yet, the founding fathers are viewed as individuals and not the noun, *Indian Founding Fathers.* Nevertheless, like America, the Indian founding fathers remain very popular in print, theater, and television. Their actions and thoughts are adduced to and quoted in every general election by prospective candidates. Finally, just like America, every government has its own favorite founding fathers. We may ask then that why do our present leaders seek to obtain the legitimacy for their actions from the founding fathers? Robert Kraynak has succinctly summarized this tendency of looking back at the American founding fathers which can be applied to the Indian founding fathers too. He writes

> [A] deeper reason for the perennial fascination with the American Founders is the need to justify our political principles today—to explain why the principles we live by are "legitimate" in the ultimate sense of being right, just, or true. The search for legitimizing principles takes many forms, but one form is to try to prove that "the Founders are on your side"—meaning, your view of government and vision of America are in accordance with the Founding Fathers' view, or with one of their members.[12]

So, the question arises that what exactly were the achievements of these two founding generations which have made them so relevant in the everyday lives of Americans and Indians respectively? The

British philosopher and essayist Alfred North Whitehead once remarked that 'there have been only two instances in the history of Western Civilization when the political leaders of an emerging nation behaved as well as anyone could reasonably expect. The first was Rome under Caesar Augustus and the second was America's revolutionary generation.'[13] Whitehead so remarked because the American founding generation set up many firsts. It came out with flying colors in the nearly impossible task of winning a war against the world's most powerful empire, then went on to forge a nation from thirteen states that had no common history of governance, established the world's first nation-sized republic of the modern era, established a wholly secular state, and (inadvertently) kick-started the process that led to the formation of modern political parties.[14] Had they attained success in only one of the above five undertakings, they would have still merited a prominent mention in world history for themselves. And yet, they were able to achieve all of the above in their own lifetime. They utilized the twin factors of geography (America's isolation from the Old World with unbounded territory towards the west) and the ideas unleashed during those times in what later came to be known as "the Enlightenment," to lay the foundation of the modern American nation. The political revolution started by the American founding fathers inaugurated a system of governance that has been adopted the world over in one form or another.

Commenting on India's success as a democracy, Sunil Khilnani wrote two decades ago

> [T]he history of independent India appears as the third moment in the great democratic experiment launched at the end of the eighteenth century by the American and French revolutions...Each of these experiments released immense energies...The Indian experiment is still in its early stages, and its outcome may well turn out to be the most significant of them all, partly because of its sheer human scale...[15]

The political elite of India forged common nationalism among its citizens, adopted a constitution that has stood the test of time despite the mindboggling diversity of the nation, made India the first nation in history to provide universal adult franchise while taking birth, politically integrated the 562 princely states into a single administrative unit, and successfully replaced the economically extractive British police-state colony by an economically flourishing democratic republic. Increasingly, many nations in Asia and Africa plagued with single-party domination and military dictatorships look towards India's success in democratic politics and accommodating diverse groups in the post-colonial era. In addition to the political revolution, the Indian founding fathers also played a key role in instigating and promoting social revolution along multiple axes. These included the abolition of untouchability along with making provisions for the emancipation of depressed classes, abolishing the British-instituted land ownership system to promote economic equality, and reforming ancient Hindu laws through legislation to promote gender equality.

In a way, the Indian founders utilized the shared wisdom from the American creation (epitomized in India's constitution which considerably borrowed from its American counterpart) and applied it to a much diverse and larger population at another time. Khilnani further writes

> If one looks beneath the messy confusion and black arts of India's politics, one sees in its democratic experience evidence of something that James Madison and his Federalist colleagues well understood more than two hundred years ago. Large republics with diverse and conflicting interests can be a better home for liberty, a safer haven against tyranny, than homogenous and exclusive ones. Within them, factions can check one another, moderating ideological fervor and softening power.[16]

Absorbing Madison's celebrated *Federalist No. 10* essay which detailed the above observation, the Indian founding fathers drafted a constitution that could promote unity in diversity. It is a fact that despite the occasional tensions between the two major religious communities (Hindus and Muslims), India remains the only nation with a very large Muslim population (more than 185 million) where Muslims share common citizenship with the majority community. Historian Ramachandra Guha remarks, 'Thus India provides a test case of the challenges to democracy from its critics on the left and the right; and a test case of the challenge to social harmony posed by a multi-religious citizenry.'[17]

The preeminent historian of the American founding era, Joseph Ellis claims that papers of the most prominent founders 'taken together, constitute the most complete documentation of human endeavor by any political elite in recorded history.'[18] This is not exactly true since the collected works of only two of the Indian founding fathers namely, Mohandas Gandhi and Jawaharlal Nehru, constitute more documentation than the combined documentation of many of the American founders. Irrespectively, the collected writings of these two founding generations go into hundreds of volumes of printed text. These have been diligently collected, translated, and indexed by generations of editors in both nations. Many of these writings are available free of cost and have been utilized by scholars to write biographies and histories, producing movies, documentaries, theater plays, etc. No other nation can claim to possess such a heritage of written text by leaders who not only expressed their ideas of nation-building but played prominent roles during the nation's founding era. Additionally, another parallel between the two founding generations is that the founding fathers (in both nations) were in contact with each other. This means that through their own documentation, we can discern their interpersonal relationships and their views about each other's actions.

The founding fathers in both nations wrote verbosely about their thoughts on various political, social, and economic issues of their times. It is fascinating to trace the evolution of their thoughts across time and events in their lives. They also come alive to us as human beings through their rich personal correspondence with family, friends, and close ones. Unfortunately, these personal letters have also fed an array of "scholars" in both nations who have approached the founding fathers to belittle their achievements by attacking them personally. Many of these writings, when taken out of the historical context, have fabricated controversies in the contemporary world. However, these same writings also illuminate the personal failings of the founding fathers. These writings help us bring them from the pedestal of Mount Olympus (abode of the most important gods in Greek mythology) to our world. The treasure trove of information in the writings of these founding generations has been used to conduct research across multiple domains in historiography, sociology, policy-making, linguistics, among others. With so many similarities, it is nothing but surprising then that by and large, Americans are wholly unaware of the founding generation of India, and vice versa.

Much more surprising is that among academicians, there is not a single scholarly work that I could find which shows the two founding generations under the same light. It seems like the academicians in both nations have been devotedly possessive about and possessively devoted to their own founding generation.[19] Furthermore, this ignorance has sustained even when the Indian founding fathers wrote predominantly in the English language or otherwise their works have been translated. Furthermore, both sets of founding fathers were educated (formally or informally) in the western ideas of liberty and nationalism, while they made their own contributions towards these ideas in their nation. Yet, much ink has been spilled in both nations to discuss contemporary and future foreign policy perspectives entwining the world's largest democracies while collective research on the two founding generations has been neglected. It is not out of antipathy but apathy for the other nation's history that this has been the case.

To be sure, in addition to the chronology, there are four obvious differences between the two founding generations. First, in America, none of the founding fathers were subservient to each other to the extent that many were subservient to Gandhi in India. American founders collaborated and dissented as friends and colleagues. On the other hand, many of the Indian founders deferred to Gandhi with either almost-parental or tutorial ties. If Washington can be viewed as *primus inter pares* among the American founders, then Gandhi was a central body around which many Indian founders revolved.

Second, as a consequence of the first difference, but also because of differences across culture and time, the expression of dissent among the Indian founders was never as vitriolic in language as that between the American founders. The kind of acrimonious language used by John Adams towards his colleagues and personal vilification through libeling in public newspapers encouraged by Thomas Jefferson and Alexander Hamilton against each other were wholly absent among the Indian founders. The Indian founding fathers almost never permitted their ideological differences to affect their personal relationships.

Third, the office of the president was held by multiple founding fathers in succession in America, thus shaping the nation from the executive branch of the government. By contrast, in India, Nehru occupied the office of the prime minister until his death almost seventeen years after independence, by when many of the prominent founders had already died. Age played a large role in this discrepancy. In general, compared to the Indian founding fathers when India became independent, American founding fathers were relatively much younger when the Revolutionary War culminated in America's victory.

Fourth, American founders were solely interested in the success of the political revolution while Indian founders aimed at simultaneously realizing a political as well as a social revolution. American founders left open the questions of slavery and Native Americans for succeeding generations whereas Indian founders sought to bring a social revolution as well (such as by the emancipation of the Untouchables and transforming a feudal society into a democratic one as we will read in the following chapters). In this way, the Indian founding fathers brought about not only a political but also a social revolution to vindicate Jefferson's self-evident truths that all men are created equal and endowed by their creator with unalienable rights of life, liberty, and the pursuit of happiness. These differences notwithstanding, both sets of founding fathers significantly influenced the direction taken by their respective nations.

With so much achieved by the two founding generations, it is interesting to ask that if Whitehead was to come again and look around the world (not just the Western Civilization), will he include the Indian political elite in the same group of political leaders? It is also curious to ask what opinion will Whitehead make of the present generation of leaders in both democracies? Today, with anti-democratic and xenophobic forces gaining influence across the world, as citizens in India and the U.S. debate what it means to be an Indian or an American, the founding fathers are more relevant than ever before. Historian Gordon Wood remarks

> The United States was founded on a set of beliefs and not, as were other nations, on a common ethnicity, language or religion. Since we are

not a nation in any traditional sense of the term, in order to establish nationhood, we have to reaffirm and reinforce periodically the values of the men who declared independence from Great Britain and framed the Constitution. As long as the Republic endures, in other words, Americans are destined to look back to the founding.[20]

The founding fathers were ordinary men who did extraordinary things. Just like us, they had their flaws and failings. Their failings are manifest not just in their documented views but also in their nation's history as well as the present polity. As newer political and social disruptions originate around us, it is an opportune time to go back to the lives and actions of the founding fathers in search of answers to our present dilemmas.

Politics can be defined as 'the process by which a society chooses the rules that will govern it....When there is conflict over institutions, what happens depends on which people or group wins out in the game of politics.'[21] Instinctively then, we search for the causes of our present distresses in the past. After all, it was the founding fathers who won in the game of politics and codified the rules in the constitution which governs our society. As Joseph Ellis writes

> the American [true also for India] system of jurisprudence links all landmark constitutional decisions to the language of the Constitution itself and often to the "original intent" of the framers. Once again, this legal tradition gives the American Founders an abiding relevance in current discussions of foreign and domestic policy that would be inconceivable in most European countries.[22]

This contemporary relevance of the founding fathers is what makes them ubiquitous in the nation's polity. Historians portray events around the founding of India and the United States of America as republics from various perspectives such as the so-called Whig, Marxist, and Imperialist interpretations of history. These interpretations do not agree with each other, indeed are mutually incompatible. Yet, the role of the founding fathers is prominent in all these perspectives. This is because each interpretation traces the source of our contemporary socio-political dilemmas to the actions of the founding fathers. Thus, the founding fathers continue to cast a long shadow on our present-day politics.

Both nations as democracies face a number of conundrums today. These revolve around the status of minorities, race, social and economic equality, nationalism, independence of the government institutions, highly partisan political parties, among others. Instead of democracy being a vehicle for politicians to promote social and economic inclusion, it is becoming a medium to gain power by fanning fears of "the other" among the citizens. Political rhetoric is loud and rancorous. Social distress is being fueled by populist measures leading to more anguish. However, if anything, social and economic distresses were much worse during the founding of these two democracies. In both nations, the debates around minorities, race, equality, nationalism, etc. raged during the founding era too, and were molded by the founders as they thought would be best for the future of their nation. Furthermore, the founding fathers had no precedents to guide them—they did not have the luxury to scrutinize and imbibe the history of their democracy and learn from it. They had to get things right at the first attempt with a very limited margin for error. If they would have failed, they would perhaps not have encountered another chance since many forces antithetical to democracy were also concurrently at play. Thus, it is natural to ask: what can we learn from the founding era to guide us in our present dilemmas as democracies? This book is a quest to answer the same.

Reading through the writings of the American founding fathers, one quickly gets familiar with two words frequently used by them—*Providence* and *Posterity*. It is manifest from their writings that they interpreted their own times as if bequeathed to them by Providence. They also aspired to be remembered by posterity through their actions. In old age, years after the American Revolution but when the rest of the world was still hostile to the republican ideals, Jefferson addressed posterity in what became the last letter of his life. This letter shows the sheer confidence and grandiosity of the aspirations of the founding generation. Jefferson wrote

> may it be to the world, what I believe it will be, (to some parts sooner, to others later, but finally to all,) the signal of arousing men to burst the chains, under which monkish ignorance and superstition had persuaded them to bind themselves, and to assume the blessings & security of self-government.[23]

Similarly, John Adams wrote in his old age: 'The American Revolution was not a common event. Its effects and consequences have already been awful over a great part of the globe. And when and where are they to cease?'[24] Clearly, both Jefferson and Adams were implying that the fruits of the American Revolution especially the establishment of a republic will propagate across the world. Yet, the American founding fathers were wise enough to be unwilling to bind the future generations with the tenets set by them. Jefferson had earlier written, 'We may consider each generation as a distinct nation, with a right, by the will of its majority, to bind themselves, but none to bind the succeeding generation, more than the inhabitants of another country.'[25] We get an allusion here that though the American founding fathers were very optimistic about the political institutions created by them, they were willing to let posterity judge for itself the suitability of these institutions. Contrastingly, the Indian founding fathers were not satisfied only with gaining independence from the British. Rather, they wanted to bring about a social revolution in a highly unequal nation ridden with many prejudices and superstitions. Jawaharlal Nehru's "Tryst with Destiny" speech on the eve of India's Independence has been much celebrated. But, this dithyramb delivered in English was actually a follow-up of his oration in Hindustani. In this now forgotten Hindustani speech, Nehru optimistically proclaimed

> Generally, countries wrest their freedom after great bloodshed, tears and toil. Much blood has been spilt in our land, and in a way which is very painful. Notwithstanding that, we have achieved freedom by peaceful methods. We have set a new example before the world....Big problems confront us and at their sight sometimes our heart quivers, but, then again, the thought that in the past we have faced many a big problem and we shall do so again, gives us courage. Shall we be cowed down by these?...All Indians shall have equal rights, and each one of them is to partake equally in that freedom. We shall proceed like that, and whosoever tries to be aggressive will be checked by us. If anyone is oppressed, we shall stand by his side.[26]

These examples show that in both nations, the founding fathers were confident about achieving their aims and were self-aware that they are setting an example for the world. They were conscious that their actions will determine the future of their nation and beyond.

The founding fathers faced many "problems" as faced by the two nations today. It is only from a few decades that America has become a truly multi-racial society guaranteeing equal political and judicial rights for all its citizens. The nation is still far from being able to secure social equality among all its citizens. In recent years, the fear of "the other" has made many Americans view the immigration system with suspicion. America has also seen multiple foreign military engagements in recent times and is still embroiled in them. In addition to all these concurrent happenings, the effects of globalization have led to huge income inequality, leading to a second "Gilded Age." Some of the debates around these issues today were also conducted by the American founding generation in different forms.

The American founding fathers confronted the question of race in twin forms of slavery and Native Americans. They failed to answer the latter in a peaceful manner and left the former one unresolved which ultimately resulted in a civil war. Fortunately, their record on other such questions was more impressive. They participated in the debates around the freedom of religion and instituted a wholly secular state. When they confronted the dilemma of choosing a side in the Napoleonic wars, they chose neutrality which remained the core of the American foreign policy for more than a century.

Similarly, today India suffers from religious communalism, poverty, income inequality, and caste-based conflicts. These issues were tackled by the Indian founding fathers too—with varying degrees of successes and failures. For example, even after the wounds of the partition, they were able to forge a common nationalism not dependent on religion or language. But, they failed in destroying the seed of religious communalism itself in the process. Similar to the American founding generation, the Indian founding generation chose neutrality as the foreign policy during the Cold War. This tendency towards neutrality still dominates the nation's foreign policy. While making comparisons with the founding fathers, what must be kept in mind is that taken overall, the conditions were much worse during the founding era than they are now. As discussed above, those times were highly turbulent and there would be neither India nor the United States today in its present form, without the actions—fruitful or futile—of the founding fathers. This is to say that there would be no "founding" of the nation without the founding fathers. This is what makes in both nations the tendency to learn from the founding fathers an irresistible and incessant process.

At the end of the Cold War, Francis Fukuyama optimistically proclaimed the "End of History." Fukuyama wrote that 'liberal democracy may constitute the "end point of mankind's ideological evolution" and the "final form of human government"....the *ideal* of liberal democracy could not be improved on.'[27] [emphasis original.] Since then, the ripples originating from the 2008 financial crisis, the further rise of Islamic fundamentalism, and the increasing gap in income equality has led to an upsurge in populist forces, identity-based hatred, and anti-democratic movements across the world. This upsurge has been stimulated further by various fast-pacing developments in technology—the effects of which we are still trying to comprehend and catch up with. Across the world, divisive political figures have capitalized on these changes.

On top of all these, we are now witnessing the catastrophic effects of the COVID-19 pandemic and Global Warming which are making the world increasingly unstable. The institutions of governance conceived by the American founding generation are once again under threat. However, unlike last time when the threat was posed from the outside by an ideology (Communism), this time the threat originates from within those same institutions. As a consequence, many citizens of America and India are being forced to reassess their democratic ideals—indeed, are being forced to question the aims of the democratic system itself. Thus, it is natural for the present generation to look for answers to the founding era of their nation—to the times when these democratic institutions were established—and to the "original intent" of the founding generation. As India seeks to become a global power in the 21st century and as America plans to prepare for a post-COVID world with its hegemony being challenged by China (an authoritarian nation-state), it may be helpful to look back at their respective founding eras. Such navel-gazing would ensure that these nations do not lose sight of their democratic ideals that have brought them here in the first place.

It is said that all historians write with an eye to the present. However, we must also not delude ourselves with the notion that we can just bring back the democratic ideals from the founding times and solve our problems. Making historical comparisons can be notoriously misguiding since historiography can never provide us a complete picture of those times. For example, even today Americans discuss not just the Second Amendment to the Constitution but also the "original intent" of the founding fathers behind the same. This amendment codified that "the right of the people to keep and bear Arms, shall not be infringed." But, most contemporary debates around the amendment do not focus on the preceding phrase: "A well regulated Militia, being necessary to the security of a free state." This is because it is quite difficult for our contemporary sensibility of a well-organized military force to envisage the times when militias were required to be raised by the government for the security of the state. Thus, it is hopelessly misleading to paint either a thoroughly bright or a perfectly dark picture of the founding generation since it is difficult to properly situate the sensitivities of the founding fathers and the times they lived in. It may be true on a higher level that History repeats itself. But, History can never duplicate itself since each generation has to make its own choices based on its own moral values and prejudices. Hagiographical writing about the founding fathers with the belief that if they could be transplanted today, they would solve our problems is no more than a farcical fantasy. The modern values of gender and race equality, transparency, inclusiveness, secularism, equality before the law, etc. had different meanings during the founding era. The founding fathers imbibed the moral values of their times and modern ethics would be inexplicable—if not repugnant—to them. Thus, we should only search for answers to our dilemmas in the actions of the founding fathers while situating ourselves in their shoes as best as possible. This is to say that there is a lot we can learn from the founding fathers but only after reconciling ourselves with the fact that we cannot and must not attempt to imitate them.

Around the early second century, the Greek biographer Plutarch published his magnum opus, a multi-volume biographical work named *Parallel Lives*. It chronicles biographies of some famous Greeks and Romans, arranged in a pair-wise manner (each pair consisting of one Greek and one Roman). Plutarch presents a biographical portrait of each personality while also comparing the common moral virtues and vices among the constituents of each pair. In his *Life of Alexander,* Plutarch writes, 'I have chosen rather to epitomize the most celebrated parts of their story, than to insist at large on every particular circumstance of it. It must be borne in mind that my design is not to write histories, but lives.'[28] Thus, Plutarch mainly focused on his subject's life and not the events around the subject. Many of the famous Greeks and Romans chronicled by Plutarch were what we can call the founding fathers of Greek and Roman Empires respectively. These Greek and Roman founding fathers were separated by both time and territory. Due to the lucid analogy with this work, a strong temptation while writing this book was to follow the example set by Plutarch and present biographical portraits of the American and the Indian founding fathers while comparing their characters and making the readers familiar with their achievements. But, on serious reflection, I concluded that writing a book in Plutarch's format will lead to three problems. It would require multiple volumes of printed text to write detailed biographies of the remarkable leaders comprising the two founding generations. This would limit the reach of the work by taking it outside the purview of the general audience. Second, presenting multiple biographies may overwhelm the reader with the information, biography after biography. Thus, the reader may find it difficult to distinguish between the chief characters. Furthermore, in either nation, scores of biographical works already exist for every founding father. Third, a biography, because of its very nature, suffers from its focus on a single figure around which the plot revolves. This is not an ideal way to discuss multiple figures who collaborated frequently with or against each other. This meant a format needed to be conceived which could weave together the two founding generations in a decent-sized single-volume work. Thus, I deduced that the best way to convey the thoughts and actions of the two founding generations would be to weave the narrative around themes relevant to a democratic system rather than personalities. This was also desirable from the point of view of familiarizing the historical parallels between these two nations.

    The aim of the book is, first and foremost, not to denigrate or compare the founding generation of one nation with that of the other. Rather, it is to show how the two founding generations were composed of the political elite the likes of which have never else been seen in the world. Second, it is also to revisit the founding era and show how events from the distant past are still relevant in the two democracies—both facing many political and social dilemmas in the present time. Hence, my approach will be to narrate a story from each nation in every chapter. These stories will revolve around historical events in which the founding fathers played the central role in shaping the destiny of their nation. Each pair of stories (one from America and one from India) will be followed by a short discussion on how these accounts from the founding of each nation are still relevant today. Furthermore, the stories are so selected that each chapter will only focus on a single contemporary socio-political theme. To introduce the founding fathers who feature prominently in a chapter, their short biographies will be presented, amalgamated in the narrative itself. In this manner, the book will be centrally focused on events (shaped by the founding generations) that still have tangible effects on the lives of the two nations. Consequently, the chapters will not follow the order of chronology. Finally, the closing chapter of the book focuses on the failings of the two founding generations—whereby their compromises too shaped these democracies. By reading this single-volume work, I hope that the reader will become familiar with the founding fathers of each nation and will be able to appreciate their legacy. I also hope that by exploring the past through the actions of the founding fathers, the reader will be able to reflect more thoughtfully on the contemporary political debates of her nation.

The members of the American founding generation are nostalgically looked to in multiple scholarly works as a bouquet of colorful flowers. By contrast, the Indian founding fathers are still viewed separately as flower stems not threaded together into a collective i.e. there is a tendency to not view them as the "Indian Founding Fathers." Thus, another aim of this book is self-reflection on the part of Indians to learn from their American brethren and look to the founding generation as a collective political leadership.

Finally, the last aim of the book is to present a new text which entwines the histories of these two nations. One of the casualties of the Cold War has been the amount of good historiographical research conducted in India and America on each other. This was fueled by the insulation between these two democracies during the Cold War.

Serious scholarship on India is scarce in the United States as evident from the number and genre of books present on India in any decent bookstore in the nation. It is also unfortunate that the same goes for scholarship on the United States of America in India. Most of the present works featuring these two democracies together revolve around economics or foreign policy, and not much effort has been put into the field of historiography. This is despite the fact that the United States continues to be the most preferred foreign destination for opportunities in academia and industry for Indians. This book is a humble attempt to open another avenue to historiographical research between these two diverse democracies through the example of the founding generations.

Due to chronology, American founding fathers can only be depicted in the form of drawings and portraits whereas we possess audio-visual recordings of the Indian founding fathers. Thus, the American founding fathers appear tangibly more remote—it is hard to think of Washington without his piercing eyes and almost pursed lips. Despite this difference in caricature, the founding fathers in both nations have fallen victims to all sorts of theories of re-evaluation. Consequently, the founding fathers have been forced to oscillate on a swing between adulation and incineration by generations of scholars. This book is then an attempt to bring these figures to the earthly pedestal of human beings—complete with their weaknesses and failures. Another challenge to portraying the two founding generations n a single-volume work is that their collective works span hundreds of volumes of printed text. Their works are still widely read, quoted, edited, and referenced. Multiple biographies have been written about each one of them. This makes it excruciatingly hard to selectively focus on their long political careers and personalities by filtering out the irrelevant information. Hence, it is through a few chosen themes that I intend to familiarize the founding generations and discuss their relevance towards our present quandaries.

Since there is not (and cannot be) an agreed definition about whom all belongs to the elite coterie called the Founding Fathers, I have followed the example of other works and taken the liberty to select them as per my own predilections. The six American founding fathers chosen are the usual suspects: George Washington, John Adams, Thomas Jefferson, Alexander Hamilton, James Madison, and

Benjamin Franklin. To be impartial, the number of Indian founding fathers chosen is also six. These are Mohandas Karamchand Gandhi, Jawaharlal Nehru, Vallabhbhai Patel, Bhimrao Ramji Ambedkar, Chakravarti Rajagopalachari, and Subhas Chandra Bose. Of course, there are many other names in both nations belonging to the same generation which could have been included in the above lists, such as John Jay and Thomas Paine in America, and Abul Kalam Azad and Rajendra Prasad in India. But, alas, one must make a choice to restrict the scope of this book. All the twelve men chosen above contributed through their political acts as well as philosophical ideas towards the nurturing of these two upstart democracies.

It should be pointed out that all American founding fathers in the above list were white Christian men whereas with one exception (Ambedkar was from the lowest Hindu caste) all Indian founders featured above were upper-caste Hindu men. Thus, almost all founding fathers came from privileged social backgrounds, though their economic backgrounds varied considerably.

It is especially very unfortunate that no woman is featured in these two lists. To be sure, some women did play influential roles in the founding of each nation (like Abigail Adams and Mercy Otis Warren in America, and Sarojini Naidu and Kamaladevi Chattopadhyay in India). History has been unfair to them and many other women who played major roles during the founding of these nations by overlooking them. I am myself culpable of the same crime since being dependent on other scholarly works, I could not find enough material to highlight more the roles played by women during the founding era of each nation. A chief reason for this bias is that being highly unequal times, in both nations during the founding era, women were sidelined by men in politics. However, I have taken care to include the role of women wherever possible in various chapters of the book especially in the Indian case where women contributed substantially toward the nation's founding.

All founding fathers are long busy being dead. But, their tryst with legacy still continues. The legacy and fame of most of these figures have modulated with time and circumstances. John Adams has been much reviled as a monarchist and it is only in recent years that his reputation is being restored. Nehru, much loved when he was alive is today vilified as never before. Vallabhbhai Patel who was put to the background for years has now been resurrected in the main political arena. Jefferson has been alternatively glorified and denounced whereas Rajagopalachari awaits rebirth in the popular consciousness of India. Madison's legacy has been mostly restricted to the field of law whereas Ambedkar has become even more influential as the pioneer against the caste system after his death—to the point of being revered alongside Buddha in many households. Franklin is remembered much more for his contributions to science than politics, while Bose is still romantically looked to with the wish that he should not have died right before the Independence. Washington, "the Father of His Country" and Gandhi, the Father of India have been reviled by successive generations of scholars but are still (by and large) accepted as the foremost among the founding fathers.

Historians still seek answers to many "what if" questions around the actions of the founding fathers. These questions are spun around the political narratives of our times—such as what course India would have taken if Patel would have been elected the first prime minister; what would have happened to India if Gandhi's village model of governance would have been adopted; if the rise of America would have been possible without the leviathan financial system established by Hamilton; was it possible for Adams to get re-elected and forestall the Jeffersonians if he had not instituted the Alien and Sedition Acts, etc. The contemporary political forces in both nations have had and will always politicize and capitalize on the legacy of the founding fathers. In the loud democracies that America and India are, this is expected yet unfortunate. It is expected because as discussed before, the thoughts and actions of the founding generation pervade every aspect of the polity of the nation, whether in India or in America. This makes the founding fathers easy scapegoats for our failures and justifications to vindicate our actions. We must be careful when blaming them for our present troubles since as we shall see in the book, much more could have gone wrong. Whether deified or denounced in the present, the only thing that we can be reliably sure of is that, in the long-term, the invisible and all-powerful forces of history will never let any of these twelve names fall into oblivion.

The past and the present are forever entwined in an unending conversation. The past acts as a beam of light on the choices we face in the present, whereas we interpret the past based on our contemporary predispositions and agendas. The following chapters are a quest to look back at the past—to the founding era—in order to better formulate and answer the questions posed by the present.

---

[1] *The Oxford Modern English Dictionary*, Edited by Della Thompson (New York: Oxford University Press, Second Edition, 1996)
[2] B.R. Ambedkar's speech in the Constituent Assembly while presenting the draft constitution, 4 November 1948, *Constituent Assembly Debates: Official Report* (reprint New Delhi: Lok Sabha Secretariat, 2014), Vol. VII, p. 38
[3] The use of armed forces against the Indian population has been detailed in Stephen P. Cohen, *The Indian Army: Its Contribution to the Development of a Nation* (Oxford: Oxford University Press, Oxford India Paperback Edition 2001), chapters 2, 3
[4] Ramachandra Guha, *India after Gandhi: The History of the World's Largest Democracy* (Picador India, 2008), p. 97
[5] Joseph J. Ellis, *American Creation* (New York: Vintage Books, 2007), p. 9
[6] This expression of opinions about the executive role of the government by various members of the Constitutional Convention has been detailed in Richard Beeman, *Plain, Honest Men: The Making of The American Constitution* (New York: Random House, 2009), chapter 9
[7] Granville Austin, *The Indian Constitution: Cornerstone of a Nation* (Oxford University Press, 1966), p. 308
[8] *The Works of John Adams*, Second President of the United States: with a Life of the Author, Notes and Illustrations, by his Grandson Charles Francis Adams (Boston: Little, Brown and Co., 1856). 10 volumes. Vol. 4., p. 203
[9] Nehru on the new constitutional proposals, 3 June 1947, *Selected Works of Jawahar Lal Nehru*-Second Series-3, p. 99
[10] Paul Johnson, *A History of the American People* (New York: Harper Perennial, 1997), p. 128
[11] Barack Obama's comment in Obama: U.S., India 'Natural Allies' In 21st Century, *NPR*, 24 Nov 2009
[12] Robert P. Kraynak, The American Founders and Their Relevance Today, *Modern Age: A Conservative Review*, Winter 2015 – Vol. 57, No. 1
[13] Joseph J. *Ellis, American Creation* (New York: Vintage Books, 2007), p. 10
[14] Ibid., pp. 8-9
[15] Sunil Khilnani, *The Idea of India* (New York: Farrar Straus Giroux, paperback edition, 1999), p. 4
[16] Ibid., Foreword to the Paperback edition, p. xv
[17] Ramachandra Guha, *Makers of Modern India* (Penguin Books, 2012), p. 19
[18] Joseph J. Ellis, *American Creation* (New York: Vintage Books, 2007), p. 12

[19] This expression has been used by Ramachandra Guha, *Gandhi: The Years that Changed the World 1914-1948* (Penguin Random House, 2018), pp. xx

[20] Gordon Wood, *Revolutionary Characters: What Made the Founders Different* (New York: Penguin Books, 2006), p. 4

[21] Daron Acemoglu and James A. Robinson, *Why Nations Fail* (New York: Crown Business, 2012), p. 79

[22] Joseph J. Ellis, Introduction to *The Founding Fathers: The Essential Guide to the Men Who Made America* (New Jersey: John Wiley and Sons, Inc., 2007), pp. 2-3

[23] Thomas Jefferson to Roger O. Weightman, 24 June 1826, *The Works of Thomas Jefferson*, Federal Edition (New York and London, G.P. Putnam's Sons, 1904-5). Vol. 12, p. 477

[24] John Adams to Hezekiah Niles, 13 February 1818, *The Works of John Adams, Second President of the United States: with a Life of the Author, Notes and Illustrations, by his Grandson Charles Francis Adams* (Boston: Little, Brown and Co., 1856). 10 volumes. Vol. 10., p. 282

[25] Thomas Jefferson to John Wayles Eppes, 24 June 1813, *The Works of Thomas Jefferson*, Federal Edition (New York and London, G.P. Putnam's Sons, 1904-5). Vol. 11, p. 298

[26] Jawaharlal Nehru's speech translated in English, 14 August 1947, *Constituent Assembly Debates: Official Report* (reprint New Delhi: Lok Sabha Secretariat, 2014), Vol. V, pp. 3-4

[27] Francis Fukuyama, *The End of History and the Last* Man (New York: Avon Books, 1992), p. xi

[28] Plutarch, *Greek and Roman Lives*, translated by John Dryden, revised and edited by Arthur Hugh Clough (New York: Dover Publications, Dover Giant Thrift Edition, 2005), p. 132

1. MINORITIES

In December 1784, while serving as the United States Minister to France, Thomas Jefferson sent a letter from Paris to his protégé James Madison in which Jefferson caustically wrote, 'While Mr. Henry lives another bad constitution would be formed and saddled for ever on us. What we have to do I think is devoutly to pray for his death.'[1] Jefferson, who usually maintained a calm and composed temperament was referring bitterly to Patrick Henry, who had been frustrating various reforms proposed by Jefferson in the Virginia legislature for a long time now. One of these reforms was very close to Jefferson's as well as to Madison's heart—the revisionist provision for complete religious freedom. In his mentor's absence, Madison was now pursuing the bill to enact this provision in the state legislature. In a nation dominated by Protestants, why were Jefferson and Madison directing their energies to this cause?

In the seventeenth century, thousands of Europeans (mostly from Britain) facing religious persecution fled to America with the vision of building an other-worldly "City on a Hill." In 1620, the *Mayflower* transported the first English Puritans to America. They were utopians and zealots who 'insisted that religion was the biggest single motive in getting [them] to hazard all on the adventure.'[2] In the subsequent years, many settlers belonging to a multitude of religious sects were undertaking the transatlantic journey to freely practice their customs in America. Thus, American history is filled with stories of various religious sects such as Puritans, Quakers, Methodists, Moravians, Dutch and German Lutherans, Baptists, Calvinists, and Presbyterians to name but a few. These sects were not always at peace with each other. In fact, there were many violent conflicts between them. For example, the Puritans, who settled in New England believed in having a covenant with God. Their concept of a "City on a Hill" quickly turned into being an intolerant theocracy. Subsequently, in New England's Massachusetts, all those outside the covenant i.e. other religious sects—Anglicans, Quakers, Catholics, Baptists, and Jews—

were fervently persecuted by Puritans while the opposite was true in Virginia where Anglicans retaliated with equal vigor.[3]

Like Massachusetts, the colonies of Pennsylvania and Rhode Island were founded against a backdrop of religious persecution. Pennsylvania was founded when the Quaker, William Penn, obtained a charter from King Charles II of England to launch a "Holy Experiment" in which Christians of every denomination would enjoy religious freedom. Similarly, Rhode Island was founded by Roger Williams who was banished by the Puritans from the Massachusetts Bay Colony for his religious views. Despite the pursuit of religious liberty during the early stages, the persecuted soon became the persecutors in these colonies. In 1705, Pennsylvania retreated from Penn's idealism by barring Catholics and Jews from serving in the government. Likewise, in 1716, Rhode Island passed a law that barred Catholics and Jews from voting in the colony.[4]

The social and political tensions between various Protestant sects and even more between Protestants and Catholics spilled over in various forms. Since non-Puritans were not allowed in Boston, four Quakers were hanged between 1659 and 1661 for exhibiting resistance by returning to the city.[5] The infamous Salem witch trials when Puritans hanged nineteen people accused of witchcraft are another testimony of the mass hysteria and religious extremism of the American society during those times. Prior to the American Revolution, eleven of the thirteen states already had an established church. These recognized establishments were patronized by the state governments. Duties were imposed on the citizens to pay taxes to support a prescribed local church and to attend worship services.[6] A qualification in order to vote or hold public office was to profess a belief in the doctrines of the established church. However, prompt availability of land in the vast mostly-unpopulated continent meant that the dissenters could translocate to other places in America in order to promulgate their doctrines. Paradoxically, this fostered more parochialism in the social life of the nation since the dissenters could afford to be more conservative in their new abode.

Perhaps more precarious than Catholics was the condition of non-believers, who were another minority outside the rotunda of labyrinthine Christian sects. In 1703, South Carolina passed a law to define blasphemy as a crime and codified it as 'defaming any person of the Trinity, denying the truths of Christianity, or denying the divine authority of the Bible.' In Pennsylvania, Agnostics and atheists had restricted voting and property rights whereas only Christians could hold office. Furthermore, academic institutions were also associated with religious sects. Thus, Princeton (formerly College of New Jersey) was Presbyterian, College of William and Mary was Anglican, while Yale maintained Puritan orthodoxy. Even at the time of the American Revolution, religious persecution did not abate despite the strong currents of liberty and republicanism that had gripped the nation.

In Massachusetts, between 1760 and 1774, 'over one-half of all the criminal prosecutions were for sexual offenses or offenses against God and religion.' These prosecutions followed scripture-based wrongdoings such as 'adultery, fornication, working on the Sabbath, missing church, blasphemy, or swearing.'[7] In 1777, New York State's constitution banned Catholics from holding public office.[8] Massachusetts's Constitution guaranteed that only Protestants could hold elective office and Jews or Catholics must take oaths renouncing their beliefs. Serving in the government for Jews, Catholics, and other non-protestants was also prohibited by New Jersey, Delaware, North Carolina, Georgia, South Carolina, and Vermont.[9]

Only Pennsylvania's constitution (with Benjamin Franklin being a part of the drafting committee) provided broad suffrage rights and ensured that nobody shall be compelled to attend any religious worship or hold opinions contrary to his own will.[10] Quakers who had established Pennsylvania presented a curious case during the Revolutionary War (American War of Independence) since due to their pacifist beliefs, most of them declined to support the war. As a consequence, they suffered at the hands of non-Quakers whether the British or the American revolutionaries. With so many divisions, it was an almost impossible task to bring together all disparate sects under a single national church in America. Such an attempt would also have been ruinous since it would have instigated more insecurities and conflicts between the religious sects.

It was amidst such divisions that the founding fathers assumed the mantle to freshly consider the relationship between the state and individual faith. The founding fathers entered the picture at a junction when the ideas of Enlightenment were colliding with the religious orthodoxy in America. Most of the founding fathers discussed in this book were rational deists, skeptics, or agnostics. Their achievement in being able to establish a wholly secular state and guaranteeing religious freedom to all citizens has been succinctly summarized by the famous historian of the early American democracy, Alexis de Tocqueville. He noted about the dual nature of the American culture: 'it is the result of two distinct elements, which in other places have been in frequent hostility, but which in America have been admirably incorporated and combined with one another. I allude to the spirit of Religion and the Spirit of Liberty.'[11] But, to admirably assimilate religion and liberty was not an easy task and the two founding fathers who played the most influential roles in instituting religious liberty in America—guaranteeing religious freedom to atheists and minorities of every religious sect—were Thomas Jefferson and James Madison.

Thomas Jefferson was an introverted politician who came out best not in conversations but in written prose. Jefferson was born on a Virginia plantation in 1743 and being a member of the Virginia aristocracy had inherited 5,000 acres of land by the age of twenty-one. He grew up reading about Roman heroes in childhood and then went to the College of William and Mary to study mathematics, metaphysics, and philosophy. He then pursued law as a profession. He was also a *philosophe* and an inventor besides being interested in linguistics and paleontology. By all accounts, he was very handsome who looked even more attractive as he aged. He was influenced by the trinity of John Locke, Francis Bacon, and Isaac Newton, whom he expounded as the three greatest men who ever lived.[12] Jefferson served on the committee which drafted the American Declaration of Independence, and in fact, was its primary author. This act was his most memorable contribution to posterity. In terms of popularity, no other words (except perhaps Lincoln's Gettysburg Address) in American history match Jefferson's prose: We hold these truths to be self-evident; that all men are created equal; that they are endowed by their Creator with certain [inherent and] inalienable Rights; that among these are life, liberty & the pursuit of happiness. His biographer Joseph Ellis remarks, 'This is the seminal statement of the American Creed, the closest approximation to political poetry ever produced in American culture.'[13]

After the Revolutionary War, Jefferson served as the U.S. Minister to France. Through his life, Jefferson maintained an exceptional enthusiasm for collecting and reading books. In fact, Jefferson was America's foremost bibliophile as well as an extraordinary spendthrift. He bought thousands of books during his life and when the Library of the Congress was burned in the War of 1812, he sold his library to the U.S. Government. However, true to the Virginian aristocratic culture, he never ceased his profligate activities and was constantly debt-ridden which was another of many things that he bequeathed to posterity.

Jefferson served as America's first Secretary of State under President George Washington. After his fallout with the Secretary of the Treasury Alexander Hamilton (who enjoyed Washington's support) and the Federalists over the interpretation of the American Revolution (we shall discuss this in the third chapter), Jefferson sequestered himself in his home, Monticello. From there, he collaborated with Madison to launch opposition against the Federalists and inadvertently established the two-party system in the process. Jefferson then served as the Vice President under President John Adams (at that time the candidate getting the second largest number of votes in the election was automatically elected as the Vice President). Finally, between 1801-1809, Jefferson served as the third president of the United States. The highlight of his presidency was the Louisiana Purchase which more than doubled the American territory. After his retirement, John Adams and he wrote each other letters discussing a wide array of topics including history, philosophy, governance, interpretation of the American Revolution, among others. These letters have occupied the supreme position in the history of American correspondence. Finally, an astonishing detail which nobody writing about these two founding fathers can afford to miss and which even a veteran novelist will find hard to conjure is that both Jefferson and Adams died on the 50th anniversary of the Declaration of Independence.

These are plain facts which do no justice to bringing out Jefferson's character. Perhaps the greatest dichotomy around Jefferson's legacy is that he has been relevant in every age, both because of his seminal contribution to American liberty as well as his legacy towards slavery. He has been the most elusive of the American founding fathers—in the sense that it is hardest to uncover the various façades that he donned during his life. He was the American champion of religious freedom, individual liberty, and republican ideals. He was also a utopian and an admirer of the French Revolution even after it had spiraled into violent pandemonium. His utopian vision can best be expressed in his own words: when America was dealing with the violent Shays' Rebellion, he wrote 'The tree of liberty must be refreshed from time to time with the blood of patriots and tyrants. It is it's natural manure.'[14] On at least one occasion, he doctored his correspondence to present a wiser image to posterity by toning down his affection for France after violence had consumed the French Revolution.[15]

Jefferson was also the founding father who could not live up to the ideal of "all men are created equal," that he professed in the Declaration of Independence. He owned a large number of slaves and secretly practiced miscegenation while at the same time decrying the differences between the two races. He covered his tracks so well that it took two centuries and advanced DNA analysis techniques to prove his act. On the one hand, this apostle of liberty and master of prose had once unsuccessfully proposed a provision to end slavery in all newly created states by 1800. On the other hand, despite being fully aware that slavery is the fundamental contradiction at the core of the American republic, he never again publicly voiced his opinion against slavery. Therein lies the Jeffersonian paradox. He was also an avid supporter of a free press and public education. In his twilight years, he invested time in founding and minutely designing every aspect of the University of Virginia which he envisioned as an institution free from religious influences of all kinds.

Like Jefferson, James Madison also known as the "Father of the Constitution" inherited a vast amount of wealth from his family. Madison was born in 1751 on a Virginia plantation and went to the College of William and Mary where he was influenced by its President John Witherspoon who shaped his views on liberty and morality. With dogged endurance, he completed the three-year bachelor course in two years while also finding time to become a co-founder of the American Whig Society. For most of his youth, Madison grappled with bad health and premonitions of early death. After joining politics, he willingly came under Jefferson's influence.

The growth in their friendship and political collaboration is a principal theme in the life of each.[16] Once, Madison failed to get reelected in the Virginia Convention because of his refusal to furnish the voters with free whiskey. From being such a novice in American politics, he went on to play the most important role in the success of the Constitutional Convention, co-authored the Federalist Papers, and drafted the Bill of Rights. His deft maneuvering and influence helped in ratifying the Constitution in Virginia which led John Marshall (later, President Madison's bête noire and one of the most influential justices in Supreme Court's history) to remark that if eloquence included 'persuasion by convincing, Mr. Madison was the most eloquent man I ever heard.'[17] During the debate to ratify the constitution, Madison came out as the most ardent proponent of the separation of powers between the three branches of the federal government i.e. executive, legislature, and judiciary (known today as the Madisonian model) as well as between states and the federal government. He was also a passionate advocate of religious freedom and of separation between the church and state. Madison also served as a close advisor to President Washington during the early years of Washington's presidency. In an amusing tale that shows Washington's trust in Madison as well as the political indispensability of the latter, Madison drafted the inaugural address of the first American president and then replied to his own discourse by preparing the official response of the House to the president's address. He achieved all of the above before the age of forty! After his fallout with Washington, he formed the Republican faction with Jefferson, served as the Secretary of State during Jefferson's presidency, and as the fourth president of the United States from 1809 to 1817.

However, Madison has been overshadowed in history by Jefferson as the latter's chief aide. This is unfair since Madison's finest moments were during the Constitutional Convention and subsequent ratification debate, when Jefferson was ensconced in France and Madison was acting on his own. If Jefferson was the foremost apostle of liberty, Madison was the most meticulous politician of his time. Appearances can be deceiving in the case of Madison. His weak constitution, frail voice, pale face, and short figure concealed a fanatic determination towards achieving his goals. He was always 'invariably the best-prepared person in the room,' the kind of which with whom you do not wish to engage in a debate.[18] He was punctilious and logically pursued his targets in a systematic manner. Be it the drafting and ratification of the Constitution, the ascent of the Republicans, or the Louisiana Purchase which he oversaw as the Secretary of the State, Madison was always on the winning side. His biographer Noah Feldman writes that over the course of his life, Madison changed the United States three times: by designing the Constitution and the Bill of Rights, by co-founding the original Republican party and by pioneering a foreign policy based on economic sanctions.[19] His transformation from being an ardent federalist i.e. an advocate of a strong federal government and Hamilton's chief collaborator during the ratification debate to becoming the most inveterate enemy of the Federalists remains inexplicable to a degree and has been widely debated for two centuries. It took the disastrous War of 1812 to again persuade Madison of the necessity of a stronger federal government. He remained one of the largest slaveholders in Virginia and reticent about slavery in his public discourse. Worrying about posterity, he tampered with many of his letters in the old age which presents a most disturbing picture of his final years and casts doubt on the integrity of his personal records.[20]

In the summer of 1776, while drafting the Declaration of Independence, Jefferson was physically present in Philadelphia but mentally he was in Virginia. At the time, he considered the drafting of the Declaration as a routine work that had fallen into his lap through the machinations of John Adams. The Declaration itself did not garner the iconic position by which we view it today for many years to come. Jefferson's mind was decidedly fixed at "my country," Virginia. The state of Virginia was drafting a new constitution and Jefferson was focused on preparing a draft of the same. Virginia was the most heavyweight of the states with almost one-fifth of the Americans living in Virginia alone. Thus, demography made Virginia, politically the most influential state and any constitutional measure adopted by it was bound to garner interest and foment debates across the nation.

Virginia's treatment of Baptists was barbaric. Baptist ministers were beaten, imprisoned, and taxed. In 1768, three Baptist preachers were arrested and sent to jail for breach of the peace when they refused to promise that they will not preach again in the state.[21] The condition of other religious minorities was also perilous. Against this background, Jefferson prepared three drafts of the constitution of Virginia between late May and early June. He proposed the separation of powers between branches of the government, an independent judiciary, and a bicameral legislature. He also proposed a radical provision to provide complete religious freedom to all inhabitants.[22] Jefferson suggested that 'All persons shall have full & free liberty of religious opinion nor shall any be compelled to frequent or maintain any religious institution.'[23]

Thus, by a single stroke, Jefferson aimed at establishing the right to follow any religious sect (or none) and also at minimizing the government's interference in the matters of self-beliefs. The scheme would have provided refuge to all religious minorities in Virginia. It was a thoroughly Jeffersonian scheme: lofty in design, noble in intention but impractical in contemporary politics. Jefferson, who was still in Philadelphia, sent the draft of the constitution but it reached Virginia too late for thorough consideration. Hence, it was broken to be proposed as a series of amendments to the already prepared document. The amendment containing the provision of religious freedom being too revisionist was quietly dropped by the legislature.[24]

Despite this setback, Jefferson continued his activism to safeguard religious minorities after returning back to Virginia. He was not content with mere toleration between various religious sects as advocated by many others. In his opinion, the idea of toleration was not binding on the citizens through the force of law and also that society should follow the higher ideal of equality than mere toleration. He wanted Virginia to endorse complete religious freedom in its Constitution since only then the protection for religious minorities could have been secured by the law. Quoting John Locke, he iterated that where Locke, the "Father of Liberalism," stopped short of the idea of complete religious freedom and advocated mere toleration, 'we may go on.'[25] Back in Virginia, Jefferson served as the governor between 1779 and 1781 but could not be successful in getting his bill guaranteeing religious freedom passed in the Assembly. Between late 1781 and early 1782, Jefferson wrote *Notes on the State of Virginia*. These notes were later translated into French and published during his stay in France. It would remain the one and only book he ever published during his lifetime. It created a wide sensation since it contained many desultory references about religion in addition to his liberal ideas regarding the protection of religious minorities. He wrote

> Is uniformity attainable? Millions of innocent men, women, and children, since the introduction of Christianity, have been burnt, tortured, fined, imprisoned: yet we have not advanced one inch towards uniformity. What has been the effect of coercion? To make one half the world fools, and the other half hypocrites. To support roguery and error all over the earth. Let us reflect that it is inhabited by a thousand millions of people. That these profess probably a thousand different systems of religion.[26]

Earlier in 1776, when Jefferson was drafting the Declaration of Independence in Philadelphia, young James Madison still in his mid-twenties was a delegate to Virginia's Constitutional Convention. In the Convention, the drafting committee had adopted an article proposed by George Mason that stated, 'all men shou'd enjoy the fullest Toleration in the Exercise of Religion, according to the Dictates of Conscience.' Like Jefferson, Madison was convinced that "toleration" was an invidious and relative term. He also foresaw that this article would not lead the way to complete religious freedom since it was possible to use this article for persecuting dissenting religious sects under the garb of "toleration." This is because "toleration" implied the onus of maintaining religious freedom on the populace whereas guaranteeing religious freedom by law made it binding for the government to ensure the same. Thus, he sought to have the noxious word excised from the article to establish the foundation for complete religious freedom and safeguards for all minorities.

Following some political machinations and legal ingenuities, Madison was successful in substituting "toleration" for "full and free exercise" of religion. However, the enacted clause did not guarantee the free exercise of religion which could only be enforced by getting Jefferson's earlier bill passed. For now, Madison had to be content with partial victory and complete religious freedom accompanying the protection for all minorities had to wait. Later in life, Madison wrote that he had proposed the change with a view to substituting for 'the idea expressed by the term "toleration," an absolute and equal right of all to the exercise of religion according to the dictates of conscience.' Historian George Bancroft has called Madison's partial success in his early political career as 'the first achievement of the wisest civilian in Virginia.' In this way, Madison kickstarted his political career by providing a clear expression of imbibing and implementing the ideas of Enlightenment towards safeguarding religious minorities.[27]

After serving in the Confederation Congress[α], Jefferson had left for Paris in 1784. In his absence, Madison came forward to fill the leadership void and spearhead the activism for Jefferson's bill for religious freedom. The conservative and fiercely oratorical Patrick Henry turned out to be the chief opposition for Madison. Henry was a revolutionary firebrand, one of the greatest orators in America, famous for his unbearably long and impassioned speeches. Henry believed that despite the absence of an established church in Virginia, every citizen should pay a mandatory tax to support all churches in the state. This would have obviously infringed the people's right to support (or not support) religious institutions as they deem fit.[28] While planning to tackle Henry, Madison was in continuous contact with Jefferson through letters. In addition to acting as the primary source of news for Jefferson and receiving the latter's advice, Madison was also fulfilling Jefferson's idiosyncratic requests to send exquisite American commodities that Jefferson wanted to display for the enjoyment of his French audience. It was in reply to one of Madison's letters that Jefferson wished to devoutly pray for Henry's death (as we read at the start of this chapter) so that a constitution agreeable to Jefferson's beliefs could be formed. However, a partial victory was not enough for Madison. He decided to take on Henry's resistance with diligent political skills which he had perfected by now. The battle lines were drawn.

The immediate bone of contention was that the Episcopalian clergy in Virginia had introduced a project to re-establish their independence of the laity. Patrick Henry had frustrated Madison's hopes when Henry's talents 'preserved from a dishonorable death,'

[α] Confederation Congress was the legislative branch of the government established in 1781. It had delegates sent by various states and it succeeded the Second Continental Congress.

the bill to support all religions in Virginia from funds collected by a state-wide tax—which would have primarily benefitted the Episcopalians.[29] Henry had persuaded the Assembly to resolve to support the clergy by the religious tax. Madison conveyed the news about Henry's designs to Jefferson. Jefferson was pleased that the Episcopalians were demonstrating their true colors by overtly demonstrating their dominance in the Assembly. He advised Madison to garner support from the dissenters—Baptists, Methodists, Quakers and others, and unite them against the Episcopalian ventures. Closer to home, Madison's concern was to not let any religious sect shake hands with the Episcopalians and thus fully dominate the other religious minorities. He found it unconscionable that a majority sect (Episcopalian) should force Virginians of other denominations to contribute to the Episcopalian church.[30]

Madison started to muster support from other religious sects to restrain Episcopalians. At the same time, Madison shrewdly schemed on three fronts to neutralize his opposition. First, he intrigued behind the curtains to have the assembly elect Henry as the governor of Virginia. This step may seem counter-intuitive but it was essential to Madison's plan. For Henry, the appeal of governorship was to be able to move to Richmond and find suitable suitors for his daughters. Thus, by securing the governorship for Henry, Madison executed Henry's departure from the Assembly. Clearly, it was a more practical and potentially less drastic approach than to devoutly pray for Henry's death. Second, to mollify the opposition from Episcopalians, Madison voted with Henry's allies in support of a different legislation favored by Episcopalians which allowed them to hold and manage the property of the Church. This legislation was passed by a majority of forty-seven to thirty-eight. Finally, to buy time for mobilizing support for Jefferson's bill, Madison persuaded the Assembly to delay the final vote on his bill for a year so that the Assembly could ascertain the opinions of the state's voters.[31]

Madison drafted *Memorial and Remonstrance against Religious Assessments* as the bulwark of propaganda against Henry's pending bill. He took pains to keep his authorship of the document secret so as to achieve more space for political maneuvering. The *Remonstrance* assembled fifteen reasons detailing the support for freedom of religion as well as a complete separation of church and state. It is a purely political document that has been termed as 'one of the most eloquent statements on religious freedom in history.'[32] In the first article, Madison proclaimed religious liberty as an 'unalienable right.' He further wrote that religion is 'wholly exempt' from the cognizance of civil society. He added that though every question in a civil society is determined by the will of the majority, in certain cases, the majority may trespass on the rights of the minority. This is a clear expression of Madison's concern for the protection of religious minorities from the tyranny of the majority. In Article 4, he declared that if the freedom of religion is abused, 'it is an offence against God, not against man: To God, therefore, not to men, must an account of it be rendered.' Madison proposed that the right to not believe in any religion should be respected and must not be violated by imposing a religious tax. He also criticized Henry's bill for its explicit favoring of one faith over others since it violated the principle of equality before the law.[33]

The *Remonstrance* was successful in bringing Madison's ideas home to other legislators and persuade them to sign the same—without their knowledge of who the author of the document was. As he wrote to Jefferson with delight, 'The opposition to the general assessment gains ground. At the *instance of some of its adversaries I drew up the remonstrance* herewith inclosed. It has been *sent* thro' the *medium of confidential persons in a number of the upper Counties*, and I am told will be pretty extensively signed.'[34] [emphasis original.] When George Washington received a copy of the *Remonstrance*, he conveyed his sentiments on this volatile issue. In a remarkable premonition of his belief in religious freedom which he upheld later during his presidency, Washington remarked that he strongly feels about not having 'any kind of restraint upon religious principles.' He added that he is not opposed to people paying tax towards their own sect whether they be 'the denominations of Christians…Jews, Mahometans, or otherwise.'[35] Thus, Washington expressed his approval for a religious tax as long as religious minorities (from Christianity or other religions) were provided appropriate exemptions. Reflecting on the *Remonstrance*, Madison later wrote that, 'the number of Copies & signatures presented displayed such an overwhelming opposition of the people,' that Henry's bill to mandatorily tax citizens for religious establishments was 'crushed under it'[36]

Thus, assessing correctly that his proposals have garnered enough momentum, Madison resurrected Jefferson's earlier *Bill for Establishing Religious Freedom*. Madison planned to use all tricks in his sleeve to get it passed this time. A revealing dispute now arose over the preamble of the bill. Jefferson had written in the preamble that any attempt to influence people by civil power or punishment only begets hypocrisy and is a departure from the plan of 'the holy author of our religion.' An amendment was proposed in the legislature to add the words "Jesus Christ" before the phrase 'holy author of our religion.' Madison viewed this proposal as a threat to the principle of universal freedom of religion. He feared that this would imply a restriction of the liberty defined in the bill only to those who profess the Christian religion. Due to Madison's opposition, this proposal was shelved. This episode shows that Madison's concerns for religious freedom extended to Non-Christians as well.[37] Years later, Jefferson reacted approvingly when he wrote that the protection of religious opinion was meant to be universal in his preamble and hence the omission of explicitly Christian language from the law was meant to comprehend within the government's protection 'the Jew and the Gentile, the Christian and Mahometan, the Hindoo, and Infidel of every denomination.'[38]

By now, Madison's *Remonstrance* had had its effect on the legislators. Not only Henry's bill was crushed by Madison's activism but Jefferson's bill was also passed. The Assembly passed the Virginia Statute for Religious Freedom on January 19, 1786. Madison was jubilant on achieving the first big victory of his political career. He remarked to Jefferson, 'The enacting clauses [passed] without a single alteration and I flatter myself [we] have in this country extinguished forever the ambitious hope of making laws for the human mind.'[39] Madison's biographer Ralph Ketcham writes, 'Of all his accomplishments as a legislator, Madison took greatest pleasure and pride in this victory….In fact, religious liberty stands out as the one subject upon which Madison took an extreme, absolute, undeviating position throughout his life.'[40] Jefferson was elated, to say the least. Years later, Jefferson explicitly requested that his authorship of the Statute of Virginia for religious freedom should be etched on his tombstone since he wanted to be remembered most for it along with two other achievements: authorship of the Declaration of Independence and founding of the University of Virginia.[41] The Statute was a major step in the development of America's religious freedom. Thus, with victory in Virginia ended one segment of the battle. Subsequent events of the battle to institute religious freedom were fought by this duumvirate at the federal level.

Madison was the chief architect in sketching the path of the Constitutional Convention as well as the greatest ingredient in its success—hence honored with the title "Father of the Constitution." Madison was the leader of the federal bloc of the Convention i.e. he desired a strong federal government. The Revolutionary War had witnessed pathetic coordination between the states. The Confederation Congress had failed in providing adequate support to the army. There were also apprehensions that with the waning of the revolutionary spirit, the states may fall into the machinations of European powers by pursuing an independent foreign policy. Without a centralized form of governance, it was also impossible for the states to pay back the war debt. However, in the Constitutional Convention, the states were unwilling to let go of their power. The Convention underwent multiple compromises (most famous being the Connecticut Compromise[α]) between the advocates of a strong federal government and those who opposed depletion in state power.

At the Convention, Madison was also incessantly vigilant in the cause of religious freedom. The Constitution's draft prepared by the Convention proved to be a remarkably secular document with the only reference to religion being the injunction that 'no religious test shall ever be required as a qualification to any office or public trust under the United States.' This particular clause was proposed by Charles Pinckney and was vigorously advocated by Madison. It was a clear break from the past since in Britain, anybody aspiring for public office was required to profess allegiance to the Church of England.[42] More interesting is the fact that Madison himself was not an atheist but

---

[α] A compromise arrived at by large and small states in the Constitutional Convention in 1787 that defined the legislative structure and representation that each state will have in the future United States Constitution.

rather a rationalist. Just a few months after the Convention adjourned, he proclaimed 'it is impossible for the man of pious reflection not to perceive in [the Constitution] a finger of that Almighty hand which has been so frequently and signally extended to our relief in the critical stages of the revolution.'[43] This lucidly means that Madison's personal motives were driven not by atheism or animosity towards deists but by careful consideration of protecting religious minorities and establishing a secular state. As he summed up his philosophy later in his life, '[R]eligion and Gov[ernment] will both exist in greater purity, the less they are mixed together.'[44] There you have it in a nutshell what Madison advocated throughout his legislative career. His defense of religious liberty was not based on hostility to any religion but was an expression of his rational views. However, an issue in which Madison could not go against the states for the Convention to be a success was that of voting rights. The constitution left the voting requirements to be instituted by individual states. Madison was dismayed but accepted it in a series of other compromises to not let the Convention fall apart.[45]

After the Constitution was drafted and sent to the states for ratification, Madison prepared to get it ratified in his home state, Virginia. His earlier struggle in Virginia to defeat Episcopalian measures had impressed upon Madison the importance of competing factions. Madison now understood that the presence of multiple religious sects afforded the protection of religious freedom if instituted by the law and not left to mere toleration. He deemed the competition between religious sects essential without which declarations in favor of religious freedom such as his *Remonstrance* were mere 'parchment barriers.'[46] To provide momentum for the ratification of the Constitution (especially in the crucial New York), Madison collaborated with Alexander Hamilton on the latter's *The Federalist* essays. The importance of competing factions became the foundation of Madison's celebrated *Federalist 10* essay in which he advocated that the presence of multiple competing factions in a nation may in itself provide protection to liberty. Madison specifically wrote about religious sects in *Federalist 10* that a single religious sect may degenerate to be the source of a political faction but the competition between the sects in a nation would secure the government 'against any danger from that source.'[47] Thus Madison envisioned how in the

American Republic, the government may facilitate and also benefit from the existence of competing religious sects and other political factions. This was his seminal contribution to the idea of diversity in a republic. In *Federalist 52*, Madison wrote that Congress's door must be 'open to merit of every description…without regard to…any particular profession of religious faith.'[48]

When the constitution's draft was sent to the states for ratification, many states objected to the absence of a bill of rights in the constitution. Such a bill of rights would have explicitly guaranteed particular rights to the citizens such as the freedom of religion, press, speech, etc. Jefferson who was still in Paris was dismayed at this omission when he received the draft of the Constitution from Madison. Jefferson complained that he did not like this omission and the bill of rights should be drafted to provide safeguards 'for freedom of religion, freedom of the press, protection against standing armies…'[49] Jefferson wanted to codify these rights in the Constitution since he considered such text as a safeguard against evil 'which no honest government should decline.'[50] Madison was of a different opinion. He had not pushed for a bill of rights earlier since he felt that by codifying these rights, their validity could be challenged in the court of law which was anathema to him. He felt that according to the present draft of the Constitution, 'There is not a shadow of right in the general government to intermeddle with religion. Its least interference with it would be a most flagrant usurpation.' When questioned about the bill of rights in the Virginia Convention, Madison answered, 'Is a bill of rights a security for [religious liberty]?...If there were a majority of one sect, a bill of rights would be a poor protection for liberty.'[51] None of the Madisonian arguments worked in the face of complaints about the omission raised by many state conventions considering the document. The Anti-Federalists i.e. those wanting more rights to be vested in the states rather than the federal government specifically found in this omission another point to attack the Constitution's draft. Six of the thirteen states, worried about the hostility between various religious factions in the new republic, actually proposed specific amendments to guarantee the freedom of religion.[52]

By this time, Patrick Henry was again plotting against Madison since the former was an Anti-Federalist and wanted to thwart the

Constitution's ratification in Virginia. Henry got a hold of one of the letters Jefferson had sent to a Richmond merchant expressing his displeasure at the omission of a bill of rights. Henry used this letter to publicly attack Madison by portraying Jefferson to be a friend of his cause. After Madison crafted a compromise between the Federalists and Anti-Federalists, Virginia Convention ratified the Constitution by a narrow majority of 89 to 79 with the recommendation that proposed amendments will be added to the document. The ratification further embittered Henry against Madison. It was clear knowledge to everyone that Madison enjoyed Washington's support and will thus be the most influential legislator in the future Congress. Henry now plotted to scupper Madison's election to the Congress. As the governor of Virginia, Henry first convinced the Virginia legislature to not appoint Madison to the U.S. Senate. When Madison then decided to run for the House of Representatives, Henry exemplified skullduggery by redrawing the legislative map so that Madison's home county was placed within a stronghold of Anti-Federalists (the first instance of gerrymandering$^\beta$ in America even before the term was coined). To achieve another layer of security, Henry convinced James Monroe—Madison's friend and Jefferson's other protégé—to run against him. It looked for a moment that the chief Federalist will not be able to get elected to the first Congress of the nation—the Congress for whose inception he toiled more than anybody else.[53]

In the face of this opposition, Madison changed tactics to consolidate his support and proposed to support the drafting of a bill of rights. Many observers have called this event the most important campaign promise in American history. In a series of letters, Madison performed a volte-face by suggesting that the same amendments to the Constitution which he had previously opposed were now appropriate. The pledge worked, and Madison was able to defeat Monroe. Personally, Madison was still not fully convinced about the need for a bill of rights. He wrote to Jefferson that he feared not being able to ensure 'the most essential rights' by such a step since the rights of conscience in particular 'if submitted to public definition would be narrowed much more than they are likely ever to be by an assumed

---

$^\beta$ The manipulation of the boundaries of an electoral constituency to favor a political party. This unfair practice continues to this day in the United States.

power.'⁵⁴ Jefferson assuaged Madison's worries by reversing the equation and explaining that the inclusion of a bill of rights would mean that judicial review could be exercised by religious minorities for their own protection. He also made a personal appeal to Madison: 'You omit one which has great weight with me, the legal check which it puts into the hands of the judiciary.'⁵⁵

When the first Congress convened in the newly inaugurated government, Madison prepared a list of all the amendments proposed by the state conventions and compressed them into a bill of rights which he proposed to the Congress. Absorbing Jefferson's argument regarding judicial scrutiny, Madison declared, 'independent tribunals of justice will consider themselves in a peculiar manner the guardians of those rights; they will be an impenetrable bulwark against every assumption of power in the Legislative or Executive; they will be naturally led to resist every encroachment upon rights expressly stipulated for in the Constitution by the declaration of rights.'⁵⁶ Thus, the Bill of Rights was incorporated inside the American Constitution as the First Amendment. It became a motivation behind enumerating the fundamental rights enjoyed by a citizen in constitutions across the world (including the Constitution of India). Madison's original draft read, 'The civil rights of none shall be abridged on account of religious belief or worship, nor shall any national religion be established, nor shall the full and equal rights of conscience be in any manner, or on any pretext, infringed.'⁵⁷ This language was condensed by Congress after repeatedly sending the bill between the House and Senate. The Senate did not pass the injunction that "No state shall violate the equal rights of conscience, or the freedom of the press, or the trial by jury in criminal cases." The state interference with religious liberty had to wait until 1940 to get scrapped by the Supreme Court. The Bill of Rights was passed by Congress codifying that "Congress shall make no law respecting an establishment of religion, or prohibiting the free exercise thereof."

With the passing of the First Amendment to the Constitution, Madison ensured the protection for all religious minorities in the new republic from the federal government by forbidding it from favoring one church or sect over another. The First Amendment also precluded the possibility of the rise of a national church. This is not to say that the amendment achieved total separation between church and state *in practice* at this point. The complete separation between church and state had to wait for a few decades and is still debated. But, the First Amendment secured *de jure,* religious freedom for all the citizens of the American republic. In fact, Madison went a step further by opposing the provision to inquire about a man's profession in the national census since the answer to this question would have infringed the right to absolute religious privacy.[58] With the inauguration of George Washington as the first president and the federal government now in place, it was up to Washington to ensure religious freedom and strengthen safeguards for religious minorities in the American republic.

President George Washington was acutely aware that any action that he would take (or would not undertake) will set up a first in the republic—a standard against which future presidencies would be evaluated. As he wrote to Madison, 'As the first of everything, in *our situation* will serve to establish a Precedent, it is devoutly wished on my part, that these precedents may be fixed on true principles.'[59] [emphasis original.] As the Commander-in-Chief of the Continental Army, Washington had given the freedom to the local military units of attaching with them their chosen chaplains so that no denominational character could be imposed on the army from the top.[60] Washington's inaugural speech to the Congress was first prepared by his secretary David Humphreys. Washington asked Madison to review the draft. Madison was appalled to read it and started drafting an altogether new speech. Significantly, Humphrey's draft had used explicit Christian language, referring to 'the blessed Religion revealed in the word of God.' Madison excised such language and though his draft still retained religious imagery, Madison included nothing that was uniquely Christian.[61] As president, Washington addressed different religious sects about his conviction to religious liberty and inclusion. Washington wrote to assuage fears of religious denominations by saying that if he had 'the slightest apprehension that the Constitution framed in the Convention,' at which he had presided might possibly 'endanger the religious rights of any ecclesiastical Society,' he would not have signed such a document. He claimed that 'no one would be more zealous than myself to establish effectual barriers against the horrors of spiritual tyranny, and every species of religious persecution.' Thus, Washington clearly led the way from the front—as he had done in the Revolutionary War—in the struggle of various denominations to achieve complete religious freedom and for the protection of religious minorities.[62]

Since Catholics were one of the most persecuted religious minorities in America, they looked up to Washington for assimilation into American society. In reply to a Catholic priest who expressed his apprehensions about religious liberty, Washington wrote that as mankind is becoming more liberal, it will be more accommodating in ensuring that 'worthy members of the Community are equally entitled to the protection of civil Government. I hope ever to see America among the foremost nations in examples of justice and liberality.'[63] Washington advocated an atypical position in the late eighteenth century about the assimilation of Catholics into the American Christian community. He anticipated that these and other such letters of his will be shared with the general masses and will create precedents for future administrations. Quakers were another community that had been earlier suspected of disloyalty during the Revolutionary War. Due to their pacifist beliefs, Quakers had refused to support any military action in the War. Thus, the prevailing mood in the new republic was of distrust towards Quakers. As a result, hundreds of Quakers had moved to Canada after the War and many had been expelled from the faith for siding with the British. General Washington too had been acerbic towards the Quakers during the War. But, as president, while expressing his past disappointment in a letter to Quakers, Washington reassured them that he has sworn to protect their religious liberty. Washington declared, 'Government being, among other purposes, instituted to protect the Persons and Consciences of men from oppression, it certainly is the duty of Rulers, not only to abstain from it themselves, but according to their Stations, to prevent it in others.'[64] Washington had transcended from being the General to being the President.

Washington also wrote similar letters addressing Jews in America hoping that the people of 'every denomination' could share in the 'temporal and spiritual blessings' of the Jews. When Washington was visiting Rhode Island after it had joined the Union, a Jewish Congregation seeking words of reassurance from him expressed their ordeal about how the Congregation had formerly been deprived of equal rights as free citizens of the state.[65] In reply to the Jewish Congregation, Washington expressed (though there is considerable evidence that Jefferson actually wrote the draft) his views referring to the matter of "toleration" earlier debated by Jefferson and Madison in Virginia. Washington wrote: 'It is now no more than toleration is spoken of, as if it was by the indulgence of one class of people, that another enjoyed the exercise of their inherent natural rights.' In this way, he coherently distilled the essence of religious freedom as not being built only on the concept of mere toleration. He went further to express his vision of religious equality in the American republic, adding that 'For happily the Government of the United States, which gives to bigotry no sanction, to persecution no assistance requires only that they who live under its protection should demean themselves as good citizens, in giving it on all occasions their effectual support....while every one shall sit in safety under his own vine and figtree, and there shall be none to make him afraid.' Thus, at a time when Jews were persecuted across Europe, Washington was quoting the Jewish prophet, Micah, while assuring them that America would be different.[66]

As the paramount American icon, Washington traveled through all the states of the Union and crowds everywhere thronged to the streets cheerfully to get a glimpse of their favorite hero. During such travels, when visiting cities with multiple religious sects, Washington followed an unusually idiosyncratic practice of praying in churches of various denominations. On a visit to orthodox Boston, he went to churches of Episcopal, Presbyterian, and Congregational denominations. Patently, he did not want his behavior to show any preference for a particular religious sect over others since that may have fueled animosity between them.[67]

On his last full day as president after eight years at the nation's helm, Washington complimented his countrymen by saying that he viewed the harmony and brotherly love between clergy of various denominations 'with unspeakable pleasure,' while adding that they are 'exhibiting to the world a new and interesting spectacle, at once the pride of our country, and the surest basis of universal harmony.'[68] Though somewhat exaggerated, Washington's address did exemplify his own efforts towards ensuring peace and liberty for religious minorities. He had facilitated the creation of an environment of religious freedom in the newly-born American republic. Various aspects of Washington's leadership and his ability to renounce power have been glorified in the past two centuries. However, the ideals of religious liberty that he established for the future—in a series of administrative policies and traditions—have not been sufficiently appreciated. As Paul Boller wrote, 'Washington unquestionably deserves major credit, along with Jefferson and Madison, for establishing the ideals of religious liberty and freedom of conscience...for Protestants, Catholics, and Jews—and for Deists and freethinkers as well—firmly in the American tradition.'[69]

Washington, Jefferson, and Madison together served as presidents for twenty-four years during the first three formative decades of the republic. All three of them upheld the principles of religious liberty and did not discriminate between various sects in their policies. These learned men were products of Enlightenment who were in power at a time when the personal liberty of human beings expanded more than at any other time in human history. Riding the philosophical current, they implemented the ideals of religious freedom. However, the ideals of complete separation between church and state differed during the first four presidencies. There were occasional proclamations recommending public days of thanksgiving and fasts (except during Jefferson's presidency), official days of prayer, and the use of religious imagery in the speeches made by these founding fathers. With electoral politics also came the practicality of indulging in such acts. What was clear though is that the general view of the government towards protecting religious minorities—no federal administration should discriminate between religious denominations—had been firmly established by the end of Washington's presidency. The actions of these founding fathers ensured the assimilation and protection of religious minorities of all denominations.

The personal beliefs of the founding fathers have been much debated and varied considerably among the group—from being devoutly religious to putting their faith in Providence to being atheist. To focus on the personal beliefs of the founding fathers is to diverge from the central point: Their faith in religious liberty for all sects and religions triumphed their personal faith. They advocated for religious freedom and protection for all religious minorities irrespective of their personal beliefs. They were anxious to not make the American Republic another Europe where nation-states were associated with particular religious denominations and minorities were actively persecuted. President Madison was especially worried about churches accumulating vast amounts of property. He did not desire that like the Catholic church in Europe, any religious sect in America should accumulate immense wealth which may foster abuse, corruption, and persecution of other sects. He vetoed down such bills that incorporated the church's attempt to gain personal property or sanction for charitable activities.[70] However, what should also be pointed out is that since Christianity was perceived as a moralizing force having a civilizing influence on the people, the early administrations of the nation indulged in policies to convert Native Americans to Christianity. Numerous times in their presidencies, the founding fathers appropriated federal funds to promote Christianity among the Native Americans in order to 'civilize them.' In this sense, the ideals of religious freedom (like many other ideals) only applied to the white citizens of the American Republic (more about this in the final chapter).[71]

For millennia, the caste system has dominated the social, economic, and political life of India. The origins of the caste system are shrouded in myth and speculation. It is speculated that as the Indian civilization diversified from agriculture towards other specialized professions such as artisans and merchants i.e. the society became more complex, the political organization of the society took the form of arrangement along the lines of one's profession. With time, this system started propagating along hereditary instead of professional lines.[72] Paradoxically, on the one hand, this institution of caste provided extraordinary stability to the Indian society across centuries while on the other hand, it degraded into an instrument of oppression. From the Greek historian Megasthenes in the third century BC to the French anthropologist Louis Dumont in the twentieth century, foreigners have found the caste system confounding as well as repulsive. Dumont went on to characterize Indians as *Homo Hierarchichus* and detailed the mindboggling complexity of the caste system, just like Megasthenes had characterized castes long ago. To put it briefly, the caste system is hereditary and there are four primary castes: Brahmins, the priests; Kshatriya, the warriors and nobility; Vaishya, farmers and merchants; and Shudra, tenants and servants. Then, there were the Untouchables—the so-called "fifth caste." They were below the caste system and were crushed under the burden of the social pyramid of the above four castes. The Untouchables constituted about a sixth of India's population and it can be said without exaggeration that they enjoyed no right as fellow human beings alongside the other four castes. They were not allowed to worship with or marry a person from another caste. Any kind of physical contact with them was deemed impure and they were marginalized to the periphery of the society in occupations such as manual scavenging, leather-tanning, and killing pests. If one is to go by ancient texts, even the shadow of an untouchable could pollute a Brahmin, while for an untouchable the punishment of reading (or even hearing) sacred Hindu texts was to chop off his ears, tongue, etc.[73]

In the nineteenth century, while opposing the British colonial rule, Indians began self-reflection towards their own society. The old structure of society based on caste as the fundamental unit collided with the enlightened notion of the human self as the basic constituent. From this clash between the old and new sprang new social reformers like Gopal Ganesh Agarkar, Jyotirao Phule, Savitribai Phule, Ishwar Chandra Vidyasagar, Ram Mohan Roy, Syed Ahmad Khan, and Tarabai Shinde who worked towards correcting various social ills. These reformers worked for the emancipation of various subaltern sections of Indian society such as untouchables, widows, and the uneducated. What made them different from other reformers before them was that many of them were products of Western education (formally or informally) and thus received sympathy (if not support) from the British in their endeavors. Before this time, due to the almost complete illiteracy and backwardness of the Untouchables, no leader had come forward from their community itself who could use the dual weapons of mass mobilization and education towards their emancipation. At the turn of the century, the struggle for freedom from colonial rule gained momentum through the rising influence of the Indian National Congress (the political party to which Gandhi belonged and referred from now on as Congress). When Mohandas Gandhi assumed the leadership of the Indian freedom movement, he earmarked the emancipation of the Untouchables through reforming the minds of the upper Caste Hindus (hereafter referred to as Caste Hindus) as a chief target on the way to Independence. At the same time, a young leader started the process of mobilizing the Untouchable minority from the bottom.[χ]

Bhimrao Ramji Ambedkar was born an untouchable in the Mahar community on 14 April 1891. From childhood, Ambedkar had learned that his existence was defined by his position in the caste system. There are multiple childhood stories of his humiliation by the Caste Hindus such as being beaten while drinking water from a public watercourse not meant for the Untouchables, being refused by a barber to shave his head, being segregated by other students who used to put their tiffin boxes away from the fear of getting polluted, not being allowed to take up Sanskrit (the language of sacred Hindu texts) as a subject,[74] and not being allowed to touch the common water vessel in the school.[75] Such cruel upbringing during childhood

---

[χ] The problem of Untouchability was that of Minorities as well as Equality. The Untouchables (also known as the Scheduled Castes) have been treated as minorities by the Indian Constitution in the sense that they have been provided safeguards for their emancipation. Their struggle for equal rights is also a part of this process. B. R. Ambedkar, the father of the Indian Constitution and an Untouchable himself by birth, believed that the Scheduled Castes should be dealt with as minorities. He had said clearly expressed that 'Scheduled Castes are more than a minority and that any protection given to other citizens or to the minorities will not be adequate for the Scheduled Castes. [They require safeguards against] the tyranny and discrimination of the majority.' (B.R. Ambedkar, 'States and Minorities' in Dr. Babasaheb Ambedkar: Writings and Speeches, Vol. 1, compiled by Vasant Moon, p. 383) I have followed Ambedkar's view in this chapter by treating the historical problem of Untouchability as that of Minorities though later chapters also comment on the Equality aspect of the issue. Another way to approach this chapter would have been to draw the parallels between race in the U.S. and caste in India but I have kept the former for the final chapter. This was done intentionally to draw the reader's attention toward the failures of the founding fathers in that chapter.

imprinted an indelible impression on Ambedkar's delicate young mind against Hinduism. Yet, it was a Brahmin teacher who became so fond of the young boy that in the class records, he changed the surname of the young 'Ambavadekar' to his own surname 'Ambedkar.' Since the last name in Hindus also reflects one's caste, this meant that Ambedkar would be confused by some as being a Caste Hindu during his life. Such was the sad state of Ambedkar's community that it celebrated his achievement of passing the fourth-grade examination by holding a public meeting because they considered it as having reached a 'great height.'[76] Ambedkar's father always supported him with all he could by buying new books for him and encouraging him to continue his studies after he graduated from high school. Ambedkar enrolled in Elphinstone College in Bombay to study economics and political science. After graduation, Ambedkar still wanted to study further and once expressed his adulation for Shakespeare's immortal lines: "There is a tide in the affairs of men, Which, taken at the flood, leads on to fortune; Omitted, all the voyage of their life is bound in shallows and in miseries." If these lines are anything to go by, fate intervened, and he soon received a unique opportunity to ride the flood to fortune for himself as well as for his community.[77]

The Maharaja of the princely state of Baroda was a generous ruler who decided to send Ambedkar to the United States for further education in lieu of working for the Baroda state for ten years after his return. Ambedkar arrived in the United States at the age of twenty-two and in two years graduated from Columbia University with a master's in economics. He then presented another thesis next year to earn another master's degree and a third thesis for which he later received a Ph.D. in Economics in 1927. Among the founding fathers of India discussed in this book, Ambedkar was the only political leader who received an education in the United States. A voracious reader all his life, Ambedkar collected more than 2,000 books from second-hand bookstores during his stay in New York and continued to buy hundreds of books during overseas trips throughout his life.[78] After studying at Columbia University, Ambedkar enrolled for the Bar course at Gray's Inn in London and simultaneously started working on a doctoral thesis at the London School of Economics (LSE). In the meantime, his scholarship ended, and he was summoned back to Baroda by the Maharaja. He took up a job in Baroda state where despite his academic qualifications, he faced discrimination due to his caste. He quit the service in disgust. After accumulating some savings, he went back to London in 1920 to resume his studies. He received a doctorate from LSE in 1923 for his thesis on *The problem of the rupee: Its origin and its solution* and was also called to the Bar.

Having studied more than anybody else in his community (in fact, being the first Indian to receive a doctorate in Economics from a foreign university), Ambedkar concentrated on the emancipation of his community. He launched a periodical to put forward his views and advocate rights for his community, led movements against untouchability in Mahad and Nasik, launched a party to fight elections for gaining political power, was appointed in the Viceroy's Executive Council in 1942, and became the first law minister of India after independence. From being defined only by his caste, he rose to become the Chairman of the Constitution Drafting Committee and thus received the honorific title "Father of the Indian Constitution." As Ramachandra Guha writes, 'He was, at various times, a lawyer, teacher, legislator, educational organizer, party builder and cabinet minister. Through all these roles and assignments, he continued to be a prolific writer. He published important books on many topics, including federalism, theology and philosophy, finance, language, constitutionalism and, not least, the sociology, politics and history of the caste system.'[79]

Throughout his life, Ambedkar remained a critic of Gandhi and the Indian National Congress. At times, he could become extremely piquant while exhibiting pungent humor and obstinacy in his views. He could also be pompous (he once compared himself with Moses in leading his followers towards freedom; he signed many of his letters with the salutation "Jai Bhim" that his followers used in his praise) and vilifying towards his political opponents.[80] However, the genius of Ambedkar was to understand that the emancipation of Untouchables could not come about until they would themselves stand up and fight for their rights. "Educate, Agitate, Organize," was the mantra that Ambedkar asked from his community to imbibe. For his contributions to the eradication of untouchability and emancipation of the Untouchables, he is fondly called *Babasaheb* meaning "respected father." Ambedkar advocated for the eradication of the caste system itself. He renounced Hinduism before his death and embraced Buddhism along with thousands of his followers. While Gandhi worked for the Untouchables from the above i.e. by reforming the minds of Caste Hindus, Ambedkar worked for the same cause from below i.e. by organizing the Untouchables to struggle for their rights. At various times during their activism, both of these social reformers influenced each other but could not fully reconcile their differences over religion and caste system as we shall see in this chapter. The compromise between the two in 1932 (known as the Poona Pact) and subsequent events in the Constituent Assembly (where major roles were played by Ambedkar and Vallabhbhai Patel) led to the provision of reservation for Scheduled Castes (erstwhile Untouchables) in the Indian Electoral System. In many aspects, the debate between these two founding fathers (Gandhi and Ambedkar) has received a central status in the life of the nation.

The first meeting between Gandhi and Ambedkar happened on August 14, 1931, before they left to attend the Second Round Table Conference (R.T.C.). The British had released Gandhi from the prison hoping to persuade Gandhi to attend the R.T.C. which was being convened to draft a new constitution for British India. By this time, Gandhi was the undisputed leader of the Indian freedom struggle and just a few months back he had concluded the most notable civil disobedience movement of his remarkable life—the Salt Satyagraha. Gandhi had already become a Mahatma (great soul) for millions of Indians. The meeting between the two was called by Gandhi who had invited Ambedkar to fathom his views. Gandhi wanted to understand Ambedkar's demands before going to the R.T.C. Apparently, Gandhi did not know at this point that Ambedkar was himself an untouchable. Both had, of course, heard about each other. Gandhi had earlier praised Ambedkar's 'Mahad Satyagraha' in his journal *Young India*. At an indirect level, Gandhi had already influenced Ambedkar since Satyagraha was a key Gandhian technique that was utilized by Ambedkar in Mahad to demand the use of a public water tank for the Untouchables. However, the first meeting between the two did not go well.[81]

As per the summary provided by Ambedkar's biographer Dhananjay Keer, 'The interview sounded the beginning of a war between Gandhi and Ambedkar.'[82] Gandhi started by asserting his dominance and said that even before Ambedkar was born, he has been thinking about the issue of untouchability. Gandhi went on to point out that the Congress under him has undertaken enormous efforts for the emancipation of the Untouchables. Ambedkar replied that 'All old and elderly persons always like to emphasize the point of age....But let me tell you frankly that Congress did nothing beyond giving formal recognition to this problem....We are not prepared to have faith in great leaders and Mahatmas. Let me be brutally frank about it. History tells that Mahatmas, like fleeting phantoms, raise dust, but raise no level.' One can only wonder how flabbergasted Gandhi would have been hearing this. Here was a fellow Indian, twenty-two years younger, giving back to Gandhi as good as he was getting. Ambedkar favored separate electorates for the Untouchables while Gandhi considered the political separation of the Untouchables from the Hindus as 'absolutely suicidal,' at which point Ambedkar took his leave. The two could not find common ground.[83]

The issue of separate electorates was close to Gandhi's heart because, in some provinces, the British had provided separate electorates to other religious communities like Muslims, Sikhs, and Christians. This meant that only those communities could choose their representatives. This scheme worked well for the British divide-and-rule policy. It led to a feeling of alienation and animosity among the communities since their leaders were not answerable to the public at large. Gandhi did not wish to exclude the Untouchables from the Hindu fold by the way of separate electorates since this would have stimulated more friction between them and the Caste Hindus. In such a conflict, the Untouchables had much to lose because of their economic and social weaknesses. Additionally, their livelihood, as well as social life, was intimately connected with the Caste Hindus and separate electorates would have created a further division in every village. The next clash between Gandhi and Ambedkar happened when the British convened the R.T.C. in London. The winter of 1930-31 in London was cold. The atmosphere, anything but.

At the R.T.C., the atmosphere became heated around the question of separate electorates for the Depressed Classes (Untouchables). Ambedkar fiercely advocated for separate electorates which would have meant that only the Untouchables could elect their own representatives. He considered this essential for the emancipation of his community since only its own representatives could understand their suffering. As discussed before, this was not acceptable to Gandhi who feared that this would divide the Hindu community within itself and further stimulate inter-caste violence. On being asked by a reporter to clarify his position, Gandhi said tactfully

> I do not mind Dr. Ambedkar. He has a right even to spit upon me, as every untouchable has, and I would keep on smiling if they did so. But I may inform you that Dr. Ambedkar speaks for that particular part of the country where he comes from. He cannot speak for the rest of India and I have numerous telegrams from the so-called 'untouchables' in various parts of India assuring me that they have the fullest faith in the Congress and disowning Dr. Ambedkar...[I]f they were to be given special electorates, as Dr. Ambedkar persists in demanding, it would do that very community immense harm. It would divide the Hindu community into armed camps and provoke needless opposition.[84]

Thus, Gandhi the politician attempted to underplay Ambedkar's representation of Untouchables while reinforcing his own position. They confronted each other on at least four occasions during the R.T.C. Gandhi made it clear that though due to historical reasons, Congress has reconciled itself to the special treatment of the Hindu-Muslim-Sikh tangle, Congress will not extend 'that doctrine in any shape or form.'[85] On November 13, in a speech at a meeting of the Minorities Committee, Gandhi said that he would not mind if the Untouchables shall convert 'to Islam or Christianity. I should tolerate that, but I cannot possibly tolerate what is in store for Hinduism if there are two divisions set forth in the villages...I want to say with all the emphasis that I command that, if I was the only person to resist this thing, I would resist it with my life.'[86] Thus, Gandhi warned everybody that if separate electorates would be extended to the Untouchables, then in the true Gandhian way of opposition, he would starve himself to death. Visualizing an impasse, the British prime minister ruled that each committee member should sign a request that his decision would be acceptable to them. Gandhi signed this request but Ambedkar did not.[87]

Within a week of his return to India, Gandhi was incarcerated again since he had planned to relaunch the Civil Disobedience Movement. He had also devised elaborate plans about how the movement should go on despite his incarceration. After his arrest, he was sent to Yerwada Jail along with his chief lieutenant Vallabhbhai Patel. Six months after the R.T.C., Ambedkar paid another visit to London asking the British Government not to yield to Gandhi.[88] Gandhi wrote to the Secretary of State reminding him about his vow of resisting separating electorates with his life. On 17 August 1932, the British announced their decision in which they accepted Ambedkar's suggestion of a separate electorate for the Depressed Classes. Receiving the news, Gandhi declared that he would undergo 'a perpetual fast unto death from food of any kind save water with or without salt and soda.' He also announced that he would begin the fast on 20th September, unless 'the British Government, of its own motion or under pressure of public opinion, revise their decision.'[89] Ambedkar felt that Gandhi's stand was immoral since, at the R.T.C., Gandhi had signed the requisition asking the prime minister to arbitrate. Thus, Gandhi was bound to accept the prime minister's reward.[90] Anticipating to find himself in a difficult position, the British Prime Minister Ramsay Macdonald had left a window for negotiation open by mentioning that 'only agreement of the communities themselves can substitute other electoral arrangements.'[91]

Gandhi did not relent from his resolve to fast because of two motives. The first motive was the same that he had iterated before—he was against the separation of the Untouchables from the 'Hindu fold,' since it would have created animosity between Hindu caste groups.[92] The second motive was more political. When Vallabhbhai Patel asked Gandhi why he was ready to put his life on the line for this comparatively trivial issue (compared to India's freedom), Gandhi replied that separate electorates 'fill me with horror. Separate electorates for all other communities will still leave room for me to deal with them, but I have no other means to deal with "untouchables." These poor fellows will ask why I who claim to be their friend should offer Satyagraha simply because they were granted some privileges..."Untouchable" hooligans will make common cause with Muslim hooligans and kill caste-Hindus.'[93] Hence, Gandhi the Mahatma, who didn't want the Untouchables to go out of the Hindu fold made common cause with Gandhi the politician, who foresaw that separate electorates would mean the weakening of the Congress politically against the British Raj by dividing its Hindu support base. In this manner, the stage was set for Gandhi's fast unto death. The coming week would be the longest week in Ambedkar's life.

As Gandhi started his fast, to save his life, Caste Hindus and Untouchables organized a conference where, outside the British auspices, for the first time they discussed the political rights of the Untouchables.[94] Reacting to the fast, Ambedkar, who regarded the argument as an ideal form of conversation, declared that 'I do not care for these political stunts' and that Gandhi should put forward an alternative proposal for him to ponder.[95] He also firmly proclaimed that though Gandhi's life is precious, he would not trade the interests of his community to save Gandhi's life. In the time-honored Ambedkarite tradition of brutal excoriation, he further pointed out that Gandhi is not immortal by saying 'Mahatmas have come and Mahatmas have gone. But the Untouchables have remained as Untouchables.'[96]

As a reaction to Gandhi's fast, Caste Hindus started offering demonstrations of repentance by opening temples overnight to the Untouchables and dining with them across the nation. Ambedkar left to meet Gandhi on 21 September. He categorically made it clear that he had nothing to do with other Untouchable leaders that Gandhi wished to meet. He also declared that he would not accept any proposal brought to him from Gandhi by another untouchable. By these actions, Ambedkar preempted Gandhi's plan of utilizing other Untouchable leaders during negotiations and made sure that 'They were the two leaders who mattered; the rest were peripheral or inconsequential.' Ambedkar who was an obscure leader until now was planning to face Gandhi on an equal footing. But, since the responsibility for change in the agreement lay with these two leaders and one of them was a Mahatma to millions of people, the onus of Gandhi's possible death lay directly on Ambedkar's shoulders. Thus, Ambedkar became a cynosure in the whole country.[97]

Ambedkar met Gandhi in prison on 22 September. Gandhi was weak and lay in bed. Ambedkar complained, 'Mahatmaji, you have been very unfair to us.' 'It is always my lot to appear to be unfair,' replied Gandhi, 'I cannot help it.'[98] Ambedkar asked Gandhi that if he would entirely devote his life to the welfare of the Untouchables, he would become 'our hero.' Gandhi replied that 'You are born an untouchable but I am an untouchable by adoption. And as a new convert I feel more for the welfare of the community than those who are already there.' Gandhi acknowledged that nothing is dearer to Ambedkar than the welfare of his community and asked him to come back with a nice scheme that could 'inspire life into a person who is willingly courting death.'[99]

In a meeting the next day with Caste Hindus, Ambedkar demanded 197 seats reserved for the Depressed Classes in the joint electorate as opposed to 71 seats earlier provisioned by the British under a separate electorate. Census figures were then analyzed. While Ambedkar was demanding the number of reserved seats on the basis of the proportion to the total population of each province, the Caste Hindus calculated the number as the percentage of seats against the population of Hindus. The eventual compromise was to use an average of both numbers and thus arrived the figure of 148 seats. However, there were two issues on which negotiations seemed to break down: the time limit up to which the reservation should continue and how the referendum would be held after that time limit to decide the question of separate vs. joint electorate in the future. Ambedkar wanted the agreement to not be binding forever and put to a referendum among Depressed Classes after ten years.[100] More than three days had already passed since Gandhi (who was almost sixty-three) had commenced the fast. As news started trickling in about his worsening health, Gandhi's youngest son Devdas made a strong appeal before Ambedkar with tears in his eyes to save Gandhi's life. Devdas pleaded that the agreement should not be paralyzed on the question of a referendum. Ambedkar was adamant and decided to take the matter to Gandhi. It was past nine at night when Ambedkar reached the prison and found Gandhi on a bed under a mango tree. Gandhi communicated to Ambedkar that he did not oppose a referendum though it should take place after five years instead of ten.

Suddenly, when Gandhi's voice started to weaken, the doctors intervened and Ambedkar had to go back.[101]

As discussions continued the next day, despite Gandhi's nod, the Caste Hindus persisted in opposing the clause of the referendum. Ambedkar decided to again meet Gandhi in the prison and went to do so along with Gandhi's confidant Chakravarti Rajagopalachari (Rajaji). Ambedkar was not sure if five years would be a sufficient time to judge the merit of joint electorates over separate ones. Gandhi turned Ambedkar's logic back on him by retorting that if Ambedkar was unsure, then the referendum should be held sooner rather than later. Gandhi asked Ambedkar to give Hindus a chance for expiation while the Caste Hindus should 'give a good account of themselves within five years or not at all.' In the end, Gandhi added with a firm tone: 'There you are. Five years or my life.' Gandhi's health was rapidly deteriorating by now. His voice 'scarcely rose above a whisper.'[102] The government was considering moving him outside the prison so that it could not be blamed in case he died.[103]

After coming back from the prison, Ambedkar assembled his advisory group in a separate room to continue the discussions. Thought must have crossed Ambedkar's mind that what would happen if Gandhi died. Ambedkar would have been blamed for the death of the most esteemed Indian of the time whereas the cause of Depressed Classes would also have received a big blow due to the distrust Gandhi's death would have spawned. Already, Ambedkar was being excoriated from all sides of the Hindu community—even many members of the Depressed Classes were cursing him since they felt that Gandhi is staking his own life for their cause. After a whole hour, he returned and announced that the group was unable to agree on less than ten years! Despite seeing for himself how feeble Gandhi had become, Ambedkar was adamant about his position. Gandhi, devoid of energy, was still equally adamant and conveyed that 'My stand is: either agree to referendum after five years or let me die.'[104]

At this juncture, Rajaji took initiative on his own to save his mentor's life. Rajaji suggested to Ambedkar and got his acquiescence to altogether drop the question of a referendum for the moment. One wonders if Rajaji coerced Ambedkar into accepting his viewpoint by cunningly pointing out that if Gandhi would die, Ambedkar's political career would have been over and that he would be excoriated by posterity. Getting Ambedkar on board, Rajaji then went to convey the news to Gandhi. Rajaji explained that the compromise does not go against Gandhi's resolve and future course of events may decide the question of the referendum. According to an eyewitness, Gandhi asked Rajaji to repeat the proposal and 'expressed himself only in one word, "Excellent."'[105] Ambedkar was himself filled with joy on hearing the news. The Poona Pact was then drafted, and signatures were gathered on the evening of September 24. Ambedkar signed on behalf of the Depressed Classes along with other leaders whereas many Congress leaders (except Gandhi himself) signed the pact on behalf of the Caste Hindus. Rajaji was so overjoyed that he exchanged his fountain pen with Ambedkar.[106]

After signing the Poona Pact, Ambedkar and caste Hindu leaders reached back Bombay and the pact drafted inside one of His Majesty's prisons was cabled to the British Cabinet for its approval. In a speech in Mumbai, a mellowed Ambedkar said

> I believe it is no exaggeration for me to say that no man a few days ago was placed in a greater dilemma than I was. There was placed before me a difficult situation in which I had to make a choice between two difficult alternatives.
>
> There was the life of the greatest man in India to be saved. There was also before me the problem to try to safeguard the interests of the community which in my humble way I was trying to do...I think in all these negotiations a large part of the credit must be attributed to Mahatma Gandhi himself. I must confess that I was surprised, immensely surprised, when I met him that there was so much in common between him and me.[107]

But, Gandhi did not yet break his fast. Gandhi communicated that he will break the fast only if the Cabinet will accept the settlement in *toto*. Urgent messages were sent to His Majesty's Government appealing that it should lose no time in ratifying the pact. Gandhi's condition was worsening and there was no sign of action from the British government. A cable from Reuter's informed that the Cabinet would meet on Wednesday (September 28) and nothing decisive could be done before then. Another unnerving report said that the Cabinet might first satisfy itself by receiving feedback from all the concerned parties before accepting the pact. Such propaganda was having its effect on Gandhi's admirers who were becoming increasingly restless due to the delay. The doctor overseeing Gandhi was of the opinion that he is entering 'into the danger zone.' On receiving the news about the Poona Pact, Ramsay Macdonald hurried back to London and after prolonged deliberations extending to midnight, the government ratified it.

The whole of 26 September passed in anxiety in the Yerwada prison. The renowned poet and Nobel laureate Rabindranath Tagore arrived at noon from Calcutta to meet Gandhi. At last, the Poet conveyed the good news about the ratification of the Poona Pact by saying that 'I am so glad that I have come and that I have come in time.' Finally, in another show of firmness, Gandhi postponed the breaking of the fast until being fully satisfied by studying the actual text of the government's communique. He also remarked that the document should go to the leaders of the Depressed Classes too for their acceptance as a whole in *toto*. Everyone around him was flabbergasted and protested that this would mean 'holding another conference,' to which Gandhi replied, 'Then a conference it must be.' After anxious consultation and assurance by leaders present around him that the leaders of the Depressed Classes will have no objection, Gandhi succumbed to the pressure. Amidst recitation of a poem by Tagore and prayers, Gandhi broke his fast by drinking some orange juice handed to him by his wife Kasturba.[108]

The Poona Pact was a watershed moment in the history of Indian politics. It had three significant effects. First, it brought together the Caste Hindus and the Depressed Classes face to face in a way that had never happened before. With his fast, Gandhi averted the animosity between the two groups which would have taken root if the upcoming elections would have taken place by separate electorates. Second, Ambedkar emerged as an indisputable representative of the Depressed Classes—someone who could also challenge Gandhi. Ambedkar broke the cardinal rule of India's politics that one should not go against Gandhi and came out not just unscathed but with increased political weight. Third, and most significantly, every single election in India from 1932 to the present day, whether at the central, state, or district level has been conducted broadly on the basis of reservation for Depressed Classes in a joint electorate on the basis of this pact. Finally, it was also the highest point of the Gandhi-Ambedkar relationship. The challenge that Ambedkar threw at

Gandhi had profound effects on the latter. Both were working for the emancipation of the Untouchables, but the events of September 1932 made Gandhi drop his patronizing attitude towards the Untouchables. The recent encounter with Ambedkar also forced him to reassess his views about the caste system itself. Gandhi had had his way over Ambedkar by undertaking the fast. But at what cost? Deep inside he felt that he had coerced Ambedkar. From now on, for the next few years, he placed the emancipation of the Untouchables at the front among the goals of the freedom struggle. Independence from the British would mean nothing to him if the Untouchables were to continue to be held in bondage.

In February 1933, barely five months after the Poona Pact, Gandhi started a new weekly named *Harijan*. The term meant "Children of God" and from now on Gandhi used this euphemism to address the Untouchables. The inaugural issue contained seven pieces written by Gandhi and another contributed by Ambedkar on Gandhi's request. In his piece, Ambedkar first made it clear that he did not believe he has sufficient worth in the eyes of Hindus that they will take 'any message from me with respect.' He further clarified that he is only writing as an individual to another. Ambedkar stated that 'The out-caste is a bye-product of the Caste-system. There will be outcastes as long as there are castes. Nothing can emancipate the Out-caste except the destruction of the Caste-system.' Gandhi was distressed by Ambedkar's message of renouncing the caste system. Beneath Ambedkar's short statement, Gandhi wrote a much longer explanation about how Ambedkar has every right to be bitter towards Hinduism. To divert attention from the caste system, Gandhi then underplayed the role of the caste system by instead focusing on 'the distinction of high and low that has crept into Hinduism and corroding it.' Each issue of the *Harijan* contained pieces about the emancipation of Harijans by reporting news of the opening of temples and wells to them as well as about the literature celebrating their cultural traditions. The government had given permission to Gandhi for editing the weekly from the jail. For now, the campaign for India's Independence was put to the background by Gandhi and all focus was on the emancipation of Harijans.[109]

Many of Gandhi's own followers were skeptical about Gandhi's efforts for Harijans at a time when the struggle for freedom demanded Gandhi's unmitigated leadership. However, for Gandhi, it was like 'one time in my life an emphasis on one thing, at another time on [an]other,' though Gandhi conceded that, 'Full and final removal of untouchability…is utterly impossible without swaraj [self-rule].'[110] With time as Gandhi felt that the Harijan movement is waning, he declared that he would go on another fast, this time for three weeks, commencing on May 8. The stated aim of this fast was self-purification. It was also aimed at shaming the Caste Hindus at their treatment of the Harijans. As we saw, Gandhi's last fast of less than a week had been perilous for his health. Thus, everybody was shocked by Gandhi's recent announcement. Perhaps Gandhi realized that his last fast had a measure of coercion (towards Ambedkar) associated with it. Gandhi stated that another fast was needed for himself and asked his fellow-workers to pray that 'whether I live or die, the cause for which the fast is to be undertaken may prosper.'[111] After Gandhi commenced his fast, the British government released him from the prison fearing that his likely death may fall upon their shoulders. Across the nation, to save Gandhi's life, hundreds of temples were opened to the Harijans and joint luncheons were organized by the Caste Hindus as a sign of penance. Despite his fragile health during the last fast, Gandhi bore this fast well. The fast ended after twenty-one days as planned.

The encounter with Ambedkar had a profound effect on Gandhi's thoughts and methods towards emancipating the Untouchables. Gandhi's views regarding the caste system also substantially changed. He had never been a proponent of inter-caste marriages but next month, his youngest son Devdas got married to Rajaji's daughter Lakshmi (who was Brahmin whereas Devdas was Vaishya) with Gandhi's permission. In 1926, Gandhi had declared that 'All I have advocated is abolition of the fifth varna [caste]. The untouchables should, therefore, merge in the fourth division.'[112] By the end of 1935, Gandhi wrote an article titled 'CASTE HAS TO GO' in *Harijan*, and proclaimed that 'The sooner public opinion abolishes [caste] the better.'[113] Going a step further in years to come, Gandhi said in 1947 that he had 'long ago made it a rule not to be present at, or give his blessings for any wedding unless one of the parties was a Harijan.'[114]

Gandhi started a 'Harijan tour' on November 7, 1933, which covered 12,500 miles and lasted for nine months. The goal of the tour was to foster love and break down animosity between Harijans and Caste Hindus. He collected an enormous sum of money on the tour to be spent on Harijan welfare work. Gandhi also emphasized the importance of economic advancement for Harijans and treated it as a question of the rejuvenation of village life in India. He successfully mobilized women from all sections of society to undertake cotton spinning and weaving in order to become economically more self-reliant. However, with his active campaign against the caste system, he also became a target of the orthodox Hindus. In 1934, there were attempts on his life. In Poona, a bomb was thrown at a car thought to be carrying him. Seven others were injured in this failed assassination attempt. In Karachi, a man planning to use his ax against Gandhi was apprehended.[115]

Ambedkar, on the other hand, became increasingly bitter towards Caste Hindus and the Poona Pact. The Doctor also published a booklet *Annihilation of Caste* which was a tract criticizing Hindu religion, its caste system and traditions. He advocated that the only remedy for demolishing the caste system is to promote inter-caste marriages. Until now, Ambedkar had viewed the emancipation of the Untouchables as a purely economic and social problem. But, he now observed that Hindus follow the caste system chiefly because of being deeply religious. This was a departure from his previous beliefs since he had always been opposed to considering the question of untouchability as a religious matter. In 1935, Ambedkar went a step ahead and declared that he will not die a Hindu. The encounter with Gandhi had changed him too. As a cultural critic has presciently written, Gandhi had 'taken over economics from Babasaheb [Ambedkar] and Ambedkar had internalized the importance of religion.'[116]

In the provincial elections of 1937 held under restricted franchise under the Government of India Act 1935, Ambedkar's party won fifteen out of seventeen seats reserved for the Depressed Classes in the Bombay Province. Despite his reputation of taking on Gandhi and the Congress, Ambedkar's Independent Labour Party was confined to the Bombay Province. Elsewhere in the nation, Congress championed support of the Depressed Classes. Gandhi's campaign against

Untouchability and Congress's zestful campaigning were successful in gathering their support. However, Ambedkar ascribed Congress's performance to caste Hindu voters. As things appeared to settle down with the capture of power by Congress and Ambedkar's party, an event of world significance occurred not much later. In 1939, Europe descended into the chaos of war which expanded into engulfing the whole world in its fold.[117]

During the Second World War, after the failure of the Cripps Mission, Congress launched the Quit India Movement in August 1942. As Gandhi and other Congress leaders commenced another prison term, Ambedkar supported British policies and was elected to the Viceroy's executive council. In 1945, Ambedkar published *What Congress and Gandhi Have Done to the Untouchables*—a book whose chief aim was to criticize Gandhi and the Congress. In this stinging critique, Ambedkar stated that the Harijan emancipation work by Congress has been motivated by the desire to prevent the Untouchables from becoming a separate element in the national life which would hurt the Congress. He also deplored Gandhi's philosophy as a reactionary one. He excoriated Gandhi by suggesting that Gandhi was using 'religion as an opiate to lull the masses into false beliefs and false security.'[118] Instead of replying himself, Gandhi deputed Rajaji to refute Ambedkar's book. Rajaji published *Ambedkar Refuted* in which he demonstrated that Ambedkar has been very selective in his attack and that Gandhi's efforts have brought a revolutionary upheaval in the mindset of Caste Hindus and Harijans in addition to tangible social reform. Alas, Ambedkar could not have chosen a more inopportune time to publish his book. The transfer of power from the British to the Congress was around the corner.

Having collaborated with the British, Ambedkar had burned his bridges with the general populace. Consequently, his political party fared miserably in the elections of 1945-46. By now, it was certain that the transfer of power from the British would take place in a few months and hence Ambedkar sought to reach out to the Congress Party. Because of the Quit India Movement, the leadership of Congress had endured imprisonment for more than three years. This sacrifice combined with increased Hindu-Muslim polarization around the issue of partition meant that Congress swept the Hindu votes across the nation. Vallabhbhai Patel who was incarcerated with

Gandhi in Yerwada Jail during his fast was a silent spectator at the time of the Poona Pact. However, now Patel was the most influential leader within the Congress organization. Ambedkar met Patel through an intermediary and discussed a possible alliance between Congress and his Scheduled Caste Federation. Patel took an active interest in neutralizing this 'former adversary.'

But the talks failed when Ambedkar advocated the demand of 20 percent of all seats to be reserved for his party in the alliance which was not acceptable to Patel. Patel was in continuous contact with Gandhi during this time and the latter had advised about exercising caution. Gandhi was wary of Ambedkar's commitment. Ambedkar sent Patel a memorandum and proposed 'reservation for Depressed Classes in public services (as well as in the legislature), state support for them in high school and university, and state funding for the foreign education of their best students.' Ambedkar also thought that this is a good opportunity to resurrect the demand for separate electorates and pointed out how in his view the present system has proven to be detrimental for the interests of the Depressed Classes. Patel wrote back to Ambedkar and expressed his disagreement by noting that Congress had a different approach to the problem. Patel reiterated that Congress aimed at the assimilation of the Depressed Classes into the Hindu community while Ambedkar's proposals will 'perpetuate the separation' of the two communities. Being one of Gandhi's closest disciples, Patel also expressed his resentment over Ambedkar's past attacks on Gandhi. Ambedkar replied to Patel after more than a month in which he defended himself and questioned if Patel's sense of nationalism meant that one should be a Congressman to be a nationalist. In this way, the first round of talks between the two ended on a bitter note.[119]

Ambedkar then tried to launch another satyagraha against caste Hindu oppression. But, in the nationalistic fervor of the time, this movement fizzled out. He then left for London where he met many politicians in the hope of gaining support for his views back home. The British knew well that Congress would soon be in power in an independent India and wisely decided to not encourage Congress's adversary. Back in India, Ambedkar mellowed down in the face of isolation. He realized that as the British would soon be out of the picture, he needs to realign himself in the Indian political landscape or face political extinction. He became keen to come to terms with the Congress and talked privately with Amrit Kaur who was among Gandhi's close disciples. Amrit Kaur passed the gist of their talk to Gandhi who replied that Ambedkar's demand for separate electorates cannot be conceded. Ambedkar then dropped the demand for separate electorates. Subsequently, Ambedkar had a conversation with Prime Minister Jawaharlal Nehru and agreed to join the Cabinet. Such reconciliation between Ambedkar and the Congress would not have come to fruition without Gandhi's nod.[120]

What made Ambedkar's inclusion in the Indian Cabinet acceptable to Gandhi? One explanation is that Ambedkar had dropped the most contentious of his demands—separate electorate for the Depressed Classes—which would have annulled the Poona Pact. A second explanation says that Gandhi viewed Ambedkar's inclusion as an atonement that India had to make to the Untouchables. A third observer notes that initially Nehru and Patel were not receptive to the idea of inducting Ambedkar due to the lack of trust. Gandhi then convinced Nehru by reminding him that freedom has come to India and not only to the Congress.[121] Whatever the case may have been, it is certain that it was only due to Gandhi's acquiesce that Ambedkar could serve in the Cabinet. Thus, Gandhi exemplified large-heartedness by reconciling with Ambedkar despite all the attacks the latter had mounted on Gandhi in the previous years. Gandhi had also similarly proposed to Nehru, names of eminent lawyers who were earlier loyal to the British, and later with Gandhi's acceptance served in the Constituent Assembly.[122]

To serve in the Cabinet, Ambedkar had to first get elected to the Constituent Assembly. With the Partition of India, he had lost his earlier seat. Patel intervened at this juncture to get Ambedkar elected by compelling a Congress member to vacate his seat. Ambedkar was then made the first law minister of independent India and was also appointed as the Chairman of the Drafting Committee of the Constitution.[123] In this way, a member of the Untouchable community—which was discriminated against in innumerable ways codified in ancient legal texts—became the chief draftsman of the Constitution of free India. A so-called untouchable drafted the Constitution that ensured equal rights to all in a society plagued with inequalities. Ambedkar would become a symbol of emancipation for his community and would receive the honorific title "Father of the Indian Constitution." It would be poetic justice that a nation dominated by Caste Hindus would adopt the Constitution chiefly drafted by an untouchable.

Our story would have already ended had there been no hiccups in the Constituent Assembly. In 1945, Sir Tej Bahadur Sapru headed a committee to prepare a report on the constitutional scheme to be adopted after independence. This report, known as the Sapru Committee Report, suggested that for the seats reserved for the Scheduled Castes (a term comprising various disadvantaged groups including the Untouchables) in the legislature, the candidate must win at least 20 percent of the Scheduled Caste votes to get elected. This was similar to a scheme that Ambedkar had earlier proposed. It was advocated by Ambedkar so that a Scheduled Caste candidate could get elected by the say of the community itself and not only by the wishes of the caste Hindu majority. Ambedkar's proposal was accepted by the committee. In the same report, a Congressman and a leader of the Untouchables, Jagjivan Ram, had advocated the stipulation to be 25 percent votes. Jagjivan Ram explained in his memorandum that the current system containing no such stipulation 'gives a chance to the caste Hindus or interested parties of theirs to set up dummy candidates and get them returned by caste Hindus' votes.'[124]

In the Constituent Assembly, Ambedkar tried his best to add as many extra safeguards as he could for the Depressed Classes while advocating for more reservations. At the same time, India was being partitioned and communal riots had broken out in various parts of the nation. Many princely states had to be integrated into the Union while some of them were planning a military revolt to remain outside the Union. Among all this insanity that had gripped the just-born nation, the last thing Nehru and Patel wanted was to further create separation between various communities based on religion or caste. Simultaneously, Patel firmly controlled the Congress organization and thus his writ ran almost unchallenged in the Constituent Assembly. Patel was also the Chairman of the Sub-Committee on Minorities.

The task of the Sub-Committee on Minorities was to institute safeguards for the minorities in independent India. In July 1947, one of the first things the Committee did was to vote by a majority of 28 to 3 that there should be no separate electorates for elections to the legislatures. With this decision, the Committee made sure that India would be politically integrated unlike before when the British had provided separate electorates based on religion. These separate electorates had done much damage to India's unity and bring about the nation's Partition. Then, the committee decided by a majority of 26 to 3 that there should be reservation for recognized minorities in various legislatures. It was also decided that this stipulation should be fixed for a period of ten years, thereafter it could be reconsidered for further extension. The minorities that could avail this reservation were identified and listed: Anglo-Indians, Parsees, Plains tribesman in Assam, Indian Christians, Sikhs, Muslims, and Scheduled Castes. Just like the Sapru Committee Report, Ambedkar proposed that the candidates of the majority community (such as Caste Hindus) should also poll a minimum number of votes from the minority community. This was another ploy by Ambedkar to introduce the concept of separate electorates from the backdoor, in a diluted form, by giving sort of a veto to the minority over the majority. This proposal was defeated since only Ambedkar voted for it. Such was the influence of Patel that even Jagjivan Ram who had brought the same proposal in front of the Sapru Committee did not vote for it. The proposal regarding reservation of seats in the Cabinet found some favors but ultimately lost by a majority of 8 to 7. These were setbacks for Ambedkar.

On the positive side, the provision for reservation in Services for Scheduled Castes was carried by a large majority of 16 to 1. It was also agreed that such reservation should be extended to the cases where the recruitment was made by competitive exams (a much-debated topic today). The committee also provided the right to the members of the minority community to contest from unreserved seats as well, in addition to the seats reserved for them. Another of Ambedkar's proposals was accepted: the President should appoint an independent officer at the Center and by the Governors in the provinces to oversee the working of the safeguards provided for the minorities. Additionally, a proposal put forward by a Congressman was accepted which provisioned for setting up a commission to regularly investigate the conditions of socially and educationally backward classes.[125] The Draft Constitution also abolished Untouchability and its practice in any form through the force of law by deeming it a criminal offense. There is a pattern here. There were two forces at work simultaneously. Ambedkar wanted more rights for the Depressed Classes while Patel and the Congress were willing to provide them but not at the cost of any provision which may foster division between the communities and weaken the nation's unity.

In August 1947, Patel defended the Committee's proposals while presenting the report in the Constituent Assembly. Patel showed his concern for the unity of India. He started by saying that, 'An attempt has been made in this report to enumerate those safeguards which are matters of common knowledge, such as representation in legislatures, that is, joint versus separate electorates…[F]ortunately we have been able to deal with this question in such a manner that there has been unanimity.'[126] When another Depressed Classes leader Sardar Nagappa moved an amendment to again bring back the stipulation of a fixed percentage of votes from the majority community for minority election, Patel said bluntly that Nagappa already knew that he would have to later withdraw his amendment since 'a majority of the Scheduled Castes representatives in this House, except one or two or three…were all against this amendment.' He went further and appealed to the Scheduled Castes that

> You have very nearly escaped partition of the country again on your lines. You have seen the result of separate electorates in Bombay, that when the greatest benefactor of your community [referring to Gandhi] came to Bombay to stay in bhangi [an untouchable community] quarters, it was your people who tried to stone his quarters. What was it? It was again the result of this poison, and therefore I resist this only because I feel that the vast majority of the Hindu population wishes you well. Without them where will you be? Therefore, secure confidence and forget that you are a Scheduled Caste…let us stand as one, and together.[127]

With Patel's backing, the report was adopted. However, soon afterward, India was engulfed in widespread riots, vast and violent migration, and a refugee crisis. Five months later, in January 1948, Gandhi was assassinated by a Hindu extremist. The whole nation was reeling from religious tensions and conflicts. Amidst a civil war-like situation in the nation, in December 1948, Patel summoned a meeting of the Advisory Committee on Minorities. The meeting again opened the question of reservation in legislatures for religious minorities. Many members of the committee suggested doing away with reservation altogether. Patel deftly proposed that each member should confine the proposals to his/her community so as to not force another minority to give up their rights. On May 11, 1949, the committee presented its report in the Constituent Assembly. The report advocated for the abolition of all kinds of reservations based on religion except for the Hindu and Sikh members of the Depressed Classes and tribal communities which should continue for a period of ten years. The nationalistic fervor in the nation was such that the report stated, 'The committee are fully alive to the fact that decisions once reached should not be changed lightly. Conditions have, however, vastly changed since August 1947 and the committee are satisfied that the minorities themselves feel that in their own interest, no less than in the interests of the country as a whole, the statutory reservation of seats for religious minorities should be abolished.'[128] Patel wanted to make sure that religious communalism will not engulf India again on the issue of reservations. He rebuked Muslim delegates to the Constituent Assembly when they expressed resentment towards the abolition of reservations.

The details are murky about what happened behind the curtains. The report above had mentioned that the reservation for the Depressed Classes in legislature and services would be instituted as provisioned before. It is believed that at some point in time before this report was presented in the Constituent Assembly, Patel had conveyed to Ambedkar that the reservation for Depressed Classes too would be diluted. It might have just been a ploy for Patel to see Ambedkar's response. We do know that Patel was in contact with S. K. Patil (a Congressman from Ambedkar's home state) who was reporting about Ambedkar to Patel. Perhaps it was through Congressman like Patil and K. M. Munshi that Patel floated the proposal to abolish reservations altogether.[129] Patel felt that with the abolition of untouchability through the law, there will not be any need for reservation in legislatures. One source says that at this juncture Ambedkar decided to walk out of the Constituent Assembly saying that 'he had laboured for three years in preparing the Constitution on the cost of his health so that he could do something for the welfare' of his community. He made it clear that if seats were not kept reserved for the Depressed Classes in the Constitution, he would walk out of the Constituent Assembly so that 'in the pages of history it would remain written that how the Hindus opposed the question of the welfare for untouchables.' Following this threat, Ambedkar did not attend the Assembly for the next few days. By this time, Ambedkar had mostly completed the work on the Draft Constitution and had garnered respect from across the party lines for his talent. Indeed, it would have been a source of great humiliation for India if the Chairman of the Constitution's Drafting Committee would have resigned like this. At this point, Patel backed off and the report retained the clause of reservation for the Depressed Classes.[130]

With its passing, the reservation for Depressed Classes was enshrined in the Constitution with joint electorates on the model of the Poona Pact. Both Nehru and Patel showed over-confidence at the time by forecasting that the Depressed Classes would be uplifted in the next ten years. Ambedkar was more prescient when he used Edmund Burke's saying, "Large Empires and small minds go ill together" as a retort since he was convinced that it would take much more than ten years. Nehru himself extended the reservations in 1960 for another ten years and they have been further extended ever since.[131]

Finally, Ambedkar moved an amendment towards the special treatment of the Depressed Classes in recruitment to the public services while also extending its scope to the states. Many delegates in the Assembly opposed this amendment. They wanted the amendment to also include religious minorities. Here, Ambedkar found an ally in Patel who gave an impassioned reply to forcefully convey that no religious minority in the country needs so much emancipation as the Depressed Classes. Of course, the article was adopted by the Assembly as proposed. In this manner, through the rule of law and legislation, India started on the path to becoming a more democratic society by assimilating caste-based minorities that had been persecuted for centuries.[132]

But a more insidious form of nationalism is the narrowness of mind that it develops within a country, when a majority thinks itself as the entire nation and in its attempt to absorb the minority actually separates them even more.
-Jawaharlal Nehru

All, too, will bear in mind this sacred principle, that though the will of the majority is in all cases to prevail, that will to be rightful must be reasonable; that the minority possess their equal rights, which equal law must protect, and to violate would be oppression.
-Thomas Jefferson

Both America and India still strive toward providing equal opportunities in all spheres to their minorities. In America, African Americans, Native Americans, Muslims, and Immigrants face various kinds of discrimination in their daily lives. In India, the same is true for Dalits (erstwhile Untouchables), Tribals, and Muslims (we will read more about the latter two in the final chapter). Other minorities may also be added to this list such as those classified by language, sexual orientation, and culture. The record of these nations in safeguarding their minorities has varied across their history. Thankfully, we can say that the minorities in both of these nations are substantially better in almost every way than they were at the nation's birth.

America remained a safe haven for religious minorities persecuted in Europe whereas a lot of progress has been made in India towards dismantling the oppressive caste system. Of course, much still needs to be done in both nations. The actions of the founding generations shaped the institutions of governance empowered to deal with the minorities. It is up to the present generation of political leaders and citizens to keep the populist forces at bay. The rise of populist forces is generally attributed to the stoking of fears of "the other" and in recent times some such tendencies have unfortunately surfaced in both nations.

Focusing on the Indian subcontinent after the departure of the British, we see that Pakistan, Sri Lanka, and Myanmar have had bloody civil wars, caused due to or fueled by inequalities in the legal/social status of linguistic and/or religious communities (Bengali Muslims, Sri Lankan Tamils, and Rohingya Muslims respectively). Despite being much more diverse and having seen its own share of violent conflicts, India escaped a similar fate because its founding fathers enshrined safeguards for the minorities in the Constitution as well as worked towards peacefully assimilating them. In fact, the leadership of the Indian National Congress during the freedom struggle itself reflected the nation's diversity. Gandhi understood very well that independence from the British is merely political freedom whereas real freedom would come when justice and equal rights could be availed by every Indian citizen. On the other hand, America assimilated immigrants from Europe for more than two centuries belonging to various religious sects and ethnicities. Though, as we shall discuss in the final chapter, non-White races continued to face extreme discrimination for a long time in America.

There was a notable difference in the approach of the two founding generations in emancipating the minorities discussed in this chapter. The American founding fathers ensured equality for religious minorities in the republic by taking steps towards the separation of the church and state. Utilizing their political influence, Jefferson and Madison enacted safeguards for religious minorities in the founding documents while Washington ensured as the first president that these safeguards were followed to the letter. In contrast, the Indian founding fathers had to confront the question of religion head-on by rejecting the bondage of the orthodox caste system and framing policies aimed at the emancipation of the Depressed Classes. Gandhi and Ambedkar understood that just enacting the safeguards in the founding documents would not be enough in bringing down the age-old tradition. The result was the social movements that these founders participated in and led to a change in the mindset of the masses. As we read in this chapter, though the approaches taken by these founding generation were different, a central theme of their effort was that there could be no real democracy without flourishing minorities.

It is clear from this chapter that both founding generations worked in their own ways to frame governmental policies for specific minorities. The successes and failures of those policies in the following decades are outside the present discussion.[133] What is sure is that the founding fathers acknowledged the right of equality for minority groups and their intentions reflected in the success of the nation in assimilating those particular minority groups. This led to the flourishing of diversity in these two nations as well as a more cosmopolitan worldview. In fact, leaders in both nations appreciated the founding fathers of the other when it came to the protection of minorities. In 1932, while introducing his daughter to world history, Nehru wrote that the idea behind the American Declaration of Independence stating that "all men are born equal" was 'clear enough and praiseworthy.'[134] In 1959, while touring India to better understand Gandhi's passive resistance methods and apply them for the emancipation of African American minority back home, Martin Luther King Jr. met Gandhi's disciples Nehru, Jayaprakash Narayan, and Rajendra Prasad. King's wife remembered her husband comparing their itinerary to 'meeting George Washington, Thomas Jefferson, and James Madison in a single day.'[135]

With the conclusion of the Second World War and the fall of Imperialism, African Americans imbibed the spirit of liberty that was seeping throughout Asia. As they galvanized together during the Civil Rights movement and achieved full voting rights along with other safeguards, a long-overdue demolition of the racial barrier started. Similar to African Americans, Asiatic immigrants were treated as second-class citizens in the American republic. This policy of discrimination against minorities also received a blow with the Immigration and Naturalization Act of 1965. Since then, America has become much more diverse with the influx of skilled labor from around the world. Today, America has minorities representing every nationality, ethnicity, culture, and language of the world and they have contributed significantly to America's rise during the era of globalization. However, both the 2016 and 2020 Presidential Elections saw the use of vitriolic language against ethnic and religious minorities. In January 2017, the newly inaugurated U.S. administration passed the Executive Order 13769, popularly referred to as the Muslim ban. The Order specifically banned citizens from seven countries to enter the United States under the garb of terrorism.

The terrorist attack of 9/11 was cited as a justification for the ban. But, the irony is that none of the 9/11 hijackers were from any of the seven predominantly Muslim countries that were named in the ban. The ban was challenged in the Judiciary which forced the Federal Administration to retreat from many of its stipulations.

The ideals of religious liberty of the American founding fathers are also being challenged in today's America due to increasing hate towards Muslims. Race-motivated hate crime is still a big and much-debated issue in the nation impacting mostly African Americans but also immigrants. Similarly, Latino and Hispanic minorities in the country continue to be among the most politically underrepresented and economically weak sections of society. Finally, around 2045 it is forecasted that Whites will become a statistical minority but will continue to wield political and economic power more than any other group in the country. This may cause further backlash towards weaker minorities, thus placing the idea of "the American Dream" for immigrants into question.

From the establishment of India as a Republic, minorities divided along caste, culture, language, and ethnicity have by and large flourished in India while enthusiastically participating in the democratic process. The voter turnout rate of the electorate in India is one of the highest in the world. At the same time, in the past seven decades, despite its own multitude of problems, India has become a home for more than twenty-five million refugees fleeing persecution in their own homelands. They have further added to India's diversity and contributed towards its prosperity. Many of these refugees such as Tibetan Buddhists have been able to save their culture from extinction only because of the refuge provided by India. However, the demolition of Babri Masjid in 1992 and riots against Sikhs and Muslims in 1984 and 2002 respectively were great blows to the idea of a secular India safe for religious minorities. Closer to the present, with the rise in identity politics, the incumbent Indian administration recently passed the controversial Citizenship (Amendment) Act 2019 to selectively provided refuge to persecuted minorities based on their religion. This legislation sparked protests across the nation and many people died in the same, yet the government remained adamant. The violence against religious and caste minorities exemplified by the so-called "cow-vigilante" attacks against Muslims and the Scheduled

Castes have also increased in the past few years. Additionally, renewed attempts have been made to push the Hindi language spoken by the majority over non-Hindi speaking regions of the nation. All this goes against the ideals and institutions established by the Indian founding fathers. Finally, the reservations instituted by the founding fathers for the backward castes have transmuted to become a political tool for gaining power. The debate has moved from the utility and effects of reservations (the presence of which in any case should be viewed as a failure of the nation's policy in ensuring equality) to the creation of vote banks around caste. This has further increased hatred between various communities. In 1955, Ambedkar had himself proposed the annulment of reserved seats for the Scheduled Castes to garner support from other social groups and not let them go adrift from the rest of the society.[136] As India continues to be one of the fastest-growing large economies, it will be all the more essential to ensure that the fruits of development reach all segments of the society, especially the minorities. Only then, the idea that immense diversity makes India resemble the "United States of Europe" i.e. diverse nations connected together in a Union, can survive and flourish.

Looking back from the present, irrespective of how things have turned out today, the founding generations played the paramount roles in establishing institutions to flourish religious minorities in America and to uplift the Untouchables in India. These were revolutionary steps for those times. The American idea that Christians of all sects, Jews, and non-believers, can live together under a state imposing no official religion created the World's first secular nation-state. Similarly, the Indian republic took the responsibility of making amends for many centuries of oppression on the Untouchables while also ensuring safeguards in the Constitution for all religious, ethnic, and linguistic minorities.

The founding fathers were imperfect men and products of their own times. American founding fathers could not accept the idea of co-existence with African American minority possessing equal rights while the Indian founding fathers might have despised the thought of accepting LGBT minorities into the society. Yet, in their own ways, they understood that the success of the republican experiment lies in the protection of minorities and constantly working for the same ideal. It is unfortunate then that many of our contemporary political leaders respond only to their vote base rather than to the whole nation. In doing so, they may secure power but are unable to become moral representatives of the whole nation.

---

[1] From Thomas Jefferson to James Madison, 8 December 1784, *The Works of Thomas Jefferson*, Federal Edition (New York and London, G.P. Putnam's Sons, 1904-5). Vol. 4, p. 383 (Hereafter, referred to as Jefferson Papers)

[2] Paul Johnson, *A History of the American People* (New York: Harper Perennial, 1997), p. 30

[3] Brooke Allen, *Moral Minority: Our Skeptical Founding Fathers* (Ivan R. Dee, 2006), pp. 149-150

[4] Michael I. Meyerson, *Endowed by Our Creator: The Birth of Religious Freedom in America* (New Haven and London: Yale University Press, 2012), pp. 21-22

[5] K. C. Davis, America's True History of Religious Tolerance, *Smithsonian Magazine*, October 2010

[6] Mark Douglas McGarvie, *One Nation Under Law: America's Early National Struggles to Separate Church and State* (Illinois: Northern Illinois University Press, 2004), p. 4

[7] Ibid., pp. 25-29

[8] K. C. Davis, America's True History of Religious Tolerance, *Smithsonian Magazine*, October 2010

[9] Michael I. Meyerson, *Endowed by Our Creator: The Birth of Religious Freedom in America* (New Haven and London: Yale University Press, 2012), pp. 78, 82

[10] Mark Douglas McGarvie, *One Nation Under Law: America's Early National Struggles to Separate Church and State* (Illinois: Northern Illinois University Press, 2004), p. 43

[11] Alexis de Tocqueville, *Democracy in America: The Complete and Unabridged Volumes I and II* (Bantam Classic Edition, 2000), pp. 47-48

[12] Douglass Adair, *Fame and the Founding Fathers* (New York: W.W. Norton and Company, 1974), p. 13

[13] Joseph J. Ellis, *American Sphinx: The Character of Thomas Jefferson* (New York: Vintage Books, 1998), p. 63

[14] From Thomas Jefferson to William Stephens Smith, 13 Nov 1787, Jefferson Papers, Vol. 5, p. 362

[15] Joseph J. Ellis, *American Sphinx: The Character of Thomas Jefferson* (New York: Vintage Books, 1998), p. 128

[16] Ralph Ketcham, *James Madison: A Biography* (Charlottesville and London: University of Virginia Press, 1990), p. 84

[17] *The Founding Fathers: The Essential Guide to The Men Who Made America* (New Jersey: John Wiley and Sons, 2007), p. 153

[18] Ron Chernow, *Washington: A Life* (New York: The Penguin Press, 2010), p. 516

[19] Noah Feldman, *The Three Lives of James Madison: Genius, Partisan, President* (New York: Random House, 2017)
[20] Ralph Ketcham, *James Madison: A Biography* (Charlottesville and London: University of Virginia Press, 1990), p. 158
[21] Michael I. Meyerson, *Endowed by Our Creator: The Birth of Religious Freedom in America* (New Haven and London: Yale University Press, 2012), p. 37
[22] Joseph J. Ellis, *American Sphinx: The Character of Thomas Jefferson* (New York: Vintage Books, 1998), p. 55
[23] Proposed Constitution for Virginia, June 1776, Jefferson Papers, Vol. 2, p. 180
[24] William Sterne Randall, *Thomas Jefferson: A Life* (New York: Harper Perennial edition, 1994), p. 271
[25] Notes on Religion, 1776, Jefferson Papers, Vol. 2, p. 267
[26] Notes on the State of Virginia, Query XVII, 1782, Jefferson Papers, Vol. 4, p. 80
[27] Ralph Ketcham, *James Madison: A Biography* (Charlottesville and London: University of Virginia Press, 1990), pp. 72-73
[28] Brooke Allen, *Moral Minority: Our Skeptical Founding Fathers* (Ivan R. Dee, 2006), p. 90
[29] From James Madison to Thomas Jefferson, 3 Jul 1784, *The Writings of James Madison*, comprising his Public Papers and his Private Correspondence, including his numerous letters and documents now for the first time printed, ed. Gaillard Hunt (New York: G.P. Putnam's Sons, 1900). Vol. 2, p. 59 (Hereafter, referred to as Madison Papers).
[30] Brooke Allen, *Moral Minority: Our Skeptical Founding Fathers* (Ivan R. Dee, 2006), pp. 109-110
[31] Michael I. Meyerson, *Endowed by Our Creator: The Birth of Religious Freedom in America* (New Haven and London: Yale University Press, 2012), pp. 101-102
[32] Ibid., p. 106
[33] Memorial and Remonstrance Against Religious Assessments, Madison Papers, Vol. 2, pp. 183-191
[34] From James Madison to Thomas Jefferson, 20 Aug 1785, Madison Papers, Vol. 2, p. 163
[35] From George Washington to George Mason, 3 Oct 1785, George Washington, *The Writings of George Washington*, collected and edited by Worthington Chauncey Ford (New York and London: G. P. Putnam's Sons, 1890), Vol. X, p. 506
[36] *The Papers of James Madison, Retirement Series*, vol. 1, 4 March 1817–31 January 1820, ed. David B. Mattern, J. C. A. Stagg, Mary Parke Johnson, and Anne Mandeville Colony. Charlottesville: University of Virginia Press, 2009, pp. 600–627
[37] Michael I. Meyerson, *Endowed by Our Creator: The Birth of Religious Freedom in America* (New Haven and London: Yale University Press, 2012), pp. 113-114
[38] Thomas Jefferson's autobiography, *The Writings of Thomas Jefferson* (The Thomas Jefferson Memorial Association of the United States, Memorial Edition, 1907), Vol. 1, p. 67

[39] From James Madison to Thomas Jefferson, 22 Jan 1786, Madison Papers, Vol. 2, pp. 214-216
[40] Ralph Ketcham, *James Madison: A Biography* (Charlottesville and London: University of Virginia Press, 1990), p. 165
[41] William Sterne Randall, *Thomas Jefferson: A Life* (New York: Harper Perennial edition, 1994), p. 595
[42] Brooke Allen, *Moral Minority: Our Skeptical Founding Fathers* (Ivan R. Dee, 2006), pp. 112-113
[43] Richard Beeman, *Plain, Honest Men: The Making of the American Constitution* (New York: Random House, 2009), p. 179
[44] From James Madison to Edward Livingston, 10 Jul 1822, Madison Papers, Vol. 9, p. 102
[45] Michael I. Meyerson, *Endowed by Our Creator: The Birth of Religious Freedom in America* (New Haven and London: Yale University Press, 2012), pp. 133-134
[46] Federalist No. 48, *The Federalist Papers* (New York: Dover Publications, Dover Thrift Edition, 2014), p. 242
[47] Federalist No. 10, *The Federalist Papers* (New York: Dover Publications, Dover Thrift Edition, 2014), pp. 41-47
[48] Federalist No. 52: The House of Representatives, *The Federalist Papers* (New York: Dover Publications, Dover Thrift Edition, 2014), p. 258
[49] From Thomas Jefferson to James Madison, 20 Dec 1787, Jefferson Papers, Vol. 5, p. 371
[50] From Thomas Jefferson to Alexander Donald, 7 Feb 1788, *The Papers of Thomas Jefferson*, vol. 12, 7 August 1787–31 March 1788, ed. Julian P. Boyd. Princeton: Princeton University Press, 1955, pp. 570–572
[51] James Madison's speech in the Virginia Convention, 12 Jun 1788, Madison Papers, Vol. 5, p. 176
[52] Mark Douglas McGarvie, *One Nation Under Law: America's Early National Struggles to Separate Church and State* (Illinois: Northern Illinois University Press, 2004), p. 57
[53] Michael I. Meyerson, *Endowed by Our Creator: The Birth of Religious Freedom in America* (New Haven and London: Yale University Press, 2012), pp. 159-160
[54] From James Madison to Thomas Jefferson, 17 Oct 1788, Madison Papers, Vol. 5, p. 271
[55] From Thomas Jefferson to James Madison, 15 Mar 1789, Jefferson Papers, Vol. 5, p. 461
[56] Madison's speech: June 8, Amendments to the Constitution, Madison Papers, Vol. 5, p. 385
[57] The Founders' Constitution Volume 5, Bill of Rights, Document 11 Annals of Congress. *The Debates and Proceedings in the Congress of the United States.* "History of Congress." 42 vols. Washington, D.C.: Gales & Seaton, 1834--56.

[58] Ralph Ketcham, *James Madison: A Biography* (Charlottesville and London: University of Virginia Press, 1990), p. 165
[59] The Papers of George Washington, Presidential Series, vol. 2, 1 April 1789 – 15 June 1789, ed. Dorothy Twohig. Charlottesville: University Press of Virginia, 1987, pp. 216–217.
[60] Ron Chernow, *Washington: A Life* (New York: The Penguin Press, 2010), p. 294
[61] Michael I. Meyerson, *Endowed by Our Creator: The Birth of Religious Freedom in America* (New Haven and London: Yale University Press, 2012), pp. 180-181
[62] *The Papers of George Washington*, Presidential Series, vol. 2, 1 April 1789 – 15 June 1789, ed. Dorothy Twohig. Charlottesville: University Press of Virginia, 1987, pp. 423–425.
[63] Ibid., vol. 5, 16 January 1790 – 30 June 1790, pp. 299–301.
[64] Ibid., vol. 4, 8 September 1789 – 15 January 1790, pp. 265–269.
[65] The Papers of George Washington, Presidential Series, vol. 5, 16 January 1790 – 30 June 1790, ed. Dorothy Twohig, Mark A. Mastromarino, and Jack D. Warren. Charlottesville: University Press of Virginia, 1996, pp. 448–450.
[66] Ibid., vol. 6, 1 July 1790 – 30 November 1790, pp. 284–286.
[67] Ron Chernow, *Washington: A Life* (New York: The Penguin Press, 2010), p. 611
[68] George Washington, *Maxims of Washington* (Collected and Arranged by John Frederick Schroeder, Third Edition, New York: 1854), p. 374
[69] Quoted in Michael I. Meyerson, *Endowed by Our Creator: The Birth of Religious Freedom in America* (New Haven and London: Yale University Press, 2012), p. 198
[70] Brooke Allen, *Moral Minority: Our Skeptical Founding Fathers* (Ivan R. Dee, 2006), pp. 118-119
[71] Mark Douglas McGarvie, *One Nation Under Law: America's Early National Struggles to Separate Church and State* (Illinois: Northern Illinois University Press, 2004), p. 59
[72] John Keay, *India: A History* (New York: Atlantic Monthly Press, 2000), pp. 52-54
[73] For detailed information on the caste system, among others see: G. S. Ghurye, *Caste and Race in India* (Bombay: Popular Prakashan, 1996)
[74] Dhananjay Keer, *Dr. Babasaheb Ambedkar: Life and Mission* (Mumbai: Popular Prakashan, Reprint May 2018), pp. 13-18
[75] B. R. Ambedkar, Waiting for a Visa, *Dr. Babasaheb Ambedkar: Writings and Speeches*, Vol. 12, edited by Vasant Moon (Bombay: Education Department, Government of Maharashtra, 1993), Part I, pp. 661-691
[76] B. R. Ambedkar's unpublished Preface (text provided by Eleanor Zelliot), *The Buddha and His Dhamma: A Critical Edition* (Oxford University Press, 2011)
[77] Dhananjay Keer, *Dr. Babasaheb Ambedkar: Life and Mission* (Mumbai: Popular Prakashan, Reprint May 2018), p. 27

[78] Ramachandra Guha, *Makers of Modern India* (Penguin Books, 2012), p. 205; Various instances of Ambedkar buying many books during his trips are chronicled

in Dhananjay Keer, *Dr. Babasaheb Ambedkar: Life and Mission* (Mumbai: Popular Prakashan, Reprint May 2018)

[79] Ibid., p. 207

[80] Dhananjay Keer, *Dr. Babasaheb Ambedkar: Life and Mission* (Mumbai: Popular Prakashan, Reprint May 2018), pp. 469, 493

[81] Ramachandra Guha, *Gandhi: The Years that Changed the World 1914-1948* (Penguin Random House, 2018), pp. 391-392

[82] Dhananjay Keer, *Dr. Babasaheb Ambedkar: Life and Mission* (Mumbai: Popular Prakashan, Reprint May 2018), p. 168

[83] Ibid., pp. 165-168

[84] *The Collected Works of Mahatma Gandhi (CWMG)*, Vol. 48: September 12, 1931 – January 3, 1932, Answers to Questions, pp. 160-161

[85] Ibid., Speech at Federal Structure Committee, p. 34

[86] Ibid., Speech at Minorities Committee Meeting, p. 298

[87] Raja Sekhar Vundru, *Ambedkar, Gandhi and Patel: The Making of India's Electoral System* (New Delhi: Bloomsbury, 2018), p. 34

[88] Rajmohan Gandhi, *The Good Boatman: A Portrait of Gandhi* (Penguin Books, 1997), pp. 250-251

[89] CWMG, Vol. 50: June 1, 1932 – August 31, 1932, Letter to Ramsay Macdonald, August 18, 1932, pp. 383-384

[90] B. R. Ambedkar, *What Congress and Gandhi have Done to the Untouchables* (Bombay: Thacker and Co., 1945), p. 82

[91] Ibid., p. 86

[92] *CWMG*, Vol. 51: September 1, 1932 – November 15, 1932, Letter to Ramsay Macdonald, September 9, 1932, p. 31

[93] *The Diary of Mahadev Desai*, Vol. 1 (Ahmedabad: Navajivan Publishing House, 1953), August 21, 1932, p. 301

[94] Eleanor Zelliot, *Ambedkar's World: The Making of Babasaheb and the Dalit Movement* (New Delhi: Navayana, Second reprint 2016), p. 137

[95] Quoted in Raja Sekhar Vundru, *Ambedkar, Gandhi and Patel: The Making of India's Electoral System* (New Delhi: Bloomsbury, 2018), p. 41

[96] B. R. Ambedkar, *What Congress and Gandhi have Done to the Untouchables* (Bombay: Thacker and Co., 1945), p. 326

[97] Ramachandra Guha, *Gandhi: The Years that Changed the World 1914-1948* (Penguin Random House, 2018), pp. 433-434

[98] Quoted in Dhananjay Keer, *Dr. Babasaheb Ambedkar: Life and Mission* (Mumbai: Popular Prakashan, Reprint May 2018), p. 211

[99] *CWMG*, Vol. 51: September 1, 1932 – November 15, 1932, Appendix 1 (B) Discussion with B. R. Ambedkar, September 22, 1932, pp. 458-460

[100] Ramachandra Guha, *Gandhi: The Years that Changed the World 1914-1948* (Penguin Random House, 2018), pp. 436-437

[101] Dhananjay Keer, *Dr. Babasaheb Ambedkar: Life and Mission* (Mumbai: Popular Prakashan, Reprint May 2018), p. 212-213
[102] Pyarelal, The Epic Fast (Ahmedabad: Navajivan Press, 1932), p. 71
[103] Ramachandra Guha, *Gandhi: The Years that Changed the World 1914-1948* (Penguin Random House, 2018), p. 438
[104] *CWMG*, Vol. 51: September 1, 1932 – November 15, 1932, Appendices (E) Message to M. M. Malviya, M. R. Jayakar and Tej Bahadur Sapru, September 24, 1932, p. 461
[105] Pyarelal, *The Epic Fast* (Ahmedabad: Navajivan Press, 1932), p. 72
[106] Dhananjay Keer, *Dr. Babasaheb Ambedkar: Life and Mission* (Mumbai: Popular Prakashan, Reprint May 2018), p. 214
[107] Quoted in Ramachandra Guha, *Gandhi: The Years that Changed the World 1914-1948* (Penguin Random House, 2018), pp. 438-439
[108] Pyarelal, *The Epic Fast* (Ahmedabad: Navajivan Press, 1932), pp. 76-80
[109] *Harijan*, 11 February 1933, Journal Volume Number 1, Issue 1
[110] *CWMG*, Vol. 55: April 23, 1933 – September 15, 1933, Letter to C. F. Andrews, June 15, 1933, p. 199
[111] *CWMG*, Vol. 55: April 23, 1933 – September 15, 1933, Statement on Fast, April 30, 1933, p. 75
[112] *CWMG*, Vol. 31: June 15, 1926 – November 4, 1926, A Catechism, October 14, 1926, p. 493
[113] *CWMG*, Vol. 62: October 1, 1935 – May 31, 1936, CASTE HAS TO GO, November 16, 1935, pp. 121-122
[114] *CWMG*, Vol. 87: February 21, 1947 – May 24, 1947, Talk with Harijan Workers, April 24, 1947, p. 350
[115] Rajmohan Gandhi, *The Good Boatman: A Portrait of Gandhi* (Penguin Books, 1997), p. 256
[116] D. R. Nagaraj, *The Flaming Feet and Other Essays* (Ranikhet: Permanent Black, 2010), p. 56
[117] Dhananjay Keer, *Dr. Babasaheb Ambedkar: Life and Mission* (Mumbai: Popular Prakashan, Reprint May 2018), pp. 292-293
[118] Ibid., p. 371
[119] Ramachandra Guha, *Gandhi: The Years that Changed the World 1914-1948* (Penguin Random House, 2018), pp. 784-788
[120] Ibid., pp. 841-842
[121] Rajmohan Gandhi, *The Good Boatman: A Portrait of Gandhi* (Penguin Books, 1997), p. 260
[122] B. Shiva Rao, *India's Freedom Movement: Some Notable Figures* (New Delhi: Orient Longman, 1972), p. 70
[123] Ramachandra Guha, Gandhi: *The Years that Changed the World 1914-1948* (Penguin Random House, 2018), pp. 842-843

[124] *Constitutional Proposals of The Sapru Committee* (Bombay: Padma Publications, 1945), pp. 220-222, 230-231

[125] B. Shiva Rao, *The Framing of India's Constitution: Select Documents* (New Delhi: The Indian Institute of Public Administration, 1967), Vol. II, pp. 396-400

[126] Sardar Vallabhbhai Patel's speech in the Constituent Assembly while presenting the report on Minority Rights, 27 August 1947, *Constituent Assembly Debates: Official Report* (reprint New Delhi: Lok Sabha Secretariat, 2014), Vol. V, pp. 198-199

[127] Ibid., 28 August 1947, pp. 270-272

[128] B. Shiva Rao, *The Framing of India's Constitution: Select* Documents (New Delhi: The Indian Institute of Public Administration, 1968), Vol. IV, pp. 601-602. Also available in Appendix A of *Constituent Assembly Debates: Official Report* (reprint New Delhi: Lok Sabha Secretariat, 2014), Vol. VIII, p. 312

[129] *The Diary of Maniben Patel: 1936*-50 (Edited by Prabha Chopra, Vision Books, 2001), p. 244

[130] Prem Parkash, *Ambedkar: Politics and the Scheduled Castes* (New Delhi: Ashish Publishing House, 2002), pp. 150-151; Also mentioned in Raja Sekhar Vundru, *Ambedkar, Gandhi and Patel: The Making of India's Electoral System* (New Delhi: Bloomsbury, 2018), pp. 138-139

[131] Ambedkar in the Constituent Assembly, 25 August 1949, *Constituent Assembly Debates: Official Report* (reprint New Delhi: Lok Sabha Secretariat, 2014), Vol. IX, p. 697

[132] B. Shiva Rao, *The Framing of India's Constitution: A Study* (New Delhi: The Indian Institute of Public Administration, 1968), pp. 777-778

[133] For a more detailed study of the effects of reservation in India, the reader can refer to (among others): K. S. Chalam, *Caste-based Reservations and Human Development in India* (New Delhi: Sage Publications, 2007)

[134] Jawaharlal Nehru, *Glimpses of World History* (Penguin Books, 2004), p. 418

[135] Quoted in Nico Slate, *Colored Cosmopolitanism* (Cambridge and London: Harvard University Press, 2012), p. 225

[136] Christophe Jaffrelot, *Dr. Ambedkar and Untouchability: Analysing and Fighting Caste* (London: Hurst & Company, 2005), p. 85

2. POWER

When George Washington died, the most memorable eulogy to him was paid by a fellow Virginian, Henry Lee, who proclaimed that Washington was 'First in war, first in peace, and first in the hearts of his countrymen.'[1] It isn't too much of an exaggeration to say that America's founding revolved around George Washington. Over his lifetime, Washington changed America's destiny at least four times. First, he was at the front of the events that started the French and Indian War causing an economically broken Britain taxing the American colonies which ultimately led to the Revolutionary War. Second, against all odds, he led the army to triumph in the Revolutionary War against the world's most powerful empire. Third, by presiding over the Constitutional Convention, he was instrumental in bringing together the states to form a Union. Fourth, as the first American president, he administered the first nation-sized republic in world history and did not let the republican experiment fall into pandemonium. For all his contributions to America's destiny, Washington still adorns the first place in the annals of American history. He is the paramount American icon. This chapter will focus on Washington's rise to power, his understanding of how to wield and when to renunciate power.

Among the many celebrated American founding fathers, the name of George Washington shines and shines distinctively—like the sun illuminating its surroundings by igniting itself. He was the indispensable founding father who despite his many failings was the *primus inter pares* among the founding fathers. As his biographer, Joseph Ellis writes, '…Benjamin Franklin was wiser than Washington; Alexander Hamilton was more brilliant; John Adams was better read; Thomas Jefferson was more intellectually sophisticated; James Madison was more politically astute. Yet each and all of these prominent figures acknowledged that Washington was their unquestioned superior.'[2] The same impression was conveyed more than two centuries ago by one of the most brilliant American women of the time (and surely one of the most influential first ladies of the United States), Abigail Adams, who wrote about Washington, 'Take his Character all together, and we Shall not look upon his like again...'[3]

Another Washingtonian feature is that he was most conscious among all the founding fathers to court posterity's judgment. Like a mathematician, he arrived at each of his major life decisions by factoring in all present turn of events, subsequently modeling all possible actions, and aimed at attaining that optimal solution which shall make him beloved in posterity. Among others, this impression is bolstered by the fact that after owning slaves all his life, in his will, Washington expressed the desire to free them after his and his wife's death and provisioned for their support as well.

Throughout his life, Washington maintained an inscrutable countenance as if the world was a stage on which he could not let his real self unfold. During his childhood, he had hand-copied 110 maxims from *The Rules of Civility and Decent Behavior in Company and Conversation*. It included rules such as "Every action done in company ought to be done with some sign of respect to those that are present," and "Do not puff up the cheeks, loll not out the tongue rub the hands, or beard, thrust out the lips, or bite them or keep the lips too open or too close." Legends say that Washington followed these maxims to the letter. Neither in conversations nor in letters did he open himself to posterity's examination. Notably, from the fear of divulging his personal facet, he instructed his wife Martha to burn all their correspondence after his death—which she duly did. Even Washington's personal diary provides us no clues about his thoughts. It is filled with daily observations of weather or business transactions. Nobody understood the ways more than Washington or did more to levitate himself into a legend. Thus, it is difficult to separate Washington the man, from Washington the monument. As multiple scholars have pointed out, unlike other monuments on the National Mall, the Washington Monument stands silent—no words, no eulogy, no praise. Washington is just there like one of Jeffersonian self-evident truths.[4]

George Washington was born on February 22, 1732, in Virginia. Though he acquired wealth in his youth, possessed British oriented aristocratic tastes, and died one of the wealthiest men in America, Washington was brought up in a poor household. He never received formal education and his hope to receive education abroad died with the death of his father when he was eleven. He taught himself practical surveying and map-making. He also taught himself to write prose with a clear and forceful style but could never acquire grammatical sophistication. In 1751, he accompanied his half-brother Lawrence to Barbados when the latter came down with tuberculosis. Washington hoped that the tropical climate would cure Lawrence. This was the only time in his life that Washington ventured into the ocean and outside the limits of the future United States. During this trip, he contracted smallpox which made him immune to the disease in the future—a coincidence with great consequences during the Revolutionary War when thousands of soldiers died from smallpox, the greatest killer of the War. But then, as we shall see, coincidences were not rare in Washington's life throughout which he enjoyed immunity from many human fallibilities. After Lawrence's death, Washington leased and eventually inherited a 2,500-acre plantation (which he later named Mount Vernon) and sought an appointment in Lawrence's place as the adjutant general of the Virginia militia. Washington did this in the true Virginian fashion of the time: not by passing any examination to display his proficiency in military matters (which was non-existent) but by calling on the 'influential members of the government.' This well-built young man of twenty attained 'the responsibility of training a militia in skills he did not himself possess.'[5]

Washington's schooling was done on the battlefield. In February 1754, he was appointed as a special envoy to the Ohio Country to demand French withdrawal from the territory claimed by the British. He was also given the assignment to make peace with the Native American Iroquois Confederacy. Having received the rank of lieutenant general, Washington ventured towards the savage Ohio Country as the second in command. At this time, Britain and France were engaged in a cold war for the domination of the North American continent. Ohio Country was inhabited by Native Americans who were trapped between the French marching from Canada and the

British impinging from the Allegheny Mountains located along the Virginian side. At the head of 160 troops, Washington received the news that the French had begun to construct a fort (Fort Duquesne). This fort would have provided a bastion to the French forces for occupying the areas to the west of Virginia which the British Ohio Company wanted. Washington planned to attack the French detachment with his Native American allies.

What followed is disputed but most certainly Washington's Native American allies killed and scalped the Frenchmen even when the latter had thrown down their guns in an attempt to surrender. Thus, controversially, Washington's graduation from the school of the battlefield was actually the event of overseeing a massacre. This attack ignited the French and Indian War which later became part of the larger Seven Years' War between the two world powers—Britain and France. Ignoring the massacre that he oversaw, Washington romantically wrote in a letter to his brother: 'I heard Bullets whistle and believe me there was something charming in the Sound.'[6] This self-aggrandizing statement was taken hold of by the Virginia newspapers and thus started the process of myth-creation around Washington. However, King George II was not convinced. By what he heard about Washington, he dismissed Washington's remark by noting that Washington would not have said so about bullets 'if he had been used to hear many.' In this way, Washington's first thrust onto the world stage was purely coincidental yet started the process of making him an American celebrity—America's first war hero.[7]

After the French and Indian War was on in full force, Washington, now at the head of a much larger militia, found himself about a month later in a defensive posture when a French force attacked with 900 men. Washington had placed his troops in a precariously vulnerable position and his side suffered one hundred casualties compared to only five on the French side. On July 4 (another coincidence), Washington surrendered with his force to the French. He was compelled to acknowledge in the instrument of surrender that the initial hostilities of the War were launched by the British who were responsible for murdering a diplomatic emissary of the French crown. Ironically, despite this tragic defeat in War as well as on the diplomatic front, Washington was celebrated in Virginia. The French had projected him as a villain who had overseen a treacherous massacre of the French force but this notorious designation boosted Washington's patriotic image in America.[8]

Back in Virginia after his surrender, Washington was offered captaincy, but he refused the demotion and preferred to serve voluntarily as an aide to General Edward Braddock. General Braddock led an expedition to expel the French from Fort Duquesne. In a confrontation between the two forces at Monongahela, the British suffered heavy casualties and General Braddock was mortally wounded. In another feat of fortune, during the engagement, two horses were shot beneath Washington and four musket balls pierced his coat and hat, all the while he himself escaped without a scratch (another coincidence). Thus, after another defeat on the battlefield, Washington came back beleaguered and dejected. After a few more assignments and skirmishes, Washington resigned his commission and returned to Mount Vernon in 1758. He courted Martha Custis who had inherited two children and a significant fortune from her deceased husband. The two were married in early 1759. They enjoyed a long and happy married life although they could not conceive any children. Since Martha already had children from her previous husband, it is probable that the future "Father of His Country" was sterile (though Washington claimed otherwise throughout his life). He spent the next decade and a half, pleasantly sequestered at Mount Vernon.[9]

During these peaceful years in his life, Washington expanded his estate to make it one of the largest in Virginia. He also inherited a large amount of land for his military service and increased the size of his slave population to more than a hundred. In effect, he owned a small village and ran it meticulously in a business-like manner. He acquired aristocratic tastes and continuously looked to Britain for acquiring the most fashionable commodities. At the same time, he held local offices and was elected to the Virginia provincial legislature. Hunting fox on horseback became a hobby.

Let us pause here for a moment and reflect on what we know about Washington until now. Washington's military record was poor. He had been at the losing end in the battle at least twice and had been forced to surrender once. Multiple times, he had placed his life on the battlefield for the English crown. He had repeatedly tried and failed to get commissioned in the British crown forces. He had acquired British patrician tastes and looked to England as his mother country.

All in all, Washington was an English patriot and an undistinguished military man who would have never imagined in his wildest dreams that soon he would become the symbol of the American Revolution.

When the British imposed the Stamp Act in 1765 and the Townshend Act in 1767, Washington mostly maintained measured silence. While Americans protested against these taxes, he was probably in the belief that the wave will pass under the ship. As resistance against the British taxation grew in America and the epoch-changing Boston Tea Party event happened, Washington was forced to make a decision. As an army veteran and innate pragmatic, half-hearted acts of reconciliation were alien to his nature. He wrote to a friend that, 'the cause of Boston…ever will be considered as the cause of America (not that we approve their cond[uc]t in destroy[ing] the Tea.)'[10] With an increase in British repression, Washington progressively augmented his association with the American cause. As he became increasingly radicalized, he perceived the British repression as an evil conspiracy against American liberty. He was elected to and served rather inconspicuously in the First Continental Congress in 1774 which was called to discuss the colonies' collective response to the British government's coercive policies. The First Continental Congress was convened by legislatures of the colonies to discuss the path forward after the Boston Tea Party event. Interestingly, despite not having entered a battlefield for years, at this time he ordered silk and epaulets for his military uniform and a copy of Thomas Webb's *A Military Treatise on the Appointments of the Army*. The veteran was clearly thinking about the possibility of war and was preparing for it. By Spring 1775, the eventuality of war was brewing in the air. It was common knowledge that the decisions taken by the Second Continental Congress would be crucial to America's destiny. Washington was made a delegate to the same by the Virginia Convention and he sped north towards Philadelphia with a premonition of what would follow.[11]

At Lexington and Concord in Massachusetts, the British had launched hostilities against the colonists in April 1775. This marked the beginning of the conflict between Britain and the thirteen colonies. Following these battles, the Second Continental Congress met in Philadelphia amidst a surcharged atmosphere. George

Washington was the only delegate who was attending the Congress in his military attire as if to brandish his credentials to gain the highest military job. He had always been celebrated as an American war hero, but truth be told, he had never commanded any unit larger than a regiment. He had absolutely no experience in planning the larger tactics of war, deploying artillery, maneuvering cavalry, and coordinating between different constituents of an army. He was an amateur compared to the British officers he was aspiring to face. Despite all these disabilities which made him unqualified for the job, he had one thing in his favor—an astute sense of timing. His deportment conveyed a resolve that augmented his martial credentials and other candidates for the job such as Horatio Gates and Charles Lee did not command such gravitas. More importantly, Washington was born in America unlike the other two who were born in Britain. John Hancock, who was another serious competitor, had even lesser military experience and was incapacitated with gout at the time. Finally, the deciding factor was that Washington was a Virginian. The support of the most populous and wealthiest state was politically indispensable (without Virginia fully on board, there could be no war) and made his appointment a fait accompli. As John Adams sarcastically wrote later while enumerating the talents that propelled Washington to fame in 1775, 'Virginian Geese are all swans.' After getting elected as the Commander-in-Chief of a still nonexistent Continental Army to fight a still undeclared war, Washington gave a speech in which he modestly admitted that he did not feel qualified for the honor and that he would serve without pay. In effect, he gambled his present fortune and future reputation on his leadership skills which had never been adequately evaluated.[12]

We see here that in addition to the conscious pursuit of glory, Washington's rise to power was filled with fortunate coincidences. Having been elected as the Commander-in-Chief, Washington was on the battlefield for the next eight years during which he emerged as a father figure to not just his fellow military men but also to the American cause. The winter of 1777-78 that the Army spent at Valley Forge amidst disease, snow, and suffering, held together by loyalty to General Washington has entered popular American mythology. Crucially, it is also true that during the War, he lost more battles than he won. Given his hawkish instincts, it took much time for

Washington to understand that the factor of geography i.e. distance from Britain meant that he only had to ensure not losing the War in order to win it. It was only after this realization that he changed his tactics from being exceedingly aggressive to following a more Fabian strategy. He learned from his mistakes and displayed composure with high moral and incorruptible behavior throughout the War. After the French entered the War on the American side, American victory became a foregone conclusion. By the end of the War, Washington had become the face of the American Revolution and the only American who was loved and respected across the thirteen states.

When the War ended, everyone looked towards Washington to gauge his next move. History had taught the American citizenry that military dictatorships had taken over the Roman and British republics during their formative phases. Washington was the only man in the nation who commanded the stature and power of becoming a monarch. The world of the late eighteenth century was filled with monarchies. Truth be told, if Washington would have expressed his intention to be a monarch backed with his military might, Americans would have accepted him as their king without much dissension. Washington had never received adequate support from the Continental Congress in waging the War. Many times, he had been forced to plead to the delegates for basic provisions for the Army such as boots, clothing, blankets, and gunpowder. Raising militia remained a problem throughout the war since some states were unwilling to proactively recruit militiamen. Furthermore, at times adverse circumstances had forced the Army to suffer the indignity of feeding itself by snatching food from the farmers. Thus, it was natural to wonder if Washington would now seek to correct the ills plaguing the nation because of the ineffectual Confederation Congress by taking power into his own hands. Amidst, the rumors of Washington's inauguration as the king, he had already made up his mind.

Washington had always admired the Roman hero, Cincinnatus, who had served the republic in times of crisis with selfless devotion only to voluntarily retire when the crisis was over. During the Revolutionary War, Washington had willingly submitted to the Continental Congress's authority. He had always insisted that he had been given a mandate by Congress and hence he is subordinate to the will of the American citizenry as represented by the Continental Congress.[13] Washington was determined to not be another King George III. In 1782, at the Newburgh encampment, rumors about a coup were being circulated by some officers who were disgruntled by Congress's conduct of the War. Their complaints were not meaningless since they had been through pathetic living conditions during the War only to find that the Congress was now reneging on its post-war promises. It was being whispered that Washington should declare himself the king to save America from a catastrophe since the weakness of the republic in ensuring the nation's security had been exposed during the War. When Washington got to know of these rumors, he responded sternly to the officers to 'banish these thoughts from your Mind.' He further condemned them for thinking of such a plan that was 'big with the greatest mischiefs that can befall my Country.' On hearing these words, George III—who surely knew something about monarchy and absolute power—remarked that if he could resist the temptation of becoming a monarch and retire, Washington would be 'the greatest man in the world.' Washington was facing the greatest personal challenge of his life. The enticing option from the perspective of wielding power was to listen to his officers, declare himself the king, and join the ranks of hundreds of sovereigns reigning across the world while starting his own dynasty along the Roman example. The judicious option which was also the correct one for the American Republic was to reprimand the officers and retire to Mount Vernon in the footsteps of Cincinnatus. By choosing one of the two options, he would have either killed the newborn American Republic or given it a chance to take root. Thus, this event has also been called "the Last Temptation of Washington." More mundanely, it is known as the Newburgh Conspiracy.[14]

On the morning of March 15, 1783, seventeen months after Americans had delivered the decisive blow to the British forces at Yorktown, General George Washington strode towards the Newburgh encampment to address disgruntled soldiers. Due to the criticality of the situation that Washington sought to defuse, it was perhaps 'the most important single gathering ever held in the United States.'[15] He was nervous, angry, frustrated, and uncertain. While the peace negotiations had dragged on in Paris, the soldiers had remained disgruntled and unpaid. The promises by the Confederation Congress of a generous pension were not fulfilled since the War had made the nation bankrupt. The calamitous combination of aggrieved soldiers combined with a weak American government was a sure foreboding of a potential tragedy. Some officers had already decided to take matters into their own hands. There was a rumor in the air of an upcoming coup against the government. Pamphlets were being circulated advising the soldiers to not submit to an uncaring Congress and if needed, even throw off Washington's leadership in their quest for redressal. Throughout the War, he had been a father figure to the officers and such loose talk on their part was heresy. Washington had spent the preceding day drafting the most impressive speech he ever wrote. As he walked inside the building where the officers were assembled and traversed the length of the long hall, the atmosphere became restive. More than five hundred officers sat there gazing at him. The penurious condition of the officers was evident from their torn and soiled uniforms and worn-out boots. 'Their wives and children back home were reduced to begging' in the state of penury. Any talk of American liberty was a farce to their sensibilities. Washington could feel the gloom and was visibly uneasy when he assumed the stage. He took out from the pocket of his coat the speech he had written the previous day.[16] He started by genuinely sympathizing with the officers' demands and said further

> By an anonymous summons, an attempt has been made to convene you together—how inconsistent with the rules of propriety! how unmilitary! and how subversive of all order and discipline—let the good sense of the Army decide....But as I was among the first who embarked in the cause of our common Country—As I have never left your side one moment, but when called from you, on public duty—As I have been the constant companion & witness of your Distresses, and not among the last to feel, & acknowledge your Merits—As I have ever considered my own Military reputation as inseparably connected with that of the Army—As my Heart has ever expanded with joy, when I have heard its praises—and my indignation has arisen, when the Mouth of detraction has been opened against it—it can scarcely be supposed, at this late stage of the War, that I am indifferent to its interests....And let me conjure you, in the name of our common Country—as you value your own sacred honor—as you respect the rights of humanity, & as you regard the Military & national character of America, to express your utmost horror & detestation of the Man who wishes, under any specious pretenses, to

overturn the liberties of our Country, & who wickedly attempts to open the flood Gates of Civil discord, & deluge our rising Empire in Blood.[17]

In this way, Washington made his stand clear and gave expression to his thoughts that a nation's military power is derived from the legitimate consent of the public. But, he sensed that his evocative appeal did not have much of an impact on the gathering. The officers seemed moved but not convinced. He needed to do something more. At this point, he took out another piece of paper from his pocket which was a letter written by one of his friends to express sympathy with the soldiers' plight. The letter was poorly scrawled and was barely legible. Finding it difficult to read, Washington stumbled and reached for his pockets once more. He took a dramatic pause and then pulled out a pair of spectacles. Probably nobody had publicly seen him wearing spectacles before this time. Washington adjusted the glasses and said in a breaking voice, 'Gentlemen, you will permit me to put on my spectacles, for I have not only grown gray, but almost blind in the service of my country.' With this theatrical performance, Washington read the letter and left the room. This simple thespian gesture did what Washington could not do through his words. The plans of the coup died the moment the officers saw their Commander-in-Chief visibly broken and remembered his service to the nation. The officers realized that Washington, a father figure to them on the battlefield, sympathized with their condition and had made great sacrifices for the nation. Many of them started to sob. After regaining composure, they gave a vote of thanks to Washington, repudiated the talk of a coup, and placed their faith in him to secure the rewards for their service. No other man in America could have pulled off such a performance since nobody else was so revered as Washington had been during the Revolutionary War. The message went home to the Confederation Congress which at last took partial financial measures to placate the officers. Washington's sense of how to utilize his power served as a critical turning point in American history. It saved a political revolution from descending into chaos.[18]

In Cincinnatus's footsteps, Washington then planned a final gesture to reiterate his subordination to the Confederation Congress and display the proclivity to commence a hard-earned retirement. In other words, General Washington planned for a final exit. On

December 4, he participated in a final gathering with his officers and was moved at the sight. He said in a breaking voice 'With a heart filled with love and gratitude, I now take leave of you. I most devoutly wish that your latter days may be as prosperous and happy as your former ones have been glorious and honorable.' With these words, tears swelled in his eyes as well as in his comrades' eyes. They hugged each other and remembered the hard days of the battle when all hope was lost—of winning as well as surviving. After this meeting, Washington left for Annapolis where Confederation Congress was sitting temporarily. He had planned to resign his commission by personally reporting to the legislature to convey his humility and subservience to the will of the people. He minutely prepared for the resignation ceremony to convey a message to the wider world that the American Republic would not descend into a monarchy because of him. At the State House where the delegates had assembled, Washington gave a short speech in which he said: 'Having now finished the work assigned me, I retire from the great theater of Action....I here offer my Commission, and take my leave of all the employments of public life.' He then formally bowed and shook hands with each member of the Congress. Hundreds of spectators cheered him as he came outside the State House. Washington took his leave from them and from public service—for now, though in his eyes it was his last farewell.[19]

The most powerful man in America (not just of that generation but of all subsequent generations) voluntarily chose to renounce power that had come knocking at his feet. Unlike so many other military men before him across the world, he did not lose his senses by the intoxicating allure of power. As Jefferson later wrote to Washington, 'the moderation and virtue of a single character [Washington]...probably prevented this revolution from being closed, as most others have been, by a subversion of that liberty it was intended to establish.'[20] For this renunciation of power, another tribute to Washington went like this: '"the man who unites all hearts," the American Zeus, Moses, and Cincinnatus all rolled into one.'[21]

Back at Mount Vernon, Washington sequestered himself away from the politics of the nation. He also got afflicted by rheumatism which reduced his agility. He again spent his days following the aristocratic traditions of rich Virginia planters such as getting himself sculpted and obtaining exquisite commodities from Europe. He also became the first president of the Society of Cincinnati—a fraternal order of the officers of the Continental Army. This act created a political firestorm since primogeniture was the criterion for passing the membership of the Society and thus, naturally, it triggered the fears of monarchy. This controversy aside, Washington's days in retirement were filled with peace but came to an end in less than four years.

Since the War had ended with the American victory, the glue of nationalism connecting the states together had weakened and they had started to drift apart. The Confederation Congress was reduced to a powerless body. It was so much neglected by the states that it was rarely the case that a quorum could be obtained by the attendance of the state delegates. In violation of the Articles of Confederation, the states had started to pursue their own foreign policies. No state wanted interference with its own laws or financial systems and thus there was no way that the economically broken and heavily indebted American nation could pay back the war debt. The currency issued by Congress had reduced to triviality. Congress was unable to coerce the states to pay their share of the debt. It could also not regulate trade between the states. Developing friction with Spain over the Peace Treaty posed another threat to American freedom. Furthermore, the federal army had reduced to less than a thousand men and there was no way for Congress to raise a sizeable army for the nation's security. To put it shortly, America as a nation was on the verge of failure. The singular "United States of America" was at the brink of becoming "the many states in America." America would have disintegrated into the constituent states in the short term and may have fallen prey to the stratagems of European powers in the long term. "Join, or Die" slogan to bring the colonies together before the Revolutionary War was again becoming relevant. Washington was very concerned about these developments and termed the Confederation Congress as 'wretchedly managed' and the Articles of Confederation as 'fatally flawed.' However, he had no intention of interfering by coming out of retirement.[22]

In autumn 1786, an outbreak of violence occurred in rural Massachusetts where the state had increased land taxes. These taxes combined with dislocations in the currency of Massachusetts (as mentioned earlier, each state was directing its own financial system) had worsened the condition of the farmers who could not pay their debts and had to forfeit their land. Thousands of farmers took to arms and the mob marched towards courthouses to assault judges and block their foreclosures of land. The mob activity came to be known as the Shays' Rebellion (after its leader Daniel Shays). Many among the mob donned their earlier Continental Army uniforms and planned to march on a big army arsenal at Springfield. Appeals were made to Washington to pace towards Massachusetts and terminate the rebellion at its bud. Veteran Henry Lee beseeched to Washington by saying: 'In one word, my dear General, we are all in dire apprehension that a beginning of anarchy, with all its calamities, has approached.' Washington was struck with horror and remarked: 'I am really mortified beyond expression that, in the moment of our acknowledged independence, we should by our conduct verify the predictions of our transatlantic foe and render ourselves ridiculous and contemptible in the eyes of all Europe.' Though Shays' rebellion petered out after a bloody blow it received in a confrontation with privately financed Massachusetts force, it convinced Washington that overhauling of the Articles of the Confederation must be done soon.[23]

One young man who was convinced about the same even before Washington and was already planning to overhaul the government was James Madison. Already in Fall 1785, Madison had spent time at Mount Vernon and had started the process to persuade Washington to come out of the retirement (a propitious sign). Without Washington's activism, any step towards reforming the Articles of Confederation would not have come to fruition. Washington was the only man in the nation who was respected across all the states and to challenge his views politically would have amounted to buying a one-way ticket to obscurity. In January 1786 i.e. before the Shays' Rebellion, Madison had been a delegate to the Annapolis Convention (another gathering of delegates to discuss the future form of government in America) which deliberated on the rules governing interstate commerce. But, the Annapolis Convention had failed since only five of the thirteen states had shown up. Alexander Hamilton had audaciously proposed to meet again by calling another convention to discuss all salient issues. We will encounter Hamilton in detail in the next chapter.

Suffice it to say here that he was a trustee of Washington, learned in law, and a very forceful character. The proposal to meet again initiated by Hamilton was a wild move. The present convention in Annapolis to discuss a single trivial matter could not even reach a quorum. Yet, here was Hamilton, proposing to meet again to discuss all problems at once. After Shays' Rebellion, the Confederation Congress had been forced to appoint delegates for another convention at Philadelphia.

Madison renewed his efforts to cajole Washington to come out of the retirement and requested him to participate in the convention. Only the legitimacy provided by Washington's presence would have ensured that the states would have taken the proposed convention in all seriousness. Additionally, Madison knew that a strong Federal government supported by Washington presiding over the convention would not be explicitly objectionable to other delegates of the convention. Washington, chiefly occupied with courting posterity's judgment, was noncommittal and wavered due to two reasons. First, he could foresee that the chances of success of the future convention were not very high since many states would resist any diminution in their power—the chief reason behind the failure of the Annapolis Convention. Hence, to cast his reputation on the success of the future convention seemed unwise to him. Second, if the convention would be a success, he speculated that in the eyes of posterity, he may be vilified as somebody who came out of retirement to gain power. This is because it was a foregone conclusion that by attending the upcoming convention, he would be re-entering public life and would be the natural choice for presiding over the subsequently established American government. He was also worried about resuming public life once again on a personal level since no other male in his family had lived beyond fifty. Thus, he thought that at fifty-four he may not live long especially under the physical exertion which would accompany public office.[24]

At the same time, Washington was also receiving letters from other friends to impinge upon him the necessity of attending the Philadelphia Convention. Thus, John Jay argued that nothing less than absolute reform from the bottom-up would do. Edmund Randolph urged that 'From the gloomy prospect still admits one ray of hope that those who began, carried on & consummated the revolution, can yet rescue America from impending ruin.' While on the one hand, Madison tactfully promulgated the news without Washington's approval that he was on board, on the other hand, Madison was conversing with Benjamin Franklin to be appointed as the chair if Washington backed out. Washington was still not ready to risk his reputation on the question of attending the convention. He wrote to Henry Knox: 'In confidence, I inform you, that it is not, at this time, my purpose to attend.' While many were requesting him to take charge, others forced upon him the view that if the convention would succeed, he would almost surely be asked to head the new government and hence would have to say goodbye to his retirement. Subsequently, it took much more than Madison's arguments about impending doom to pursue Washington to attend the convention. Only one consideration swung Washington's resolve—posterity's judgment.[25]

Ever the indefatigable and persuasive, Madison, was continuously sending reports to Washington about developments in each state and conveyed that unlike the previous Annapolis Convention, this time surely the proposed Philadelphia Convention would attain a quorum. Henry Knox who had earlier advised Washington to not attend the convention changed his advice based on reports about the attendance of different states. Knox now wrote evocatively that 'But were an energetic and judicious system to be proposed with your Signature, it would be a circumstance highly honorable to your fame, in the judgment of present and future ages; and doubly entitle you to the glorious republican epithet—the Father of Your Country.' The question of legacy was thus formulated in the reverse by Knox. By not attending the convention which now had a higher probability of success due to Madison's machinations, Washington would be risking his reputation in the eyes of posterity. Madison's political maneuvers and Knox's appeal about legacy finally pushed Washington over the edge. He agreed to attend the Philadelphia Convention which would come to be known as the Constitutional Convention (since the constitution drafted in the Philadelphia Convention was ratified by the states and officially became the Constitution of the United States of America). Washington's days of retirement were over.[26]

Washington presided over the Constitutional Convention but did not participate in any major debate. His presence at the Convention was in itself an expression of his wish to see the formation of a strong Federal government. After the Constitution was drafted and ratified, it was inevitable that Washington would become the first president of America. He was of course chosen unanimously and remains the only president in American history who did not belong to any political party. Throughout the process of voting, he maintained calculated aloofness so as to not present himself as eager to gain power. In his first inaugural address, as per his wont, he expressed reluctance in accepting the presidency since he thought himself inexperienced for holding the highest public office in the nation. He did not delve into trivial policy matters but rather outlined the larger themes of his administration. Acknowledging that the success of the republican experiment now depended on his administration, he said that 'the sacred fire of liberty, and the destiny of the republican model of government, are justly considered as *deeply*, perhaps as *finally* staked, on the experiment entrusted to the hands of the American people.' He also made up his mind to only serve for one term as president, nurture the infant republic, and retire again to spend the rest of his days under his vine and fig tree (a phrase borrowed from Hebrew scriptures which he quoted almost fifty times in his life). Power had come to Washington again despite all the overtures he had made in the opposite direction.[27]

As president, Washington took many overreaching decisions such as backing up Alexander Hamilton's economic program to pay back war debt and consolidate the financial system, secured Jay Treaty which averted a war with Great Britain, instituted the provision of neutrality which remained the centerpiece of American foreign policy for more than a century, and crushed another mob uprising known as the Whiskey Rebellion (we will read more about these events in the next chapter). By any standards, his presidency was an unqualified success. During the presidency, Washington consciously took steps to avoid any impression of overt use of power. He did not interfere with the freedom of various institutions of governance nor did he express any preference for his successor. Throughout most of his presidency, he was concerned with the partisanship in his government. His restrained exercise of power can be gauged from two facts. One, he only used the power to veto congressional proposals twice during the eight years of his presidency.[28] Second, he was irked by a section of the press which was highly partisan and hostile to his administration's policies. Specifically, in his second term as president, Washington was being vilified and attacked in the press by Jefferson and Madison who were by now in the Opposition (about which too we shall read in the next chapter). But Washington never tried to curtail the freedom of the press through the power vested in him as the president. Remember that we are talking about the late nineteenth century when in politically sophisticated Europe, similar criticism of the king in the press would have almost surely led the writer to gallows.

Washington's initial days in office were dominated by establishing presidential customs. Nobody had the slightest idea about what should be the proper way to address the president. At the time, all sorts of fashionable titles were popular in Europe to address the head of the government. The Senate appointed a committee to devise a suitable title for Washington. The committee discussed a wide range of titles, many of them highfalutin and proposed by Vice President John Adams, such as "His Highness, the President of the United States of America, and Protector of the Rights of the Same," "Excellency," and "His Mightiness."[29] Finally, the Senate decided that the title should be austere and proposed that it should simply be "the President" which Washington gladly accepted. Even the matters of etiquette and symbolism became issues of debate. During his initial days as president, he was flooded with visitors to the point that he could not do any administrative work. He then inquired about the policy for meeting visitors that was pursued earlier by the presidents of the Confederation Congress as well as followed by the kings in Europe. After soliciting written opinions from his cabinet members and other advisers, he concluded that he would hold public levees every Tuesday afternoon. During his first presidency, he also fulfilled his promise to visit every state of the Union. He utilized these tours to proclaim the ideals of religious freedom and unity among the states (as we read in the previous chapter). He traveled unostentatiously and exhibiting his showmanship, always posed for the public as well as for portrait artists. In no way did Washington wanted to convey an impression that could have been construed as a step towards monarchy. True to his style of leadership, he displayed himself as a monument to the masses but never became too familiar with his subordinates. He feared that excessive warmth in the relationship with his subordinates may weaken his power over them and thus was never a cozy figure.[30]

After the end of his first term in 1792, Washington was eager to retire back to Mount Vernon. He was convinced that his administration had already established a strong and stable federal government and so he could now retire back to his abode, just like Cincinnatus had retired a second time after coming out of retirement once. At the same time, he complained about partisan squabbles afflicting his cabinet and his physical decline due to old age. Both Hamilton and Jefferson, the two opposite poles of this cabinet, appealed to Washington to stay for another term. Jefferson warned Washington that the regional tensions created by Hamilton's economic program meant that 'North and South [northern and southern states] will hang together, if they have you to hang on.'[31] They also apprised him of the fact that the French Revolution and subsequent wars in Europe have made the times volatile and Washington was the only leader who could unite the nation in such partisan times. In the end, Washington did not put forward his name for the presidency but did not resent either. He was again unanimously elected to serve another term.

By the end of his second presidency, Washington personally kept despairing of the two political factions that had grown from his cabinet and were now "plaguing" the nation. The concept of political factions and parties was anathema to the sensibilities of the founding fathers. Having no precedent to take note of, they could not conceive a healthy two-party system in a democracy. Washington felt helpless in checking the growth of this phenomenon. It must be pointed out here that renouncing power was Washington's personal resolve and not a decision enforced on him by the political considerations. If he had not chosen to retire, rest assured, he would have served a third time by getting elected either unanimously or with a highly dominant majority. Washington had earlier asked Madison at the end of his first term to draft his farewell address. Ironically, by now Madison had become one of his chief opponents. Hence, Washington sent Madison's earlier draft to Hamilton for making changes after making a few additions. Hamilton was a gifted wordsmith and was like a surrogate son to Washington. In the earlier draft from 1792, Washington had written

> I did not seek the office with which you have honored me…[and now can show] only the grey hairs of a man who has…either in a civil or military character, spent five and forty years—All the prime of his life—in serving his country…[who only wanted to] be suffered to pass quietly to the grave, and that his errors, however numerous; if they are not criminal, may be consigned to the Tomb of oblivion, as he himself will soon be to the Mansion of Retirement.[32]

This excerpt never made it to the final draft but provides us a glimpse of Washington's state of mind at the end of his first term. If anything, by the time his second term ended, he had become even more morose and grumpy. Washington's additions to Madison's draft were filled with criticism of the political factions. He also wanted to pour his heart out against newspapers for discharging 'all the invective that disappointment, ignorance of facts, and malicious falsehoods could invent to misrepresent my politics.' Hamilton saw to it brilliantly that this and other such sections do not make it to the final draft. He wanted to present Washington's grand and father-like stature to the public and not an old curmudgeon lachrymose man. The farewell address thus drafted was a collaborative effort between Washington and Hamilton where Hamilton gave words to and refined Washington's ideas. It was aimed by Washington to directly address posterity.[33]

Washington wanted to publish his farewell address in June itself i.e. full half a year before his term ended. Hamilton cautioned against doing so by pointing out that a national emergency such as a possible military clash with France might happen in the Fall, in which case Washington would have to assume a third term as president. The editing of the draft between the two was successfully maintained as a secret and the farewell address was published in the newspaper *American Daily Advertiser* on September 19, 1796. It was by reading the newspaper that the citizens came to know of Washington's ineluctable retirement. That's it! No big commemoration, no political rally, no paraphernalia of renouncing power. The "Father of the nation" quietly announced his retirement through a write-up in a newspaper! With time, Washington's farewell address became one of the most important founding documents of America. For a long time, it remained alongside the Declaration of Independence as a most celebrated document and an "ideal" guide for future presidents and citizens of the United States.[34]

The "Farewell Address" as it came to be known started with the warm words 'Friends and Citizens.' Washington then expressed his grudge 'that it would have been much earlier in my power…to return to that retirement, from which I had been reluctantly drawn.' He made it clear that he wanted to retire at the end of his first term but did not do so due to the criticality of foreign affairs at that point. The central message that American leadership for many years afterward took from the farewell address was the idea of American isolationism. Washington wrote: 'Europe has a set of primary interests, which to us have none, or a very remote relation. Hence she must be engaged in frequent controversies, the causes of which are essentially foreign to our concerns. Hence, therefore, it must be unwise in us to implicate ourselves, by artificial ties, in the ordinary vicissitudes of her politics, or the ordinary combinations and collisions of her friendships, or enmities.' Much else of the document was dedicated to sounding a call for unity among the citizens (which also meant that it excluded any mention of slavery and Native American policy). The document expounded that being an American should triumph above all other identities, 'The name of AMERICAN, which belongs to you, in your national capacity, must always exalt the just pride of Patriotism, more than any appellation derived from local discriminations.' Finally, Washington justified the formation of a federal structure of government as the fulfillment of the American Revolution by saying that the respect for the authority of the Government, 'compliance with its laws, acquiescence in its measures, are duties enjoined by the fundamental maxims of true Liberty. The basis of our political systems is the right of the people to make and to alter their Constitutions of Government—But, the Constitution which at any time exists, till changed by an explicit and authentic act of the whole people, is sacredly obligatory upon all. The very idea of the power and the right of the people to establish Government presupposes the duty of every individual to obey the established Government.'[35]

Having explained himself to the American citizenry, Washington was ready to set up a new precedent by abdicating the presidency after two terms. Joseph Ellis summarizes Washington's decision to retire: 'Our obsession with the two-term precedent obscures the more elemental principle established by Washington's voluntary retirement—namely, that the office would routinely outlive the occupant, that the American presidency was fundamentally different from a European monarchy, that presidents, no matter how indispensable, were inherently disposable.' Thus, Washington's greatest act as the president was ironically his voluntary retirement.[36]

In his final address to the Congress, Washington delved into more detail about the Native American policy and also suggested the need to raise a small navy for policing the coastline and set up a military training academy. This was a time when there was mass hysteria against a standing military since it was seen as a doom for the republic—another Roman precedent. His advice on other matters was also related to expanding the federal power which he did not himself carry out during his presidency. Much of his last days as the president went in hosting official dinners and dances in his honor.[37]

Washington maintained total reticence regarding his preference for his successor between the two realistic choices: John Adams and Thomas Jefferson. It is certain though that Washington would have felt delighted when Adams defeated Jefferson in America's first presidential contest. This is because Adams was a federalist like Washington whereas in previous years Jefferson (along with Madison) had become his most embittered opponent.

True to his nature of not expressing his feelings, his diary entry for his last day as president simply reads: 'Much such a day as yesterday in all respects. Mercury at 41.' Adams's inauguration which Washington attended while presenting a short address witnessed much sobbing by the spectators whose greatest patriarch was exiting the stage. In fact, the ceremony turned from being a joyful transfer of power to become another sorrowful farewell. At the end of the ceremony, Washington made 'an exquisite gesture' by insisting that President John Adams and Vice President Thomas Jefferson exit the chamber before him. By this gesture, Washington wanted to convey the symbolism that the person who was the nation's most powerful man a few minutes ago was now a private citizen. Thus, even during this last exit from active public life, Washington did not forget to exhibit his acute sense of theatrics and symbolism.[38]

Washington's retirement and return to Mount Vernon served as a template for future presidents to only serve two terms until this unwritten law was broken by Franklin Roosevelt in the 1940s. It was only after Roosevelt's death that the law was codified into the Constitution. Washington's achievements during the presidency were breathtaking. He united the nation under the federal government and kept peace at home and abroad, fixed the American financial system, showed that the republic can handle tensions without threatening civil liberty, and did everything while abiding by the Constitution. In his view, he failed to stop the rise of political parties since he considered them vicious for the republic. He could never understand the inevitability of the rise of the political parties and their role in guaranteeing stability in a democratic form of government. He was content by his return to Mount Vernon after willfully abdicating the "crown of thorns" and all the power associated with it. It may seem unreal to our contemporary sensibilities that the most powerful leader of the nation willfully abdicated his power and did so by simply publishing a farewell address to apprise the citizens.

Washington's last years were spent devoting time to his plantation and business ventures. He found himself quite lonely since many of his former associates had passed away and the condition of transport during those days ensured that farewells actually meant never being able to set eyes upon many people again. Unlike other Virginian aristocrats who almost as a rule lived and died in debt, Washington amassed a fortune through his life's service and died a very rich man. An old man now, he took pleasure in conversing with his guests for hours and inviting them to stay for long. When war with France became likely in 1798, Adams persuaded Washington to resume his generalship which he did but only symbolically while Hamilton managed the nitty-gritty. Expectedly, during his last days, the wish to court posterity's favor became even more dominating on Washington's mind. Worrying about his legacy, he decided and wrote in his will to free all his slaves after his and Martha's death. He was the only slave-owning founding father and the only president who owned slaves while in office to do so.

The overwhelming practice in Virginia's plantations was to bequeath a large portion of one's wealth to one of the heirs, thus keeping the core intact. This was done so as to perpetuate one's dynasty and wealth over many generations. However, Washington decided to divide his wealth equally among twenty-three heirs. This effectively meant that no Washingtonian dynasty came into existence to flourish under the patriarch's name and legacy.[39] Once, the Earl of Buchan sent Washington an antique and valuable box connected with British history asking him to pass it on to whomever he would choose as his political heir. Washington politely returned it. Perhaps, Washington understood more than anybody else how power could be misused in his name should he declare somebody as his heir.[40]

Historian Garry Wills has noted that Washington 'gained power from his readiness to give it up.'[41] After the Revolutionary War, General Washington who had wielded immense power during the War as Commander-in-Chief had started the transition towards maintaining an aloofness from it. Again as president, Washington gave up the highest public office in America and retired despite all the temptations of power that the office brought to him. Thus, Washington's life story is a story of assuming power with some support from the factor called luck, wielding it through self-restraint, and its renunciation in the larger interests of the nation. His readiness to give up power has ensured that he shall always be the first in the hearts of his countrymen.

One of the Indian founding fathers, Subhas Bose, once remarked, 'India is a strange land where people are loved not because they have power, but because they give up power.'[42] Nobody understood this more than Mohandas Gandhi. Gandhi gained absolute power over the Indian freedom movement by renouncing all kinds of power—personal or privileged. Gandhi's life is an open book accessible to everyone. He remains perhaps the most exhaustively exposed public figure of all time. Everything about him—thousands of letters and other writings, medical history, documentation of daily meetings, diary entries, dietary idiosyncrasies, and excretory records—has been in the public domain for decades now. He appears so much down-to-earth that it is hard to mythologize him. On the one hand, his life is a story of gaining power and influence over millions of Indians who adored him, while on the other hand, it is a story of continuous and willful (some may say strategic) renunciation of power to uphold moral principles. He self introspectively titled his autobiography, "The Story of My Experiments with Truth," but could have as well titled it, "The Story of my Experiments with Power."

Throughout his life, Gandhi played many roles—lawyer, politician, writer, quacksalver, journalist, philosopher, and activist for civil rights, vegetarianism, and peace—and had various agendas—India's freedom, the emancipation of the Untouchables, reform in Hinduism, bridging the gap of animosity between the East and West, Hindu-Muslim unity, village renewal, political decentralization, women empowerment, coalescing nationalism with multiple social identities, etc. Throughout all roles played by him, all the agendas that he undertook, and all the struggles he participated in, three features pervaded every single decision that he made: non-violence, self-control, and respect for the opponent. This man's frail body, disarming smile, playful eyes, and scant clothing may give an impression of being just another saint from the East, but Gandhi was also a formidable politician, shrewd fundraiser, and strict disciplinarian with exemplary fortitude. Indians with all their diversity usually deferred to him as their Bapu (loving father), mostly deified him as a Mahatma (great soul), while sometimes defied him as senescent, only to come back to him later.

Mohandas Karamchand Gandhi was born on 2 October 1869 in Porbandar, a coastal town in today's state of Gujarat. His father, Karamchand, served as the chief minister in the princely state of Porbandar while his mother, Putlibai, was a devoutly religious housewife. Gandhi imbibed discipline from his father and spirituality from his mother. In his childhood, he was 'restless as mercury…either playing or roaming about…One of his favorite pastimes was twisting dogs' ears.' Through his mother, Gandhi was introduced to vegetarianism and to an intermingled culture that had elements from multiple religions.[43] As per the tradition of arranged marriage in his family, he was married at the age of thirteen to coetaneous, Kasturbai.

She was a woman of tremendous fortitude who later in life became Gandhi's strength in many ways. Gandhi has himself written in his autobiography about the charm of lust that possessed him when 'Even at school I used to think of her, and the thought of nightfall and our subsequent meeting was ever haunting me.' He has also written about the tendency of controlling her due to which 'she could not go anywhere without my permission…More restraint on my part resulted in more liberty being taken by her and in my getting more and more cross.' Evidently, Gandhi's concept of power at this point flowed from regressive societal concerns.[44]

Without any inhibitions, Gandhi wrote about how he was tricked by his friend to visit a brothel and was "saved" by God's mercy and how another time he was persuaded by his friend to eat meat. Two incidents that had bearing on young Gandhi's mind need mention. First, aged fifteen, he stole a bit of gold out of his brother's armlet. Unable to suffer regret and shame, he decided to write to his father and confess his error. His father was understandably agonized but taking note of his confession, Karamchand forgave him. In this way, Gandhi learned the power of truth. The second incident happened during Gandhi's sixteenth year when his father was bed-ridden. Gandhi used to massage his father's legs and retire to bed only after his father used to fell asleep. However, one day, carnal passion took better of his senses and Gandhi retired back to his bedroom where 'My wife, poor thing, was fast asleep. But how could she sleep when I was there?' Kasturba was pregnant at this time and as Gandhi wrote, it 'meant a double shame for me.' He also wrote that 'Every night whilst my hands were busy massaging my father's legs, my mind was hovering about the bed-room,—and that too at a time when religion, medical science and common sense alike forbade sexual intercourse.' As he retired back to his room, news came that his father had passed away. The regret and shame that he harbored due to this incident taught him a lesson in self-control.[45]

After graduating from high school, Gandhi enrolled in college but soon dropped out. A family friend advised sending the young boy to London for studying law. With monetary help from his elder brother and family, Gandhi got ready for pursuing studies in London since 'the desire to go to England…completely possessed me.' Before leaving he made three promises to his worried mother: to not touch a strange woman, or drink wine, or eat meat. However, as per the traditions of his caste, he was treated as a pariah by members of his community for taking the decision to go overseas since doing so would have supposedly polluted him.[46] He attended University College London and was invited to enroll at Inner Temple to become a barrister. He tried to blend himself in the English sartorial traditions and also started to refine his English writing. His first rendezvous with activism happened when he joined the Vegetarian Society. He was soon elected to its executive committee and started a chapter of the society in his own locality. At this time Gandhi also started to read theosophical texts from different religions which he continued throughout his life. Another habit which he acquired in London, and rejoiced pursuing forever in his life was to walk daily for many miles. With activism and reading also came the desire to write. It was at this time that he started to take himself seriously as a writer. He acquired a diary and also started writing for a magazine, *The Vegetarian*.[47] Though it appears that he did not take any interest in politics at this time, his worldview had started to expand rapidly. This is because in India he had never enjoyed reading newspapers 'but in London, he spent an hour a day reading *The Daily Times, The Daily Telegraph* and *The Pall Mall Gazette.*' Despite always being mindful of his living expenses, he never allowed any reduction in newspaper reading.[48]

After being called to the Bar in 1891, Gandhi returned back to India and learned that his mother had died in his absence. Having become a lawyer, he tried to set up a law practice in Bombay—the most cosmopolitan and industrialized city in India. For almost a year he tried to establish himself but due to his mediocre oration skills, he failed. He then moved back to Gujarat and started making only a modest living. At this time, he received a message from a merchant whose distant cousin based in South Africa needed a lawyer, preferably somebody who knew the Gujarati language. The compensation that was offered was quite good and Gandhi who described it as a 'tempting opportunity of seeing a new country, and of having new experience,' readily agreed. The opportunity was actually an escape route for him from his failure to establish himself in India during the past year.[49]

It was in South Africa that Gandhi really evolved to thrust himself on the world stage. His time in South Africa built the foundation on which he later stood as the leader of the Indian freedom struggle. The initial discrimination that he faced in South Africa especially the incident when he was thrown off a train because of his color—emphasized as the point of his transformation and made famous by the movie *Gandhi*—marked in his words, the beginning of his 'active nonviolence.'[50] The case that brought him to South Africa concluded in a year and Gandhi prepared to return back. During his farewell party, he noticed an article in the newspaper about the government's bill to deprive Indians of their right to elect members of the legislature. Gandhi advocated the idea that this move must be opposed and on being nudged by his friends, he consented to stay for a month. That supposedly one month's stay turned out to be of twenty years in the end.[51]

Through petitions, Gandhi opposed the discriminatory bill but failed in blocking its passage. He then helped in founding the Natal Indian Congress in 1894 and became its secretary the next year. He started mobilizing the Indian support as well as raising funds for the organization. Being the only London-trained lawyer in Durban, he acted as a bridge between the discriminated Indian community and the privileged Europeans. He also started to write pamphlets and articles supporting the Indians' cause. Knowing that his stay would be prolonged, he went on a short trip to India to bring back his wife and children. During this trip, he sought to meet the rising leaders of the Indian National Congress—Gopal Krishna Gokhale and Bal Gangadhar Tilak—to gather support for the overseas Indian community in South Africa. By the time he reached back and landed in Durban, he had already become notorious among the Europeans in South Africa for his activism. As soon as he landed, a mob of white men attacked him, and he was beaten. Fortunately, the wife of the police superintendent—a white woman—came to his rescue. This incident further strengthened Gandhi's view regarding making a distinction between opposing injustice vs. opposing the adversary. The earlier incident of being thrown out from the train was an act of racism by a single person but this was Gandhi's first experience of targeted antagonism by an organized group.[52]

With leadership came power which Gandhi used to mend the relationship with the British. In 1900, during the Boer War, Gandhi volunteered to raise an ambulance corps to take care of the sick and the wounded and help the British in a non-violent manner. Despite his disagreements with the British policies, he was a loyal subject of the Empire. He was able to persuade a few hundred reluctant Indians to serve the British in the War with him in non-violent roles. For his service, he and thirty-seven other Indians were awarded the Queen's South Africa Medal. At this time, he decided to migrate back to India. His law practice was prospering but perhaps he wanted to provide better education to his four sons in India rather than in South Africa. At the farewell meeting this time, he was presented with costly jewels and such luxury items by the grateful Indian community. Kasturba wanted to keep the items for future needs, but Gandhi staged a protest and demanded to return them and donate them to the Natal National Congress. In the end, Kasturba had to yield.

Back in India, Gandhi again forayed into the activities of the Indian National Congress. He willingly came under Gokhale's influence and started to see Gokhale as his mentor. He again tried to initiate a legal practice in Gujarat and Bombay and again he failed. Despite his failures, he was in continuous contact with friends in South Africa. They informed him of the end of the war, the establishment of a new regime, and requested Gandhi to return for taking up the activism for their rights. He agreed in no time. Gandhi's biographer, Ramachandra Guha, writes that 'the decision to leave for South Africa was mandated not by the mysterious ways of fate [as Gandhi explained in his autobiography], but by the mundane facts of failure.' In the world of the judiciary, Gandhi may have been a blue whale in the Indian community pond that was South Africa but he was only a minnow in India's vast sea.[53]

In 1906, the Transvaal government in South Africa sought to install a law which compelled all Indians in the colony to register for obtaining a certificate. It further stipulated that if somebody would be found without the certificate in the Transvaal province, s/he could be imprisoned, fined, or deported. In the adjacent province of Natal, this was not so even when there too the Indians were not allowed to vote or own property in designated places. It was at this time that Gandhi first experimented with his still-evolving ideology of Satyagraha (truth-force). He made a stirring speech at a mass gathering where he first urged Indians of all religions to come together in opposing the government. He then warned them that following his lead, they may lose their jobs and wealth, they may be imprisoned and beaten, but 'I can boldly declare and with certainty that so long as there is even a handful of men true to their pledge, there can be only one end to the struggle—and that is victory….There is only one course open to me, to die but not to submit to the law. Even if the unlikely happened and everyone else flinched, leaving me to face the music alone, I am confident that I will never violate my pledge.'[54]

When a visit to London failed in thwarting the Transvaal government in instituting the new act, Gandhi and his followers prepared to offer Satyagraha (passive resistance). He had already started the journal *Indian Opinion* to promulgate his views and he was now preparing for a confrontation with the government. Gandhi and his followers started the movement to defy the government by not applying for the permits. As a result, Gandhi was sentenced to two months' imprisonment. This was his first encounter with life in gaol. Throughout his life, Gandhi maintained a willingness to compromise with the adversary if such a compromise could be arrived at without sacrificing his principles. Hence, in the subsequent round of talks with the government, he accepted the proposal that the law will be repealed if the Indians would register voluntarily. This was construed as an act of deception on Gandhi's part by one of his fellow Pathan supporters. He felt so much betrayed that he mercilessly attacked Gandhi. Gandhi lost two teeth and much blood from the nose and forehead but fortunately, his life was saved because of a quick response from others nearby.[55]

When the government reneged on the promise and reintroduced compulsory registration, Gandhi and his followers organized bonfires of the certificates and were again imprisoned. The final precipitation came in 1913 when a judge ruled that only Christian marriages were valid in South Africa. This was the biggest affront yet against the Indian community since it invalidated Hindu, Muslim, and Parsi marriages and turned all Indian wives into concubines in the eyes of law. Five thousand strikers under Gandhi's leadership assembled and planned to court arrest after a long march. The government was rattled and finally agreed to negotiate. An agreement amenable to both parties was agreed on which validated all Indian marriages, abolished an annual tax on indentured Indian laborers, and provided them the freedom to move freely between provinces of the Union. Gandhi had won his South African battle. His method of Satyagraha had been vindicated.

During his stay in South Africa, he had also taken the vow of celibacy and was already experimenting with a simpler lifestyle by raising everything required for himself and his followers on a small farm. All power that he possessed on the Indian community in South Africa flowed through his activism for their betterment. He had renounced all sources of personal strength in their cause and cared 'nothing for sensual pleasures, nothing for comfort or praise or promotion, but [was] simply determined to do what he believes to be right.' His stay in South Africa had made him a leader who could bring together Indians (living in South Africa) of many religious and linguistic groups together in a single cause. While leaving for India, Gandhi was also highly self-confident and ambitious. From being a leader of a few thousand Indians in South Africa, Gandhi now aspired to be the leader of more than 300 million Indians back in his much more diverse country—where he had earlier failed twice in establishing himself.[56]

India of 1915 had stalwart leaders associated with the Indian National Congress such as Gopal Krishna Gokhale, Bal Gangadhar Tilak, Annie Besant, Madan Mohan Malaviya, Lala Lajpat Rai, among others. After his return, Gandhi was just one of the leaders in the Congress, who had gained popularity through his activism overseas. He was totally unknown to the masses. Congress was an elite organization at this time with no base support among the general populace. It was a party with minimal presence in villages and in the hearts of poor, illiterate Indians. It was also a party of moderation and legislation. At this time, Gandhi considered himself to be a loyal British subject who had faith in the Empire's ideals. In the next five years, he became the most notorious and inveterate enemy of the British Empire. Gandhi also emerged as the most powerful leader in India and widened the base of the Congress by taking it to the masses to make it a truly national organization. Three astute observations made by him based on his experience of rising as a leader in the culturally diverse Indian community in South Africa helped him in this venture. First, he understood the influence of the mother tongue and broke down the Congress organization according to linguistic regions in India rather than administrative boundaries defined by the British. Simultaneously, he encouraged the use of local languages to communicate Congress's agendas. This helped in taking Congress's proposals to the peasants who could not understand English—the language of the elite. Second, there is a saying that Gandhi 'could fashion heroes out of common clay.' He cultivated young leaders throughout India who in turn became bridges between him and their own provinces. When Independence came, these leaders took center stage during the transfer of power and the drafting of the Constitution.[57]

Third, Gandhi understood very well that he could not at this time relate to the problems of common Indians nor could he relate personally with life in India's villages where most Indians lived. Perhaps, he had never spent a single night in a village in India until this point in his life. Earlier in South Africa, Gandhi's clients and other acquaintances belonged to many regions in India representing different religious and linguistic groups. This gave him a much more cosmopolitan and pan-Indian view than he would have gathered if he had stayed in India during his formative years as a politician. Gandhi knew about the culturally diverse palimpsest that was India but had not himself lived a life closely related to that of the common folk. In his book *The Discovery of India,* Jawaharlal Nehru wrote about Gandhi's coming to India, 'And then Gandhi came. He was like a powerful current of fresh air that made us stretch ourselves and take deep breaths…He did not descend from the top; he seemed to emerge from the millions of India, speaking their language and incessantly drawing attention to them and their appalling condition. Get off the backs of these peasants and workers, he told us, all you who live by their exploitation; get rid of the system that produces this poverty and misery.' Flowery prose can be misleading. Nehru had written these lines years later from the vantage point of nostalgia. The mundane reality is that on his return in 1915, Gandhi sought to discover India for himself.[58]

Gandhi had already acknowledged Gokhale—the leader of the moderate section of the Congress which advocated reforms by working with existent institutions of governance—as his mentor in politics. Later, he dedicated three successive chapters of his autobiography to his stay with Gokhale during his earlier visit to India. In fact, it was Gokhale who had asked Gandhi to return back and work for India's freedom. But how could Gandhi understand the common Indian man and his problems when he was away from India for years? Hence, Gokhale extracted a promise from him that he would not indulge in politics for one year so as to understand India anew. Gandhi spent most of the year traveling across the nation including few days of stay with Gokhale. He also established an ashram in Gujarat and was backed by wealthy businessmen in the endeavor. Through his travels, which as a rule were in the third-class compartments in trains so as to be close to the peasants, Gandhi was able to appreciate India's problems in a much more intimate and plebeian manner. In the same year, Gokhale died at the relatively young age of 48. Gandhi was deeply anguished but an unexpected outcome of Gokhale's unfortunate demise was that now Gandhi was free in promulgating his views without looking to Gokhale for his assent. As Gandhi wrote later that it was 'blasphemous to conjecture what would have happened if he [Gokhale] were alive today. I know that I would have been working under him.'[59]

After the one-year self-imposed exile was over, Gandhi came out as a new and revitalizing force in India's politics in Banaras. He was participating in the inauguration ceremony of the Banaras Hindu University organized by Annie Besant and Madan Mohan Malaviya. Any other newcomer foraying for the first time into an unfamiliar political landscape would probably have been coy and surely not combative. This was not Gandhi's way. He started his speech by excoriating the British education system and then accused the princes of being loyal to the British and enjoying their luxurious lives when millions in India did not have enough food to eat. Not stopping here, he then criticized Hindus in one of the most ancient and holiest Hindu cities for the filthy condition of the streets. He said: 'If a stranger dropped from above on to this great temple and he had to consider what we as Hindus were, would he not be justified in condemning us?....If even our temples are not models of roominess and cleanliness, what can our self-government be?' Some princes started to leave the stage as a mark of protest. Annie Besant intervened to stop Gandhi by yelling: 'Stop! Please Stop!' The audiences were enjoying Gandhi's salvos and shouted to go on. After Gandhi continued and the situation became uneasy for Besant and other leaders, the meeting was declared closed. Gandhi had made it clear that he was not an elite leader but that he aspired to be a leader of the masses and that he would not shy away from criticizing his countrymen's faults. Gandhi was not willing to put all the blame on the British for all problems tormenting Indian society.[60] Word now started to reach every part of the subcontinent about a leader who lived like a poor man, had renounced all worldly objects of luxury and desire, and who defended the poor against the rich. India had seen many such renunciates before. But, Gandhi's renunciation was not for the mere sake of it. It was aimed at cleansing his own society and religion from ills while also freeing India from the British-rule on the way. In the process, power itself started to come toward Gandhi.[61]

Gandhi was looking keenly for an opportunity to launch mass opposition on a nation-wide level and emerge as the leader of the Indian freedom movement. He was lucky that such an opportunity soon came knocking at his feet. After the First World War, Indians were aspiring to receive more generous treatment from the British due to their support in the war. Over one million Indian soldiers had fought from the British side during the war and naturally, they thought that they will be rewarded for their service. Alas, all they got in return was the Rowlatt Act of 1919 which gave the government enormous powers of indefinitely extending the emergency measures of preventive detention and imprisonment without trial or judicial review. For Indians, this came as a breach of faith that they had shown in the British. This law turned India into a police-state in every sense of the term. The leader of the Congress extremists, Tilak, was at this time away in England to fight a court case. This fortuitous circumstance provided more room to maneuver for Gandhi since it is sure that if Tilak would have been in India, being a much more popular leader than Gandhi, he would have spearheaded the agitation against the Rowlatt Act. Gandhi launched a nationwide mass movement (known as the Rowlatt Satyagraha) which raised his stature as a pan-Indian leader.[62]

The British government's response to the Rowlatt Satyagraha was to brutally crush the Indian spirit of freedom by force. The

Jallianwala Bagh massacre that followed in April 1919 was a turning point in India's history. Hundreds of peacefully gathered Indians were shot at close quarters by troops of the British Indian Army. All hopes of moderation between the rulers and their subjects ended that day. With hopes also died any semblance of trust in the British government and its ideals. Gandhi ceased to be a loyal subject of the throne and as a mark of his conversion, he returned the three medals that had been awarded to him by the emperor for his services in the Boer, Zulu, and World Wars. It was also a coincidence that the day Gandhi returned these medals, Tilak, who had by now returned to India, passed away. Gandhi attended his funeral and helped in carrying Tilak's body for cremation. It was an event symbolizing the passing of the torch and was taken note of by everyone. As Ramachandra Guha writes, 'Tilak's death in 1920 allowed Gandhi to emerge as the leader of the militant tendency in the Congress-led national movement.'[63]

Gandhi's response to the Jallianwala Bagh massacre was to launch the Non-Cooperation Movement of 1920 with the aim of self-governance and obtaining independence from the British. With this mass movement, he was successful in emerging as the undisputed leader of the freedom movement. His rise to power had been founded on the shoulders of the giants of Congress before him (most notably Gokhale and Tilak). He would use his power through the next quarter-century in multiple ways, mostly democratic, sometimes authoritative, but without making any compromise with his ideals of truth and non-violence. The Non-Cooperation Movement itself was an example of Gandhi's adherence to his principles. In the words of the Governor of Bombay, George Lloyd, it 'was the most colossal experiment in the world's history, and it came within an inch of succeeding. But he [Gandhi] couldn't control men's passions. They became violent, and he called off his programme.' Gandhi called off the Movement because of violence that happened at a small hamlet in a corner of India. Ideals would not be compromised on the way to gain self-rule for Indians.[64]

In the mid-1930s, while witnessing the unprecedented pace of development in the Soviet Union, many young Indians were developing an attraction towards socialism. Congress was an amalgam of diverse ideologues and activists including young socialists, communists, trade unionists, conservatives, and capitalists. Encouraged by the Soviet Union's example, Communists outside the Congress were expanding their violent activities. In the ranks of the Congress too, there was an increasing pressure from young minds to adopt socialism as Congress's economic agenda. Socialists in the Congress were increasingly coming to odds with Gandhi's efforts for village renewal and his social work. Gandhi increasingly felt that a gap was developing between his ideas and those of other Congress leaders. Further unrest in Congress was brewing because with Gandhi as the most popular leader in India and a figurehead in the party, there was almost no room for dissent inside the organization. To challenge Gandhi's leadership within the organization was to witness one's support melting away only to find oneself land on an isolated island. Gandhi sensed these unhealthy trends. At the same time, Gandhi was devoting most of his efforts in the mid-1930s towards the emancipation of Harijans and village renewal. Thus, he wrote to Patel in 1934 that

> [t]he best interests of the Congress and the nation will be served by my completely severing all official or physical connection with the Congress, including original membership....There is a growing and vital difference of outlook between many Congressmen and myself. My presence more and more estranges the intelligentsia from the Congress....Then there is the growing group of socialists....That group is bound to grow in influence and importance...I have fundamental differences with them on the programme published in their authorized pamphlets. But I would not, by reason of the moral pressure I may be able to exert, suppress the spread of the ideas propounded in their literature. My remaining in the Congress would amount to the exercise of such pressure.[65]

Expressing his views like this, Gandhi resigned from the membership of the Congress. He also made it clear to the party workers that his retirement 'was neither a threat nor an ultimatum.'[66] However, Congress could not abandon him, and he did return back later to steer the party for achieving his aims. But, this episode shows us how Gandhi understood that his position in the party was stifling the growth of young leadership which differed from his ideology. Congress was his vehicle of choice to attain freedom for India and he renounced his power over the party when he found that his own popularity is becoming detrimental to the organization. Being shrewd that he was, soon after his resignation, he got Jawaharlal Nehru elected as the Congress president which served twin purposes. Nehru was the leader of the Congress Socialists and yet was fiercely loyal to Gandhi despite many differences in their viewpoints. Hence, Nehru served as a bridge between Gandhi and the socialists in addition to keeping the extreme faction among the Congress socialists in check.

We have seen in the last chapter how Gandhi's views about the caste system evolved over time. The same can be said about his views towards women. For the most part in his early life, Gandhi viewed women in the traditional role of homemaker. At the same time, he campaigned for the emancipation of women by opposing child marriage, dowry, and *purdah*β. By the 1920s he was actively seeking women's support for the freedom movement. Women had started to come out of their domestic life in large numbers and were actively taking part in the patriotic cause. On Gandhi's call, it was common to witness women participate in acts like picketing liquor shops, burning foreign-manufactured clothes, and weaving and selling khadi (handspun cloth). Gandhi had got Sarojini Naidu (civil rights activist, poet, and social reformer) elected as the president of the Congress in 1925—at a time when probably no mainstream political party in the West had a woman president.

However, at this time, Gandhi was not in favor of women courting arrests. Despite his resentment, it was not possible for him now to enforce his absolute will. Women had already tasted the sweet nectar of nationalism that had earlier been fomented among them by Gandhi. During the Salt March in 1930, Gandhi had restricted the group who would march to the sea and break the salt law to men. When a feminist leader tried to persuade him to allow women to march with him and court arrest, Gandhi replied, 'if impatient sisters will be a little patient, they will find ample scope for their zeal and sacrifice in the national struggle for freedom.' After breaking the salt law, he appealed to women to not take part in the movement by breaking the law since 'they will be lost among the men.'[67] But, some women did not heed his advice and did court arrest by breaking the

---

β The regressive practice of secluding women in the society behind a curtain or by using a veil to conceal the face.

salt law. In the next three years, a large number of women participated in the next far-reaching mass movement orchestrated by Gandhi (the Civil Disobedience Movement). Kasturba herself courted arrest twice. Women had gone ahead of Gandhi's views and by the Quit India Movement of 1942, Gandhi was himself encouraging women to participate in the struggle. In his historic Quit India Speech, he declared

> Here is a *mantra,* a short one, that I give you...The *mantra* is: "Do or Die." We shall either free India or die in the attempt; we shall not live to see the perpetuation of our slavery. Every true Congressman or [Congress] woman will join the struggle with an inflexible determination not to remain alive to see the country in bondage and slavery. Let that be your pledge....Let every man and woman live every moment of his or her life hereafter in the consciousness that he or she eats or lives for achieving freedom and will die, if need be, to attain that goal.[68]

As a result of the evolution in Gandhi's views because of the pressure from women and his ceding power to them, thousands of women participated in the Quit India movement, often playing leadership roles after their husbands were imprisoned. In fact, Gandhi's reluctant and yet definite relinquishment of power to women meant that more women participated in the Indian freedom struggle than in any other political movement across the globe at the time.

Historian Rajmohan Gandhi points out that among the numerous leaders in Asia and Africa whose nations gained independence in the twentieth century, only Gandhi did not assume office. He had cultivated a score of leaders across the nation each of whom played distinct and significant roles when Independence came. As early as 1931, Gandhi had made this clear in an interview.

> *Journalist:* Do you expect Purna Swaraj [complete self-rule] in your lifetime?
> *Gandhi*: I do look for it most decidedly. I still consider myself a young man of sixty-two.
> *Journalist*: Would you agree to become the Prime Minister of the future Government?
> *Gandhi*: No. It will be reserved for younger minds and stouter hearts.[69]

After Independence, Gandhi's self-imposed restraint on power went a step further. He not only favored his chief lieutenants Nehru and Patel to serve as the prime minister and deputy prime minister but also desired that talented men who had earlier supported the British should also serve in the government. Thus, the first Cabinet of India consisting of fourteen members had seven non-Congressman. Irrespective of their political differences with him, Gandhi wanted competent men to serve in the nation's cause. He made this clear when he remarked a month before Independence that talented men who had been loyal to the British 'have not become our enemies...Please remember that they are at heart patriots...If we seek the advice of such old and experienced persons, they will show their genius...Our country will suffer if we don't take their help.' Gandhi could not only restrain himself but also accommodate his erstwhile antagonists in sharing power.[70]

As India became independent on 15 August 1947, Indians rejoiced across the nation. Freedom had come at last and Nehru announced India's arrival as a sovereign nation-state on the world stage through his famous *Tryst with Destiny* speech. Delhi was decorated like an Indian bride and all ceremonies associated with the transfer of power were underway. But, the leader of the freedom movement who had ruled Indians' hearts for three decades, the acknowledged "Father of the Nation," was mourning in a derelict house in Calcutta, a thousand miles away from the nation's capital. 'I cannot participate in the celebration of 15 August,' declared Gandhi.[71] He chose to spend the day fasting and praying with the poor and oppressed. When a government spokesperson asked him for a message for Indians, he only said that 'he had run dry.' He was saddened that the masses had not been following his principle of non-violence and had indulged in riots across the city. Hindus and Muslims of the nation were rioting since a section of Muslims were demanding partition of the nation into two based on religion. From the past few months, Gandhi was utilizing all power under his command towards stopping the widespread violence.[72]

In August 1946, one year before the Independence, Calcutta had witnessed widespread Hindu-Muslim rioting when Mohammad Ali

Jinnah's[x] Muslim League had called for the Direct Action Day—a political measure to demand the partition of India followed by the establishment of Pakistan. More than 4,000 people died and 100,000 were displaced within 72 hours. While Muslims had started the conflagration under the aegis of the Muslim League, they themselves became victims in the Hindu-majority megapolis. Then started the call for attrition and the cycle of revenge between the two communities. Widespread attacks on Hindus took place in the Noakhali area of East Bengal. Hindu-Muslim rioting in India had earlier been restricted to urban settlements only. Rioting in rural Noakhali had the potential to flare up tensions across rural India. Villages had always been the backbone of inter-religious harmony in India and so Gandhi was distressed beyond measure. He wanted to go to Noakhali in the endeavor to stop rioting. However, he was in poor health and the Congress leaders wanted him to be in Delhi where negotiations for the transfer of power from the British were progressing. 'All I know is that I won't be at peace unless I go there [to Noakhali]' insisted Gandhi. At the same time, he was unsure if he could make a difference by calming down the paranoia that had gripped people's minds in Noakhali. Amidst the cycle of murder, rape, loot, forceful conversion, abduction, and incineration, Gandhi left for Calcutta on the way to Noakhali.[73]

Reaching Calcutta, Gandhi was shocked at the desecration of the city he witnessed, '…entire rows of gutted shops and burnt-out houses in the side-streets and by-lanes as far as the eye could reach, one felt overcome with a sinking feeling at the mass madness that can turn man into less than a brute.' Worse news came from Bihar where to avenge Noakhali's killings, Hindus had gone berserk with communal frenzy. As Gandhi wrote to Nehru, 'If half of what I hear is true, it means that Bihar has lost all humanity.' He appealed to the people of Bihar that 'A bad act of one party is no justification for a similar act by the opposing party…And is counter-communalism any answer to the communalism of which Congressmen have accused the Muslim

---

[x] Mohammad Ali Jinnah was the president of the Muslim League and the chief orchestrator of India's Partition. He vigorously advocated the so-called "two-nation theory" that Hindus and Muslims constituted two separate nations and cannot coexist peacefully. We will read more about this in the final chapter.

League?' He tried to put sense in the minds of the people of Bihar by telling them that they were 'honor bound to regard the minority Muslims as their brethren requiring protection, equal with the vast majority of Hindus.'[74] He also declared that as a penance he would keep himself 'on the lowest diet possible,' which would become a 'fast unto death if the erring Biharis have not turned over a new leaf.'[75]

In Noakhali, Gandhi gave many speeches and addressed meetings every evening. After an initial good response from the Muslim community which came to hear him, hope soon started to fizzle out as their attendance began to decline. Gandhi asked his disciples to go to different rural settlements as his messengers. He established himself in a village named Srirampur which despite its Hindu name had a Muslim majority and which had presently only a single Hindu family left—all others were either dead or had fled the village. Amidst all this, Gandhi, who was seventy-seven but ever a student, wanted to impart his message on people's minds in their own tongue and thus started to take daily lessons to learn writing Bengali. On November 20, in his first press statement after reaching the village, Gandhi said: 'I do not propose to leave East Bengal till I am satisfied that mutual trust has been established between the two communities and the two have resumed the even tenor of their lives in their villages. Without this there is neither Pakistan nor Hindustan—only slavery awaits India, torn asunder by mutual strife and engrossed in barbarity.' Gandhi's daily routine was to tour nearby villages and address villagers to calm down the religious animosity. To bring peace and harmony between the two communities, Gandhi was willing to utilize all his power capital and sacrifice everything in the quest.[76]

Gandhi continued to propagate his message with verses from the religious texts of Hinduism, Islam, and Christianity. After spending forty-three nights in the village hamlet of Srirampur and having calmed down things to his satisfaction, he resumed his walking tour. Congress leaders were still urging him to at least move to Calcutta where it would have been easy for them to consult him regarding the transfer of power. But, for Gandhi, everything else had to wait. Walking barefoot in the pursuit of a higher ideal, Gandhi felt that Hindu-Muslim unity deserved his undivided attention.[77] Altogether he lived in forty-nine villages during his pilgrimage. He would wake up at four in the morning, walk for three to four miles barefoot to a village, hold meetings and prayers, and move on to the next village. Wherever possible he would spend the night at a Muslim's place. It was by no means an easy task. Many times, he was rebuffed and some rogue elements who were disgruntled by their past tragedies 'strewed broken glass, brambles and filth in his path.' He was also asked by politicians to propagate that the populations of the region should just abandon their region and settle elsewhere but Gandhi 'rejected such defeatism' and endured everything with great fortitude. It was his innate belief that love and tolerance exist in the heart of men and he was endeavoring to bring them out. Often the old man had to deal with bad health and was unable to keep his balance on poor roads and bridges. His co-workers were also scared about their safety in remote villages, but his instruction was to 'unflinchingly face whatever comes in the natural course.' As a result of his pilgrimage, many Hindus felt secured and returned back to their homes in Noakhali.[78]

From Bengal, he moved to Bihar where his target was to save Muslims from the atrocities of Hindus. He promised to return back to Noakhali since the Hindu-Muslim brotherhood that he had been able to establish there was still fragile. He rebuked the Hindus in Bihar as he had done the Muslims in Bengal since 'to me the sins of the Noakhali Muslims and the Bihar Hindus are of the same magnitude and equally condemnable.' He followed the same demanding routine daily as he had done in Bengal to bring peace in Bihar. But, with the inauguration of a new viceroy in Delhi, Gandhi had to leave for the capital. Shortly after the Partition of India and the beginning of the worst rioting that the nation had witnessed, Gandhi utilized all his power to initiate what have been called his greatest fasts.[79]

Punjab and Bengal, the two provinces that had been partitioned at Independence were engulfed in widespread rioting. Gandhi was in Calcutta on Independence Day and was attempting to do everything possible to stop the violence. For the moment, peace had returned to the city on 15 August as all Indians rejoiced in the celebration of Independence. In the evening, Gandhi asked to be driven anonymously around the city in order to see for himself the joy in everybody's eyes and whether the peace that had come was a 'Miracle or Accident.'[80] Unfortunately, it was only a temporary respite. Soon,

Gandhi started receiving news of atrocities from Punjab and was being requested to come there to calm the religious tempers and stop the violence. In the event, fresh rioting broke out in Calcutta on the last day of August. Amidst huge violence in the city, the rioters reached where Gandhi was staying. The crowd started throwing stones at the windows and attempted to cut the electricity supply. Gandhi himself went outside with folded hands to dissuade them. A brick that was thrown at him hit a friend standing by his side. A stick aimed at his head narrowly missed him. Fortunately, police arrived on time and the intruders were ousted.[81]

Gandhi then started an indefinite fast the same evening. Amidst the celebration of Independence in most parts of India and the transfer of power to Indians, Gandhi was willing to renounce his life to bring back sanity to people's minds. He said in a press statement that 'if India is to retain her dearly won independence all men and women must completely forget lynch law,' and that his fast would 'end only if and when sanity returns to Calcutta.' Rajaji who was serving as the Governor of West Bengal tried hard to dissuade Gandhi from staking his life by saying that with his death 'the conflagration would be worse.' Gandhi was adamant and said: 'At least I won't be there to witness it. I shall have done my bit. More is not given a man to do.' There were many instances in his life when Gandhi had used fasting as a political instrument or as a show of penance. Now he was attempting to use it to secure peace in the country. Unlike many of his earlier fasts which had been for a fixed duration and against the oppression by an adversary, he was adamant this time—thus he commenced a fast unto death which was aimed at the reunion of hearts between people.[82]

From September 2, many political leaders started to visit Gandhi and assure him that peace and normalcy had started to return. There were fewer reports of violence that day and around 5000 students marched through the city as a symbol of peace. The fear of losing their Mahatma meant that people were willing to go through all sorts of penances to save his life. The next morning, a bunch of hooligans visited Gandhi to surrender their weapons and ask for his forgiveness. He suggested that they should 'go immediately among the Muslims and assure them full protection. The moment I am convinced that real change of heart has taken place, I will give up my fast.'[83] As normalcy started to return and Gandhi received appeals from leaders of both communities, he asked them to sign a pledge that they will desist from any rioting or encouragement of such activities. He also told them that if this promise will be broken, he would commence 'an irrevocable fast' which nothing but his death would stop.[84]

With the signing of the pledge and calming of tempers, Gandhi broke his fast. He had saved Calcutta from destroying itself in communal delirium. Gandhi's fast led Lord Mountbatten, the last viceroy of India and presently serving as the Governor-general of India (the representative of the British monarch and the highest serving official in India) to remark that 'in Punjab we have 55 thousand soldiers and large scale rioting on our hands. In Bengal our force consists of one man [Gandhi], and there is no rioting.'[85] A single frail unarmed man had brought peace and normalcy to Bengal by wielding the power of love that he possessed over the masses. Gandhi had himself said once that 'Power is of two kinds. One is obtained by the fear of punishment and the other by acts of love. Power based on love is a thousand times more effective and permanent than the one derived from fear of punishment.'[86] Having thus calmed tempers in Bengal, he now planned to go to Punjab and perform the same dramatic feat. To Bengal, Gandhi wrote in his farewell message before leaving for Delhi, 'Amar Jibani Amar Bani' (My Life Is My Message). It was a fitting tribute to his endeavors.[87]

On his seventy-eighth birthday, the poet Sarojini Naidu had spoken about Gandhi's personality which also has bearings on the way Gandhi wielded power: 'Today, there is Gandhi, a tiny man, a fragile man, a man of no worldly importance, of no earthly possessions, and yet a man, greater than emperors....This man, with his crooked bones, his toothless mouth, his square yard of clothing, or of cloth rather, that just covers his nakedness, where nakedness must be covered, he passes meekly through the years, he faces embattled forces, he overthrows empires, he conquers death.' Gandhi had willingly renounced everything material and was loved by his countrymen for the act of renunciation itself. He wielded absolute power in the nation and at a time when there was a civil war-like situation developing in the nation, he was utilizing his power towards fostering peace and unity.[88]

On his way to Punjab, Gandhi reached Delhi. There as his wont, he wanted to stay in the Harijan locality but Patel and others vetoed him because of the considerations regarding his safety during Hindu-Muslim rioting. Gandhi wanted to proceed to Punjab soon but violence in Delhi stopped him from doing so. In Delhi, Muslims were the victims of rioting and they had taken shelter in various ancient monuments in the capital. Gandhi visited them and asked Hindus to be more accommodative of their Muslim brethren. At the same time, he asked Muslims who had stayed and not gone to Pakistan to 'open-heartedly declare that they belong to India and are loyal to the Union.' Gandhi sought to eliminate the existential threat to the lives of Delhi's Muslims. He was also dejected and bleak from the hatred he was witnessing. He told his audience on his seventy-eighth birthday: 'I am surprised and also ashamed that I am still alive. I am the same person whose word was honoured by the millions of the country. But today nobody listens to me. You want only the Hindus to remain in India and say that none else should be left behind. You may kill Muslims today; but what will you do tomorrow? What will happen to the Parsis and the Christians and then to the British? After all, they are also Christians.' He further said that 'if you really want to celebrate my birthday, it is your duty not to let anyone be possessed by madness and if there is any anger in your hearts you must remove it.'[89]

Gandhi's appeals were not all futile but they could not yet eliminate the violence in the city. In early January 1948, as fresh rioting broke out, Gandhi had had enough. For many days he was witnessing the animosity between the two communities first hand during his evening prayer meetings. There were always hooligans who were objecting to his use of verses from the *Koran* during these meetings. Gandhi now decided to fast again. On 12 January, he declared that he would commence a fast the next day which would end only when he would be 'satisfied that there is a reunion of hearts of all communities brought about without any outside pressure, but from an awakened sense of duty.' Gandhi was frail after his last fast and the announcement of this one came as a surprise even to his closest associates. One of the aims of Gandhi's fast was to force the Indian government's hand to release Pakistan's share of sterling balances that the British had owed to undivided India. This has fueled many debates among historians over the decades that Gandhi fasted in Pakistan's cause. The plain truth is that even after Nehru and Patel assured Gandhi that the funds would be released to Pakistan, he did not break his fast. This shows that his fast was chiefly directed at securing peace in the nation's capital. Hindus in Delhi had become so fanatic by then that every day there were demonstrations with slogans against Gandhi. On 14 January, demonstrators were shouting 'Let Gandhi Die' in front of Birla House where he was staying. Elsewhere, the members of the Hindu right-wing group Rashtriya Swayamsevak Sangh (RSS) were also shouting 'Boodhé ko marné do' (Let the old man die). Meanwhile, Gandhi's health was worsening. He could barely speak from the third day of the fast during the evening prayers. Congress leaders across the capital and the country were appealing to the masses to abjure violence and save Gandhi's life.[90]

Nehru addressed a crowd of more than a hundred thousand in the capital and appealed to them to save Gandhi's life: 'We must not allow Gandhiji to suffer for our sins.' Gandhi laid down seven conditions on whose fulfillment he would break his fast. These included safeguards of worshipping, travel and economic security for the Muslims as well as returning their places of worship. As his health further deteriorated, the same soothing effect that was earlier seen in Bengal started to ignite in the capital. Two hundred thousand people signed a peace pledge, Hindus started welcoming Muslims back to their localities, the mosques that had been taken away were returned to them, and they again started to freely move in the capital. The magician's magic had once again succeeded in doing what the government could not. Having convinced himself of the assurances provided by the leaders and masses, Gandhi broke his fast on the sixth day. Gandhi's fast had applied a healing ointment on people's wounds. Thousands of people came to Birla House where he was staying to pay homage to the magician.[91]

Willing to renounce his life for the ideals of non-violence and Hindu-Muslim unity, Gandhi saved thousands of people from massacring each other. He still wanted to proceed to Punjab and do what he had done in Delhi and Bengal. But, fate would not have him do so. Extremist Hindus were grudging against Gandhi for his supposed "appeasement" of the Muslims. They saw his fast as an act of coercion aimed at them. Gandhi's earlier pilgrimage in Noakhali where he had gone to save Hindus from Muslims had been forgotten by them in the communal frenzy. On the evening of 30 January, a Hindu extremist shot three bullets at Gandhi and assassinated him. In death, as in life, Gandhi achieved what appeared to be impossible. Rioting and violence suddenly came to a halt and all hearts across the nation mourned his death. The fact that his assassin was a Hindu made most of them bow their heads in shame. By sacrificing his own life, Gandhi had again saved thousands of other lives.

In the radio broadcast that fateful night, Nehru said: 'The light has gone out of our lives and there is darkness everywhere.... The light has gone out, I said, and yet I was wrong. For the light that shone in this country was no ordinary light...For that light represented something more than the immediate present; it represented the living, eternal truths reminding us of the right path, drawing us from error, taking this ancient country to freedom.'[92] It can rightly be said that Gandhi derived his power from the love he received from the people and the ideals of truth and non-violence that he professed. Through constant experimentation with himself throughout his life and some fortuitous circumstances along the way, Gandhi had assumed leadership of millions of Indians and had attained absolute power. He still never shied away from renouncing everything in order to uphold those ideals that he considered as embodying the ultimate truth.

Power tends to corrupt and absolute power corrupts absolutely.
-Lord Acton

The lust for power, for dominating others, inflames the heart more than any other passion.
-Tacitus

At the outset, it may seem absurd, if not entirely foolish, to put together a General and a Mahatma in the same chapter. In many ways, Washington and Gandhi could not be more different. Washington was taciturn, cold, and kept a distance from everybody whereas Gandhi was loquacious, light-hearted, and everything about his life was open.

Where Washington wanted to court posterity's judgment by memorializing himself, Gandhi wanted to be remembered by nakedly exhibiting everything about his life. Though fortune played a role in the rise to power for both, one rose to fame through victory in a bloody war while the other through the creation of a non-violent struggle against Imperialism. In appearance too, one was over six feet tall, well-built, fluffed his hair from the side, powdered them regularly, and had immaculate sartorial preferences for both military and non-military surroundings while the other was a short, frail, toothless man who after assuming power, wrapped as much white cloth around himself as was needed to cover where it needs to be covered.

But, one quality that connected the Fathers of both nations was that in their lives they repeatedly proved Lord Acton and Tacitus wrong—they knew something about the judicious exercise of power. They could wield immense and absolute power without falling prey to its corruption. They could keep away the lust for power and in the pursuit of higher ideals, they could willingly renounce their power. Both could be authoritative at times and could force their wishes on others but even then, they understood their place in history and appreciated the difference between right and wrong. Instead of lust for power, their passion was to achieve their aims without being corrupted by power in the process. And, in both cases, the will to renounce power brought them more power and love from their countrymen.

Fortuitous circumstances played at least part role in the rise to power for both Washington and Gandhi. Having gained power, both played the central part in the founding of their nation—they were the *primus inter pares* amidst the two founding generations. When he had achieved absolute power, Washington renounced it after the Revolutionary War and again after two terms as the president. If not for him, the American Revolution would have degenerated either into anarchy or monarchy. Washington's rise to power amidst hardships of war and sacrifices that he made for America was legendary even in the eyes of Gandhi who had written in 1907 that 'By suffering endless hardships, George Washington made America what it is today. This again shows that one must pass through suffering before tasting happiness. For the public good, men have to suffer hardships even to the point of death.'[93] And, that is what Gandhi sought to do. He suffered hardships for the public good and embraced death while utilizing his moral authority to quell the Hindu-Muslim rioting following the Partition of India. Through all the hardships that Gandhi bore during his life, he always kept his humor and optimism. After meeting Gandhi in Noakhali while the latter was on his pilgrimage to foster Hindu-Muslim unity, Nehru had remarked 'It is always a pleasure and inspiration to meet this young man of seventy-seven. We always feel a little younger and stronger after meeting him and the burdens we carry seem a little lighter.'[94] Perhaps it was light-heartedness and his display of self-effacing humor that sustained Gandhi amidst the demanding struggle he led. He was at the vanguard of the national life for three decades and was never corrupted by power. While during his life, Washington was often compared with Greek and Roman heroes, Gandhi was equated with Buddha and Jesus—Gandhi was simultaneously leading a social and a political revolution. Gandhi's non-violent methods of struggle are so much relevant in our contemporary world that more living people across the world today remember him as a symbol against oppression than have ever heard the names of other American or Indian founding fathers.

Another defining trait that connects these two figures is that their views evolved throughout their lives, though a strong case can be made to argue that such evolution was just not enough. Washington's views on slavery evolved from being a typical Southern slave-owner to not selling any slave which would break a family to taking care of infirm slaves to freeing all his slaves in his will. Similarly, his views toward Native Americans evolved from treating them as savages to endeavoring (and ultimately failing) towards achieving a long-lasting peace with them (more about this in the final chapter). We have already seen in the last chapter and this one how Gandhi's views towards the caste system and women evolved. Similar cases can be made regarding his views on inter-religious dining and marriages, and race. Gandhi was initially adamantly opposed to dining with or marrying somebody outside one's religion while for most of his stay in South Africa he addressed Africans pejoratively as *Kaffirs* and imbibed racial stereotypes prevalent at the time. By his death, Gandhi was willfully advocating and participating in inter-religious marriages and had become an inspiration to, was supporting the cause of, and had many personal friends among Africans and African Americans.

In this, we see that with changes in circumstances both Washington and Gandhi evolved by changing their views and thus they could retain moral authority in posterity's judgment.

The legacy of both Fathers has varied across history. There have been repeated attempts to undermine the political achievements and amplify the personal flaws of both Fathers. These reinterpretations of history are welcome since no public figure should escape the scrutiny of historical judgments. However, in recent years, such attempts have gone to the extreme. Though Washington was and is still a symbol of American government and bipartisanship, there are some attempts by White Supremacist groups to hijack him as an icon for their cause. In India, Hindu extremist groups have never "forgiven" Gandhi for standing up to Hindus and save India's Muslims during the Partition. Such groups have erected temples to honor Gandhi's assassin and in recent years, on Gandhi's death anniversary they recreate the horrific event of Gandhi's murder. In mid-2019, a terror-accused politician was elected to the Parliament of India despite her remark before the elections that Gandhi's assassin was a patriot. It is true that such extremist elements in both nations' polity were always present at the fringe but in the recent vitriolic political climate, they are increasingly receiving official accreditation. Due to Gandhi being relatively fresh in Indian minds than Washington has been in American folklore (since the latter lived more than two centuries ago), more attempts are being made at tarnishing Gandhi's legacy.

Perhaps great nations need great founders and then they can be sustained by lesser men (and women). In a world where the administrations of many nations have become far more authoritative and dictatorial in the past decade, both India and the U.S., being plural democracies that they are, must act as adamantine bulwarks against the trend. This can only be done by strengthening the constitutional safeguards that aim to maintain checks and balances of power in these democracies. In the U.S., though the Constitution restricts the president to two terms, President Donald Trump openly expressed his admiration for China's President when the latter was elected for life. This goes against the values of George Washington as well as those of American polity. In India, the judiciary and many public intellectuals have raised concerns against increasing authoritarianism in recent times. On the other hand, most of the opposition parties in India including Gandhi's very own Indian National Congress have long suspended the tradition of inner-party democratic elections.

It is said that people make history, not in the circumstances of their own choosing but rather those that have been bequeathed by the past. Washington and Gandhi lived at times when destiny bequeathed the opportunity on them to become the "Fathers" of their respective nations. They shaped themselves according to the public opinion but subsequently also led from the front to shape the public opinion for making theirs a better society. They represented the people's hopes, thoughts, and emotions and in return gave courage and hope to the masses. Not always were they ahead of the public opinion since going too much ahead of the same would have weakened their absolute power by creating dissensions and factions. While Washington's achievements are associated with novelty since he played the central role in establishing the world's first nation-sized republic and renounced his power to uphold the principle of rotation of power, Gandhi's achievements are associated with conceiving a non-violent freedom struggle along with bringing social change simultaneously in a poor, illiterate, and colonized society. Consequently, their ways were quite different from each other but they worked selflessly towards the founding of their nation and commanded moral authority in their nation that has never been surpassed since.

---

[1] Joseph J. Ellis, *American Dialogue: The Founders and Us* (New York: Alfred A. Knopf, 2018), p. 233

[2] Joseph J. Ellis, *His Excellency: George Washington* (New York: Vintage Books, 2005), p. xiv

[3] Abigail Adams to Thomas Boylston Adams, 8 Nov 1796, *The Adams Papers*, Adams Family Correspondence, vol. 11, July 1795 – February 1797, ed. Margaret A. Hogan, C. James Taylor, Sara Martin, Neal E. Millikan, Hobson Woodward, Sara B. Sikes, and Gregg L. Lint. Cambridge, MA: Harvard University Press, 2013, pp. 394–398.

[4] Joseph J. Ellis, *His Excellency: George Washington* (New York: Vintage Books, 2005), p. x-xiii

[5] James Thomas Flexner, *Washington: The Indispensable Man* (Little, Brown and Company, First Back Bay Edition, 1974), pp. 3-9

[6] From George Washington to John Augustine Washington, 31 May 1754, *The Papers of George Washington*, Colonial Series, vol. 1, 7 July 1748 – 14 August 1755,

ed. W. W. Abbot. Charlottesville: University Press of Virginia, 1983, pp. 118–119 (Hereafter, referred to as Washington Papers).
[7] Joseph J. Ellis, *His Excellency: George Washington* (New York: Vintage Books, 2005), pp. 14-15
[8] Ibid., pp. 17-18
[9] Ibid., p. 42
[10] From George Washington to George William Fairfax, 10-15 June 1774, Washington Papers, vol. 10, pp. 94-101
[11] Ron Chernow, *Washington: A Life* (New York: The Penguin Press, 2010), pp. 174-176
[12] Ibid., pp. 183-186
[13] Joseph J. Ellis, *His Excellency: George Washington* (New York: Vintage Books, 2005), p. 82
[14] Ibid., pp. 139, 141
[15] James Thomas Flexner, *Washington: The Indispensable Man* (Little, Brown and Company, First Back Bay Edition, 1974), p. 174
[16] Richard Beeman, *Plain, Honest Men: The Making of the American Constitution* (New York: Random House, 2009), pp. 3-5
[17] From George Washington to Officers of the Army, 15 March 1783, Washington Papers
[18] Richard Beeman, *Plain, Honest Men: The Making of the American Constitution* (New York: Random House, 2009), pp. 5-6, Joseph J. Ellis, *His Excellency: George Washington* (New York: Vintage Books, 2005), pp. 143-144
[19] Ron Chernow, *Washington: A Life* (New York: The Penguin Press, 2010), pp. 452-456
[20] Gordon Wood, *Revolutionary Characters: What Made the Founders Different* (Penguin Books, 2006), p. 42
[21] Joseph J. Ellis, *His Excellency: George Washington* (New York: Vintage Books, 2005), p. 147
[22] Ibid., pp. 168-169
[23] Ron Chernow, *Washington: A Life* (New York: The Penguin Press, 2010), pp. 517-518
[24] Joseph J. Ellis, *The Quartet: Orchestrating the Second American Revolution 1783-1789* (New York: Alfred A. Knopf, 2015), pp. 104-106
[25] Ibid., pp. 107-111
[26] Ibid., pp. 111-112
[27] Ron Chernow, *Washington: A Life* (New York: The Penguin Press, 2010), p. 569
[28] Harry C. Thomson, *Presidential Studies Quarterly,* Vol. 8, No. 1 (Winter, 1978), pp. 27-32
[29] David McCullough, *John Adams* (New York: Simon and Schuster, 2001), pp. 404-406

[30] Ron Chernow, *Washington: A Life* (New York: The Penguin Press, 2010), pp. 575-579, 608-613
[31] Thomas Jefferson to George Washington, 23 May 1792, *The Papers of Thomas Jefferson*, vol. 23, 1 January–31 May 1792, ed. Charles T. Cullen. Princeton: Princeton University Press, 1990, pp. 535–541.
[32] Joseph J. Ellis, *His Excellency: George Washington* (New York: Vintage Books, 2005), p. 233
[33] Ron Chernow, *Washington: A Life* (New York: The Penguin Press, 2010), pp. 752-753
[34] Ibid., pp. 753-755
[35] George Washington, To the PEOPLE of the UNITED STATES, 19 September 1796, Washington Papers
[36] Joseph J. Ellis, *Founding Brothers* (New York: Vintage Books, 2000), p. 125
[37] Joseph J. Ellis, *His Excellency: George Washington* (New York: Vintage Books, 2005), pp. 238-239
[38] Ron Chernow, *Washington: A Life* (New York: The Penguin Press, 2010), pp. 767-768
[39] Joseph J. Ellis, *His Excellency: George Washington* (New York: Vintage Books, 2005), p. 264
[40] James Thomas Flexner, *Washington: The Indispensable Man* (Little, Brown and Company, First Back Bay Edition, 1974), p. 396
[41] Gordon S. Wood, *Revolutionary Characters: What Made the Founders Different* (Penguin Books, 2006), p. 47
[42] Sugata Bose, *His Majesty's Opponent: Subhas Chandra Bose and India's Struggle Against Empire* (Penguin Books, 2013), p. 165
[43] Ramachandra Guha, *Gandhi Before India* (Penguin Books, 2014), pp. 22-24
[44] Mohandas Karamchand Gandhi, *An Autobiography or The Story of My Experiments with Truth*, translated from Gujarati by Mahadev Desai (Ahmedabad: Navajivan Publishing House, 1927; October 2010 Reprint), pp. 11-12
[45] Ibid., pp. 24-28
[46] Ramachandra Guha, *Gandhi Before India* (Penguin Books, 2014), pp. 32-35
[47] Ibid., pp.42-48
[48] Rajmohan Gandhi, *The Good Boatman: A Portrait of Gandhi* (Penguin Books, 1997), p. 59
[49] Mohandas Karamchand Gandhi, *An Autobiography or The Story of My Experiments with Truth*, translated from Gujarati by Mahadev Desai (Ahmedabad: Navajivan Publishing House, 1927; October 2010 Reprint), p. 95
[50] *The Collected Works of Mahatma Gandhi (CWMG)*, Vol. 68: Before October 15, 1938 – February 28, 1939, Discussion with John R. Mott, On or before 4 December 1938, p. 171
[51] Louis Fischer, *The Life of Mahatma Gandhi* (London: Granada Publishing Limited, 1982), p. 63

[52] Ramachandra Guha, *Gandhi Before India* (Penguin Books, 2014), pp. 102-117
[53] Ibid., p. 150
[54] Louis Fischer, *The Life of Mahatma Gandhi* (London: Granada Publishing Limited, 1982), pp. 100-101
[55] Ibid., pp. 105-108
[56] Ibid., pp. 141-153
[57] Ramachandra Guha, *Gandhi Before India* (Penguin Books, 2014), p. 544
[58] Jawaharlal Nehru, *The Discovery of India* (Penguin Books, 2004; First published by The Signet Press, Calcutta, 1946), p. 392
[59] CWMG, Vol. 20: April 15, 1921 – August 19, 1921, A Confession of Faith, 13 July 1921, p. 371
[60] Ramachandra Guha, *Gandhi: The Years that Changed the World 1914-1948* (Penguin Random House, 2018), pp. 30-32
[61] Louis Fischer, *The Life of Mahatma Gandhi* (London: Granada Publishing Limited, 1982), pp. 174-175
[62] Ramachandra Guha, *Gandhi: The Years that Changed the World 1914-1948* (Penguin Random House, 2018), pp. 73-77
[63] Ibid., pp. 112-113
[64] Rajmohan Gandhi, *The Good Boatman: A Portrait of Gandhi* (Penguin Books, 1997), p. 110
[65] *CWMG*, Vol. 58: May 18, 1934 – September 15, 1934, Letter to Vallabhbhai Patel, Before 5 September 1934, pp. 403-406
[66] Ramachandra Guha, *Gandhi: The Years that Changed the World 1914-1948* (Penguin Random House, 2018), p. 492
[67] Ibid., pp. 338, 348
[68] *CWMG*, Vol. 76: April 1, 1942 – December 17, 1942, Speech at A.I.C.C. Meeting, 8 August 1942, p. 392
[69] Rajmohan Gandhi, *Understanding the Founding Fathers* (New Delhi: Aleph Book Company, 2016), p. 126
[70] CWMG, Vol. 88: May 25, 1947 – July 31, 1947, Talk with Dr. Syed Mahmud, 26 July 1947, p. 434
[71] Louis Fischer, *The Life of Mahatma Gandhi* (London: Granada Publishing Limited, 1982), p. 587
[72] Sugata Bose, *The Nation as Mother and Other Visions of Nationhood* (Penguin Random House, 2017), p. 142
[73] Louis Fischer, *The Life of Mahatma Gandhi* (London: Granada Publishing Limited, 1982, pp. 552-553
[74] Ramachandra Guha, *Gandhi: The Years that Changed the World 1914-1948* (Penguin Random House, 2018), pp. 796-797
[75] Louis Fischer, *The Life of Mahatma Gandhi* (London: Granada Publishing Limited, 1982), pp. 554-555

[76] Ramachandra Guha, *Gandhi: The Years that Changed the World 1914-1948* (Penguin Random House, 2018), pp. 798-800
[77] Ibid., pp. 806-808
[78] Louis Fischer, *The Life of Mahatma Gandhi* (London: Granada Publishing Limited, 1982), pp. 557-561
[79] Ramachandra Guha, *Gandhi: The Years that Changed the World 1914-1948* (Penguin Random House, 2018), pp. 822-823
[80] Rajmohan Gandhi, *The Good Boatman: A Portrait of Gandhi* (Penguin Books, 1997), p. 352
[81] Louis Fischer, *The Life of Mahatma Gandhi* (London: Granada Publishing Limited, 1982), p. 592
[82] Ramachandra Guha, *Gandhi: The Years that Changed the World 1914-1948* (Penguin Random House, 2018), pp. 846-847
[83] Ibid., pp. 848-850
[84] Louis Fischer, *The Life of Mahatma Gandhi* (London: Granada Publishing Limited, 1982), p. 593
[85] Ramachandra Guha, *Gandhi: The Years that Changed the World 1914-1948* (Penguin Random House, 2018), p. 849
[86] CWMG, Vol. 25: August 16, 1924 – January 15, 1925, Presidential Address at Kathiawar Political Conference, 8 January 1925, p. 563
[87] Sugata Bose, *The Nation as Mother and Other Visions of Nationhood* (Penguin Random House, 2017), p. 143
[88] V. B. Kulkarni, *The Indian Triumvirate: A Political Biography of Mahatma Gandhi, Sardar Patel, and Pandit Nehru* (Bombay: Bharatiya Vidya Bhavan, 1969), pp. 238-239
[89] Ramachandra Guha, *Gandhi: The Years that Changed the World 1914-1948* (Penguin Random House, 2018), pp. 851-856
[90] Ibid., pp. 866-869
[91] Ibid., pp. 870-872
[92] Jawaharlal Nehru, *Selected Works of Jawaharlal Nehru*-Second Series-5, The Light Has Gone Out, 30 January 1948, p. 35
[93] *CWMG*, Vol. 07: June 1, 1907 – December 31, 1907, Divine Law [From Gujarati] Published in *Indian Opinion*, 27 July 1907, p. 122
[94] M. Chalapathi Rau, *Gandhi and Nehru* (Allied Publishers, 1967), p. 143

3. OPPOSITION

'If I could not go to heaven but with a party, I would not go there at all,' remarked Jefferson in 1789.[1] American founding fathers' aversion to political parties was so extreme that in his farewell address, President Washington had warned his countrymen 'in the most solemn manner against the baneful effects of the spirit of party.'[2] Similar sentiments were conveyed by John Adams who wrote: 'There is nothing I dread So much, as a Division of the Republick into two great Parties, each arranged under its Leader, and concerting Measures in opposition to each other. This, in my humble Apprehension is to be dreaded as the greatest political Evil, under our Constitution.'[3] Likewise, Alexander Hamilton had written in the first of *The Federalist* essays that 'nothing could be more ill-judged than that intolerant spirit which has at all times characterized political parties.'[4]

These statements may sound unusual to us but are just some of the many expressions that the founding fathers used to convey their abhorrence to the idea of political parties in a republic. With no precedent of a healthy democratic opposition or the practice of rotation of power between political parties, the founding fathers could not conceive that dissent could be expressed legitimately through the creation of political parties. The Roman Republic to which the founding fathers always looked to as an aspiration had a Senate whose members were not elected along the lines of political parties by the citizens. Another reason amplifying the founding fathers' antipathy towards political parties was that their contemporary French Revolution which had started on high hopes for humanity had descended into The Reign of Terror due to the multifarious factions that had devoured it. Thus, to the founding fathers, the emergence of political factions was evil and could only steer the American Republic towards anarchy by fueling animosity and conflicts. In their inherently moral world, the system of government could propagate with harmony and stability only by elected legislators expressing their individual opinions on various subjects. Such a unipolar system was ideal for a republic in their view but, of course, in politics, especially in the presence of forceful personalities amidst turbulent times, the emergence of organized opposition in America was inevitable. The founding fathers themselves despite their avowed disapproval of political factions inadvertently caused the rise of political parties and the establishment of a two-party system in the American Republic. However, they did not view this feat as something to be proud of. In fact, their response to the rise of political parties varied from interpreting it as a temporary phenomenon that shall terminate in due course of time to perceiving it as a personal failure.

Founding fathers' reactions to the "failure" in forestalling the rise of political parties could reach extreme degrees of expression. Washington went to his maker believing that the greatest failure of his presidency was that he could not stop the rise of political parties whereas Jefferson went to his grave without accepting that he was the chief force behind the Democratic-Republican Party (not to be confused with the present-day Democratic or Republican parties). Though their views towards political parties remained myopic, the fact is that by instituting an outlet for legitimate expression of opposition through the creation of a two-party system, America achieved extraordinary political stability in the long run. Dissent being central to the working of democracy, the rotation of power between political parties became the mainstay of Republican expressionism in America and later across the world. When Washington had been unanimously elected as the president in 1789, he had no inkling that his own cabinet will be troubled with partisan warfare which he so dreaded. Even remote was the thought for him that the actions of his own son-like protégé, Alexander Hamilton, would contribute most to the rise of political parties and opposition to his government.

The first word that comes to mind after reading Alexander Hamilton's life story is "ambition." The story of his life is so tempestuous that not even in the wildest dreams can an adroit novelist formulate it. It is plainly impossible to truly capture his tumultuous life in writing or theatre. Hamilton was born on 11 January 1755 on a small Caribbean island. Caribbean islands were hellish sugarcane-growing British colonies where lashing slaves to death and other such bloodcurdling scenes were commonplace. On most islands, the population of slaves far exceeded that of whites which made whites even more brutal in their quest for domination. In such a sadistic island named St. Croix, his mother, Rachel Faucette, had been accused of adultery by her husband and spent several months in a dark, cramped prison. At the first opportunity, she escaped from the island abandoning her husband as well as their son. Alexander Hamilton and his older brother James were born out of wedlock on the island of Nevis after Rachel started living with a Scotsman James Hamilton who had come to the West Indies in search of a fortune. After a few years, James abandoned them and fled. In the meantime, Rachel's earlier husband filed for divorce accusing her of whoring. When Alexander was 13, Rachel died and the two boys were left to fend off for themselves. Briefly, they were taken in by one of their cousins but soon after that cousin committed suicide and they were left alone once more. Due to his illegitimate birth, Alexander Hamilton was also barred from formal schooling by the Anglican Church. There were also insinuations that he was a mulatto and thus her mother was portrayed as a prostitute. Such an upbringing in a nightmarish society left emotional scars on Hamilton's mind which never healed. Throughout his life, he never owned slaves and remained a passionate advocate for the abolition of slavery. He also continued to be hypersensitive about the question of the legitimacy of his birth, painfully conscious about class and social hierarchy, and reticent about his early life. Obsession with prevailing over what destiny had served him in West Indies kindled inside him an unbridled ambition to succeed.[5]

From the depths of misery, Hamilton rose and rose. Except for some tutoring by a Jewish headmistress, he taught himself while at the same time working as a clerk at a local firm. Subsequently, he became an avid reader and writer. Even at the young age of fourteen, he detested his life of being a mere clerk and wanted to gain fame. Perceiving war as the surest way to earn distinction and respect, he looked forward to becoming a soldier and wished that 'there was a War.'[6] When a hurricane struck and devastated the St. Croix island in 1772 where he was living, he wrote a letter to his father giving a detailed account of the hurricane. This letter was published by a journalist in a newspaper and became Hamilton's passport to glory. It was a custom in Europe and America among wealthy gentlemen to become patrons for young minds who showed precocious signs of distinction (Edmund Burke and Benjamin Franklin also owed their rise in-part to such support). Hamilton's letter was extraordinarily sophisticated for a teenager. Impressed by the young boy's learning and intelligence, community leaders collected money to send him to America for higher education.[7]

Arriving in America aboard a ship that had been charred when it had caught fire during the voyage, Hamilton enrolled at King's College (now Columbia). Understanding very well that the coming conflict between Britain and her American colonies would become his vehicle to fame, he started to publish articles in the Revolutionary cause even at the pre-war stage. The first act of Hamilton's public life came in 1775 when he saved his college president Myles Cooper, a British Loyalist, from an angry mob. The same year even before the fighting had broken out, Hamilton had written in an eighty-page pamphlet *Farmer Refuted* what Washington could only understand with time: 'The circumstances of our country put it in our power to evade a pitched battle. It will be better policy to harass and exhaust the soldiery by frequent skirmishes and incursions than to take the open field with them…'[8]

Hamilton could not complete his studies due to the college getting closed when the British occupied the city after the Declaration of American Independence. When hostilities broke out, he joined the New York militia and was offered a position as an aide to a brigadier general but Hamilton declined it. He had an inherent dislike for becoming a subordinate in a non-combat role instead of taking charge from the front which had a higher probability of providing fame and glory. Interestingly, soon an appointment in a non-combat role was proposed to him which he could not decline—to become General Washington's aide-de-camp with the rank of lieutenant colonel. For four years, Hamilton diligently served as Washington's chief staff aide and handled Washington's correspondence while enjoying the General's complete trust. During this tiring service, he somehow also found the time to write detailed notes on Plutarch's *Lives*. He had probably already started to imagine himself in line with ancient Greek and Roman heroes.[9] Due to his restless nature and pursuit of glory, he continued to seek field command and participation in active combat. On being reprimanded by the General on a minor misunderstanding, he sulked and left Washington's staff. Finally, Washington had to relent from his earlier stand and Hamilton got the opportunity to command an assault from the front. After the War, Hamilton along with Madison became the chief force behind calling the Constitutional Convention and ratification of the Constitution in New York for which he authored 51 of the 85 *The Federalist* essays.

Once in life, Hamilton had written about the love of fame as being 'the ruling passion of noblest minds.'[10] During Washington's presidency, Hamilton's rise to fame and power commenced. He served as the first Secretary of the Treasury between 1789-1795. It was in this role that he made the most far-reaching contributions to the American government. He presented the first report on public credit which analyzed America's poor financial situation after the War and made recommendations to reorganize the national debt. He then drafted an audacious economic program to pay back the war debt and consolidate the federal government's monopoly by establishing a national bank, a Mint, and a system of tariffs. To secure America's commercial interests, he also founded the United States Coast Guard. Resigning from Washington's cabinet in early 1795, he became the leader of the Federalist Party. When war with French became likely under John Adams's presidency, Hamilton became the senior major general of the army (effectively in control of the army with a retired Washington only serving as a figurehead) and subsequently proposed highfalutin plans of "liberating" European colonies in the American content and marching towards South America.[11] His ambitions took better of his judgment and he started viewing himself as another Julius Caesar—whom he once expounded as the greatest man who ever lived to the horror of Jefferson.[12] '[G]reat ambition, unchecked by principle, or the love of glory, is an unruly tyrant,' he wrote once but could not follow.[13] Adams was successfully able to negotiate peace with France and thus, in the end, Hamilton's over excesses decimated his public standing. Throughout his career, Hamilton continued to be a prominent lawyer, essayist, and political theorist. Remaining touchy about the question of honor throughout his life, in 1804, he agreed to participate in a duel with the then Vice-President Aaron Burr, his arch-nemesis and another prodigy. Hamilton died in the duel after he was mortally wounded by Burr who shot him in the lower abdomen.

This is in four paragraphs is a short sketch of Hamilton's roller-coaster life which does no justice to him. With well-chiseled features, a prominent nose, powdered hair, and impeccable dressing preferences, Hamilton conveyed an impression of self-confidence and finality by his demeanor. He was the most restless and assertive founding father who needed a great leader (such as Washington) for controlling and channeling his overabundant energy. As he wrote himself, 'the passions of a revolution are apt to hurry even good men into excesses.'[14] Even after never assuming the presidency, this self-taught economist's contributions made America a major financial power and laid the foundation of modern America. He was not only the lone immigrant among the founding fathers but also the only one among them to die at a relatively young age. His principal biographer, Ron Chernow writes: 'Hamilton was the supreme double threat among the founding fathers, at once thinker and doer, sparkling theoretician and masterful executive....an exuberant genius who performed at a fiendish pace and must have produced the maximum number of words that a human being can scratch out in forty-nine years.'[15]

While assuming the presidency, Washington would have probably never thought that he would be sullen and dejected when he would retire. He would have never imagined even in his wildest dreams that two men he was very fond of, Hamilton and Jefferson, would inadvertently become the orchestrators for his gloom. Organized opposition to the government could be beneficial for a republic was an idea as alien to Washington as to other rulers in the eighteenth century. It caused him immense pain to see Jefferson and Hamilton, the pillars of his cabinet, were charging at each other as if they were the leaders of opposing political parties.

Jefferson and Hamilton met each other perhaps for the first time in 1790 when Jefferson came back from Paris and assumed the office of the Secretary of State while Hamilton was serving as the Secretary of the Treasury in Washington's administration. From the moment both met, they became obsessed with each other. Jefferson assumed office in March and by June their views had so much digressed that a compromise was brokered between them with far-reaching consequences for the nation. The previous year, the House of Representatives had instructed Hamilton to prepare a report on the greatest problems facing the new government—improving the nation's public credit and coping with indebtedness. Hamilton had toiled hard to prepare a forty-thousand-word report with references ranging from philosophers to economists which proposed an economic plan for the newborn nation. He estimated the total federal and state debt owed by Americans to be $79 million. It was such a large amount that annual interest payments on the national debt exceeded the revenue of the federal government!

To retire the national debt, Hamilton proposed two policies that proved to be highly conflagrant at the time but chartered the course of the American republic for the next several decades. First, he proposed that the federal government should assume the state debt. This would have substantially augmented the power of the federal government over the states. To pay the debt that states had incurred during the American Revolution would have meant that the federal government could expand taxation in avenues previously reserved for the state governments and thus assume authority over their economies. This was not acceptable in the least to those who had only a couple of years ago vehemently opposed the concentration of federal power at the Constitutional Convention.

Second, Hamilton suggested to consolidate and propagate the debt over many years by recommending that the federal government should refinance it. In simple terms, his proposal was to eliminate the foreign debt by utilizing a sinking fund and thus creating new debt to pay off the old—something that is common in today's world. This was again not tolerable to those advocating for greater states' rights since it appeared as another ploy to consolidate the power of the federal government by prolonging the time frame of payments. Furthermore, Hamilton's scheme of refinancing the debt would have tied the wealthiest Americans with the stability of the government by attracting them to purchase Treasury securities. This was his intention all along. Hamilton wanted to ensure that the loyalty of the wealthiest Americans (thus creditors) was tied with the national government since it would have boosted America's credit rating by enticing European investors. But these Hamiltonian proposals got trapped in a congressional gridlock contrived by southern congressmen with the support from an influential politician who had earlier been an ardent federalist and Hamilton's collaborator—James Madison.[16]

Hamilton's proposal for the federal assumption of state debts was chiefly opposed by the southern states and especially by the most influential of them all, Virginia, for three reasons. First, fluid forms of capital such as securities were not considered wealth and were looked at with suspicion by southerners. Only land was considered as a financial asset whereas monetary institutions such as financial securities and banks were despised. In fact, southerners took their complete aloofness of understanding Hamilton's scheme with pride. Second, southern states due to their plantation-based economy and aristocratic habits of consumption and expenditure were under much higher debt than the northern ones. The assumption of debt by the federal government thus became a source of friction divided along geography since southern states were wary of losing their power and dominance. Shifting their debt to the federal government would have increased its responsibilities, making the southern states more dependent on it. Third, Virginia contained many ardent anti-federalists. Any concentration in the power of the federal government was unacceptable to them just like they had opposed the same in the Constitutional Convention. Approval for Hamilton's program would have stimulated the decline of the southern way of life by taking the nation towards sophisticated and centralized financial institutions which would have promoted industrialization. Thus, this issue had the explosive capacity of dissecting the newborn nation into two camps if Hamilton's program was to be adopted. If not adopted, America was facing the perpetuity of foreign debt with a broken financial system. To make way for Hamilton's plan, something big was needed to placate the southern states in return for greater control over their economies. As it turned out, there was just one such thing.[17]

When Washington's government was inaugurated, the seat of the federal government was New York and no decision had been made over where the national capital would be established. The Constitution had stipulated that Congress should identify a location not exceeding a hundred square miles to be purchased from the proximate states for establishing the national capital. Two likely competitors due to being big cities were New York and

Philadelphia—both in the north. The issue of locating the national capital had been bruited for almost a decade and Virginia being the most populous state had repeatedly expressed the desire that the capital should be located on the Potomac River within its boundaries. While given the geographical centrality, some location in Pennsylvania seemed to be the obvious choice. However, Madison deftly argued that Washington's estate Mount Vernon was the exact midpoint of the nation along the north-south axis—since how could anybody question something associated with Washington. Backdoor talks by Madison with other congressmen started to lay the foundation of what has been called the "Compromise of 1790."[18]

Hamilton was invited to a dinner party by Jefferson at his house on Broadway probably on 20 June. Madison too was present. The details of the so-called "The Dinner" are murky. What came out of the dinner was a bargain made between the trio that charted the course of the nation thence. Jefferson's later account of the dinner went like this

> Going to the President's one day I met Hamilton, as I approached the door, his look was sombre, haggard, & dejected beyond description, even his dress uncouth & neglected, he asked to speak with me, we stood in the street near the door, he opened the subject of the assumption of the State debts, the necessity of it in the general fiscal arrangement & its indispensible necessity towards a preservation of the union....On considering the situation of things I thought the first step towards some conciliation of views would be to bring Mr. Madison & Colo. Hamilton to a friendly discussion of the subject. I immediately wrote to each to come and dine with me the next day, mentioning that we should be alone, that the object was to find some temperament for the present fever....They came, I opened the subject to them, acknowledged that my situation had not permitd. me to understand it sufficiently but encouraged them to consider the thing together. They did so, it ended in Mr. Madison's acquiescence in a proposition that the question should be again brought before the house by way of amendmt. from the Senate, that tho' he would not vote for it, nor entirely withdraw his opposition, yet he should not be strenuous, but leave it to it's fate. It was observed, I forget by which of them, that as the pill would be a bitter one to the Southern States, something should be done to soothe them, that the removal of the seat of Government to the Patowmac was a just measure, & would probably be a popular one with them and would be a proper one to follow the assumption.[19]

The Jeffersonian account of a "somber, haggard, and dejected" Hamilton requesting Jefferson to save the Union partly rings true since indeed the question of assumption had the capability to break the Union. As a whole though, the self-serving account is deceptive since backdoor discussions being undertaken by Madison with southern congressmen were key to the whole enterprise. Madison was able to persuade the southerners to swallow the bitter pill of Hamilton's financial plan in lieu of getting the national capital established in Virginia. This was to ensure the South's continued dominance in national politics. The bargain or rather the "Compromise of 1790" averted the threat of survival hanging over the infant republic. Sectarian tensions between the north and south even without the issue of slavery in the picture—which led to a civil war seven decades later—could have dissected the nation right after it took its first breath. As a result of the compromise, the newly inaugurated and vulnerable federal government got breathing space to consolidate itself before it attained the power to suppress the schism between the north and south during the Civil War.[20]

While the trio had to be content with a compromise, Washington was doubly delighted since he wanted Hamilton's plan to go through as well as the national capital to be on the Potomac (which was falsely believed by many to be a gateway to the vast American interior in the west) in his home state of Virginia. Naturally, the patriarch decided the location of the national capital (which was named in his honor) himself and chose it to be as close to Mount Vernon as possible. Nobody had the temerity to question Washington's judgment no matter that the chosen location was just a piece of swampland. It took decades to clear the land, construct a city, and sufficiently populate it so as to look like a national capital. As a sop to Pennsylvania—a location inside which would have been the natural choice of the capital based on geography, Philadelphia was made the national capital for ten years until major buildings in the new capital were erected and the government moved there. Washington, the master of symbolism, named the central street of the future capital Pennsylvania Avenue—where today stands the White House so that the president still resides in Pennsylvania.

One unintended outcome of choosing the seat of government to be far away from a major metropolis was that it separated the political and financial capitals of the nation—unlike European nations. This meant that the corrupt nexus between politicians and financiers was harder to forge and the same practice of separating political and financial capitals was followed in states too. While for now, the compromise had satisfied both Jefferson and Hamilton, the latter's financial plan was the first wedge in their relationship and the start of partisan troubles. Later in life, the orchestrator of the compromise, Jefferson, denounced the compromise while claiming that he had been deceived by Hamilton.[21]

Hamilton's upcoming financial proposals marked the beginning of political factions and the origin of organized political opposition in America. While Hamilton was all for expanding the government, promoting business, and increasing the sources of revenue, Jefferson's conviction was that America should develop primarily as an agricultural society. The sectarian divisions kindled by Hamilton's economic policies created in Jefferson's words, 'the real ground of the opposition' to the so-called Hamiltonians. Having tasted success in the assumption of state debt by the federal government, Hamilton sought to increase the sources of revenue to keep his debt repayment plan on track. His aim was to limit the direct tax as much as possible and so instead he proposed an excise on a luxurious commodity—liquor. Hamilton's intention was to monopolize this source of revenue by introducing what came to be known as the "whiskey tax" before the states could tap it. As was expected, many states, especially the southern ones, revolted at this proposal since the tax on domestically distilled whiskey would have fallen the most on their farmers who raised corn. However, since the proposal to tax liquor was essential to Hamilton's economic program, Washington backed it and the bill passed in Congress while both Jefferson and Madison steered clear of the issue due to the fear of challenging Washington.

As if harsh musical notes were being played one after the other, Hamilton's next step agitated Jefferson and Madison beyond measure—the proposal to establish a national bank. This was the moment when Jefferson fathomed the complete depth of the Hamiltonian financial program and labeled the bank as the 'engine' that will drive everything else in Hamilton's juggernaut. Hamilton had urged Congress to establish a national bank in Philadelphia with a charter of twenty years. This was a momentous step in a nation where at the time the capital in the three banks totaled only two million dollars while Hamilton proposed 'that the national bank be capitalized at ten million, with one-fifth of its startup money provided by the government, the remainder coming through the sale of bank stock. It was to be managed by private citizens.' By establishing the federal bank, Hamilton aimed at stimulating the economy, increasing the supply of money, and promoting investment and loans. Nevertheless, to Virginian planters like Jefferson who lived and died in perpetual debt, and acknowledged land as the only source of wealth, this Hamiltonian scheme was the very definition of evil. As a general rule, Virginian planters detested commerce and financial speculation, and considered banks as consisting of sophisticated tricksters duping people by manipulating entries on paper.[22]

Jefferson's vision of America was an agricultural paradise in which there was no space for banks. In his view, the introduction of a banking system would have unleashed the forces that would have subverted the republican simplicity of the nation. There were also concerns that Hamilton's economic program which promoted *laissez-faire* economics as advocated by the Scottish economist Adam Smith[α] would take America on the same path as Britain. The concept of an industrialized society like Britain with centralized administration, intricate bureaucracy, and high commercial activity was antithetical to the southern way of life. As Jefferson maintained, 'our governments will remain virtuous for many centuries as long as they are chiefly agricultural.' The fear of big government was ingrained in the psychology of the South. As a result, the Virginia legislature had formally denounced the assumption of state debts as a way for the federal government to assert influence over the states similar to the British monarch.[23] Small instances such as Hamilton's one-time remark at a dinner with Jefferson that the British government was 'the most perfect…which ever existed' due to the sway of parliament over

---

[α] A contemporary of the American founding fathers, Adam Smith, was a Scottish economist, philosopher, and author. He is also known as "The Father of Economics" and the "Father of Capitalism." Two of his classic works are *The Theory of Moral Sentiments* (1759) and *An Inquiry into the Nature and Causes of the Wealth of Nations* (1776). His contributions to Economics and free-market theory laid the foundations of Capitalism.

monarchy and commercial interests may have contributed to exacerbating Jefferson's worst fears regarding Hamilton's intentions.[24]

Because of Washington's unwavering backing, Hamilton's *Report on Public Credit,* the legislation to establish the national bank sailed through Congress. As a dernier resort, both Jefferson and Madison then appealed to the president that the establishment of a bank would be unconstitutional since Congress was explicitly empowered only to tax but not charter a bank. Washington then sent their written opinion to Hamilton who wrote a detailed rebuttal. Hamilton took a hard line which later became the centerpiece of the so-called Federalist Party: Governments possess the 'right to employ all the means requisite, and fairly applicable to the ends of such power; and which are not precluded by restrictions & exceptions specified in the constitution; or not immoral, or not contrary to the essential ends of political society.' Washington, who as we have seen in the previous chapter already wanted a strong federal government, concurred with Hamilton and signed the bill into law.[25]

This gave the first big blow to the Jefferson-Madison duumvirate. The establishment of the national bank marked the starting point of overt partisan battles. From now on, as per their strengths, Jefferson planned the larger strategy whereas Madison took care of the dirty work. This helped in keeping Jefferson above the fray while Madison handled the messier political skullduggery. As Hamiltonians noted, Madison geared to become 'the General' and Jefferson 'the Generalissimo.' In fact, the two were so close that many times they conversed with each other in coded language so as to be discreet about their moves.[26]

The first step taken by Jefferson to organize opposition was to discreetly recruit Philip Freneau, "the Poet of the American Revolution," a journalist and polemicist with a radical outlook, to start a newspaper for criticizing the actions of the government in which Jefferson himself was serving as the Secretary of State. Within a few weeks, the newspaper *National Gazette* was widely circulating in the country. Jefferson managed to keep his sponsorship of the newspaper secret (or at least not conspicuous). At the same time, he noticed that due to his financial plan, Hamilton had acquired the support of powerful friends across the nation for his schemes, especially in New

York which had already started on the path to becoming the financial capital of the nation. To counter this, Jefferson started a New York tour. He could not overtly declare his real intent due to the fear of undermining Washington's authority and hence the purpose of the tour was shielded behind the euphemism, "botanizing tour," being undertaken 'to study flora and fauna.' In total, Jefferson and Madison spent thirty-three days traveling and rallying support against the Treasury Secretary by meeting Hamilton's adversaries in the state. In time, the attacks on Hamilton in the *National Gazette* started to become more and more vitriolic. Never the one to back out from a challenge or to possess that one gift required of all politicians—self-restraint, Hamilton geared to be on the offensive and refute the attacks with his pen. All cordiality between Jefferson and Hamilton was lost not just in public but also in private and the two secretaries were 'daily pitted in the cabinet like two cocks.'[27]

The two great collaborators of the *Federalist Papers*—Hamilton and Madison—were now replying to each other's articles under different pseudonyms. In the press, the labels "Republicans" to denote Jeffersonians and "Federalists" for Hamiltonians stuck. Since Washington kept himself above the partisan lines despite his backing for Hamilton's initiatives—to the consternation of Jefferson who expected his fellow Virginian to support his cause—no side dragged Washington into the battlefield. Washington's reelection was due soon and the only thing that Jefferson and Hamilton agreed on at this time was that Washington was the adhesive keeping the government and the nation together. Washington had earlier threatened to retire unless the partisanship in his government came to a halt and had been continuously making honest efforts to reconcile the differences between the two factions in his government. Amidst all this, Jefferson received a treasure trove of information about Hamilton which could be used in partisan warfare.[28]

What came to be known as the *Reynolds Affair* eventually marked the beginning of Hamilton's downfall. Maria Reynolds, a twenty-three old woman had lured Hamilton into a sexual affair while his family was away from the city. As per Hamilton's account, multiple times he tried to end the affair but she would always overcome his resentment. At the same time, her husband was blackmailing Hamilton and duping him of money in lieu of maintaining silence. Hamilton kept falling into the endless cycle of licentiousness and extortion even after his family's return. On being confronted privately about his sense of honor by some congressmen who suspected the Treasury Secretary of embezzling funds to Maria's husband, Hamilton had a Freudian slip and unwisely divulged everything about the affair to them. Perhaps his insecurities about honor originating from his miserable childhood played a part (as they would play later when Hamilton accepted the offer of a duel and eventually died in it to preserve his sense of honor). One of these congressmen to whom Hamilton had disclosed the privileged information and had entrusted the records of the conversation was James Monroe—Jefferson's protégé. For now, the records of the conversation were kept secret but in time they were divulged to sully Hamilton's reputation.[29]

Jefferson's current plan was to demolish Hamilton's financial integrity. He made many attempts through his proxies in the press and Congress to discredit Hamilton by accusing him of embezzlement and wrongdoing while beseeching Washington to start an official inquiry against Hamilton. Washington spurned this proposal and Hamilton was vindicated when he labored zealously to prepare and present a long report to Congress in a remarkably short time. In this report, Hamilton minutely detailed the transactions which had taken place under his authority and subsequently completely satisfied the Congress. His acquittal further irked Jefferson who had already sentenced Hamilton in the depths of his mind. Until now we have seen that partisan warfare was on between the two factions in Washington's government based mostly on sectarian interests and fueled by personal enmities. But, the turn of events across the Atlantic in Europe, triggered in America the beginning of what we are familiar with in today's democracies—organizing political parties along the lines of differences in ideologies and advocating opposite policies.[30]

What transpired in Europe during the French Revolution[β] between 1789-99 changed the course of world history. When the

---

[β] The French Revolution overthrew the monarchy in France, established a republic, disintegrated into violent political turmoil, and created social and political upheavals across the world. It instigated conflicts across the world leading to a

Girondins' political faction assumed power in the French Revolution, it issued a decree declaring war on monarchies across the world. A young prodigy, Edmond Charles Genêt, was appointed as the Ambassador of France to the United States. Citizen Genêt as he was called in consonance with Girondins' ideals was earlier serving as an ambassador to Tsarist Russia where he had become a *persona non grata* because of his radical views against monarchy. When Britain and France declared war on each other, President Washington was concerned about the effect of the conflict on America due to its fraternal ties with both nations. Considering that the future prosperity of the nation could only be ensured by peace, he wisely declared neutrality. The French Revolution was a matter of intense argument and created a wide gulf between the two factions in America.

Republicans under Jefferson viewed the French Revolution as a continuation of the American Revolution which ought to be supported and so they extended their solidarity with France. In their view, France had helped America during the Revolutionary War and so America was bound to support France due to the treaties that had been signed between them during the Revolutionary era. Federalists under Washington and Hamilton were horrified at the anarchic turn that the French Revolution had taken when more than 1,400 political prisoners were slaughtered in the so-called September Massacres. Such a bloody revolution was being declared by its famous champion Robespierre as 'the most beautiful revolution that has ever honored humanity' while another famous French leader Marat clamored: 'Let the blood of traitors flow. That is the only way to save the country.' Federalists also pointed out that the Revolutionary Era treaties had been signed with the French King Louis XVI and the demise of his administration along with his decapitation by guillotine had rendered them void. Here were the beginnings of a healthy democratic opposition aimed at a specific policy—America's stance towards the war in Europe—and backed up by opposing ideologies—interpreting the French Revolution as the continuation of the American Revolution or as an unrelated event.[31]

---

decline in monarchies with their replacement by republics. Ironically, it finally culminated in a dictatorship under Napoleon Bonaparte.

As soon as Citizen Genêt arrived in America, even before presenting his credentials to the government, he started to foment revolutionary fevers by summoning Americans to 'erect the *Temple of Liberty* on the ruins of *palaces and thrones.*' He started encouraging privateers to prey on British commerce and went forward with enlisting Americans for service in the French armed forces. He also began to establish Democratic-Republican societies across America. These secret societies mirrored those that had come into existence during the American Revolution and were influencing the public opinion towards aiding France in the war.[32] Jefferson's followers were so much elated in their support of the French cause that they had started to address each other as "Citizen" to emphasize the 'egalitarianism of republicanism' and had begun to parade singing "Marseillaise." All these developments were in complete opposition to Washington's proclamation of neutrality. Federalists like Vice President John Adams were petrified by the 'Anarchy, Licentiousness and Despotism' of the French Revolution which were making their way into America.[33]

Just when Genêt's efforts were turning the tide of the public opinion towards France from neutrality, in a feat of conceit, he committed the cardinal mistake of American politics: threatening Washington with impunity. Genêt asked Washington to formally suspend his proclamation of neutrality while he kept raising militia and privateers to capture British ships. Even Jefferson who had been initially supportive of Genêt could not but be embarrassed at this and 'found himself with a migraine—a recurrent complaint of Jefferson's in moments of crisis and perplexity—and took to his bed.' The final breaking point in the Washington-Jefferson relationship had come and Jefferson resigned just before a cabinet meeting which decided to demand France that it should recall Genêt. However, as it happened later, Genêt never left since the Reign of Terror in France had begun by then. Hence, from the fear of being guillotined on his return, he sought asylum in America which was granted. Having left the government, Jefferson geared to start his "retirement" and to direct the policies of his Party from his home via Madison.[34]

During the Genêt affair, Republicans portrayed American neutrality as a betrayal of France and the ideals of the American Revolution. To them, American neutrality was a pro-British policy and Washington who had until now escaped direct criticism from the Republican press came under attack. He was accused of ruling the nation like a monarch, listening to only one faction inside his government, and a tyrant who had no respect for public opinion.[35] Demonstrations were organized by Republicans against the president marking the commencement of the tradition which holds no leader in democracy above criticism. As Adams recalled vividly later in his life (undoubtedly with some exaggeration), the Republican opposition was so frenzied that there was a sheer terror on the streets of Philadelphia: 'Ten thousand People in the Streets of Philadelphia, day after day, threatened to drag Washington out of his House and effect a Revolution in the Government, or compel it to declare War in favour of the French Revolution, and against England.'[36]

In trying to navigate a neutral position between the two world powers, America came close to a war with Britain. This event emerged as the 'greatest crisis of the Washington presidency.' The Treaty of Paris which had been signed after the American Revolutionary War had left some loose ends. Even after more than a decade since the signing of the treaty, British troops were still stationed in the American northwestern frontier in response to America's refusal of paying back the pre-War era debt to British creditors (most of which was owed by Virginia's planters). This presence of the British military on the American soil had provided security to Canadian traders for monopolizing the fur-routes. The British were also providing arms to Native Americans in armed conflict against the settlers of the Ohio Valley region. These problems were compounded by the war between Britain and France and the public opinion in America tilting towards France. British cruisers started to scupper American merchants from trading with the French.[37] Britain was still America's largest trading partner by far and naturally America wanted to preserve friendly relations with it but fast-changing circumstances made it difficult. Things came to a head when the British Royal Navy captured 250 neutral American merchant ships in the Caribbean which were carrying goods from the French colonies. To achieve a compromise between British and American interests and avert war, Washington dispatched Chief Justice John Jay to London for negotiations. Republicans were outraged since they perceived Washington's diplomatic decision as a step that sold American dignity and interests to the British.[38]

Washington's thinking was clear: America could not afford a war with Britain for at least a generation. Such a conflict would have been disastrous both economically and militarily for the infant nation and might have as well killed it. The Republican press was so furious by the president's diplomatic gesture as to suggest that by sending the Chief Justice to London, Washington is securing immunity from being impeached over his neutrality policy. When Jay returned with the terms of the treaty, matters got worse. The treaty brought back by Jay codified that America would receive the most favored nation trading status by Britain, stipulated the removal of all British troops from the American territory while providing America limited rights to trade in British West Indies. In return, Britain demanded the most favored trading status and asked America to acquiesce in anti-French maritime policies. Considering the American dependence on trade with Britain, these terms were generous. But, as Republicans pointed out, by the acknowledgment of British naval supremacy, it would have given American neutrality a decidedly British tilt. Such was the opposition faced by the Federalists that John Jay claimed to be able to walk the entire length of United States at night with 'his way illuminated by protestors burning him in effigy.'[39] Buildings were being defaced defaming John Jay with enormous rhetorical phrases such as 'Damn John Jay. Damn everyone that won't damn John Jay. Damn everyone that won't put up lights in the windows and sit up all night damning John Jay.'[40]

According to a newspaper *Independent Chronicle* published in Boston—despite being a Federalist stronghold—fifteen thousand people had met to denounce the treaty whereas only seven hundred had approved it. In New York City, a stone struck Hamilton when he started to address a crowd about the treaty. Public protests were organized throughout the nation and Federalists including Hamilton and Washington were decried as monarchists. Washington wrote to Hamilton who had resigned from the Cabinet to ascertain his views on the treaty. Alarmed by the opposition's outpouring, Hamiltonians started organizing their own protests with backing from the merchant community whose interests were tied with the trade with Britain. Federalist newspapers *Minerva* and *Argus* made their readers aware of the meetings where citizens had unanimously voted for the treaty. This was an early example of how the rise of political parties based on specific issues could foment meaningful debates, encourage propaganda, and engage citizens in the decision-making process.[41]

Hamilton was writing in favor of the treaty under various pseudonyms and had become its champion in the press. Slowly, as Federalists rallied support under Washington, the public opinion started to tilt towards their side. Sequestered at his home in Virginia, Jefferson was simultaneously decrying Washington through a whispering campaign as a senile old man who was being manipulated by Hamilton to descend America into a monarchy. Hamilton was proving to be a master pamphleteer. As Jefferson privately wrote to Madison to encourage him for taking on Hamilton in the press: 'Hamilton is really a colossus to the anti-republican party. Without numbers, he is an host [an army] within himself....In truth, when he comes forward, there is nobody but yourself who can meet him.' When Washington signed the treaty in mid-August 1795, Madison came up with 'an interpretation of the Constitution so unorthodox as to provoke a full-blown constitutional crisis.'[42]

Madison argued that the Treaty could not become a law unless it was passed in the House of Representatives since it dealt with regulating commerce and exercised powers granted to Congress. This was a complete violation of the separation of powers between the arms of government enshrined in the Constitution. As Washington wrote: to interfere in the executive domain in this manner 'would be to establish a dangerous precedent' which would also violate the Constitution that granted the right to make treaties only to the president and Senate. Such a precedent would have made it impossible for the federal government to direct the nation's foreign policy. Instead, the president would have become hostage to Congress's veto on every major issue. Effectively, Madison's novel interpretation of the Constitution would have killed the executive branch.[43]

With completely partisan motives, the "Father of the Constitution," Madison, assumed the floor in the debate in Congress to defend his innovative interpretation of the Constitution. He was very confident of his victory at the start of the debate but as Adams incisively noted, Madison looked 'worried to death. Pale, withered, haggard' by the end. All Madisonian political maneuvers and Jeffersonian strategic campaigns were not enough to surmount Washington's support and the treaty passed by a thin majority of 51-48. Jefferson consoled Madison by telling him that the treaty passed only due to Washington, 'the one man who outweighs them all in influence over the people.'[44] In retrospect from a historian's perspective, Jay's Treaty proved to be extremely beneficial for America. It provided America an ally in Britain which remained the preeminent world power for more than a century. Thus, it ensured America's rise without being engulfed in the British-French conflict, and provided America the space to emerge as an economic powerhouse while its security was being guaranteed by the British fleet. As historian George Herring writes, 'It bought for a new and still weak nation that most priceless commodity—time.'[45]

The debate over Jay's Treaty also marked the consolidation of political parties in American democracy. Washington was now regularly bombarded in the press by language that would have been inconceivable and heresy just a few months back. He was charged with tyranny, having plans of establishing a monarchy, was called 'the scourge and misfortune of our country,' and was even accused of being 'a secret British agent' during the American Revolution![46] The genie of political opposition had come out of the bottle and it was not possible now to put it back. After Washington published his farewell address, the first real presidential election in American history due later in the same year (1796) was fought along partisan lines.

'I am heir apparent, you know,' wrote John Adams to his wife, Abigail, in early 1796. Adams had been a faithful vice president to Washington—which Jefferson would not be to Adams—and was senior to both Jefferson and Hamilton. He was also a New Englander and so there was support for him from the northern states to put their own man in the capital after Virginian Washington's eight years as president. As per the unwritten custom of the day, neither Adams nor Jefferson was willing to openly announce his candidature or seek support from the voters. Both maintained aloofness from the campaigns being run by both parties in their names across the nation. Adams had been Jefferson's senior in the Continental Congress and the two had become very close in Paris. However, in the past few years, with partisanship troubles inside and outside the government, they had started to grow distant. Both Adams and Jefferson knew the plain truth that they were in competition with each other for the president's office. Jefferson maintained that he had retired from politics to live a peaceful life whereas Adams admitted that he had become 'weary of the game [of politics]. Yet I don't know how I would live out of it.'[47]

Hamilton had wisely decided to not run for the office because his divisive personality risked dividing the federalist voter base. He went back to playing tricks behind the scenes to not let Jefferson become either the president or the vice president. At the time, the person getting the second-highest number of votes was automatically chosen as the vice president. Such was the trust in the working of the government without effective opposition that nobody had thought about the possibility of the emergence of political parties in the Constitutional Convention. This now led to the peculiar situation whereby political rivals could now be president and vice president in the same administration. Unable to trust Hamilton, Adams was worried that Hamilton's machinations may end up depriving him of the presidency. Deploring his secret initiatives, Abigail henceforth privately addressed Hamilton as "Cassius" while Adams called him 'as great a hypocrite as any in the U.S. His intrigues in the election I despise.' In the event, voting in the states showed a decided north-south divide and Adams emerged victorious over Jefferson by just three votes. It was a curious situation for the next four years since the president and vice president continued to be competitors and in opposition to each other.[48]

The first mistake that President Adams committed was to retain Washington's cabinet in the hope of providing continuity to the administration. After Washington's retirement, these cabinet members proved to be more loyal to Hamilton than Adams. As Jefferson remarked, 'Hamiltonians who surround him [Adams] are only a little less hostile to him than to me.'[49] Adams tried his best to fit himself into Washington's shoes knowing well that it would be impossible to gather as much love and support as Washington did. Three events defined Adams's presidency: XYZ Affair, Alien and Sedition Acts, and Quasi-War. All three were interconnected.

Adhering to Washington's policy of neutrality which had secured peace with Britain, Adams planned to send a peace mission to France while simultaneously calling for a military buildup in case of a war with France. Jefferson and Republicans had thought that with Washington gone, it would be easy to manipulate Adams towards the French cause and reverse Washington's neutrality proclamation. Thus, they were disappointed when Adams sent a peace mission instead of supporting France in the war. However, the peace mission sent by Adams failed since the French emissaries (codenamed X, Y, and Z) demanded enormous bribes. This failure provided fuel to the Republicans to vehemently attack Adams until he disclosed the reason for the mission's failure. Once it became clear to Americans that the French had humiliated their ambassadors by being discourteous and had tried extortion, public opinion turned behind Adams. An embarrassed Jefferson who had for many years been Adams's close friend now swiveled around to position himself behind the president by maintaining silence. Speaking about swiveling, interestingly, Jefferson was also the inventor of the modern swivel chair.[50] With the eloquent Jefferson under a self-imposed silence, this was the high point of Adams's presidency. He was enjoying the huge support of the masses and Congress in his federalist policies after the XYZ affair. But things started to go downhill for Adams not much later.

What was Hamilton doing all this while? Unbeknownst to Adams, Hamilton was pulling strings in his cabinet from outside. In summer 1797, a notorious journalist named James Callender published an account accusing Hamilton of laundering money through James Reynolds and 'wenching' while he was the Secretary of the Treasury. Callender had obtained the confidential documents which Hamilton had provided to the congressmen while disclosing his illicit affair. Hamilton was furious. The disclosure was an affront to his sense of honor. Silence, which would have been the best option to let the wave pass under the ship was not what he considered as the optimal course. Instead, he wrote and published a 100-page booklet discussing his licentiousness in exquisite detail to convey that he was only guilty of the sexual affair but not of any embezzlement. As he put it: 'My crime is an amorous connection with his [James Reynold's] wife.' Republican press had a field day with Hamilton's booklet. Ironically, by coming out clean, Hamilton marked the beginning of his decline and his sidelining from politics.[51]

A little later, when a French privateer captured an American vessel, it marked the beginning of an undeclared naval war between America and France. During this phase of Quasi-War, the massive military buildup was commenced by the government and Washington was asked to accept the command of the forces. An ailing Washington accepted the command only symbolically. It was clear that Hamilton was to be the *de facto* commander. Without Washington to restrain Hamilton's passions, he devised large and almost-surely disastrous plans to seize Spanish Florida and Louisiana in collaboration with British troops (Spain was France's ally). Adams wisely rejected such plans perceiving that Hamilton was being driven from one consideration only—personal glory.[52]

Emboldened after the XYZ affair which was a boost for Federalists, in June 1798, Congress passed the Alien and Sedition Acts which were signed into law by Adams. These were meant to enhance national security by quelling French supporters and immigrants and gave enormous powers to the president such as to expel foreigners from the Union or accuse anybody of sedition who excited "hatred" by writing against the government, Congress, or president. However, Federalists had overplayed their hand by imposing such restrictions on the freedom of the press. Republicans were waiting for an opportune time since the XYZ affair and these laws became a new rallying point for them to attack the president.[53] Jefferson and Madison secretly drafted the Kentucky and Virginia Resolutions to nullify the Alien and Sedition Acts by deeming them unconstitutional in these states.

In summer 1800, having had enough with Hamilton's cronies in his cabinet, Adams asked them to resign which further embittered Hamilton. With Napoleon Bonaparte taking over the French Government and declaring that the French Revolution was now over, peace prevailed between Britain and France for the moment. Confident that the French would not attack America despite the warlike atmosphere being created by Hamilton, Adams remarked to his Secretary of War: 'at present there is no more prospect of seeing a French army here, than there is in Heaven.'[54] Adams had continued secret negotiations with France even after the XYZ affair and to his credit, he avoided a disastrous war with France by securing peace in 1800. It would have been a political masterstroke by Adams to rally the nation behind him by inflaming nationalist passions and get reelected by declaring war when Americans were clamoring for it. But a war with France at that time would have been disastrous for the weak American economy and government. It is for this reason Adams later wrote to a friend: 'I desire no other inscription over my gravestone than: "Here lies John Adams, who took upon himself the responsibility of peace with France in the year 1800."'[55]

With no war in foresight, the army was quietly disbanded and Hamilton's ambitions were quelled. Instead of making efforts to unite the Federalists, Hamilton grudged his removal as the commander of the armed forces and inflicted a mortal wound on his own political career by publishing a fifty-four-page pamphlet titled *A Letter from Alexander Hamilton, Concerning the Public Conduct and Character of John Adams, Esq., President of the United States.* This work deplored Adams in every possible way, produced a schism in the Federalist Party, and destroyed Hamilton's credibility.[56]

The wreckage caused by the split in the Federalist Party was accumulated and disposed of by Republicans for their own gain. The only thing Jefferson had to do now for thwarting Adams's reelection was to not commit any blunder. Hence instead of showing an active interest in running for the office, Jefferson again sat calmly at his home and emerged victorious in the election of 1800 (the first and only time a president and vice president were pitted against each other). It was the first transfer of power from one political party to another in American history. The fact that it was peaceful and made the Union more stable added to the event's significance. Republicans held the presidency for the next twenty-four years. With Adams's retirement and Hamilton's death four years later, there was nobody in the nation to match Jefferson's stature to lead the Federalist Party and it gradually declined. But, the spirit of organized opposition once ignited, never died.

In our journey through this chapter, we saw how the founding fathers were concerned about the rise of political factions but contributed to the same nonetheless. The two-party system instituted inadvertently and rather grudgingly by them became a legitimate way of expressing dissent and opposition to the government. It is also notable that while Hamilton's actions and vocal mannerisms contributed most towards the rise of political parties, he himself became a victim of the same in the end. On the other hand, Jefferson who took pains to present himself publicly as being distant and aloof from the ongoing partisan warfare gained the most. Already in the first decade of the young nation, organized political opposition to different policies such as Jay's Treaty, Alien and Sedition Acts, and Quasi-War proved beneficial for the nation by forcing the ruling administration to ponder over and improvise its policies. Though Washington and Adams had to face frequent accusations of monarchical intents and tried their best to govern in a nonpartisan manner, the rise of an organized and vocal political opposition ensured that America would not descend into being a monarchical state. The emergence of the two-party system secured that the balance of power would be maintained in the American democracy, excesses of the ruling party would be contained, and dissent would be expressed in a legitimate manner.

In 1937, Jawaharlal Nehru was elected the President of the Congress Party for the third time. In the same year, an article was published in the *Modern Review* journal of Calcutta under the title *Rashtrapati* (President) and was written under the pseudonym *Chanakya*. The article brutally excoriated Nehru's presidency as well as his demeanor towards the opposition. Here are some excerpts:

> Rashtrapati Jawaharlal ki Jai [Hail President Jawaharlal]....Watch him again. There is a great procession and tens of thousands of persons surround his car and cheer him in an ecstasy of abandonment. He stands on the seat of the car, balancing himself rather well, straight and seemingly tall, like a god, serene and unmoved by the seething multitude....A little twist and Jawaharlal might turn a dictator sweeping aside the paraphernalia of a slow-moving democracy. He might still use the language and slogans of democracy and socialism, but we all know how fascism has fattened on this language and then cast it away as useless lumber....Jawaharlal cannot become a fascist. And yet he has all the makings of a dictator in him—vast popularity, a strong will directed to a well-defined purpose, energy, pride, organisational capacity, ability,

hardness, and, with all his love of the crowd, an intolerance of others and a certain contempt for the weak and the inefficient....Caesarism is always at the door, and is it not possible that Jawaharlal might fancy himself as a Caesar?....His conceit is already formidable. It must be checked. We want no Caesars.[57]

The article was much talked about in the press. Here was a courageous writer who was criticizing Nehru not only for his demeanor and conceit but was also accusing him of disregard for the opposition. It should also be kept in mind that this article was published right after the provincial elections of 1937 that were held under British aegis. Patel was the chief fundraiser for the Congress Party in the elections while Nehru was the star campaigner. To seek votes Nehru had traveled about fifty thousand miles across the subcontinent by 'aeroplane, railway, automobile, motor lorry, horse carriages of various kinds, bullock cart, bicycle, elephant, camel, horse, steamer, paddle-boat, canoe, and on foot.'[58] Congress had performed spectacularly in the elections across the nation and Nehru's stature had gained exponentially. So, who was this anonymous writer publishing in the *Modern Review* journal and why was he attacking Nehru so sarcastically and vehemently? A few years later, it was revealed by a journalist that the author of that piece was, Jawaharlal Nehru! In a self-reflective mood and desire to not be the Congress President again due to his ideological differences with the organization at the time, Nehru was criticizing himself. He had become his own opposition. A decade after the publication of his self-criticizing essay, Nehru became the first prime minister of Independent India. What course was the nation taking with him at its helm with no strong opposition to check his Congress Party?

Jawaharlal Nehru was born on 14 November 1889 in an affluent family in Allahabad—an ancient city situated at the meeting point of two major Indian rivers, Ganga and Yamuna. Jawaharlal's father, Motilal Nehru, was an accomplished lawyer who had made a fortune by his practice. Motilal modeled himself and his household after the British aristocracy. The only thing denied to Jawaharlal in his childhood was adversity. His palatial house had two swimming pools, three kitchens, gardens, tennis court, etc. along with an army of attendants. With roots in the Kashmiri Brahmin community,

Jawaharlal was in the words of his biographer, 'favored with a strikingly handsome appearance, both by Indian and Western standards....making him one of the most photogenic statesmen of the century.'[59] After receiving early schooling by private tutors at his home, the young lad was sent to study at the best academic institutions in Britain—Harrow and Cambridge. Nehru studied natural science at Cambridge and subsequently enrolled in Inner Temple Inn to study law. Returning to India in 1912, he started a law practice alongside his father. A quite unremarkable life until now for Nehru, all changed with Gandhi's arrival on the Indian political landscape. Nehru enthusiastically plunged behind Gandhi into the freedom struggle and emerged as one of the most charismatic leaders at a young age. There were no signs in Nehru's childhood that could point to such a transformation as he himself admitted that 'I have been a dabbler in many things; I began with science at college, and then took to the law, and, after developing various other interest in life, finally adopted the popular and widely practised profession of gaol-going in India!'[60] Thus, an important feature about Nehru was that he was 'not only a late developer, he was also a continuous developer.'[61]

In total, Nehru spent almost a decade in various prisons of the British Raj during the freedom struggle. A strict self-disciplinarian, he never allowed his nerves to get affected by imprisonment. During his many short and long stints in prison, Nehru matured as a master of prose, historian, intellectual, and political thinker. As he liked to quote Benjamin Disraeli, 'Other men condemned to exile and captivity, if they survive, despair; the man of letters may reckon those days as the sweetest of his life.'[62] And, so it was with Nehru who wrote three masterly books in prison which have never since gone out of publication. The first of these, *Glimpses of World History,* was written in the form of letters to his daughter in which Nehru surveyed the history of the World from an Asia-centric perspective. A prolific work written from confinement with meager resources to consult, Nehru provides a vivid picture of the history of the world in a thousand pages—the feat reflecting Nehru's intellectual breadth. On the other hand, reading *An Autobiography* feels like reading about a man with a rare tendency of self-reflection and willing to admit his failures who at the same time is not given to haughty judgments about others. The third, *The Discovery of India,* discusses many themes around the Indian civilization's past, present, and future, along with Nehru's interpretation of the many historical trends that have charted the course of the modern Indian subcontinent.

Nehru also carved for himself an international presence second only to Gandhi's. Not only did he forgo the aristocratic lifestyle by plunging himself into the freedom struggle and embracing prison, he even persuaded his father to do the same. His father, Motilal served as the Congress president twice. In the struggle to get the British out of India, while giving the reigns of the Congress presidency to Jawaharlal at the young age of 40, the Nehru père uttered a prophecy in Persian which came true in due time: *Harche Pedar natawanad, Pesar temam kunad* (What the father is unable to accomplish, son achieves).[63] In 1929, Jawaharlal was at the front among the Congress leaders who were demanding complete self-rule instead of Dominion Status as Congress Party's resolve. A momentous event in the history of India, Nehru hoisted the tricolor flag of India at the bank of river Ravi in Lahore while Congress declared 26 January to be observed as Independence Day. This date was observed as Independence Day until 1947, was chosen as the day to adopt the Constitution in 1950, and has since been celebrated as the Republic Day of India. Despite expressing fundamental differences with Gandhi on many occasions, mostly concerning Socialism (Nehru identified himself as a socialist from around the early 1930s), he remained ever-loyal and never broke up with his "Bapu." Thus, when Independence came, Nehru was Gandhi's chosen successor for leading the nation.

For seventeen years until his death in 1964, Nehru served as India's prime minister and is generally regarded as "the Architect of Modern India." A philosopher-king, Nehru retained a sense of aloofness from the general masses even when intermingling with them delightedly in public events. A specimen of good health, for years, Nehru worked tirelessly day and night for sixteen to seventeen hours each day. He retained a wide range of interests in 'Science (especially Physics and Biology), and Literature as well as over History and Statecraft. He had a fair knowledge of French. He kept up a lively, emphatic, though not always well-informed, interest in Natural History and especially in animals….Nehru's mind, moreover, was on most subjects, an open mind as well as a full mind. He had his prejudices—Maharajas, Portugal, Money-lenders, certain American ways, Hinduism, the whites in Africa...but in most things he was without dogmatism. Only occasionally did his cocksureness take on rigidity.'[64] For most of his life, Nehru needed the presence of strong and decisive men as a sense of security—a role first fulfilled by his father Motilal and later by Gandhi. After Gandhi's death, this same tendency inculcated in him a feeling of hesitation and indecisiveness in acting boldly. Assimilating influences from many civilizations and ideologies, Nehru also felt a sense of unsurety and not belonging to the shoes he was standing in.[65] As he had described himself in his autobiography, 'I have become a queer mixture of the East and West, out of place everywhere, at home nowhere.'[66]

Beloved of the masses, almost single-handedly, Nehru took India towards the path of science and modernization, democracy and pluralism, non-alignment and planning, peace and harmony. The foundations of the plural democratic Republic of India that we see today were erected by Nehru. After Gandhi's inopportune death in 1948, it was Nehru who veered India away from the course of failure like many other formerly colonized nations. But for Nehru, India would have been a less plural, a less equal, a less affectionate, and a less humane society. He stood as the adamantine bulwark against Communism on the Left and Hindu Majoritarianism on the Right. He also established a hugely successful foreign policy of non-alignment that made India gain favor from both superpowers during the Cold War while focusing solely on domestic progress. Domestically, Nehru was instrumental in enacting laws for reforming the Hindu law to criminalize caste discrimination and enact safeguards for the social freedoms of women. While in the West, democracy had been preceded by the formation of a nation-state and absorption of the forces of the Industrial Revolution, in India, Nehru achieved the confluence of all three (democracy, nationalism, and industrialization) simultaneously.

Most importantly, Nehru succeeded in instilling a sense of nationalism among his fellow Indians that transcended loyalty to their own religion, region, language, caste, culture, and other such social identifiers, while at the same time bringing together all minorities towards the project of nation-building. To again quote Nehru's biographer Michael Brecher who was writing in 1959, 'For thirty years he [Nehru] has been the idol of the Indian masses, second only to Gandhi. They literally adore him. From distant villages they come in thousands to hear him, more to see him, to have a *darshan* (communion) with their beloved "Panditji", successor to the Mahatma, champion of the oppressed, symbol of the new India of their vague dreams.'[67] Another foreigner and diplomat writing at the time noted that 'For the people of India, he is George Washington, Lincoln, Roosevelt and Eisenhower rolled into one.'[68] However, in the twilight years of his leadership, there were always speculations that India may descend into anarchy after his demise since he was the glue keeping the nation together. In the end, the institutions established by him outlived him and such forebodings of a disaster were falsified when a smooth transition of power took place after his death in 1964.

Writing in the same year as Brecher, a political analyst observed: 'As the years rolled by, the very foundations on which Nehru's prestige and reputation rested began to weigh him down. At one time, he had a solution to every difficulty; today, he faces a difficulty in every solution.'[69] The Himalayan blunder that was the debacle in the Indo-China conflict of 1962 marred Nehru's legacy forever. The ongoing Kashmir conflict too has ever been perceived as Nehru's failure. Many of the socialist policies enunciated by his government stifled the nation's entrepreneurs and private enterprise. Though Nehru conducted the government's business in a democratic manner, with time, his views started turning rigid and a coterie of followers gathered around him, impeding the process of self-introspection. Nehru's Congress was virtually dominant across the nation and an effective opposition was needed more than ever to not just challenge Nehru and force him to reflect on his government's policies but also to bolster the foundations of the young Indian democracy. There were some leaders outside the Congress like J. B. Kripalani, Jayaprakash Narayan, Ram Manohar Lohia, and Syama Prasad Mukherjee who were attacking Nehru's policies. But, the question was who in India possessed the moral authority and esteemed stature to take on Nehru as equal? There was only one answer.

The reader might recall from the first chapter "Minorities" that Rajaji's intervention was instrumental in bringing about a compromise between Gandhi and Ambedkar to save the former's life. Gandhi's biographer Louis Fischer once defined the Indian freedom struggle thus: Rajaji is the 'third outstanding figure in Indian independence—Gandhi is its prophet, Nehru, its poet, thinker and crusader, Rajagopalachari, its statesman.'[70] Chakravarti Rajagopalachari popularly known as Rajaji was born in 1878 in the south Indian province of Madras in a humble Brahmin family. Apparently, an astrologer predicted that the young boy's destiny 'includes the fortunes of a king, of an exile, of a guru, and of an outcaste. The people will worship him; they will also reject him. He will sit on an emperor's throne; he will live in a poor man's hut.'[71] When young Rajaji complained of myopic vision and requested spectacles, his father spurned the request as a child's mischief since nobody under forty-five in their city wore glasses. Thus, later at the age of thirteen when Rajaji finally acquired glasses, '[h]is life was transformed. He had not "quite known," until now, "what green was." And he found that the stars were not just "a vague mist of light" but had "points, and corners, and colors."'[72]

After studying law at the Presidency College in Madras, Rajaji set up his legal practice in Salem. He was the only Indian founding father among the six discussed in this book who did not go overseas to study. In fact, Rajaji never stepped outside the Indian subcontinent until well past eighty. He was also the first founding father to have come under Gandhi's influence, even before Gandhi returned to India from South Africa. So much was Rajaji in Gandhi's awe that he was the first Indian to review Gandhi's book *Hind Swaraj* and also reprinted *Mr Gandhi's Jail Experiences* at his own expense and labor by treading a press himself after being moved by Gandhi's arrest in South Africa.[73] When Gandhi returned back to India, Rajaji willingly made Gandhi's agendas his own and became Gandhi's southern general. After giving up his flourishing law practice, Rajaji went to jail many times during the freedom struggle.

By 1927, Gandhi was regarding Rajaji as his heir: 'I do say he is the only possible successor,'[74] while a few years later, Gandhi expounded Rajaji as 'the keeper of my conscience.'[75] Rajaji understood Gandhi's efforts towards Harijan work and promotion of the Indian cottage industry before anybody else among the Congress leadership. Gandhi, India's conscience and Rajaji, Gandhi's conscience keeper functioned together as a formidable pair of social and political activists, especially in South India. Years later, Gandhi's youngest son, Devdas, married Rajaji's daughter, Lakshmi, binding the teacher and the disciple in a familial bond.[76]

By 1942, differences between Rajaji and Gandhi over Muhammad Ali Jinnah's demand for Pakistan reached a point where Rajaji did not support Gandhi's Quit India Movement in 1942. This alienated Rajaji from the Congress organization and dismantled his public standing. The differences between them, his increasing warmth over the years towards Nehru, and Nehru's own rise in Indian politics as a unifying mass leader made Gandhi declare in 1942 that 'Not Rajaji...but Jawaharlal will be my successor.'[77] Thus, one of Rajaji's chief characteristics was that he was the first in following Gandhi, first in understanding Gandhi, and first in breaking away from Gandhi.

Short-heighted with face conveying a cunning foxlike appearance, a pointed nose, bald head, and often-sporting black round glasses as a fashion accessory, Rajaji looked like a curious mixture of Gandhi and Steve Jobs. Often showing elegant and self-effacing humor, he could also be witty and sarcastic. Rajaji's words, as well as prose, were forthright. Once when traveling on a train during a very hot day, an Englishman complained about the weather, Rajaji replied that it wasn't hot enough. To this, the Englishman asked in a puzzled tone to explain what Rajaji meant to which the latter replied smilingly that the weather is 'not hot enough to keep you gentlemen out of our country.'[78] Throughout his life, the one word everybody associated with Rajaji was "prescience." Whether it be the Partition of India, Nehru's faulty economic policies, the breakup of Pakistan into two nations, global nuclear threat, Chinese aggression, or economic liberalization, among other instances, Rajaji predicted them all accurately or foreordained the course of the future much before the events occurred.[79] It was not very uncommon for people to say things to the tune that Rajaji's views always triumph in the end or that Rajaji predicted this many years ago. Also labeled as "the wisest man in India," his uncanny knack of being wise before the event meant that often Rajaji had to pay for it in his politics.[80] However, as the writer K. T. Narasimhachar has pointed out, 'Courage was the supreme trait in Rajaji's character. Throughout his life he was never afraid to differ from others on a question of principle, being always guided by his conscience.'[81]

It is hard to classify Rajaji's character and his politics under either Liberal or Conservative banners. On the one hand, he championed the cause of Harijan welfare alongside Gandhi whereas, on the other hand, his views towards women remained reactionary. He followed Gandhi for the emancipation of the Untouchables into the society but did not favor women coming out of their traditional homemaking and family rearing roles. He also criticized birth control methods and artificial insemination as being immoral.[82] Similarly, in politics, the economic policies advocated by him were certainly liberal and stimulated personal freedom of occupation but on the other hand, he brought God into the political landscape by being unable to divorce religion from politics. He was also a passionate supporter of the prohibition of liquor and introduced a law for the same in Madras Presidency between 1937-39 which hurt the government's revenues. These contradictions and associated policies that he advocated meant that his opponents charged him with opportunism and traditionalism as opposed to being modern (even by the standards of those times).

Despite failing in his native language Tamil during his college studies, Rajaji became a profound scholar in Tamil as well as the English language. He is today perhaps most remembered for his renditions of Hindu epics *Ramayana* and *Mahabharata* and the song *Kurai Ondrum Illai* composed by him. Apart from these, he also translated Plato's *Trial and Death of Socrates* and *Crito,* and Marcus Aurelius' *Meditations* into Tamil, and *Thirukkural* into English.[83] Fond of Edmund Burke, Rajaji loved to selectively quote Burke, Plato, Socrates, Cicero, and Samuel Johnson among others from the West, as well as many characters from Hindu mythology. He was adept at Socratic questioning and logic since 'All the books that have influenced me most were accidental finds. I suppose it would be right to say that Socrates was the most important.'[84] He also wrote many short stories and books on Hindu texts like *Bhagavad Gita* and the *Upanishads*. Apart from scholarship, Rajaji demonstrated strong administrative skills during the multiple public offices he held: Chief Minister of Madras Presidency between 1937-39, Minister of Education in the interim government before Independence, Governor of West Bengal after the Independence, last Governor-General (and first Indian to be so) of India between 1948-50, Minister of Home Affairs in the Central Government after Patel's death in 1950, and another short stint as the Chief Minister of Madras between 1952-54. In 1955, he became the first Indian to be awarded the nation's highest civilian honor, the Bharat Ratna. After retiring in the mid-1950s, Rajaji plunged back again into politics at the ripe old age of eighty to mount an opposition to Nehru's government. As Rajaji's principal biographer and his grandson, Rajmohan Gandhi has written, 'From the late 1950s, when Rajaji was close to eighty, to the end of 1972, when he died at the age of 94, Rajaji was the period's most notable—and most quotable—dissenting Indian....That from time to time he contradicted himself added to his liveliness.'[85]

In 1959, Rajaji launched the Swatantra Party to organize opposition against Nehru's socialist and statist policies. Rajaji planned to teach his countrymen that no leader's policies should be taken as unquestionable and no ruler's stature as inviolable. He succinctly summarized the need for the democratic opposition as follows

> The successful working of parliamentary democracy depends on two factors: first, on a broad measure of agreement among all classes of citizens about the objectives of the government; secondly, on the existence of a two-party system...If political opinion does not succeed in crystallizing into two fairly balanced groups, the semblance of democracy may survive but real parliamentary democracy will not be there....A strong opposition is essential for the health of democratic government. In a democracy based on universal suffrage, government by the majority without an effective opposition is like driving a donkey on whose back you put the whole load in one bundle...A single-party democracy soon loses its sense of proportion. It sees, but cannot place things in perspective or apprehend all sides of a question. That is the position of India today.[86]

At the same time as advocating for a strong opposition in India, Rajaji also forcefully came out in the cause of world peace by opposing nuclear weapon testing by America and the Soviet Union. He wrote long letters to the head of states of both nations and met among others, Vice President Richard Nixon in 1954, Soviet *de facto* leader Nikita Khrushchev in 1955, and President John F. Kennedy in 1962 for this cause. Even at a very old age, his appeals were so forceful and grounded in logic that Nixon filled three pages of his diary about his conversation with Rajaji and claimed in his memoir later that the afternoon 'had such a dramatic effect on me that I used many of his thoughts in my speeches over the next several years,'[87] while Kennedy felt that 'I have seldom met a man who had a more civilizing influence on me than Rajaji'[88] and that 'Seldom have I heard a case presented with such precision and clarity and elegance of language.'[89]

Jawaharlal Nehru was a man in a hurry. He wanted to place India on an irreversible path of development by utilizing the advances in science and technology. The fastest and surest way that came to him for achieving this aim was the appeal of state-driven economic planning based on the Soviet model that had transformed the Soviet Union from a comparatively backward nation to a superpower in a single generation. Nehru, who considered himself socialist adopted five-year plans as well as heavily centralized economic policies on the Soviet model. As one of Nehru's comrade turned opponent, J. B. Kripalani who also identified himself as a socialist pointed out, 'The idea of planning had caught the imagination of Jawaharlal and socialists in India. They equated socialism with planning. The two terms came to be considered identical.'[90] Nehru worked hard to instill a sense of responsibility and admiration for planning among Indians. But, the socialist structure of economic planning, though promising quick results started to suffocate the nation's entrepreneurial spirit. Additionally, trade with other nations was discouraged by the government. An elaborate quagmire of licenses and permits had to be navigated to set up a private business and even then the production was regulated by the government. This so-called "License Raj" induced corruption by government officials while issuing the permits and was responsible for India not developing at its true potential. As the journal *The Economic Weekly* noted in 1959, 'The political problem par excellence that we face in India, in common with the peoples of new-born democracies in Asia and elsewhere, is that of reconciling the requirements of rapid industrialisation with the claims of a welfare state.'[91]

Having retired from public office in 1954, Rajaji was focusing mostly on scholarly pursuits while keeping a close eye on the government's policies. It was a gradual transformation in his views which led to the establishment of a political party to challenge Nehru's Congress Party. In 1955, Congress had formally adopted a

Socialistic blueprint—to develop India as a welfare state. As a response, in 1956, Rajaji wrote in an article titled *Value of Frank Criticism* that 'Great governments benefit by criticism, without which they are bound to deteriorate in self-complacency and unchecked self-will.'[92] This article was published in *Swarajya*, a newspaper started by one of his journalistic friends, and emerged as his mouthpiece for the next several years. A year later, Rajaji's tone had become stricter: 'If there is no prospect of a good and strong Opposition balancing the ruling party, the alternative is not to feel proud of the invincibility of the Congress but to devise measures for filling the gap by developing scope for free and open discussion and criticism, and by constructing a bridge between the party apparatus and the people. The Almighty Party Apparatus is sapping the strength of the people and that is fatal to democracy.'[93] He was now opposing the party with which he had been associated for most of his life. Three months later, Rajaji directly called for the creation of opposition against Congress: 'The domination by the Congress Party of the political scene is a product of history rather than of electoral success. Electoral successes are the result of this domination, not its cause. In order to justify the leadership that has resulted from history, the Congress Party has swung well to the Left…[Since] the Congress Party has swung to the Left, what is wanted for the body politic is…a strong and articulate Right'[94]

In calling for the establishment of a conservative party, Rajaji meant to preserve what is good while thwarting rapid change since as he liked to quote: 'survival is a proof of fitness, not worthlessness.'[95] A few months later, Rajaji published an article under the title *Wanted: Independent Thinking* in which he wrote 'What I plead for is a climate of independent thinking among citizens…Without this essential accompaniment, self-government through democracy will prove itself to be a house of cards.'[96] Indicting the government of sabotaging entrepreneurship, Rajaji wrote 'The role of the Government should be that of a catalyst in stimulating economic development while individual initiative and enterprise are given the fullest play…Many important things have been neglected because the Government has forgotten them in its obsession with "command economy." Wise planning means Government help to foster private enterprise and self-help among individuals.'[97] However, when others agreeing with him requested him to mount opposition to Congress himself, he replied to the tune: 'Impossible—a dilapidated old fogey like me?'[98]

In the words of Rajmohan Gandhi, 'In 1959, the elderly watchdog became a greyhound! Ignoring ailments and shaking off inhibitions, Rajaji, 80, decided to challenge Jawaharlal, who seemed to embody power, fame and vitality, with a new political party.' What brought about this sudden reaction from Rajaji? Having committed to the cause of Socialism in 1955, Congress had gone a step further in 1958-59 by coming up with a new agricultural policy—cooperative farming. This policy entailed that the government could takeover grain trade, maintain ceilings on landholding, and force cooperative cultivation of land, in effect a design towards disrupting the Indian economy and the biggest step yet towards socialism. Learning about this policy, Rajaji's antennae perked up and he quickly discerned that this move must be opposed with all vigor that he could command. He penned down articles such as 'Violent Socialism,' 'Retreat from Gandhism' and 'Why I Show the Red Flag,' and wrote scathingly against the policy: 'Common cultivation [was] not an idea born of experience or thought.' He added that it had been tried in countries 'where personal liberty is absent and forced labor is commandeered,' and that Congress was 'borrowing from the Communist his brush and paint.' Realizing the folly of license restrictions instituted by the government, Rajaji also coined a term to rally public opinion against the government which in time became central to Indian political debate for the rest of the century: "permit-license-quota raj."[99] Circumstances had forced his hand to once again foray into politics and come out in the leadership mode. The right to private property was sacrosanct in Rajaji's view. Thus, he advocated that forcing farmers to cultivate commonly owned land and restrict the freedom of trade were policies antithetical to the basic freedoms of a human being.

Congress's resolution on cooperative farming was indeed the proverbial last straw for Rajaji. Opposition by writing articles to Congress's policies had now culminated in Rajaji's decision to launch a political party and challenge the ruling party's ideology. But it was a Herculean task since at the time, the whole of India except one small state (Kerala) was ruled by Congress. Congress had won 371 out of 494 parliamentary seats in the 1957 general elections whereas the

Communist Party of India was a distant second with 27 seats. Praja Socialist Party which had been established by veterans of the freedom struggle and younger collaborators of Nehru and Rajaji was third with 19 seats. Ergo, based solely on numbers, there was no effective opposition in the Indian parliament while the loyalty of the Communists to the Indian state had always been dubious. Rajaji had no illusions about being able to challenge Nehru's position at this age. He knew that Nehru could not be replaced and also that it would take any political party years before it could challenge the hegemony of Congress across the nation. It had taken years for Congress and Gandhi to emerge as the undisputed national party and leader respectively across the nation due to its diversity. Rajaji's aim then was to galvanize opposition voices together on a common platform so that the tide of the public opinion could push Nehru towards rethinking his errant policies. Nehru and Rajaji were old friends and comrades and both were anxious that political differences must not affect their personal relations. Nevertheless, Rajaji now started criticizing Nehru as 'the Congress dictator' and accusing him of suppressing any dissent from within the party.

From the other side, Nehru's first comment after Rajaji's overt opposition against him was to express his 'affection and respect' for Rajaji and add 'May I perhaps venture to say one word to him with great respect; and that is, a little charity in his thinking may sometimes not be out of place.' 'We are positive friends and love each other' said Rajaji in reply to Nehru. Despite launching an opposition party, Rajaji maintained that he was an elder brother to Nehru who has erred and thus it is his job to warn the younger sibling. Expressing affection and caution in two juxtaposed statements, Rajaji wrote that it was 'God's grace that there is a good man in India who deserved to be idolized as [Nehru] is. Yet, there is nothing more important for the ruler of a great, big nation as independent, fearless advice.'[100]

It is worthwhile to ask why Rajaji did not decide to oppose Nehru from within the Congress? The answer may lie in Nehru's stern rebuke to his party men who were opposed to his land policy: 'If you do not agree with us, you can get out of the party.' As Rajaji wrote about Congress, 'The slightest attempt at dissent meets with stern disapproval [from Nehru] and is nipped in the bud.' Nehru may have written an article against his own presidency in 1937, but now as the prime minister of India, he had no plans to suffer dissent from within the Congress Party. Between 1947-50, there had been two poles in Congress—Nehru and Patel. Patel was the Deputy Prime Minister of India and had commanded much more power within the Congress organization than Nehru. Both had kept a check on each other while working together during the turbulent times accompanying India's Independence. But, after Patel's demise in 1950, Congress leaders had been following Nehru like a flock of sheep. Rajaji understood that only the power of public opinion could change Nehru's views and thus he sought to mount an opposition for shaping the public opinion.[101] On his side, Nehru tried to downplay the irreconcilable differences between him and Rajaji by flippantly remarking: 'He [Rajaji] likes the Old Testament. I like the New Testament.'[102] Once from the gloomy atmosphere of a long sentence in prison, when Rajaji was following a path at variant from the Congress Party, Nehru had written in his prison diary, 'As for Rajagopalachari—is there a more dangerous person in all India?' Now, however, Rajaji was indeed the most dangerous force working against the Congress.[103]

Rajaji named the new party, Swatantra, a word whose closest meaning is freedom. Very soon, eminent public figures such as Minoo Masani, V. P. Menon, K. M. Munshi, N. G. Ranga, Gayatri Devi, to name a few, started to get associated with the new venture. At the Party's preparatory convention in 1959, Rajaji evocatively compared the political opposition that he was orchestrating to the freedom movement by declaring:

> I have come to the conclusion that a movement, as important and as serious as the movement for independence against the British rule, has now to be inaugurated against the misconceived progress of the Congress towards what will finally end in suppression of individual liberty and the development of the state into a truly leviathan state. The state is becoming a giant entity by itself menacingly poised against the citizen, interfering with his life at all points, mistrusting the people, imposing restrictions, introducing a series of controls and regulations, stepping into the field of agriculture, industry and trade, creating an army of officials....The ruling party must be replaced by a party that will respect the freedom of the individual...[104]

Twenty-one principles of the Swatantra Party were laid out. These included respecting India's diversity and the party pledged itself to social justice 'without distinction of religion, caste, occupation, or political affiliation,' stimulating entrepreneurial energy by promoting individual initiative, and giving 'full liberty' to its members to propagate their personal views on matters not covered by the fundamental principles of the Party. The most significant principle in direct contrast to Congress's agendas was: 'The Party holds that the progress, welfare, and happiness of the people depend on individual initiative, enterprise, and energy. The Party stands for the principle of maximum freedom for the individual and minimum interference by the State, consistent with the obligation to prevent and punish anti-social activities, to protect the weaker elements of society, and to create the conditions in which individual initiative will thrive and be fruitful. The Party is, therefore opposed to increasing State interference of the kind now being pursued.'[105]

Despite accusations and paraphernalia of conservatism, the party was firmly grounded in free-market policies. Some industrialists and princes who were either disgruntled by the government's socialistic and statist policies or desired healthy opposition in the nation started to back and fund the Swatantra Party. Thus, soon the Party emerged as the second most funded party in national politics. Nehru was irritated and declared that Congress would reject donations from any company that would fund the Swatantra Party—a proclamation that in the end was never implemented since many companies wisely chose to fund Congress significantly more than Swatantra to continue being in the incumbent government's good books.[106]

In Rajaji's view, 'the Congress Party has so far run without a true Opposition. It has run with accelerators and no brakes.' With Swatantra Party, Rajaji attempted to decelerate the pace of the Congress Party's disastrous economic schemes by turning the tide of public opinion.[107] The first victory for the new party was not an electoral one. It was an example of what mounting opposition could do in a democracy by shaping public opinion. With Swatantra Party's vehement opposition and enthusiasm for the new party's ideals from the intelligentsia, Congress's resolution of cooperative farming remained a dead letter. As the President of India, Rajendra Prasad—a former colleague of both Nehru and Rajaji in Congress—privately noted: 'Rajaji commands a respect and hearing which hardly anyone else does in the country.' Nehru could have overlooked opposition from other parties and their leaders, but he was bound to engage with somebody of Rajaji's stature.[108]

India's politics was witnessing what a few months back would have been inconceivable—Nehru and Congress could be veritably challenged.

British rule in India had ended in 1947 but there were small pockets of the nation under the control of French and Portuguese. The response to the end of one such European-controlled territory created another divide in the Indian polity. Small European "colonies" being vestiges of Imperialism had continued to be psychologically abhorrent to the Indians. France had voluntarily ceded its colonies (among them the most notable being Pondicherry) by the mid-1950s. However, Portugal proved to be a lot more truculent. In fact, Portugal refused to acknowledge that Goa, with an area of 1500 square miles and located more than 5000 miles away from Lisbon, filled with beautiful beaches and a profitable seaport, was a colony that it was holding onto. Goa had been under Portuguese sovereignty for more than four and a half centuries. Despite many diplomatic efforts between the two nations in the 1950s, no resolution could be found. Portugal was holding on to its demand for carrying out a referendum in an essentially Catholic population with closer ties to Portugal than to India. The fact of the matter was that on the one hand, Portugal's retention of Goa was an anachronism since it was a clear case of still-continuing Imperialism even when most other European powers had receded from Asia after the Second World War. Thus, Goa was looked to as a continuing Imperialist insult on the Indian psyche. On the other hand, many Goans were well off in their traditional Portuguese ways and did not want to be a part of India and get subsumed in the regional politics of the nation. In previous years, Nehru had invariably maintained that a peaceful resolution would be found to the problem. However, on the night of 17 December 1961, Indian forces invaded Goa and liberated it from Portuguese rule within hours and without heavy casualties on either side.

Nehru was squarely appreciated by most of the leaders in India and by the general masses for the military action. Even forces from the Left (communist) and the Right (Hindu Majoritarianism) came together to appreciate the government's move. However, there was one problem, timing. It had already been declared earlier that the third general elections of India would be held in February 1962. Thus, Nehru could have taken the drastic step of going forward with military action in Goa either a few months earlier or after a victory for him (which was a foregone conclusion). The opposition suspected that political calculations were taken into consideration by Nehru before ordering the military campaign. To criticize Nehru for carrying out the military action would have meant to take a position against the prevailing nationalistic feeling. But, this did not deter Rajaji. As Walter Crocker writes, 'Very few Indians at any level protested against it [military action in Goa]…Rajagopalachari, great and greatly courageous once more, after so many great occasions, denounced it squarely for what it was. This was only a few weeks before the General elections; he knew that it would cost votes to the party he was leading, but he did not hesitate.'[109]

India had been proactively propagating Gandhi's principles of truth and non-violence across the world in previous years. It had been presenting itself as a "new light" in the world whose foreign-policy principles were guided by friendliness and Gandhi's non-violence. Thus, military action in Goa came as a shock to the world. Rajaji criticized it writing that by this act, India has 'totally lost the moral power to raise her voice against militarism….What faith we now profess….What message does India now carry in a world on the brink of moral collapse? Our nationalism has, I fear, led us into impatience at the wrong moment….We had a mission for promoting peace and a special qualification for fulfilling it.'[110] To Rajaji's accusations, Nehru retorted that Rajaji 'stands on a mountain peak by himself. Nobody understands him, nor does he understand anybody. We need not consider him in this connection. All his policies in regard to India, if I may say so, are bad—bad economics, bad sense and bad temper.'[111]

However, India neither suffered heavily in its reputation across the world nor was it subjected to any aggression by another nation despite attacking an American ally and founding member of the North Atlantic Treaty Organization (NATO). This was because Nehru's democratic credentials could not be questioned. Any other Asian leader carrying out such an operation against a European power would surely have had to face consequences. For example, fifteen years later, General Suharto's government in Indonesia was condemned for military action in Portuguese East Timor and Indonesian troops were expelled by UN forces. But the world community had an implicit trust that Nehru would not let nationalistic feelings go unchecked and would protect Goans' culture and way of life.[112]

It was not that Rajaji was a mindless opposition leader for whom opposing Nehru and gaining power was above any other consideration. In the steps of his master, Gandhi, Rajaji could also rise above politics in the nation's cause. Dravida Munnetra Kazhagam (DMK) party in Rajaji's home province of Madras was at the time advocating for secession from India based on a racial theory that Dravidians (south Indians) were ethnically different from Aryans (generally northerners). Rajaji tried to mollify the DMK and its leader C. N. Annadurai by trying to reach an electoral agreement before the upcoming 1962 elections. The agreement could not formally materialize fully but Rajaji kept urging Annadurai to drop the demand of an independent "Dravidaland." Simultaneously, Rajaji hoped to win over nationalists by making them believe that DMK is not a secessionist demon. Slowly, after India's conflict with China later in the year, DMK abandoned its demand for secession. Rajaji could well have shaken hands with DMK to put more pressure on Nehru before the elections. Instead, he was working in the nation's cause even from the opposition during the discordant election campaign.[113]

Gandhi's designated heirs charged at each other during the 1962 elections with the words that he may not have approved. 'Humble the Congress. Pluck its features. Maul its strength,' was Rajaji's message to the voters before the elections.[114] Rajaji at 83, himself went to campaign across the nation for the Swatantra Party though he did not contest on any seat. He accused Nehru of losing the moral stature abroad that India commanded during Gandhi's days.[115] In previous years, he had also charged Nehru with a lack of good faith and had called him 'a megalomaniac' in public.[116] From the other side of the political divide, Nehru was accusing Rajaji of being 'continually angry' and that his Swatantra Party represented 'an attitude which is so thoroughly and absolutely bad that I find it difficult to imagine that any person with intelligence can accept it.' Nehru went further to suggest that members of the Swatantra Party were reacting to his cooperative farming agenda 'like some wild animals.' He even accused them of having a tendency towards fascism and said that they were superannuated minds who were exhibiting the 'bullock-cart mentality' in the atomic age. Partisan warfare was thus on at full force.[117] However, Congress and Nehru again dominated the national parliament by winning 361 seats whereas Swatantra Party stood third after Communists with 25 seats. Nehru's popularity though declining was still substantially greater than any other public figure in India. No leader in Swatantra Party could match Nehru's appeal. 'Whether we win or not,' Rajaji had declared during the election campaign, 'making the attempt to really oppose is worthwhile.'[118]

Despite the handicaps faced by the Swatantra Party, in state legislatures, it performed well and won 207 seats (second-highest after Congress) from about a thousand and emerged as the leading opposition in some states. For a party only two and a half years old, it was no mean achievement to win seats across all regions of the nation.[119] Because of India's diversity, this feat has not been matched since by an entirely new political party established just a few months before the elections. In the words of Howard Erdman, 'Swatantra, with its distinguished (if generally superannuated) leadership, with one general issue on which it tried to capitalize, with some prospect of financial support, and with an approach to party-building which Morris-Jones has rightly termed "certainly the most flexible and realistically power-oriented" of the rightist parties, was able to rally a wide array of parties, groups, interests, and individuals (many of them erstwhile enemies) to an extent that surpassed earlier efforts…'[120]

The personal relationship between Nehru and Rajaji survived the acrimonious election campaign. Rajaji had been very vocal against nuclear testing and the arms race between the two superpowers. In humanity's cause, Rajaji had been writing to world leaders to exercise restraint. When after a hiatus, the Soviet Union exploded a 50-megaton nuclear bomb in October 1961, Rajaji planned to actively campaign against the move. In 1962, on Rajaji's continual urging Nehru agreed to send him as a representative to the capitals of many Western powers for advocating against nuclear testing and the arms race. Rajaji's arguments were appreciated by all political and religious leaders he called on. The Indian delegation was even advised to send Rajaji as their representative at the U.N. Disarmament Conference in Geneva. However, partisan considerations at home stopped Nehru from taking this further step. He said that 'Rajaji is undoubtedly a person of high ability, and we all have respect and affection for him. But I doubt very much if he will at all suit or fit in the Disarmament Conference at Geneva which consists of senior officials. Also, unfortunately, he disagrees with almost everything in the domestic or international sphere for which some of us stand.'[121]

In October 1962, China attacked India over territorial disputes and came out on top in the ensuing hostilities at the border before unilaterally declaring a ceasefire after a month. Tensions had been brewing between the two nations in the past few years. Rajaji had been cautioning against Chinese designs but Nehru remained under the impression that an armed conflict was beyond realistic expectations. In Rajaji's words, the Chinese armed forces 'outnumbered, outweaponed, outmanoeuvred and slaughtered' Indian soldiers. Indians were dejected. The nation's morale had suffered its biggest blow since Partition. Despite being in the opposition, instead of cashing the opportunity to criticize Nehru, Rajaji now sought to back him. Rajaji understood that even in this time of crisis, only Nehru still commanded people's affection and the capability to infuse fortitude in the national spirit. Hence, Rajaji now concentrated his efforts to back Nehru's leadership for boosting the nation's morale while impinging the need to revise his policies on Nehru. For Rajaji, partisan warfare took a backseat in the nation's larger interests. He variously wrote that 'The Prime Minister is standing up bravely to the reverses we have had to suffer. God bless him and give him strength,' 'Double quick change in policies is called for,' and 'It is necessary to establish friendly relations with Pakistan…We cannot fight on two fronts…[Secondly] we must build friendship and alliances with Western powers.'[122]

With defeat in the conflict, Congress's fortunes began to decline. In mid-1963, it lost two crucial by-elections which made Rajaji write 'The spell is broken. The tide has turned. The head of the government is no longer a god but a replaceable representative of the people.' Rajaji himself helped his party leader Minoo Masani to win one of these elections. At the same time, Rajaji was playing a key role in the Kashmir conflict with Pakistan by advising Kashmiri Leader Sheikh Abdullah with a new formula for settlement between the two nations.

Rajaji had naturally taken to the role of playing an elder statesman in India's cause by becoming an intermediary between Kashmir's aspirations as expressed by Sheikh Abdullah and the Government of India's views as expressed by Nehru. However, before the settlement could be worked out, Nehru was dead. Rajaji and Nehru had known each other closely for more than four decades. They had been friends turned adversaries turned collaborators. They had fired salvos at each other due to being on different sides of the political divide during the past few years. Despite all the criticism in public, their personal relationship had survived the roller coaster ride. Rajaji's eulogy to Nehru bears witness to this fact:

> Eleven years younger than me, eleven times more important for the nation, and eleven hundred times more beloved of the nation, Sri Nehru has suddenly departed from our midst and I remain alive to hear the sad news from Delhi—and bear the shock...I am unable yet to gather my wits. I have been fighting Sri Nehru all these ten years for what I consider faults in public policies. But I knew all along that he alone could get them corrected...A beloved friend is gone, the most civilized person among us all. God save our people.[123]

Rajaji continued sounding the call for a strong opposition against Congress by reminding everyone that 'It may be a nuisance to be continually told that you were wrong, but the tolerance of such a nuisance is of the essence of democracy and, indeed, what distinguishes it from other forms of government.'[124] 'We five' was a phrase Nehru had used in 1949 to refer to Gandhi's senior political team in Congress comprising of himself, Rajendra Prasad, Maulana Azad, Patel, and Rajaji. All except the last were now gone. With Nehru's departure from the political landscape, an opening presented itself for the Swatantra Party. Nehru was succeeded as the head of the government by Lal Bahadur Shastri who valiantly led India during the Indo-Pak war of 1965. However, his sudden and unexpected demise in January 1966 made the Congress Party nervous. The old guard of the Congress Party decided to bring Nehru's daughter Indira Gandhi (no relation with Mohandas Gandhi) as the head of the government. At this time, she was not an articulate leader and was dependent on support from others in the Congress for her survival in politics. Thus, in the elections of 1967, Swatantra Party doubled its tally in the national parliament and emerged as the main opposition party whereas Congress lost more than a hundred seats though it was still able to retain a majority. Additionally, the Swatantra Party also formed the government in Orissa and sent more members of parliament from some states than did Congress.[125]

Two decades after Independence, Congress's absolute monopoly was now over. For the first time, the opposition's voice could not be neglected inside the parliament. Octogenarian Rajaji's efforts had paid off at last. Though the opposition parties suffered a defeat in the next election, it did not take long before the first non-Congress government came to power in 1977. Subsequently, India embarked on a healthy democratic path with a firmly entrenched culture of a strong democratic opposition. Rajaji had the last laugh in the afterlife when many of the economic policies that he had propagated as the main opposition leader were implemented by a Congress government in 1991.

OPPOSITION, n. In politics the party that prevents the Government from running amuck by hamstringing it.
-Ambrose Bierce

The fact that a system of peaceful and legal opposition by political parties is a comparative rarity means that it must be exceedingly difficult to *introduce* such a system, or to *maintain* it, or both.
-Robert Dahl

The above lines were written by Robert Dahl in 1964 when after surveying 113 members of the United Nations, he observed that only 30 of them 'had political systems in which full legal opposition among organized political parties had existed throughout the preceding decade.'[126] Surely, the situation is better now but even old and mature democracies find that maintaining and perfecting a system of political opposition requires continuous efforts by all stakeholders in the democracy. In addition to maintaining, the introduction of political opposition in a democracy is also a challenging task. It requires an active sense of duty on the side of the opposition parties and restraint on the side of the ruling establishment. For both nations, the role of the founding fathers in planting the seed and nurturing the political opposition highlighted in this chapter needs no further commentary. Both republics bear witness to the work done by them, inadvertently or intentionally, in establishing the system of opposition to legitimately express dissent within a democratic setup.

With Jeffersonian Democratic-Republican Party ruling America for twenty-four continuous years, the Hamiltonian Federalist Party gradually faded into oblivion. With only one faction dominant in American politics, the order of the world had come to peace in Jefferson's view. It took adverse circumstances to force Republicans to recognize the merits of the policies of the Federalist Party. Despite virulent opposition to the banks during partisan warfare, President Jefferson understood the need to not disrupt the financial system and thus retained the First Bank of the United States established earlier by Hamilton. He also did not repudiate the Jay Treaty as president and followed Washington's policy of neutrality which he had so much denounced when in opposition. Similarly, after the disastrous War of 1812, President Madison was forced to revise his policies and establish the Second Bank of the United States in 1816 after the charter of the first one had ended in 1811. It was also only after the War of 1812 that Madison realized the importance of strengthening the army and navy after having drastically reduced their size earlier. This policy too had been advocated by the Federalist Party and Hamilton vocally years before the war impinged its need on Madison.

In India too, with Nehru's daughter and the incumbent prime minister, Indira Gandhi aggressively riding on the combined wave of socialism, populism, and nationalism, Swatantra Party disappeared into extinction by the mid-1970s. By the time she imposed the Emergency in 1975 and made efforts to kill dissent by imprisoning the leaders of the opposition, the tradition of political opposition had already taken root in the Indian democracy. Contrasting Indira Gandhi with her father's constructive role in engaging with the opposition, a spectator commented that had Nehru been alive during the Emergency, he would have been in political opposition to her daughter, writing letters to her from jail as he did for so many years while opposing the British.[127] Indian masses decidedly rejected Indira

Gandhi for her authoritarian turn and chose a non-Congress coalition when elections were held in 1977 after the Emergency was lifted. Before his death in 1972, Rajaji had prophesized with full confidence that Swatantra Party's policies were 'bound to become the government's policies and programs, if not now, some years hence.'[128] Two decades hence, when India was facing a disastrous balance of payments problem which triggered an economic crisis in 1991, the same Congress Party that had been catering towards socialism in the past now adopted many of Swatantra's agendas and initiated economic reforms towards the liberalization of India. The process to demolish Permit-license-quota Raj, so much criticized by Rajaji in his life, had inaugurated.

Thus, even when disappearing from the political arena, these two parties played their part in restraining the present-day government during their lives and survived in posterity because their policies were adopted by the ruling party after their demise in the respective nations. However, their lasting contributions were establishing a legitimate democratic system to foment and direct popular dissent and providing an alternative leadership option to the voters. This was crucial at a time when the culture of democratic opposition was not rooted in these two young democracies. In America, the founding fathers' actions led to the formation of political opposition despite their disapproval and dislike for the political parties. In India, in addition to Rajaji, credit must go to Nehru too who understood the value of opposition in a democracy and always engaged with leaders of other political parties inside and outside the parliament to establish a tradition of dissent and debate for the future.

Surveying the American polity today, we see that it has perhaps never been so much polarized since the days of Hamilton-Jefferson's partisan warfare with vicious personal attacks on each other. Every opportunity must be utilized to attack leaders of the other party, every aspect of the opponent's life must be attacked, and every way must be found to emerge triumphantly. Though on the one hand, such cut-throat competition usually ensures the survival of the fittest in the political sense, on the other hand, this same process leads to rarity in bipartisan measures which is a centerpiece of any democracy. Bipartisanship ensures that compromises can be secured smoothly since politics is nothing if not a game of give and take. At a time when facts are increasingly becoming meaningless and opinions are being construed as factual, there seems to be nothing bridging the gap between the supporters of the ruling party and those of the opposition. Feeling entitled to take any position irrespective of facts means that Democrats are becoming much more liberal and Republicans are taking more conservative positions than they did twenty years ago.

This rising polarization in the American polity means that the political opposition is being viewed as an adversary instead of a competitor inside the same system of governance.[129] Professors Steven Levitsky and Daniel Ziblatt have written: 'Democracies work best—and survive longer—where constitutions are reinforced by unwritten democratic norms. Two basic norms have preserved America's checks and balances in ways we have come to take for granted: mutual toleration, or the understanding that competing parties accept one another as legitimate rivals, and forbearance, or the idea that politicians should exercise restraint in deploying their institutional prerogatives.'[130] With the disappearance of the middle class and simultaneous diminution in Americans' faith in the government as has been happening in the past few years, the acrimonious political scene today doesn't inspire Americans either. The supporters of each side plainly refuse to engage with those of the other. Continuous and free-flowing dialogue between divergent political ideologies has come to a full stop since each side identifies leaders of the other with derision and contempt.

The same script is being written in the Indian polity today which is becoming increasingly loud and vitriolic while elections are being fought not on the basis of policies but rather personalities. For most of the period since India's Independence, the Congress Party dominated the nation electorally but there had always been stalwart leaders in the opposition who could mount dissent against the ruling government. Today, for the first time in more than seven decades, the opposition is devoid of leaders with indubitable moral standing and Pan-Indian presence. This is chiefly because most of the opposition political parties in India have descended to become family fiefdoms and no meritocratic structure now exists in them for young leaders to rise. Gandhi's and Nehru's Congress leads the way in this phenomenon which until recently had a fifth-generation president of the Party. It is amusing to witness that Communist-parties which were derided by Nehru and Rajaji because of their questionable adherence to the Indian Constitution are the only ones today with a semblance of maintaining inner-party democratic structures. While the opposition is fragmented and subservient to feudal interests linked with the fortunes of particular families, the ruling establishment constantly innovates new ways of decimating the opposition by any means judged solely by their efficacy. As a result, the opposition's voice is mute today, it goes unheard and unheeded. Already, many of the government's policies have started to go unopposed in the parliament. The opposition finds itself helpless in fulfilling its role of hamstringing the ruling government to prevent it from running amok. While stalwarts like Nehru and Rajaji played their part very well in introducing the system of legitimate opposition in our democracy, maintaining the same appears to be a challenge today.

The political institutions of governance and opposition in these democracies have been in an unstable equilibrium which has allowed them to adapt to fast-changing circumstances. The rise of polarizing leaders with fanatic supporters in these democracies has given way to a new era where personality-centered politics has taken the center stage—thus endangering the equilibrium. It is against this very phenomenon that in his final speech in the Constitutional Assembly, quoting John Stuart Mill, Ambedkar warned his countrymen to not 'lay their liberties at the feet of even a great man, or to trust him with powers which enable him to subvert their institutions,' and further stated that 'Bhakti in religion may be a road to the salvation of the soul. But in politics, Bhakti or hero-worship is a sure road to degradation and to eventual dictatorship.'[131] A strong opposition being antithetical to the phenomenon of hero-worship does not let the nation descend towards rule by one or a few.

The political corridors and legislatures in both Washington and New Delhi share two features: loudness and complexity. Both of these democracies are ornery vocal and public participation in expressing dissent is a quality which they treasure. Despite recent negative trends in political participation discussed above, various democratic institutions established by the two founding generations remain strong. As Nico Slate writes, 'both India and the United States…despite their many problems can claim with good reason to be bulwarks of democracy. Yet the very achievements of democracy, from regular elections to an independent judiciary to a vibrant press, can breed complacency by obscuring the persistence of inequality and oppression.'[132]

One might add that this is exactly where the role of opposition comes into play. It is the duty of the opposition to be vocal about the problems and aspirations of the masses while mounting protests against the ruling government's oppression. One thing is for sure: as long as the majority groupings in these two democracies will continue to appreciate the need for legitimate opposition, democracy will thrive. After all, without effective opposition, the institution of governance that we recognize as Democracy is as good as Majoritarianism in which there are no checks and balances to contain the ruling party's excesses. As a timeless line from the Bollywood movie *Maqbool* (an adaption of Shakespeare's *Macbeth*) reminds us: Its need being paramount, the balance of power must always be maintained in the world; Fear of water must be ever-present for the titanic force of fire [translation mine].

---

[1] From Thomas Jefferson to Francis Hopkinson, 13 March 1789, *The Works of Thomas Jefferson*, Federal Edition (New York and London, G.P. Putnam's Sons, 1904-5), Vol. 5, p. 456 (Hereafter, referred to as Jefferson Papers).

[2] George Washington, To the PEOPLE of the UNITED STATES, 19 September 1796, *The Papers of George Washington*, Colonial Series, ed. W. W. Abbot. Charlottesville: University Press of Virginia, 1983, pp. 118–119 (Hereafter, referred to as Washington Papers).

[3] From John Adams to Jonathan Jackson, 2 October 1780, *The Adams Papers*, Papers of John Adams, vol. 10, July 1780 – December 1780, ed. Gregg L. Lint and Richard Alan Ryerson. Cambridge, MA: Harvard University Press, 1996, pp. 192–193

[4] Alexander Hamilton, Federalist No. 1: General Introduction, *The Federalist Papers* (New York: Dover Publications, Dover Thrift Edition, 2014), p. 4

[5] Ron Chernow, *Alexander Hamilton* (Penguin Books, 2004), pp. 11-19

[6] Alexander Hamilton to Edward Stevens, 11 Nov 1769, *Selected Works of Alexander Hamilton* (San Diego: World Cloud Classics, 2018), p. 1

[7] Ron Chernow, *Alexander Hamilton* (Penguin Books, 2004), pp. 36-37

[8] Alexander Hamilton, Farmer Refuted, 5 February 1775, *The Works of Alexander Hamilton*, ed. Henry Cabot Lodge (Federal Edition) (New York: G.P. Putnam's Sons, 1904), Vol. 1, p. 166 (Hereafter, referred to as Hamilton Papers).

[9] Philip Stadter, Alexander Hamilton's Notes on Plutarch in His Pay Book, *The Review of Politics*, 2011, vol. 73(2), pp. 199-217.
[10] Alexander Hamilton, Federalist No. 72: The Same Subject Continued and Re-eligibility of the Executive Considered, *The Federalist Papers* (New York: Dover Publications, Dover Thrift Edition, 2014), p. 354
[11] Gordon S. Wood, *Revolutionary Characters: What Made the Founders Different* (Penguin Books, 2006), p. 139
[12] Douglass Adair, *Fame and the Founding Fathers* (New York: W.W. Norton and Company, 1974), p. 13
[13] From Alexander Hamilton to James A. Bayard, 16 January 1801, Hamilton Papers, vol. 10, p. 417
[14] Alexander Hamilton, Philo Camillus No. III, 12 August 1795, *The Papers of Alexander Hamilton*, vol. 19, July 1795 – December 1795, ed. Harold C. Syrett. New York: Columbia University Press, 1973, pp. 124–134.
[15] Ron Chernow, *Alexander Hamilton* (Penguin Books, 2004), pp. 4-5
[16] John Ferling, *Jefferson and Hamilton: The Rivalry that Forged a Nation* (New York: Bloomsbury Press, 2018), pp. 204-205
[17] Joseph J. Ellis, *Founding Brothers: The Revolutionary Generation* (New York: Vintage Books, 2002), p. 65
[18] Ibid., pp. 71-72
[19] Thomas Jefferson, The Assumption, February 1793, Jefferson Papers, vol. 7, pp. 224-226
[20] John Ferling, *Jefferson and Hamilton: The Rivalry that Forged a Nation* (New York: Bloomsbury Press, 2018), pp. 210-211
[21] Joseph J. Ellis, *Founding Brothers: The Revolutionary Generation* (New York: Vintage Books, 2002), pp. 75-80
[22] John Ferling, *Jefferson and Hamilton: The Rivalry that Forged a Nation* (New York: Bloomsbury Press, 2018), pp. 213-215
[23] Ron Chernow, *Alexander Hamilton* (Penguin Books, 2004), p. 346
[24] John Ferling, *Jefferson and Hamilton: The Rivalry that Forged a Nation* (New York: Bloomsbury Press, 2018), p. 226
[25] Ibid., pp. 220-221
[26] Ron Chernow, *Alexander Hamilton* (Penguin Books, 2004), p. 322
[27] John Ferling, *Jefferson and Hamilton: The Rivalry that Forged a Nation* (New York: Bloomsbury Press, 2018), pp. 222-223
[28] Claude G. Bowers, *Jefferson and Hamilton: A Classic Study of America's Greatest Antagonists* (The Riverside Press Cambridge, Sentry Edition, 1966), pp. 171-172
[29] Ibid., pp. 188-190
[30] Ron Chernow, *Alexander Hamilton* (Penguin Books, 2004), pp. 426-427

[31] Ibid., pp. 432-433
[32] Paul Johnson, *A History of the American People* (Harper Perennial, 1997), p. 224

[33] Gordon S. Wood, *Friends Divided: John Adams and Thomas Jefferson* (New York: Penguin Press, 2017), p. 274
[34] Paul Johnson, *A History of the American People* (Harper Perennial, 1997), pp. 224-225
[35] John Ferling, *Jefferson and Hamilton: The Rivalry that Forged a Nation* (New York: Bloomsbury Press, 2018), p. 249
[36] Gordon S. Wood, *Friends Divided: John Adams and Thomas Jefferson* (New York: Penguin Press, 2017), p. 274
[37] Joseph J. Ellis, *His Excellency: George Washington* (New York: Vintage Books, 2004), p. 226
[38] Jerald A. Combs, *The Jay Treaty: Political Battleground of the Founding Fathers* (University of California Press, 1970), p. 120
[39] Joseph J. Ellis, *His Excellency: George Washington* (New York: Vintage Books, 2004), pp. 227-228
[40] Ron Chernow, *Alexander Hamilton* (Penguin Books, 2004), p. 486
[41] Claude G. Bowers, *Jefferson and Hamilton: A Classic Study of America's Greatest Antagonists* (The Riverside Press Cambridge, Sentry Edition, 1966), pp. 277, 284
[42] Ron Chernow, *Alexander Hamilton* (Penguin Books, 2004), pp. 496-497
[43] Gordon S. Wood, *Revolutionary Characters: What Made the Founders Different* (Penguin Books, 2006), p. 58
[44] Joseph J. Ellis, *Founding Brothers: The Revolutionary Generation* (New York: Vintage Books, 2002), p. 138
[45] George C. Herring, *From Colony to Superpower: U.S. Foreign Relations Since 1776* (Oxford University Press, 2008), p. 81
[46] Gordon S. Wood, *Revolutionary Characters: What Made the Founders Different* (Penguin Books, 2006), p. 266
[47] David McCullough, *John Adams* (New York: Simon and Schuster, 2001), pp. 458-459
[48] Ibid., p. 463
[49] John Ferling, *John Adams: A Life* (New York: Henry Holt and Company, 2010), p. 333
[50] John W. Oliver, *Thomas Jefferson—Scientist, The Scientific Monthly,* Vol. 56, No. 5 (May, 1943), pp. 460-467
[51] John Ferling, *Jefferson and Hamilton: The Rivalry that Forged a Nation* (New York: Bloomsbury Press, 2018), pp. 292-293
[52] David McCullough, *John Adams* (New York: Simon and Schuster, 2001), p. 518
[53] Ibid., p. 505
[54] Gordon S. Wood, *Friends Divided: John Adams and Thomas Jefferson* (New York: Penguin Press, 2017), p. 314

[55] David McCullough, *John Adams* (New York: Simon and Schuster, 2001), pp. 566-567

[56] Ron Chernow, *Alexander Hamilton* (Penguin Books, 2004), pp. 618-622

[57] Jawaharlal Nehru, *Selected Works of Jawaharlal Nehru*, Series One, Volume 8, The Rashtrapati by Chanakya, pp. 520-523

[58] Jawaharlal Nehru, *An Autobiography* (Penguin Books, 2004), p. 628

[59] Michael Brecher, *Nehru: A Political Biography* (Boston: Beacon Press, 1962 Abridged Edition), pp. 1-2

[60] Jawaharlal Nehru, *Glimpses of World History* (Penguin Books, 2004), p. 1105

[61] A. K. Damodaran, *Jawaharlal Nehru: A Communicator and Democratic Leader* (New Delhi: Radiant Publishers, 1997), p. 14

[62] Jawaharlal Nehru, *Glimpses of World History* (Penguin Books, 2004), p. 1104

[63] Rajendra Prasad's Foreword to *A Study of Nehru*, Edited by Rafiq Zakaria (A Times of India Publication, 1959), p. v

[64] Walter Crocker, *Nehru: A Contemporary's Estimate* (London: George Allen & Unwin Ltd, 1966), pp. 136-138

[65] Michael Brecher, *Nehru: A Political Biography* (Boston: Beacon Press, 1962 Abridged Edition), p. 2

[66] Jawaharlal Nehru, *An Autobiography* (Penguin Books, 2004), p. 616

[67] Michael Brecher, *Nehru: A Political Biography* (Boston: Beacon Press, 1962 Abridged Edition), pp. 3-4

[68] Escott Reid, *Nehru: An Assessment in 1957*, International Journal, vol. 19, no. 3, 1964, pp. 279–291

[69] R. K. Laxman as quoted in Ramachandra Guha, *India after Gandhi: The History of the World's Largest Democracy* (Picador India, 2008), p. 281

[70] Vasanthi Srinivasan, *Gandhi's Conscience Keeper: C. Rajagopalachari and Indian Politics* (Permanent Black, 2018 edition; First published in 2009), p. 186

[71] Ramachandra Guha, *The Last Liberal and Other Essays* (Permanent Black, 2004), p. 36

[72] Rajmohan Gandhi, *Rajaji: A Life* (Penguin Books, 1997), pp. 4-5

[73] Ibid., pp. 17-18

[74] Ibid., p. ix

[75] *The Collected Works of Mahatma Gandhi (CWMG)*, Vol. 55: April 23, 1933 - September 15, 1933, His Will be Done, 6 May 1933, p. 120

[76] The relationship between Gandhi and Rajaji has been dealt with in detail in B. K. Ahluwalia and Shashi Ahluwalia, *Rajaji and Gandhi* (New Delhi: Allora Publications, 1978)

[77] Rajmohan Gandhi, *Rajaji: A Life* (Penguin Books, 1997), p. 229

[78] B. K. Ahluwalia and Shashi Ahluwalia, *Rajaji and Gandhi* (New Delhi: Allora Publications, 1978), p. 172

[79] Rajmohan Gandhi, *Rajaji: A Life* (Penguin Books, 1997), p. x

[80] Ramachandra Guha, *The Last Liberal and Other Essays* (Permanent Black, 2004), p. 36

[81] K. T. Narasimhachar, *C. Rajagopalachari: His Life and Mind* (New Delhi: Heritage Publishers, 1978), p. 6

[82] Vasanthi Srinivasan, *Gandhi's Conscience Keeper: C. Rajagopalachari and Indian Politics* (Permanent Black, 2018 edition; First published in 2009), pp. 191-193

[83] Ibid., pp. 13, 244

[84] Monica Felton, *I meet Rajaji* (London: Macmillan and Co Ltd, 1962), p. 48

[85] Rajmohan Gandhi, *Rajaji: A Life* (Penguin Books, 1997), p. ix

[86] Monica Felton, *I meet Rajaji* (London: Macmillan and Co Ltd, 1962), p. 52

[87] Jonathon Aitken, *Nixon: A Life* (Regnery Publishing, 2015), p. 269

[88] B. K. Ahluwalia, *Facets of Rajaji* (New Delhi: Newman Group of Publishers, 1978), p. 48

[89] B. Shiva Rao, *India's Freedom Movement: Some Notable Figures* (Orient Longman, 1972), pp. 243-244

[90] J. B. Kripalani, *My Times: An Autobiography* (New Delhi: Rupa co., 2004), p. 900

[91] The Swatantra Party, *The Economic Weekly*, Special Number July 1959

[92] C. Rajagopalachari, published in *Swarajya* on 14 July 1956, *Satyam Eva Jayate* (Madras: Bharatan Publications), vol. 1, p. 1

[93] C. Rajagopalachari, published in *Swarajya* on 29 June 1957, *Satyam Eva Jayate* (Madras: Bharatan Publications), vol. 1, p. 58

[94] C. Rajagopalachari, published in *Swarajya* on 17 August 1957, *Satyam Eva Jayate* (Madras: Bharatan Publications), vol. 1, pp. 71-72

[95] Vasanthi Srinivasan, *Gandhi's Conscience Keeper: C. Rajagopalachari and Indian Politics* (Permanent Black, 2018 edition; First published in 2009), p. 48

[96] C. Rajagopalachari, published in *Swarajya* on 10 May 1958, *Satyam Eva Jayate* (Madras: Bharatan Publications), vol. 1, p. 151

[97] C. Rajagopalachari, *Rajaji Reader: Selections from Writings of C. Rajagopalachari* (Madras: Vyasa Publications, 1980), p. 111

[98] Rajmohan Gandhi, *Rajaji: A Life* (Penguin Books, 1997), p. 366

[99] Ibid., pp. 371-372

[100] Ibid., pp. 373-377

[101] Ibid., pp. 373, 377

[102] Sarvepalli Gopal, *Jawaharlal Nehru—A Biography* (Oxford University Press, 2015 Edition), Vol. 3, p. 120

[103] A. K. Damodaran, *Jawaharlal Nehru: A Communicator and Democratic Leader* (New Delhi: Radiant Publishers, 1997), p. 333

[104] H. R. Pasricha, *The Swatantra Party: Victory in Defeat* (The Rajaji Foundation, 2002), p. 34

[105] Ibid., pp. 95-97

[106] Rajmohan Gandhi, *Rajaji: A Life* (Penguin Books, 1997), p. 382

[107] Ramachandra Guha, *India after Gandhi: The History of the World's Largest Democracy* (Picador India, 2008), p. 298
[108] Rajmohan Gandhi, *Rajaji: A Life* (Penguin Books, 1997), p. 384
[109] Walter Crocker, *Nehru: A Contemporary's Estimate* (London: George Allen & Unwin Ltd, 1966), pp. 119-123
[110] C. Rajagopalachari, *Swarajya*, 27 Dec 1961
[111] Sarvepalli Gopal, *Jawaharlal Nehru—A Biography* (Oxford University Press, 2015 Edition), Vol. 3, p. 199
[112] John Keay, *India: A History* (New York: Grove Press, 2010 reprint), p. 534
[113] Rajmohan Gandhi, *Rajaji: A Life* (Penguin Books, 1997), p. 389
[114] Ibid., p. 390
[115] C. Rajagopalachari, *Rajaji Reader: Selections from Writings of C. Rajagopalachari* (Madras: Vyasa Publications, 1980), p. 132
[116] Sarvepalli Gopal, *Jawaharlal Nehru—A Biography* (Oxford University Press, 2015 Edition), Vol. 3, pp. 119-120
[117] Ibid., p. 183
[118] Quoted in *Time* (Asia Edition), Feb. 2, 1962, p. 18.
[119] Rajmohan Gandhi, *Rajaji: A Life* (Penguin Books, 1997), pp. 390-391
[120] Howard L. Erdman, *The Swatantra Party and Indian Conservatism* (Cambridge University Press, 1967), p. 246
[121] Jawaharlal Nehru to B. Shiva Rao, Quoted in Ramachandra Guha, *The Last Liberal and Other Essays* (Permanent Black, 2004), p. 52
[122] Rajmohan Gandhi, *Rajaji: A Life* (Penguin Books, 1997), pp. 401-402
[123] Ibid., pp. 404-407
[124] Vasanthi Srinivasan, *Gandhi's Conscience Keeper: C. Rajagopalachari and Indian Politics* (Permanent Black, 2018 edition; First published in 2009), p. 38
[125] Rajmohan Gandhi, *Rajaji: A Life* (Penguin Books, 1997), pp. 408, 417
[126] Preface by Robert Alan Dahl, *Political Oppositions in Western Democracies* (Yale University Press, 1966), p. xiii
[127] A. M. Rosenthal, Father and Daughter: A Remembrance, *New York Times*, 1 November 1984
[128] C. Rajagopalachari, *Swarajya*, 1 May 1971
[129] *Political Polarization in the American Public*, Pew Research Center, 12 June 2014
[130] Steven Levitsky and Daniel Ziblatt, *How Democracies Die* (New York: Broadway Books, 2018), pp. 8-9
[131] Ambedkar in the Constituent Assembly, 25 November 1949, *Constituent Assembly Debates: Official Report* (reprint New Delhi: Lok Sabha Secretariat, 2014), Vol. XI, p. 979
[132] Nico Slate, *Lord Cornwallis Is Dead: The Struggle for Democracy in the United States and India* (Harvard University Press, 2019), p. 5

4. EQUALITY

"We hold these truths to be self-evident, that all men are created equal, that they are endowed by their Creator with certain unalienable Rights, that among these are Life, Liberty and the pursuit of Happiness," thus proclaimed the second sentence of the American Declaration of Independence adopted by the Second Continental Congress on 4 July 1776. These thirty-five words constituting the most popular and idealistic phrase in the history of American prose are the hallmark of egalitarianism. In a document whose existence is itself defined by the desire for freedom, the mention of equality between human beings has received more attention by posterity than the parts in which the subjects of the British Empire explained their grievances against the King to present a legitimate case for Independence. The document articulated these "truths" as being "self-evident." To be "self-evident" is to be obvious or apparent or needing no further explanation, justification, commentary. To be "self-evident" is to be there, by the virtue of being ubiquitous, existing since genesis and surviving until doomsday. To be "self-evident" is to be indisputable, unquestionable, undebatable, period.[1]

And so, can we dare even question the phrase "all men are created equal" before the wisdom of the founding fathers? Yet, we see so much inequality around us arising from the circumstances of birth, upbringing, and surroundings that it is commonplace to wonder what the founding fathers meant when they designated "all men are created equal" as a "self-evident" truth. Perhaps we may find refuge from this dilemma in the company of the most outspoken, curmudgeonly, grudging, haughty, conscientious, and candid founding father. Years after the Declaration of Independence was adopted, John Adams, one of the major figures of the American Revolution who also served on the committee which drafted the Declaration, wrote: 'That all men are born to equal rights is true…But to teach that all men are born with equal powers and faculties, to equal influence in society, to equal property and advantages through life, is as gross a fraud, as glaring an imposition on the credulity of the people, as ever was practiced by monks, by Devils, by Brahmins, by priests of the immortal Lama, or by the self-styled philosophers of the French revolution.'[2] He further added that 'We [Americans] may boast that we are one, the chosen people, and we may even thank God that we are not like other men, but, after all, it would be but flattery, delusion, the self-deceit of the Pharisee.'[3]

Ah! So at least perhaps we now know what the phrase "all men are created equal" does not mean. It does not mean to be born with "equal powers and faculties," "equal influence in society," or "equal property and advantages through life." For now, let us work with this much information. By referring to "powers," "faculties," "influence," "property," and "advantages," Adams is drawing our attention to the contrast between the distinguished and the commonalty. But, the Continental Congress, Constitution, and Americans, all had rejected the idea of aristocracy, hereditary titles, and statutory privileges.[4] Yet, here was Adams, at a time when other founding fathers were worried about the possibility of "the one" i.e. the rise of a monarch, this cantankerous founding father who was speaking harsh truths was warning his countrymen about "the few": 'Wherever we have seen a territory somewhat larger, arts and sciences more cultivated, commerce flourishing, or even agriculture improved to any great degree, an aristocracy has risen up in a course of time, consisting of a few rich and honorable families, who have united with each other against both the people and the first magistrate…'[5] The fear of inequality in the American society by the rise of aristocracy was then the chief force behind Adams's rejection of the "self-evident" truths in the Declaration and it proved to be prophetic. As Joseph Ellis writes, 'Adams has become relevant for our time because he is the only prominent founder who anticipated the emergence of an embedded version of economic inequality in American society, a prophecy that seemed so bizarre and thoroughly un-American to most of his contemporaries that it served for the charge that he had obviously lost his mind.'[6]

Arguably, nobody except George Washington worked as much or as hard to make reality the dream of American Independence than John Adams. Born on 30 October 1735 in Braintree, Massachusetts,

Adams was raised in a modest traditional New England household. Adams's forefathers had migrated from England as a part of the great Puritan migration while his father served as a deacon in the local church and earned a livelihood through farming and shoemaking. Right from his childhood, Adams imbibed the Puritan virtues of hard work and frugality. After receiving initial education in Braintree, Adams enrolled in Harvard College where he discovered a love for books and 'read Cicero, Tacitus and others of his Roman heroes in Latin, and Plato and Thucydides in the original Greek, which he considered the supreme language.'[7] Instead of becoming a minister in the footsteps of his father, Adams decided to pursue law as a profession. During his life, Adams published many works on constitutionalism and political theory, prominent among which were *Thoughts on Government* and *Defence of the Constitutions*. All his life, Adams opposed slavery, never owned a slave, or utilized slave labor as a principle. Fair and partially bald, with blue eyes and brown hair, short and rotund, in his own words, Adams's constitution was 'a glass bubble' beset with various illnesses and pains throughout his life.[8]

Adams's first brush with popularity came after the infamous Boston Massacre when he defended the British soldiers who were accused of killing several people while being harassed by an unruly mob. Going against the prevailing nationalistic feeling, Adams stayed true to his sense of integrity and justice, and won an acquittal for six of his clients. Subsequently, the Boston Tea Party converted him to take up the revolutionary cause and he was elected to the First Continental Congress in 1774. Shielding for some time beneath the reputation of his elder cousin and revolutionary firebrand, Samuel Adams, John Adams rose quickly as one of the leading figures in Congress. John Adams's fingerprints were then imprinted on every major event: nomination of George Washington as the commander-in-chief, drafting the olive branch petition to King George III, drafting the Declaration of Independence, and participation in the Staten Island Peace Conference. Historian John Ferling writes, 'By the fall of 1775 no one in Congress labored more ardently than Adams to hasten the day when America would be separate from Great Britain.'[9]

Adams served on many crucial committees (sitting on as many as ninety committees while chairing twenty-five of them) during his time in Congress and was generally acknowledged to be 'the first man in the House.'[10] It was Adams who delegated the task of chiefly writing the Declaration of Independence to his junior colleague, Thomas Jefferson since as Adams explained, being Virginian (support of the largest state being absolutely necessary) was enough of a reason.[11] Coming out in Congress as the most forceful advocate for declaring Independence, Adams made a powerful speech which in Jefferson's words 'moved us from our seats,' while another delegate described Adams as "the Atlas" of the hour, 'the man to whom the country is most indebted for the great measure of independency.' While Washington was fighting the British on the battlefield, Adams was single-mindedly pursuing the aim of converting the reluctant delegates of the Continental Congress into accepting Independence as their goal.[12]

After the Declaration of Independence, Adams was chosen to serve as a commissioner to France alongside Benjamin Franklin to negotiate an alliance with the French. After returning back to America, he became a member of the Massachusetts Convention in which role he became the principal author of the Massachusetts Constitution in 1779. It was the first constitution in the world to be created by a convention rather than the legislative body, to be ratified by the people, to have a bicameral legislature, and finally, it remains the oldest written constitution of the world that is in continuous effect. Adams once proudly remarked that 'I made the Constitution for Massachusetts, which finally made the Constitution of the United States.'[13]

In 1780, Adams co-founded the American Academy of Arts and Sciences which emerged as one of the most prestigious honorary societies and an acclaimed institution in policy research. After a short stay, Adams again proceeded to Europe to become the first United States Minister to the Dutch Republic in which role he was instrumental in negotiating much-needed loans from the Dutch. He also served as the American commissioner on the committee to negotiate the war-ending treaty which came to be known as the Treaty of Paris. During negotiations for the treaty, Adams's stubbornness came in handy to balance Franklin's accommodating nature in achieving favorable terms for America. As Jefferson observed: 'He [Adams] hates Franklin, he hates [John] Jay, he hates the French, he hates the English. To whom will he adhere?' yet Jefferson added further that the same features would make Adams apt for negotiations since his 'dislike of all parties, and all men, by balancing his prejudices may give the same fair play to his reason as would a general benevolence of temper.'[14]

Subsequently, Adams served as the first United States Minister to the United Kingdom in the crucial phase after the American victory in the Revolutionary War. Unfortunately, engaged in diplomatic services abroad, Adams missed capitalizing his legal erudition and vast knowledge of political theory during the drafting of the American Constitution. After returning back to America, Adams received the second-highest number of votes (beating others by a large margin) after George Washington in the presidential election and served as the Vice President under President Washington for eight years—a role in which he found himself alienated from decision-making which made him remark that 'my Country has in its Wisdom contrived for me, the most insignificant Office that ever the Invention of Man contrived or his Imagination conceived.'[15]

Finally, Adams was rewarded for his service to the nation when he succeeded Washington as the Second President of the United States to serve for one term between 1797-1801 in which his biggest achievement was to avert a war with France which would have been disastrous for the young nation (as we read in the previous chapter). The final act of his presidency which also created much controversy since he had already lost the election by then was to appoint John Marshall as the Chief Justice of the United States who went on to become the longest-serving as well as one the most influential justices in American history, to the consternation of Republicans since Marshall was a leading Federalist.

No portrait of John Adams can be complete without mentioning his beloved wife, Abigail, 'my best, dearest, worthiest, wisest friend in this world...'[16] Nearly twelve hundred letters between them survive today in which both have outpoured their feelings in a very candid and transparent manner, uncharacteristic of any other founding father. Their correspondence makes the case for the most significant correspondence between any influential couple in American history. In many ways, Abigail remained John's adviser and best friend while also keeping his excesses and ambitions in check. 'Vanity, I am sensible, is my cardinal Vice and cardinal Folly,' John Adams had written.[17] Unable to possess Washington's "gift of silence" which he much admired, Adams outpoured all his feelings in his writings and letters to Abigail and others. As he wrote in old age, 'Have mercy on me Posterity, if you should ever see any of my Letters.'[18]

Ron Chernow writes that 'One can summon up an army of adjectives for John Adams—crotchety, opinionated, endearing, temperamental, frank, erudite, outspoken, generous, eccentric, restless, petty, choleric, philosophical, plucky, quirky, pugnacious, fanciful, stubborn, and whimsical—and scarcely exhaust the possibilities.' For the most part of the American history, John Adams's legacy has been characterized by Benjamin Franklin's description of his colleague: 'He [John Adams] means well for his Country, is always an honest man, often a wise one, but sometimes, and in some things, absolutely out of his senses.'[19]

Even if one would count the three most prominent revolutionaries who midwived the birth of the American Republic, John Adams will surely be among them. Yet, there is no Adams Monument on the National Mall and no Adams's depiction on any currency note. Having succeeded Washington as president, Adams could not fill the shoes of his predecessor and his excessive verbal outpourings did not help either in cementing a legacy around his contributions to the American founding. The Alien and Sedition Acts instituted under him during the Quasi-War with France (which we saw in the previous chapter) further marred his legacy since he has ever been disgraced as the president who crushed the freedom of speech. Furthermore, due to the popularization of many excerpts of his writings and speeches in which he feared the tyranny of the majority, he has been decried as a monarchist. His excessive cantankerousness did not help either. He remained ever-fearful of how posterity will treat him and felt that he would be underappreciated (which turned out to be true). This further embittered him towards his colleagues whom he viewed as his competitors. As he wrote to a friend after Franklin passed away: 'The essence of the whole [American Revolution] will be that Dr. Franklin's electrical rod smote the earth and out sprung General Washington. That Franklin electrified him with his rod and thence forward these two conducted all the policy, negotiation, legislation, and war.'[20]

After retiring from politics, Adams lived a quiet life among his books and farm. In old age, Adams and Jefferson started corresponding with each other again after many years of mutual resentment due to the partisan struggles that we discussed in the previous chapter. Their letters which discuss a wide range of topics have achieved the paramount place in the history of American correspondence. These letters discuss the significance of the American Revolution from their differing perspectives, the likelihood of the evolution of other nations in the world based on the American principles of republicanism, slavery, and history of the world. They provide a very personal—and unparalleled—perspective of American founding as viewed by these two major founding fathers. The other significant highlight of Adams's retirement came in 1825 when his son John Quincy Adams was elected as the sixth president of the United States. Adams, the proud father, had worked very hard in early life to rise from his humble beginnings, worked even harder to establish America as an independent nation, and it was heartwarming for him to see his son become the president. Famously, dying on the fiftieth anniversary of Independence, not knowing that his dear friend turned political adversary turned pen pal had died only a few hours ago, his last words were 'Thomas Jefferson survives.' However, such has been the rendezvous with legacy for John Adams and Thomas Jefferson.[21]

A story goes that while coming out of the Pennsylvania State House after the Constitutional Convention had adjourned, Benjamin Franklin was asked by a socialite Philadelphia woman Elizabeth Powel: 'Well, Doctor, what have we got a republic or a monarchy?' to which Franklin replied: 'A republic, if you can keep it.'[22] The Constitution drafted by delegates at the Constitutional Convention had made provisions against the recognition of hereditary monarchy, and aristocracy while also abolishing titles of nobility. The draft Constitution had made no mention of social and economic classes. It had clearly stated that "No Title of Nobility shall be granted by the United States." Thus, Franklin was hopeful that as long as the current system of checks and balances would continue, the Constitution would ensure that America would be a republic. At the time, the lifestyle of elite Americans was still modest compared to the magnificence of the European aristocracy. The extreme difference in lifestyle between rich and poor in Europe was absent in America at the time.[23] This meant that Americans, in general, and founding fathers, in particular, were not ready to acknowledge the possibility of the rise of nobility or class distinctions. They were more concerned with the descent of the republic into monarchy. Around the world, most of the nations were dominated by "the one" i.e. a monarch while in many "the few" i.e. aristocracy called the shots behind the scenes. However, the possibility of the rise of "the few" in America did not cross the minds of most of the founding fathers.

The Constitution's written word was enough for Hamilton to declare that the rise of an aristocracy in America could not happen and that it was delusional to consider the ruling elite as nobility. This would prove to be ironical in just a few decades when Hamilton's financial plan would combine with the forces of the Industrial Revolution to usher America into the so-called "Gilded Age" of very high inequality of wealth. When Anti-Federalists were attacking the draft Constitution during the ratification process for the possibility of the rise of an aristocracy based on wealth, Hamilton retorted: 'This description, I presume to say, is ridiculous. The image is a phantom. Does the new government render a rich man more eligible than a poor one? No.'[24] He further argued that since the extreme difference in wealth was absent in America, 'While property continues to be pretty equally divided, and a considerable share of information pervades the community; the tendency of the people's suffrages will be to elevate merit even from obscurity.'[25] In the same vein, Madison too declared that any elite class in America might exist at the periphery as a nuisance but it could not threaten the republic: 'It may clog the administration, it may convulse the society; but it will be unable to execute and mask its violence under the forms of the Constitution.'[26] Madison was the "Father of the Constitution" and Hamilton had played a key role in calling the Constitutional Convention as well as ratification of the Constitution in New York. Both at the time labored for a strong Federal government and self-rule by citizens towards the creation of the American Republic. These credentials if nothing else made their words carry weight. Yet not everybody agreed.[27]

John Adams had initially been highly idealistic about America's future albeit with preconditions. In beautiful prose, he had written earlier that 'America was destined by Providence for the Theatre, on which Man was to make his true figure, on which science, Virtue, Liberty, Happiness and Glory were to exist in Peace.' He had high hopes from the American Revolution which in 1776 he expected to be 'an Astonishment to vulgar Minds all over the World, in this and in future Generation.' At the same time, unlike no other founding father, Adams also expressed doubts and misgivings about the future. He warned his countrymen that 'public Virtue is the only Foundation of Republics' without which no republican government could last. Without public virtue, he believed that Americans would just be exchanging one kind of tyrants for the other.[28]

America of the founding fathers' time was exceptionally egalitarian when it came to economic equality as compared to Europe. The ready availability of land in the West ensured that anybody willing to work hard could very soon own land and in time acquire a large estate. Extreme riches and poverty such as those in Europe were absent in America. This feature struck Europeans visiting America as well as Americans like John Adams when they ventured to Europe. As per an estimate, the richest American merchants were worth around £25,000 to £50,000 whereas the wealthiest merchants in London were worth £200,000 to £800,000. This meant that southern planters like Washington and Jefferson who lived in "palatial" homes and ran large plantations were only a trifle when compared to their British counterparts. The top 1 percent of Americans at the time owned only 8.5 percent of the national income. Westward expansion was continuing at such a fast pace that it was digesting hundreds of thousands of immigrants every year. While in Europe about 60 percent of the population held no property at all of any sort, in America two-thirds of the white population owned land and those who did not were usually in a state of transition after having just arrived in America.[29] It was the ready availability of land which made Jefferson propose that any unemployed person should be allowed to settle on uncultivated land and every man not having fifty acres of property must be given it by the government. Reliance on agriculture meant that most Americans were small landowners and farmers forming the backbone of a significant middle-class whose existence safeguarded the stability of the government.[30] Adams too advocated for redistribution of public lands to the landless for strengthening the middle-class while Hamilton had explicitly stated that only a strong middle-class could stimulate the economy and the businesses by becoming their chief consumers.[31]

Despite such exemplary conditions of economic equality, now serving across the Atlantic in London as the first United States Minister to the United Kingdom, John Adams was not convinced with the arguments presented by Hamilton and Madison regarding the impossibility of an American aristocracy in the future. How could the Constitution thwart the rise of an aristocracy based on wealth, beauty, or birth just by abolishing its formal acknowledgment through titles and other paraphernalia associated with it? Adams considered it to be naiveté to assume that no aristocracy could rise in America because its formal acknowledgment had been forbidden. Thus, eighteen months before Hamilton made the above speech, Adams had already started to express himself by working on his monumental three-volume *Defence of the Constitutions of Government of the United States of America*. Knowing that he is writing against the current philosophical current in America, Adams foresaw the reaction to the work he had just commenced. 'Popularity was never my mistress, nor was I ever, or shall I ever be a popular man,' wrote Adams to a friend in America. He further expressed that this book will make him unpopular but 'one thing I know, a man must be sensible of the errors of the people, and upon his guard against them, and must run the risk of their displeasure sometimes, or he will never do them any good in the long run.'[32]

Historian Gordon Wood writes, 'For too long and with much candor, he [Adams] had tried to tell his fellow Americans some truths about themselves that American values and American ideology would not admit.'[33] As early as 1763 when Adams was only twenty-eight and had just debuted in the newspaper under the nom de plume "Humphrey Ploughjogger" to write humorous essays conveying his political ideas, he had started to criticize the ruling elite. For good measure, at the same time, Adams was replying to his own essays by using a different pseudonym "U" to take forward the conversation as he desired.[34] He argued that governments must be balanced between monarchy, aristocracy, and democracy in order to be stable. By this, he was echoing the English Whig sentiments referring to the British form of government with a monarch, the House of Lords, and the

House of Commons respectively. Adams argued in these essays that only such a balanced system of governance could restrain men's pursuit of 'wanton Pleasures' while also limiting the excesses of the majority who if unchecked would rule by their 'capricious Will.'[35] To prevent the rise of European-type feudal estates in America after the Revolution, Adams had advocated for laws that forced families to divide their estates among all their children. The goal of a republic, he argued was 'the greatest happiness for the greatest number' which in his view was possible only when a ruling aristocratic elite would not rise in America. Adams was to echo these sentiments again years later when he had become much more famous and notorious.[36]

Some founding fathers most notably Franklin had believed that officials and elected representatives should serve without pay. This would have meant that only the wealthy and elite could serve the people which would have led to the political power being permanently captured by the economically strong sections of society. Adams had warned against this sentiment too by writing that without pay for those holding public office, 'all offices would be monopolized by the rich; the poor and the middling ranks would be excluded and an aristocratic despotism would immediately follow.'[37]

While leaders in America feared the possibility of the emergence of a monarch, Adams was concerned about an aristocracy. While leaders in America despised the British system of governance for concentrating too much power in hands of the monarch and viewed the hereditary House of Lords (representing the aristocracy) as mediating between the monarch and the elected House of Commons (representing the commonalty), Adams viewed the monarch as the source of mediation between House of Lords and House of Commons (together forming the legislature). By this Adams meant that a strong executive authority was needed to keep the two ends of the society (privileged and commonalty) in balance. This fundamental difference in viewpoints regarding checks and balances in the government was to haunt Adams's reputation all his life and beyond since he was decried as being a monarchist (because of advocating for a strong executive). Written hastily to get his thoughts out to Americans as soon as possible to influence the debate around drafting a constitution in America, *Defence* was a hodgepodge of text and references, a 'strange book' in his own words.[38] Writing evocatively about the need for a strong executive, Adams wrote

> Democracy, simple democracy, never had a patron among men of letters…If there is one central truth to be collected from the history of all ages, it is this; that the people's rights and liberties, and the democratical mixture in a constitution, can never be preserved without a strong executive, or, in other words, without separating the executive from the legislature power. If the executive power, or any considerable part of it, is left in the hands of an aristocratical or democratical assembly, it will corrupt the legislature as necessarily as rust corrupts iron, or as arsenic poisons the human body; and when the legislature is corrupted, the people are undone…The rich, the well-born, and the able, acquire an influence among the people that will soon be too much for simple honesty and plain sense, in a house of representatives. The most illustrious of them must, therefore, be separated from the mass, and placed by themselves in a senate; this is, to all honest and useful intents, an ostracism.[39]

For Adams, the basic construct of human nature had ever been the same and hence people were incapable of governing themselves in a perfect democracy without checks and balances. Though he opposed hereditary titles, his advocacy of a strong executive along the lines of British government came as a surprise to his fellow revolutionaries who like him had toiled during the American Revolution to separate America from the clutches of the British King. As he wrote to Jefferson, 'You are afraid of the one, I, of the few. We agree perfectly that the many should have full, fair, and perfect representation. You are apprehensive of monarchy, I, of aristocracy. I would, therefore, have given more power to the president, and less to the senate.' Adams was also not happy that the delegates to the Constitutional Convention had decided that the Senate should be elected by the people.[40]

Adams, who during the Revolutionary Era had been "the first man in the House" in the Continental Congress and whose contribution to bringing down the rule of the British monarch in America was second to none was now being decried as a monarchist. Writing along James I's famous statement "no bishop, no king," Adams argued that "no people, no king and no king, no people" since for people to maintain their sovereignty and powers it was a must to have a strong executive which could protect them against the vile aristocracy. Such ideas did not go well with Americans who wanted anything but a strong executive. A cousin of Madison and the president of the College of William and Mary, Reverend James Madison accused Adams of 'insidiously attempting to overturn our present Constitutions...plotting Revolutions' and observed that Adams had lost sight of revolutionary ideals amidst the 'Glare of European Courts.'[41] Adams's own cousin, Cotton Tufts, warned Americans to not heed such people who are trying to sow discord, favored the establishment of a monarch, and 'planned to put an English prince on the American throne.'[42] Very soon, Adams's book was being 'squibbed at in almost every paper' and being called 'one of the most deep wrought systems of political deception that ever was penned by the ingenuity of man.'[43]

Undeterred by the response he received for his first volume of *Defence*, the argumentative author started working on the second volume. Adams was not somebody who would have stopped expressing himself by the fear of backlash to his political career since he was convinced that his writings and insights would be beneficial for future American generations. In a letter to Abigail, he idealistically wrote what has since been quoted for generations: 'I must study Politicks and War that my sons may have liberty to study Mathematicks and Philosophy. My sons ought to study Mathematicks and Philosophy, Geography, natural History, Naval Architecture, navigation, Commerce and Agriculture, in order to give their Children a right to study Painting, Poetry, Musick, Architecture, Statuary, Tapestry and Porcelaine.'[44] For authoring the second volume of *Defence* which 'exclusively dealt with the history of Italian republics, Adams taught himself Italian, spent a small fortune acquiring scarce histories from London bookstores and worked such long hours at his desk that Abigail feared for his well-being.' Adams praised the popular assemblies that had been established in America and the absence of an aristocracy at this point but argued prophetically that as the wealth of the Americans will rise due to an increase in commerce-related activities, an elite ruling class will rise in the American republic. He warned that in all commercially well-doing republics, 'an aristocracy has risen in the course of time, consisting of a few rich and honorable families, who have united with each other against both the people and the first magistrate.'[45]

Specifically writing about America, Adams noted that 'All that we can say in America is, that legal distinctions, titles, powers, and privileges, are not hereditary' but this did not mean that the desire for distinction has been eliminated from the human nature.[46] Years later, Alexis Du Tocqueville made the same point: In pursuit of distinction such as titles granted by the state but without their official sanction by the Constitution (which was committed to equality), deep fissures will appear in the American society between "the few" and "the many." In the end, it was Adams rather than Madison or Jefferson who proved to be extremely prescient when Tocqueville wrote six decades after the American Revolution in his acclaimed tract *Democracy in America*: 'The surface of American society is…covered with a layer of democracy, from beneath which the old aristocratic colors sometimes peep.'[47] Adams had been highly suspicious about the future of American republicanism. Sullenly, he declared that 'Nothing but Force and Power and Strength' could restrain human passions for distinction and just formal abolitions of titles or appeals for unanimity would not reconcile the 'diversity of sentiments, contradictory principles, inconsistent interests, and opposite passions…'[48] Echoing political theorist Judith Shklar's observation, Luke Mayville has noted that sounding the call against elite groups before anybody else, Adams was 'the source of a longstanding American tradition of decrying and criticizing elite domination.'[49]

It was one thing to raise voice against what Adams felt wrong with American understanding of aristocracy by writing from London, it was another to do the same after coming back to his homeland and while serving as the first Vice President. Though Adams much detested the French Enlightenment (Rousseau was 'a coxcomb and satyr' whereas Voltaire was 'a liar and complete scoundrel'), he admired the Scottish Enlightenment which focused on emotions rather than reason to explain the human nature and its driving force. Adams admired Adam Smith, the "father of free market capitalism" and Smith's *Theory of Moral Sentiments* had a significant effect on him. Thus in 1790, Vice President John Adams published as a series of newspaper articles a book entitled *Discourses on Davila*. Having previously warned about the rise of an aristocracy in America based on wealth, beauty, and birth rather than titles of nobility, Adams now sought to explain the factors of human nature leading to that rise. Historian Joseph Ellis writes that 'The crucial Adams contribution was to recognize that Smith's analysis of the irrational urges driving the new commercial aristocracy would prove even more pronounced in the United States, where there were no vestiges of the old-style aristocracy to offset wealth as the primary measure of elite status.'

Adams felt that since the titles of nobility and other such distinctions that were prevalent in Europe were absent in America, the new elite will distinguish themselves by the way of wealth, beauty, and birth. There was no special providence for Americans in his view. Using the phrase "commercial republic" to convey what we today recognize as unbridled capitalism, Adams warned that a small number of wealthy Americans would portray themselves as virtuous philanthropists in order to achieve immortality in front of their countrymen. On the one hand, Adams believed aristocracy to be the root of avarice and corruption in a nation, while on the other hand he also thought that the elite in a society in many ways represented the best wisdom and expertise it had to offer. How then to reconcile the two extremes by containing the vices of the aristocracy?

Despite all the prescience that Adams exhibited in prophesizing the rise of inequality and aristocracy in America, his cure to this disease was bizarre: to grant titles of distinction to the elite. He believed that granting such distinctions would contain the passions of the elite Americans and would prompt the commonalty to emulate their virtues and talents rather than wealth. He believed that titles would replace wealth as the source of admiration for the American citizenry while also attracting the elite towards government and public service. He proposed that the Senate should be a body in which the elite could be ostracized for life and proposed many European-type titles be granted to the president and other ruling elite. It is because of this view that Adams had expressed that the election to the Senate should not be held by the people but rather it should be a body composed of elites just like the House of Lords in Britain. Along the lines of the British Government, he also proposed a monarch-like executive with huge power in its bosom which could overrule decisions by either legislature to maintain order in the society by balancing the interests of the elite and the multitudes.[50]

Adding to his warmth towards titles, Adams also wrote against suffrage for all since in his view (and the view of many other political philosophers of the time), giving voting rights to those without property would descend the republic to anarchy since uneducated men would elect demagogues by voting solely based on human passions. Thus, Adams provided no palliative worth serious consideration by his fellow countrymen who had moved ahead with the times in America and were dead against adopting the British form of governance. The prevailing national spirit of the time was vehemently against any ideas sympathetic to formal recognition of aristocracy. Perhaps Adams who for years had been serving as a diplomat in Europe was unable to grasp the fundamental undercurrents the American Revolution had unleashed against the recognition of any elite privileges in his absence. Expectedly then he was ridiculed from all sides of the political spectrum since they perceived Adams's proposals as being antithetical to the ideals of the American Revolution.

Other founding fathers, however, disregarded Adams's views about the possibility of an American aristocracy despite showing their concern for the poor. Equality to them was limited to equality of wealth in their contemporary time since they did not believe that wealth could be accumulated in a highly unequal manner in the future. In his proposed Virginia "Bill for Support of the Poor" and *Notes on Virginia,* Jefferson wrote about the care of the poor assigned to suitable persons and county government instead of the Anglican church along the lines of the principle of the separation of church from state. Jefferson's plan also proposed that all suitable persons looking for employment should be helped by the government to learn 'some art, trade, or business' after they had attended public school for at least three years, if necessary, at public expense. Years later, Jefferson also proudly wrote to Adams about how he had labored in Virginia to put an end to the law of primogeniture and entail, and thus ensured that one's wealth could be redistributed among all heirs after his death. These laws enacted by Jefferson expanded the use and ownership of private property by abolishing the last remnants of feudalism. As he boasted to Adams years later, these laws that were drawn by him 'laid the axe to the root of the pseudo-aristocracy.'[51]

Another time, Jefferson justified his conviction that redistribution of income between the rich and poor by the government may be the correct policy: 'I am conscious that an equal division of property is impracticable. But the consequences of this enormous inequality producing so much misery to the bulk of mankind, legislators cannot invent too many devices for subdividing property...Another means of silently lessening the inequality of property is to exempt all from taxation below a certain point, and to tax the higher portions of property in geometrical progression as they rise.'[52] But, his sentiments were not shared by Benjamin Franklin—the perfect example of a self-made man (we will read more about him in the next chapter). When Franklin observed the huge inequality of wealth in Britain, he contrasted it with the conditions of relative equality in America. Franklin's diagnosis of the condition of the poor was based on his personal experience. He wrote about how the poor should be made self-supporting by the policies of the government instead of turning the government into becoming a welfare state. At odds with Jefferson's ideas but visionary in their conception, Franklin's proposals nonetheless showed his concern for economic inequality especially in Europe:

> I am for doing good to the poor, but I differ in opinion of the means. I think the best way of doing good to the poor, is not making them easy in poverty, but leading or driving them out of it. In my youth I travelled much, and I observed in different countries, that the more public provisions were made for the poor, the less they provided for themselves, and of course became poorer. And, on the contrary, the less was done for them, the more they did for themselves, and became richer. There is no country in the world where so many provisions are established for them [as in England],...with a solemn general law made by the rich to subject their estates to a heavy tax for the support of the poor....[Yet] there is no country in the world in which the poor are more idle, dissolute, drunken, and insolent...In short, you offered a premium for the encouragement of idleness, and you should not now wonder that it has had its effect in the increase of poverty.[53]

While the ideas of the founding fathers differed when it came to the rise of aristocracy in America or the role of government in the emancipation of the poor, they were on the same platform on two topics—inequality of sexes and that the principle of equality should not be extended to those without property. The founding fathers agreed that women should not enjoy equal rights with men. For them, ownership of property was the primary condition to possess any legal rights and thus for women and children to ask for equality seemed absurd to them. No consideration was given by them towards voting rights for women in the Constitutional Convention. Abigail Adams, who is sometimes portrayed as the first American feminist, wrote to his husband John Adams in 1776:

> I long to hear that you have declared an independancy—and by the way in the new Code of Laws which I suppose it will be necessary...Remember the Ladies, and be more generous and favourable to them than your ancestors. Do not put such unlimited power into the hands of the Husbands. Remember all Men would be tyrants if they could. If perticuliar care and attention is not paid to the Laidies we are determined to foment a Rebelion, and will not hold ourselves bound by any Laws in which we have no voice, or Representation....That your Sex are Naturally Tyrannical is a Truth so thoroughly established as to admit of no dispute,...[54]

John Adams's response to the letter was to disregard it as 'the first Intimation that another Tribe more numerous and powerfull than all the rest were grown discontented,' while observing flippantly that it was only in practice that we (men) carry the name of 'Masters' while in reality 'We are the subjects.'[55] In the founding fathers' view, women were like children who were subordinate to their masters. Abigail's call for equality between the sexes was well ahead of the time and the fundamental argument that she raised about men being tyrannical was not even acknowledged for more than a century after she wrote the above letter.[56]

Adams had high admiration for intellectual women like Abigail and Mercy Otis Warren, a political writer, whom he corresponded with in adulation and a sense of equality similar to his correspondence with Jefferson. He was ready to accept and encourage intellectual achievements by women in his family and close friends. Unlike Jefferson who confessed that education for women 'has never been a subject of systematic contemplation with me,' Adams endorsed 'the principle that women should receive the same education as men.' He also advocated that equality in education between the sexes is beneficial for America since women will take up the responsibility of educating the next generation of male leaders in the republic.[57] Despite these views on the equality of sexes, Adams found it impossible to extend his personal admiration towards women to the question of women suffrage. When a few weeks after the above correspondence with Abigail, a fellow revolutionary James Sullivan opened the question of suffrage for women with Adams, his response was that he dreaded the possibility of providing voting rights to all. Specifically referring to the suffrage for women, Adams wrote

> But why exclude Women? You will Say, because their Delicacy renders them unfit for Practice and Experience in the great Business of Life, and the hardy Enterprizes of War, as well as the arduous Cares of State. Besides, their attention is So much engaged with the necessary Nurture of their Children, that Nature has made them fittest for domestic Cares…Is it not equally true, that Men in general in every Society, who are wholly destitute of Property, are also too little acquainted with public Affairs to form a Right Judgment, and too dependent upon other Men to have a Will of their own?…The Same Reasoning, which will induce you to admit all Men, who have no Property, to vote, with those who have…Women and Children, have as good Judgment, and as independent Minds as those Men who are wholly destitute of Property: these last being to all Intents and Purposes as much dependent upon others, who will please to feed, cloath, and employ them, as Women are upon their Husbands, or Children upon their Parents.[58]

Many of the founding fathers were ready to publicly express their indignation towards slavery but they could not look forward to advocating equality of sexes. The status of women continued to be governed by the law of coverture and thus after marriage, the couple was recognized as a single entity in the eyes of law with the man "owning" his wife as property. Though the Constitution barred no group (not even slaves) from voting in the elections based either on sex, wealth, property, race, etc., it gave the right to states to form their own laws concerning the same and so the dream of universal suffrage for women remained a dream whose significance was not realized by either men or women for generations to come.

While on the one hand, women were considered as "property," on the other hand, those who had no economic property at all were not considered citizens with complete civil rights. The states had enacted laws barring men from voting if owned no property. The founding fathers believed not in the democracy as familiar to us today but that providing voting rights (and thus equality before the government) to all would mean the capture of the government by primitive passions. Thus, to them, a precondition to participating in the process of democracy was the ownership of property without which men would not have a stake in the society to keep it stable. Men without property were equated with men without principles. The principle of equality before the government was thus extended only to men who could demonstrate that they have a permanent common interest with the community i.e. they own a sufficient amount of property. Hamilton charged the 'turbulent and changing' masses that they 'seldom judge or determine right' for the nation and proposed that the government should 'check the imprudence of democracy.' He also envisioned Congress to be 'composed of landholders, merchants, and men of the learned professions' without many exceptions so that only the well-to-do who had stakes in the stability of the government could influence it. Washington, who presided over the Constitutional Convention, also warned the delegates to not produce a document that would simply 'please the people.' Too much devolution of power was seen as disastrous since a perfect democracy i.e. with equal rights for all was seen as the worst of all political evils.

Thus, the founding fathers had their blind spots concerning women and landless inhabitants. The laws arising from these blind spots have fomented much debate around the founding fathers' intentions concerning equality in democratic participation. These debates have been clamorous, to say the least. Charles A. Beard's iconic work *An Economic Interpretation of the Constitution of the United States* published in 1913 has for more than a century divided historians and scholars into two groups. The first group appreciates Beard's analysis that the founding fathers were elite white male whose chief aim was to further their own interests. Since the Articles of the Confederation had provided too much power in the hands of the people (poor agricultural labor), too much devolution of power had created the conditions of anarchy for which the new constitution became a necessity. The Constitutional Convention itself met in secrecy with an elite group of leaders not chosen directly by the citizenry. The founding fathers' preoccupation was with containing the excesses of the populism such as the Shays' Rebellion to capture power in their own hands. The other group of historians counteracts these claims by focusing on the practical decisions and compromises that the founding fathers had to make in the Constitutional Convention to balance the federalists and anti-federalists. This group argues that the founding fathers instituted a system of checks and balances between the three arms of the government in order to contain the excesses of democracy (legislature) as well as monarchy (executive). Irrespective of this scholarly discourse, what is surely true is that the founding fathers could not foresee the coming of the Industrial Revolution. As America industrialized, not only the gap between the rich and poor became more pronounced but the increase in economic inequality also made the poor raise their voice for increased participation in the democracy. It must be kept in mind that since capitalism and communism as we know them today were in many ways the products of the Industrial Revolution, the founding fathers' notion that property should be the requirement for democratic participation and that aristocracy could not rise in America (except Adams's foreboding) must be read in the proper context.[59]

With the adoption of Hamilton's financial plan by Washington in the early 1790s, America ushered into the path of industrialization. The banking system established by Hamilton made it possible to raise credit for establishing industries and proved to be an irreversible bandwagon.[60] From $20.2 million in 1790, the country's exports rose to $108.3 million by 1807. Madison tried to erect a roadblock against the banking system in 1811 when he did not renew the charter for the First Bank of the United States but soon regretted when in the War of 1812, the economy crippled without the ability to raise credit or finance the war and he had to establish the Second Bank of the United States in 1816. Uniquely compared to European nations, the easy availability of capital and access to the market as per Hamilton's vision led to a boom in the number of patents filed and firms set up in America by entrepreneurs coming from all walks of life.[61] Paradoxically, as the nation's wealth increased manyfold in two generations since the founding fathers, wealth inequality also increased since the introduction of the heavy industry meant that employees and employers became more dissimilar unlike when most Americans lived an agriculture-dependent life.[62] While by 1820s

Americans looked favorably to the banking system and the number of banks in the nation grew many times, Adams accused his fellow Americans with an 'infatuation' with the banking system that will lead to an aristocracy 'growing out of them that will be as fatal as the feudal barons, if unchecked in time.'63

As America stood at the cusp of the Gilded Age after the Civil War when a handful of rich elite virtually ran the nation, Adams's doubts from a century ago started to come true: 'But there is So much Rascallity, so much Venality and Corruption, so much Avarice and Ambition, such a Rage for Profit and Commerce among all Ranks and Degrees of Men even in America, that I sometimes doubt whether there is public Virtue enough to support a Republic.'64 While all other founding fathers were perfectly content with the presumption that an elite group of men could not rise in America due to its contemporary equality of economic conditions, Adams was on point when he had chided Jefferson writing: 'No Romance could be more amusing' than to believe that Americans have some special virtue in their nature as if the migration from Europe had transformed them fundamentally in a way that would forever make America an exception in the world when it comes to the inequality of wealth.65 The self-evident truths concerning the phrase "all men are created equal" remained accessible only to free white men owning sufficient property, though, in the coming decades, the same phrase became the source of inspiration for all oppressed groups in the nation.

For three years during the Second World War, Vallabhbhai Patel and Jawaharlal Nehru were incarcerated in the Ahmednagar Fort by the British along with other members of the Congress Working Committee. Life in prison was gloomy. For more than two years, the prisoners were not allowed to have any interviews with their relatives or any outsiders. Thus, it struck Nehru one day 'as an odd and arresting fact that for nearly 26 months—for 785 days to be exact—I had not seen a woman even from a distance....And I began to wonder—what are women like?'66 Amidst such a dark, gloomy, and morose atmosphere of the prison, a sprawling and beautiful garden full of colorful flowers, birds, and vitality made its appearance. In the words of a fellow jail mate, Nehru was 'President of the Planning Committee' of the garden with the complete onus of 'preparing the flowerbed' and was 'all the while digging and delving, seeving and stocking, weeding and watering,' whereas Patel gave 'his expert's attention to the plants that have sprung up.'[67] But, he added: 'Like man and his home, the garden too hath its enemies.' During the days there were the birds who used to 'eat up the buds and tender leaves' while at nights the bandicoot was the culprit of uprooting young plants 'that have just sprouted.' The chief gardener, Nehru, was 'greatly upset by this vandalism' and a trap was laid to capture the intruding bandicoot.[68] With hard work from Nehru and Patel, the garden started to flourish while its enemies were banished. By the third year, it furnished seeds of all the flowers and before their release from the prison, Patel 'took pains to collect them' while Nehru sorted them to pack them 'into small envelopes' for each member of the group to share. They hoped that the seeds would spread across jails in India if they get 'transferred and to all the provinces when we may be released.'[69]

This, in short, is symbolically the story of India between the three years from Independence in 1947 to Patel's death in 1950. Both Nehru and Patel nurtured India together during this crucial phase in India's history. Nehru was the figurehead of the government as the prime minister while Patel though his deputy prime minister by rank, equaled him in influence within the Congress Party and the government, and even exceeded him at times. Just like the bandicoot in the above account, for centuries, "a few" at the top had inflicted heavy misery on the multitude in India's predominantly agricultural society. Together, Nehru and Patel wanted to ensure that not anymore. They were absolutely confident that the republic which was being conceived by them would be a less unequal society. Together, they tended to the young nation by sowing the seeds of constitutionalism and self-government while protecting it from majoritarianism and anarchic forces. They worked hand-in-hand in the Constituent Assembly to erect safeguards against the centuries-old fiefdoms of "the few." They labored hard to improve the lives of those at the bottom of the economic hierarchy. The seeds of their labor were distributed across India and blossomed all segments of the society when the Constitution came into effect on 26 January 1950.

Vallabhbhai Patel's official date of birth was never recorded and so we have to iterate here what he filled in his mark sheet (the story made him chuckle throughout his life) to be October 31, 1875. He was born into the Patidar community of Gujarat—a community of peasants. Even in his youth, Patel was a model of fortitude. Two incidents bear witness to this. Once around the age of 25, Patel was suffering from a large boil in his armpit seeing which even the barber he went for getting it removed trembled. Patel then took the searing hot iron rod from the barber's hand and scorched the boil himself while the poor soul quivered nearby. The second story shows his mental fortitude. After matriculation, he studied law and became an advocate while saving money for many years through his practice. He wanted to go to England to become a barrister and after five years of drudgery to save money, he applied for a passport. However, the passport only carried his name as Mr. V. J. Patel and thus it was delivered to his elder brother, Vithalbhai, whose name had the exact same initials. As Vallabhbhai wrote a few years later:

> My elder brother said to me, "I am older than you. Let me go to England. After I return you will get the opportunity to go, but I will not be able to go to England after you." I gave my brother fifteen days' time [to decide]. On the fifteenth day he proceeded to England.

To follow his duty as the younger brother, Patel sent his elder brother in his place to England without any regret and also covered his brother's expenses by working even harder at his law practice back in Gujarat. His principal biographer Rajmohan Gandhi presents this episode as the proof 'that something significant was happening inside Vallabh. A forging was proceeding apace, and Destiny was using unseen hammers, anvils and fires to shape and strengthen a character.'[70]

At the age of thirty-five, Patel finally got the opportunity to go to England. His wife had died by then and his children were being taken care of by relatives in India. Completing his course in thirty months while living a frugal life, Patel graduated from the Middle Temple Inn in London and returned to Gujarat. He became one of the most successful barristers in Ahmedabad and also greatly skilled at bridge. An often-quoted incident says that at this time Patel was very dismissive of that other and much more famous fellow-Gujarati lawyer, six-years older than him, Mohandas Gandhi. Patel dismissed Gandhi by observing that 'We already have too many mahatmas,' and once when Gandhi was visiting the club where Patel was playing bridge, he did not find it agreeable to pause his game and go to meet Gandhi. Only gradually did Patel understand Gandhi's ideas and methods to convince himself about Gandhi's mission. Subsequently, Patel emerged as Gandhi's chief lieutenant at the bosom of Gandhi's Independence Movement—Gujarat. Patel renounced his flourishing law practice and material ambitions to devote himself fully to Gandhi's agendas. Whether it be the Kheda Satyagraha of 1918, Bardoli Satyagraha of 1928, or Salt March of 1930, Patel was not only Gandhi's go-to man but also his chief source of strength among the peasants of Gujarat. Gandhi and Patel forged a brotherly relationship that endured throughout their lives. For his leadership, Patel was honored with the sobriquet "Sardar" (respected leader) and even today he is more often than not addressed as Sardar Patel.

A no-nonsense man, usually with a grave and stoic face, always carrying an aura of dignity by his presence, an effective fundraiser, and possessing immense organizational skills honed over decades, Patel gradually became the most powerful leader within the Congress Party despite formally assuming the presidency of the Party only once. But for advanced age and a certain lack of charisma among masses across India, he may have been the choice for Gandhi to become the first prime minister of India. Among Patel's lasting and most-remembered contributions to India was the accession of 562 princely states to the Union of India using all instruments ranging from negotiations to coercion to military action. Patel, as he liked to put it, filled his basket with all the apples that he desired by politically integrating India through the accession of more than five hundred princely states to the nation.[71] For his uncompromising attitude towards the integration of India and unqualified success in this venture, he is also known as "the Bismarck of India" and "the Iron Man of India."[72]

At the same time as overseeing the integration of India, Patel was coordinating efforts for the rehabilitation of refugees from Pakistan, maintaining law and order during communal strife, and playing a key role in the Constituent Assembly as the most powerful man within the Congress organization while chairing important committees during the drafting of the Constitution of India. While Patel had earlier excoriated the Indian Civil Services, he retained the same after Independence having understood the constructive role that bureaucratic officers from these services could play in the task of nation-building. These Services are today generally recognized as a "steel frame" strengthening and holding together the nation's administration and government. In recent years, Patel's birthday has been celebrated as the National Unity Day while the government has erected the world's tallest statue (the Statue of Unity) in his honor.

In many ways, Patel and Nehru were the two boats on which Gandhi stood, one leg in each, not letting them go apart while sailing forward toward the freedom of India. But, this balancing act was under serious strain just when freedom came to India. While both admired and felt affection toward each other, Nehru and Patel also had differences in outlook when it came to the functioning of the government and its policies. Both Patel and Nehru wanted to draft policies in the Constitution for outlawing the regressive forces that fueled inequality in every aspect of the society. But, the government of the infant nation and the nation at large could function only if these two poles could reconcile their differences and work together. No less prescient leader than Rajaji had once said that 'The Prime Minister [Nehru] and his colleague, the Deputy Prime Minister [Patel], together make a possession which makes India rich in every sense of the term. The former commands universal love, the latter universal confidence. Not a tear must be shed…as long as these two stand four square together against the hard winds to which our country may be exposed.' But, not everything between Nehru and Patel was hunky-dory in late 1947 just when India became independent. The emergence of serious differences between them was a serious concern for the newborn nation.[73]

The composition of the Congress Party and the Indian Government was such that no measure could be passed without the consent of both Nehru and Patel—the two pillars of the cabinet. But, the relationship between them was complex. Thus, before we dive into how they worked together for reducing the inequality in Indian society, we will first briefly look at their interpersonal dynamics. Right after India's Independence, there was a big crisis in the Nehru-Patel relationship. Nehru had appointed Gopalaswami Ayyangar as a Minister without portfolio in the Cabinet to assist himself in the Kashmir policy. Patel was dejected since apparently, Nehru had not consulted him regarding Ayyangar's entry into the government. Patel justly argued that the accession of Kashmir should have been dealt with by the States Ministry under him while Nehru took the line that the government's policy regarding Kashmir had already been taken out of that Ministry and would be taken care of by himself directly through Ayyangar. Nehru defended Ayyangar by saying that everything the new minister had been doing 'was done at my instance' and added regarding Patel's conversation with Ayyangar that 'May I say that the manner of approach to Gopalaswami was hardly in keeping with the courtesy due to a colleague?' Patel was furious and immediately wrote back to Nehru that his 'letter has caused me considerable pain…Your letter makes it clear to me that I must not or at least cannot continue as a Member of Government and hence I am hereby tendering my resignation.' To this, Nehru replied that night as one would to his beloved: 'I am sorry that what I wrote to you gave you pain. I am myself very unhappy about the trend of events and the difficulties that have arisen between you and me. It seems that our approaches are different, however much we may respect each other…If unfortunately either you or I have to leave the Government of India, let this be done with dignity and goodwill. On my part I would gladly resign and hand over the reins to you.' These differences in viewpoints escalated to such a contentious level that both Nehru and Patel offered to resign. On 24 December 1947, both Nehru and Patel met their acknowledged leader, Gandhi, and discussed about their inability to continue together within the government.[74]

India was in turmoil. The process of political integration of the nation was underway. The princely state of Hyderabad, as large as France, at the center of the nation had still not acceded to India. The Constituent Assembly was drafting a new constitution and a multitude of contentious issues were being discussed by delegates from across the nation. Refugees from Pakistan were pouring in millions whereas communal violence was underway in many parts of the nation (as detailed earlier in the second chapter). Communist-insurgency was another veritable threat. Amidst all this, the two pillars of the government had decided to resign while Gandhi was being asked to arbitrate between his chosen heir, Nehru, on one side and loyal brother-like, Patel, on the other. India needed both Nehru and Patel to work collaboratively or else not only the Congress Party but the fragile hope of establishing a democracy might have shattered into pieces.

Gandhi's first instinct was to tell Patel a few days later that 'either you should run things or Jawaharlal should' to which Patel replied 'I do not have the physical strength. He is younger. Let him run the show. I will assist him to the extent possible from outside.' From his side, Patel had resigned and was only waiting for Gandhi's final approval.[75] Around the same time, tensions between Nehru and Patel were exacerbated when Nehru had planned to visit Ajmer for coordinating and reviewing efforts for the rehabilitation of refugees. However, due to a bereavement in his family, Nehru had to cancel the trip and instead he sent his personal secretary to represent himself. Patel took deep offense at this since his own ministry's enquiry team was already present in Ajmer. To Patel, Nehru's decision to send a subordinate as his representative implied a lack of faith in Patel's ministry. While Nehru maintained that it was his right as the prime minister to send anybody to represent him, Patel argued that in a parliamentary system, the prime minister was merely *primus inter pares* and thus Nehru should not have nominated an underling for the inspection.[76]

Just like a few weeks back, both Nehru and Patel again ran to Gandhi for advice and instructions. With a large heart, Patel professed that 'If anybody has to go, it should be myself. I have long passed the age of active service. The Prime Minister is the acknowledged leader of the country and is comparatively young. I have no doubt that the choice between him and myself should be resolved in his favour. There is, therefore, no question of his quitting office.' Patel went on to tour Gujarat and await Gandhi's approval for leaving the government. On 23 January, Patel was informed by Gandhi about his decision: neither among the duumvirate should leave. On thinking more over this issue which affected the infant nation's future, Gandhi had by now understood that both Nehru and Patel were indispensable for the government and the nation. He proposed that the differences between Nehru and Patel must be talked over. Patel came back to Delhi and met Gandhi again on the evening of 30 January just before Gandhi's prayer meeting. Gandhi told Patel that his presence in the Cabinet is indispensable and that he had told the same already to Nehru. Gandhi decided to schedule a joint meeting with Nehru and Patel the next day to talk over their differences and bring them closer together. Saying thus he left for his evening prayer meeting bidding goodbye to Patel. Hardly a few minutes later, fate intervened. Gandhi was assassinated.[77]

When Nehru arrived at the scene and saw Gandhi's lifeless body, he started sobbing and placed his head in Patel's lap. Minutes later, Lord Mountbatten dramatically told them that Gandhi's last wish concerned their reconciliation upon which both Nehru and Patel embraced each other, still grieving for the one spirit that had forged the bond between them for decades past. That night, both of them addressed the nation together, one following the other. In the coming days, many people started to demand Patel's resignation since his ministry had been responsible for ensuring Gandhi's security. Patel decided to wait for some time to gauge Nehru's views while getting ready to leave the government. On 3 February, Nehru wrote a letter to Patel which deserves to be quoted at length:

> With Bapu's [Gandhi's] death, everything is changed and we have to face a different and more difficult world...I have been greatly distressed by the persistence of whispers and rumours about you and me, magnifying out of all proportion any differences we may have...We must put an end to this mischief.
>
> It is over a quarter century since we have closely associated with one another and have faced many storms and perils together. I can say with full honesty that during this period my affection and regard for you have grown, and I do not think anything can happen to lessen this.
>
> Anyway, in the crisis that we have to face now after Bapu's death, I think it is my duty, and if I may venture to say, yours also for us to face it together as friends and colleagues. Not merely superficially, but in full loyalty to one another and with confidence in one another. I can assure you that you will have that from me.

In reply to this affectionate letter from Nehru, Patel affirmed their friendship by writing back that they have been 'lifelong comrades in a common cause' and adding that Gandhi's last wish 'binds us both and I can assure you that I am fully resolved to approach my responsibilities and obligations in this spirit.' Just like ending communal strife in Delhi, Gandhi's death had achieved what his words might not have been capable of doing: bringing Nehru and Patel together and preventing a schism within the Congress Party and the government amidst fraught times. While both of them continued to have occasional political disagreements, from now on they remained fiercely loyal to each other. Patel publicly acknowledged Nehru as 'my leader' for the first time and added that 'I am with the Prime Minister on all national issues. For over a quarter of a century, both of us sat at the feet of our master [Gandhi] and struggled together for the freedom of India. It is unthinkable today, when the Mahatma is no more, that we would quarrel.'[78]

Seldom a day passed without them meeting each other over lunch or going for morning walks together while discussing various policies of the government and the Congress Party. Even in the Constituent Assembly, Patel reiterated on Nehru's 59th birthday in front of the delegates that 'Mahatma Gandhi chose Pandit Nehru as his political heir and it was very gratifying to see that the choice fell on the right person,' while Nehru reciprocated these kind words by declaring 'but for Sardar Patel's affection and advice, he [Nehru] would not have been able to run the state.'[79] Patel went further in his praise next year on Nehru's birthday: 'Having known each other in such intimate and varied fields of activity we have naturally grown fond of each other; our mutual affection has increased as years have advanced, and it is difficult for people to imagine how much we miss each other when we are apart and unable to take counsel together in order to resolve our problems and difficulties….No one knows better than myself how much he [Nehru] has laboured for his country in the last two years of our difficult existence.' Both Nehru and Patel trusted each other more than ever after Gandhi's death and did not let the differences in their viewpoints on a multitude of issues come in the way of alleviating the glaring inequality in Indian society.[80]

For centuries before the Independence, the Zamindari System had dominated the Indian landscape. Zamindars had earlier been middlemen between the tillers of land and the emperor to collect land revenue and keep a percentage as their commission. The British had in 1793 equated them with landowners in England and along the lines of the feudal system, they were awarded the rights and titles to the land, thus transforming them into landlords. Most of the cultivatable land in the nation was in the hands of a few Zamindars while tillers worked for them as tenants without any security of land or other financial resources. The condition of the peasants worsened with time since in their pursuit of profits, Zamindars had no incentive to take care of their tenants. Zamindars were usually absent from the land holdings, enjoying elsewhere the pleasures of life. Variants of the system prevailed around the country in which the landlords paid a fixed land revenue to the British.

At the same time, the inequality of landholdings was such that landlessness was the single greatest problem of rural India. More than three-fourths of the country's population was primarily dependent on land and lived in the villages while the great majority of the tillers did not usually own the land and instead worked for landlords. The condition of such tenants was pitiable as they were cruelly exploited by the Zamindars by levying many sorts of direct and indirect taxes 'such as *motorana* (a tax for the zamindar's new car) and *hatiana* (a tax for the zamindar's elephant)' and by not providing them enough food for subsistence. Furthermore, agricultural productivity was low as were the levels of health and nutrition while the population started increasing faster in the twentieth century due to advancements in medicine. Economic subsistence, status symbol, and dignity were all linked to the possession of only a few acres of land. The Congress Party had for many years stated that the Zamindari System would be abolished after Independence. It had charged the British with showing indifference to the poorest of the nation and hence had resolved to transform the pitiable state of the peasantry once it would come to power. It had also promised to carry out large-scale land reform by methods such as redistribution of surplus land and expanding the amount of credit to combat rural indebtedness. While a large section of Zamindars had supported the British and was rewarded for it by them, others maintained a strong and financially influential lobby within the Congress and now sought to thwart any land reform. The contentious issue of balancing between private property and general welfare came at the forefront in the Constituent Assembly.[81]

Historian Granville Austin has incisively written that 'The Indian Constitution is first and foremost a social document. The majority of its provisions are either directly aimed at furthering the goals of the social revolution or attempt to foster this revolution by establishing the conditions necessary for its achievement.'[82] If members of the Congress dominated the Constituent Assembly, Patel dominated the Congress as its chief herdsman. He had organized satyagrahas alongside Gandhi for peasant rights and understood the significance of the crucial policy of land reform perhaps more than anybody else in the Congress leadership. He aimed at utilizing the newly appointed Constituent Assembly to pass legislation for the abolition of the Zamindari System. As early as 1946, The Objectives Resolution adopted in the Constituent Assembly moved by Nehru and drafted with Patel's support called for 'social economic, and political justice, and equality of status, opportunity, and before the law for all people.'[83] The other feature of the Objectives Resolution and thus the path that the Constituent Assembly took was the omission of the word "socialism" in it which was probably due to Patel's influence over Nehru in the Assembly. Patel's conservatism helped in restraining the socialist lobby of the Congress from veering off course. In some ways, the peculiarity of Patel's politics was that he was a friend of big business, capitalists, and rich, as well as peasants and trade unionists.

When the discussion on land acquisition by the state came up in the Constituent Assembly, the Zamindars and such feudal interest groups in the Assembly brought in many amendments to safeguard their interests. The debate on property rights in the Assembly was longer and acute than any other subject except that of the national language (about which we shall read in the next chapter). Patel's speech as the chairman of the Subcommittee on Fundamental Rights sounded a note of importunity towards landlords when he sternly replied that 'the Zamindars or some of their representatives thought that their interests must be safeguarded by moving an amendment or by making a speech here. But they are not going to safeguard these interests in this way. They must recognise the times and move with the times…Zamindaris will be liquidated…we must not or need not go into the question whether the Zamindars have in the past been patriotic or a nuisance or anything of that kind. It is all irrelevant and we need not go into the past.' He thus made it clear that this feudal system of landlordism shall cease to exist in India.[84] At the same time, Article 18 of the Constitution was debated in the Constituent Assembly in November 1948 which later ensured that the titles of nobility such as *Rai Bahadur, Taluqdar, Sawai,* etc. prevalent during British times would be abolished and no such distinctions shall be made by the state.

In a speech in early 1949, Patel again warned such feudal landlords that they should move with the times and not come in the way of democracy and integration of India or else grief was inevitable for them. Not known to mince words, he sternly warned them that 'If you keep pace with the times, you can also remain in the vanguard, but if you go on as you have been going on for the last few centuries, even the position at the rear will not be available to you.'[85] While Patel as the Home Minister was coordinating between different states regarding the legislation to abolish Zamindari, the Zamindars were busy lobbying other leaders of the Congress in the hope to get "just" compensation for their land. For Patel, there was 'hardly any room for controversy on the merits of abolition' of the Zamindari System. The only point of contention for him was the question of "just" compensation. While some socialists such as Nehru and others preferred a minimal level of compensation or none at all, Patel wanted it to be fair to the Zamindars to maintain stability in the social construct of rural India. However, Patel wanted to keep the word "just" out of the Constitution since its interpretation might have slowed down or blocked the legislation in the judiciary.

Simultaneously, as we saw in the first chapter, Patel was working in the Constituent Assembly for abolishing the practice of untouchability by the force of law and safeguarding the rights of the Untouchables. He was also endeavoring toward tackling the related issues of access and discrimination. He introduced laws to ensure complete access to every citizen without any discrimination based on caste, religion, language, etc. to public places like wells, tanks, and roads. Thus, at least in the eyes of the law ended centuries-old regressive customs that discriminated between human beings based on the chance of birth. Being straightforward and stern particularly against the Communists and Hindu chauvinists, Patel did not extend this non-discrimination to political creeds since in his view: '[I]t is an absurd idea to provide for non-discrimination as regards a political creed...Some may not be deserving of discrimination, but may actually be deserving of suppression.'[86]

The debate over compensation raged on and off for almost two and a half years. The abolition of Zamindaris also appealed to the sentiments of nationalism and equality since it was associated with a sense of justice for the poor peasants. In the popular imagination, Zamindars were usurpers of land and thus needed no compensation. Patel was at variant with the position taken by socialist Nehru and others regarding the amount of compensation. Nehru wrote to provincial heads: 'The question of zamindari abolition has become a legal and constitutional one. It affects indeed the Constitution that we are framing...It is clear that we as a Government or as the Congress cannot put aside this abolition of zamindaris which has been a main plank in our platform for many years. Some way has to be found and that also speedily or else we shall be discredited and there will be legitimate complaint against us.'[87]

Patel's influence over Congress, in the Government, and in the Assembly was such that no decision could have been taken without his consent and for him, expropriation of Zamindars without compensation was tantamount to theft. In every village, Zamindars also acted as headmen and to crash them from sky to the ground in a single stroke might have proved to be a recipe for chaos. This was sensed astutely by Patel due to his extensive experience of working with peasants. In attempting to compensate Zamindars, Patel was closer to Gandhi's point of view. Gandhi had rejected Soviet-style socialism in which the state could forcibly expropriate private property. Gandhi had many friends among the wealthy industrialists and had, in fact, accepted his closeness to such capitalist forces. Private property was sacrosanct in his view and thus Gandhi had assured Zamindars that no forceful expropriation of their property without compensation would take place.[88]

However, when the time for voting on the resolution discussing abolition came before the Assembly, a thin majority supported to leave the compensation of Zamindars wholly on the mercy of the legislature. But, since Patel had opposed the resolution, nobody pressed forward. Instead, everyone started to build a consensus. Amidst tensions in the Cabinet over diverging ideologies for the compensation, Patel worked out a formula for the compromise (read deferred others to his wishes) which entailed that no property could be acquired for public purposes unless due procedure of law is followed and compensation was determined by the law. Various delegates in the Assembly working for different interests proposed a total of ninety-seven amendments but having once arrived at a compromise, Patel and Nehru held their ground firmly. All amendments were voted down in the face of opposition from them except a few dealing with minor technicalities.[89]

Prime Minister Nehru personally presented the compromise to the Constituent Assembly. He started the speech by observing that no other article has given 'rise to so much discussion and debate' and that so much light has been thrown by various eminent lawyers through their opinions on the issue that 'the conflicting beams of light have often produced a certain measure of darkness.' He made it clear 'that there is no question any expropriation without compensation' and that if 'property is required for public,' then the due process of law will be followed by the state to acquire it. He also sternly iterated to the members of the Assembly many of whom themselves held Zamindaris that 'It has been not today's policy, but the old policy of the National Congress laid down years ago that the zamindari institution in India, that is the big estate system must be abolished. So far as we are concerned, we, who are connected with the Congress, shall give effect to that pledge naturally completely, one hundred per cent. and no legal subtedly and no change is going to come in our way. That is quite clear.'[90] This amendment arrived after a compromise between Patel and others passed in the Assembly on 12 September 1949 and thus the Zamindaris were abolished in India by the force of law. The right to private property was also retained while some provisos were provided to the Zamindars by the Constitution through which they could question the amount of compensation fixed by the state. Having passed another hurdle toward economic and social equality among citizens, the next challenge was land reform since only Zamindaris had been abolished by legislation, but the much more complex issue of land redistribution remained. This issue was further amplified by the influx of millions of refugees after the Partition of India.[91]

The Constitution came into effect on 26 January 1950. Hearings on the validity of many provincial laws passed to acquire Zamindaris had begun in several judicial courts and Zamindars put an active front against the government in the battle. Much of the controversy was around the clause of compensation which was being challenged in many state high courts by the Zamindars. Thus, it became almost impossible for the government to be able to acquire land and redistribute it among the landless who had no other way of subsistence. In Bihar, the High Court struck down as unconstitutional the provision to be able to take over Zamindars' estates and managing them with the intent to eventually acquiring them. Some industrialists in Bombay reached the High Court to challenge the government's management of the mills. Compounding the government's anxieties, the Calcutta High Court had begun hearings in a case regarding the government takeover of property to settle refugees from East Pakistan and the compensation due for the same.[92]

Nehru had been a fierce socialist since the 1930s. He was committed to the demolition of all deep-rooted self-interests fueling inequality in the society. Nehru's long years in prisons had ignited inside him a vague idea of equality among all based on the socialist model though within a democratic establishment. Thus, all such legal obstructions by different courts were affronts in the way of Nehru's thinking and actions. Finding that the reforms he planned to unleash were being thwarted and worrying about the future course of events, Nehru wrote to the Law Minister Ambedkar to draft amendments to the Constitution's provisions relating to Zamindari abolition and nationalization of road transport.

Soon after, the Uttar Pradesh High Court issued an order to restrain the state government from acquiring property under the Zamindari and Land Reforms Act which the state legislature had passed. This was the proverbial last straw for Nehru. He was advised by experts in law that the expropriation of private property for public use is an inherent right in every country such as in the United States. In a sullen yet resolute mood, Nehru wrote to the chief ministers that 'It is the right of the judiciary to interpret the Constitution and to apply it and none of us can or should challenge that. But if the Constitution itself comes in our way, then surely it is time to change that Constitution to that extent. It is impossible to hang up urgent social changes because the Constitution comes in the way, according to the interpretation of courts.'[93] Nehru sought to amend the Constitution by excluding from its purview the compensation provided to Zamindars. Though this was to be expected from a socialist prime minister, this time he had Patel's backing as well (who was ailing by the time). When the Patna High Court struck down the government's land reforms in Bihar, the situation spiraled into a constitutional crisis.

The Bihar Land Reforms Act of 1950 had shuttled between Delhi and Patna for months before its passage by the state legislature. Bihar was one of the poorest and backward regions of the nation and so land reform was a crucial part of the state government's development agenda. An influential lobby of Zamindars in Bihar beseeched their fellow Bihari, the President of India, Rajendra Prasad, to not give his assent to the bill. The post of the president had just been inaugurated a few months back and so there were no clear conventions, practices, or precedents for the president's role in such cases. Unlike America, the President of India was only a constitutional head of the government along the lines of the British monarch and had no real and direct authority over the government's decision-making.

President Prasad raised the question that if his satisfaction was a prerequisite to ensure for himself 'that the provisions [of the bill] are fair and equitable' before providing his assent. This meant that not only the president's power included consultation with the government regarding legislative bills but also that his/her own inputs on them should be respected. The cabinet took months to ponder over this question and eventually agreed that Prasad should give his assent to the bill as is. When Prasad instead questioned certain wording of the bill, Patel cautioned Nehru to wait until the government could consider Prasad's 'rather strong convictions on this problem.' 'When I am asked to sign a document, I must satisfy myself and not sign blindly,' Prasad wrote, irked by the government's attempt to force him into signing the document.

With no precedent of what the president's role should be regarding the interpretation and signing of bills when views between the president differed from those of the government, the situation reached a deadlock. Patel was at the time ailing in Bombay and Nehru decided with other cabinet ministers to force Prasad's hand. Nehru associated so much importance with the bill to expropriate Zamindars that despite Patel's protest, he threatened his own and his government's resignation if the president would not provide his assent to the bill. Pushed to a corner, President Prasad had no way out in the face of opposition from Nehru and he duly provided his assent to the bill. In a sense, the ideal of equality took precedence over democratic niceties.[94]

With the path cleared for the government to carry out land reforms and the abolition of Zamindaris, the process was initiated to transfer the ownership of the land to peasants. Millions of acres of land changed hands due to the government's initiatives helped by Gandhian activists like Vinoba Bhave. Unlike many other nations such as the Soviet Union, China, and Cuba, the huge task of land reform was carried out in a democratic framework and in a non-violent manner. Some compensation that was provided to Zamindars (without making it fall in the purview of the judiciary) in lieu of their land as per Patel's wishes also helped in achieving this objective. Furthermore, this mammoth task was completed in a matter of only a few years. However, while a large number of peasants gained, most of them were high-caste laborers. Those at the bottom of the economic hierarchy and engaged in other miserable professions such as sanitation were left unaffected. The government was unwilling to go further by placing ceilings on landholdings and distributing the excess land so acquired, perhaps due to the fear of fomenting instability. Thus, despite its best intentions, the government was unable to go as far as it had initially aimed. The number of small/marginal farmers dropped by 3.6 per cent while the amount of land held by them could only increase by 4.6 per cent by 1960.[95]

Despite this mixed result when it came to land ownership, the abolition of zamindaris did contribute to the abolition of forced labor. The exploitation of poor peasants by landlords became harder because bonded labor was done away with. Since cultivators now had an incentive in taking care of the land (because they owned it), agricultural methods started to improve with the government's stimulus and as a result, the production started to increase. Shared property such as ponds, grazing grounds, wells, etc. which were earlier used by Zamindars as personal property now started to become communal while millions of tenants came into direct association with the government through the payment of land revenues which strengthened the democracy at the grass-root level. As a whole though, the improvement in the lives of those at the bottom was not transcending but there was another axis of equality on which the founding fathers fared decidedly better.

Whilst revolutionary changes were taking place in India of the 1940s and 50s in social, economic, and political domains, the restructuring of the society was accompanied by a transformation in its building block—family. Centuries of degradation in Hindu religious and cultural customs had most affected the position of women in society. Not only was a woman considered to be the property of her father or husband, but her status had degraded to being confined to the same regressive customs even after their death. As Historian A. L. Basham writes, 'The family [in ancient India] was staunchly patrilineal and patriarchal...Marriage was usually monogamous, and apparently indissoluble, for no reference to divorce or the remarriage of widows occur in the *Rg Veda*.'[96] While there are many historical references pointing to women education in ancient times, by the twentieth century, female literacy was abysmally low. Though the British and some Indian reformers took the initiative in the betterment of the conditions for women such as against the barbaric practices of *Sati* (widow dying by throwing herself on the deceased husband's funeral pyre) and child marriage, they could not go much further against heavy opposition from the conservative corners of the society. At this stage entered the founding fathers who were envisioning a new India while materializing their vision through the Constitution.

While Gandhi had brought millions of women into the freedom struggle, the task to formally establish equality of sexes fell upon Nehru after Independence. Nehru had always been forthcoming in demanding equality of sexes and had condemned men 'to treat woman as a chattel and a plaything to be exploited for his own advantage and amusement.' He had held the view that 'inheritance, marriage, divorce are all supposed to be parts of the personal law of various communities and this personal law is supposed to be part of religion. It is obvious that no change can be imposed from the top.' Despite saying such before the Independence, later as the prime minister, Nehru recognized that in a poor illiterate and generally-conservative society like India of the 1940s, such measures would have to be introduced from the top i.e. by the government.[97]

Talking about laws, it is impossible to get away without the mention of the nation's first lawyer. Based on an earlier draft from the British era, Ambedkar made a few revisions and presented the Hindu Code Bill to the Constituent Assembly in 1948. Despite its name referring only to Hindus, it also encompassed in itself other religions with roots in the Indian subcontinent such as Jainism, Sikhism, and Buddhism. The Bill envisioned to raise the status of women in society by abolishing disparities based on gender and caste. As Historian Ramachandra Guha has succinctly summarized, the Bill proposed:

> 1. The awarding, to the widow and daughter, of the *same share as the son(s)* in the property of a man dying intestate (which in the past had passed only to his male heirs). Likewise, a Hindu woman's estate, previously limited, was now made absolute, to be disposed of as she wished.
> 2. The granting of maintenance to the wife who chose to live separately from the husband if he had a "loathsome disease," was cruel to her, took a concubine, etc.
> 3. Abolition of the rules of caste and sub-caste in sanctifying a marriage. All marriages between Hindus would have the same sacramental as well as legal status, regardless of the castes to which the spouses belonged. An inter-caste marriage could now be solemnized in accordance with the customs and rites of *either* party.
> 4. Allowing either partner to file for and obtain divorce on certain grounds, such as cruelty, infidelity, incurable disease, etc.
> 5. Making monogamy mandatory.
> 6. Allowing for the adoption of children belonging to a different caste.[98]

These benign, logical, and rightful proposals were too radical for the conservatives at the time. The main points of opposition to the Bill were that according to the Hindu traditional laws, a husband could take multiple wives, sons were entitled to a much larger share of the property, and marriage was indissoluble. Another point of contention raised by Hindu conservatives was that Muslims and Christians were left outside the purview of the proposed Bill.

In a speech in Madras, while the debate over Hindu Code Bill was raging in the Constituent Assembly, Patel said: 'Women must have freedom as they, no less than men, had their part to play in the great task [of nation-building] that lay before the country.'[99] The tragedy was that despite such views, Patel decided to not vocally come out in support of the Hindu Code Bill.[100] While the conservative Patel who was closest to the psyche of Indian masses was unable to forcefully exert himself in support of the Bill, the British-styled Nehru was already all out in complete vigor for the emancipation of women. Prime Minister Nehru made it a matter of personal prestige to get the Bill passed in the Constituent Assembly. He expounded: 'It should be clearly understood that this is one important measure to which the government attaches importance and on which it will stand or fall' while on another occasion he expressed the opinion that 'If society has to advance, there must be this integrated advance in all fronts.'[101]

However, the prime minister had not initially anticipated that one of the chief opponents of the Bill would be the president of the Constituent Assembly itself. Rajendra Prasad warned Nehru that to bring in this legislation would be to impose 'progressive ideas' favored only by a minority of Hindus on the vast majority of the community. In Prasad's view the legislation was controversial and just to please foreigners i.e. more progressive nations, it was unwise to make changes in personal law. In addition to Prasad, religious leaders such as Shankaracharya of Dwarka and conservative Hindu organizations like Rashtriya Swayamsevak Sangh (RSS) also came out in the agitation against the Bill. RSS organized marches to protest by shouting 'May Pandit Nehru perish' while its speakers labeled the Bill as 'an atom bomb on Hindu Society' and compared it with draconian British laws.[102]

In a sullen mood, Nehru wrote to Patel, 'What is important is the difference in outlook between Parliament as a whole and me. They put up with me because of their friendliness towards me and their affection and a certain past record and habit of doing so. But they go farther and farther away from me in mind and heart. This produces unhappiness all round and frustration and work suffers' He also questioned why only women were supposed to follow society's "ideals" of purity and morality as depicted in ancient texts while men were not urged to behave piously like gods. Finally, he condemned the tendency of associating such changes in the personal code with the Western societies as if all things wrong in those societies were due to the comparatively more freedom enjoyed by women.[103]

The zeal that Nehru, the national nanny and its chief scolder, showed to reform the Hindu laws was paralleled only by that of the Law Minister Ambedkar. Ambedkar associated as much importance to the passage of the Hindu Code Bill as he had shown for the emancipation of the Untouchables. So much had Ambedkar's name got attached to the Bill that conservative Hindus who were usually staunch proponents of the caste system made anti-Ambedkarism as the rallying force against the Bill. As law minister, it was Ambedkar's duty to present the Bill and he did so in eloquent terms: 'The Hindu society has always believed that law making was the function either of God or the *Smriti* [ancient Hindu codebook] and the Hindu society had no right to change the law...It is for the first time that we are persuading Hindu society to take this big step.' On another occasion, Ambedkar proclaimed that this Bill 'will be 100 times more beneficial to India than Constitution. We are building a new society here and we are doing it by justice and law.' Having struggled against untouchability all through his life, Ambedkar was now also attacking puritans for their views toward women and wanted to restructure the Hindu society to make it more gender-equal.[104]

In September-October 1951, Nehru and Ambedkar tried hard to get the Bill passed in the parliament. But Patel had died in December 1950 and this was the last session of the parliament before the 1951-52 elections (first elections in Independent India). They faced inveterate criticism and opposition from the conservative Hindu forces, both within the Congress Party and outside. As an orthodox parliamentarian said: 'we have Pandit Nehru's administration whose representative Dr Ambedkar wants to abrogate with a single stroke all those rules which have existed since the beginning of the world.' To the criticism that the Bill had not encompassed in itself a personal code for citizens of all religions, Ambedkar retorted that it took many years to draft the Bill only for Hindus and to draft a Uniform Civil Code[α] would probably take a decade more. He also pointed out that

---

[α] Uniform Civil Code (UCC) is the proposed legislation relating to personal laws that applies to every citizen of India without making any distinction based on religion. Not adopted in the Constituent Assembly, it has been defined in India's Constitution under Article 44 of Directive Principles of State Policy. The Constitution has made it the duty of the state to secure for the citizens a Uniform Civil Code throughout the territory of India.

there are presently reformers in the Hindu community such as Nehru and other parliamentarians whereas the Muslim society had not yet produced such liberals to demand changes in their religion's personal code. Thus, in his view, to force a minority community into reforming its personal laws due to pressure from the majority one would have been disastrous for the democracy while holding up the current measure would have been to deprive reform for the majority of Indian women for years to come. However, such was the virulent opposition Nehru and Ambedkar faced that Nehru decided to break the Bill into parts and get only the essential ones passed in the parliament in the current session. Nehru thought that since the elections were due soon, he could not afford to lose the mass support and so planned to get passed certain sections of the Bill instead of letting the whole go waste. Such was the hypocrisy Ambedkar was witnessing that many opponents of the Bill overnight became supporters of a Uniform Civil Code to bring Muslims and Christians in its purview and stall the reform for years to come.[105]

President Prasad again wrote about his apprehensions to Nehru pointing out that the Bill was highly discriminatory as it applied only to Hindus. Prasad even threatened that he would exercise his presidential power and will not sign the Bill into law if it were to pass in the parliament.[106] Nehru was dismayed and taking a dig at the President's beliefs wrote to the Attorney-General: 'I regret to say that the President attaches more importance to his astrologers than to the advice of his Cabinet on some matters. I have no intention of submitting to the astrologers.'[107] In the event, the parliament session ended with the Bill getting talked out and it automatically lapsed. Ambedkar was so hurt by this failure that he resigned as the law minister. Despite four years of hard work by him on the Bill, it was in his words, 'killed and buried, unwept and unsung...' Nehru was blamed by Ambedkar as well as other progressives for not backing the Bill enough in the current parliamentary session. Ambedkar complained that while Nehru was sincere for the reform in the Hindu personal code, he lacked the earnestness and determination which was required to get the Bill passed in the parliament.[108]

'I will get the Hindu Code Bill passed, whether I win or lose the election. I am prepared to fight the election on the issue of the Hindu Code...' roared Nehru when challenged by a Hindu saint during the election of 1951-52. He let it be known before the election that should Congress return to power under him, the Bill shall be reintroduced with a few modifications by breaking it into separate bills. Getting the Bill passed before the elections might have proved to be a gamble since the Congress Party's organization itself was divided on the issue. After winning the elections by a large majority, Nehru kept his promise. He understood that getting the Bill passed as a whole may not be possible and so introduced it as separate bills. The huge margin of victory in the election had strengthened his hand inside Congress and against President Prasad.[109]

The provision of the Hindu Code Bill related to marriage and divorce was introduced in the parliament as the Special Marriage Bill in late 1953. Other parts of the Hindu Code Bill were piloted as the Hindu Marriage Act, the Hindu Succession, Minority and Guardianship, and Adoptions of Maintenance Acts. These were passed between 1954-56 in installments by the parliament. In one of his most eloquent speeches for the reform, Nehru said

> I do not know if Indian men are supposed to be perfect, incapable of any further effort or further improvement, but it is bad that this can be so. It cannot remain so, you cannot have it so under modern conditions, either modern democratic conditions or any conditions of modern life. You simply cannot have it. You cannot have a democracy, of course, if you cut off a large chunk of humanity, fifty per cent or thereabouts of the people, and put them in a separate class apart in regard to social privileges and the like. They are bound to rebel...[110]

With the Nehruvian era at its shining hour, the Bills were passed in the parliament with his backing. Unfortunately, by then, Ambedkar was a dying man and could not participate in any way in the deliberation over the Bills which in a large part were a product of his hard work. The only consolation was that he was able to witness the passage of the Bills before his death in December 1956. In tribute to Ambedkar in the parliament, Nehru said that he will be remembered most 'as a symbol of the revolt against all the oppressive features of Hindu society...[but also] for the great interest he took and the trouble he took over the question of Hindu law reform. I am happy that he saw that reform in a very large measure carried out, perhaps not in the form of that monumental tome that he had himself drafted, but in separate bits.'[111]

The debate over the Hindu Code Bill had gone on for almost eight years. It was a classic example of statesmen leading from the front by shaping the public's view while being cautious to not get too far ahead in a single stroke. Nehru and Ambedkar had superseded many hurdles in their way to reform the Hindu personal code. The opposition in the country was such that for every two steps forward, they had to take a step back. But, they did not lose their nerves and hopes. Nehru, having won the elections of 1951-52 did not comfortably sit down to focus on non-controversial measures but rather continued leading from the front to get the provisions enacted as law. Modern law supplicated ancient texts as the very basic foundation of Indian society. More than sixty million Hindu women came under the purview of these laws and unequivocally gained from them. The courage with which Nehru and Ambedkar worked on the reform for years against all opposition within and outside the Congress Party culminated in far-reaching changes which the passage of these legislations brought by restructuring the whole of Indian society. By giving power to women for choosing their partners and claiming a share in inheritance along with making monogamy mandatory, the reform has been one of the most far-reaching steps taken by the Indian democracy.

Perhaps for the first time in the history of Indian civilization, not religious texts but laws enacted by the state became the basis of organizing society. The state rather than religion became the institution through which personal laws were to be negotiated. Due to the absence of a comparatively liberal tradition among Indian Muslims at the time and their insecurities after Partition, Nehru decided (despite his sympathies) to not push for the personal reform among them. Among all his commitments regarding the nation's planning, economy, domestic and foreign policy, Nehru considered the passage of these reforms as one of his government's biggest achievements. As he wrote to the chief ministers of states after the reforms were passed by the parliament:

> One piece of good news, which has heartened me, is the passage in the Rajya Sabha and the Lok Sabha [Houses of the Parliament] of the Hindu Succession Act...It has had a long and difficult journey and it has changed shape several times. At last we appear to be reaching the end of

the journey. This Bill and the Hindu Marriage Act have a peculiar significance, not only because of the changes they bring about but chiefly because they have pulled out Hindu law from the ruts in which it had got stuck and given it a new dynamism. In that sense, the passage of this legislation marks an epoch in India. It indicates that we have not only striven for and achieved a political revolution, not only are we striving hard for an economic revolution but that we are equally intent on social revolution; only by way of advance on these three separate lines and their integration into one great whole, will the people of India progress.[112]

The road to equality was long, hard, and tedious, but the destination was reached with grit determination.

All Men are by Nature Equal
But differ greatly in the sequel.
-Nathaniel Ames

There can be no peace as long as there is grinding poverty, social injustice, inequality, oppression, environmental degradation, and as long as the weak and small continue to be trodden by the mighty and powerful.
-Tenzin Gyatso, The 14th Dalai Lama

One characteristic of these two democratic nations, America and India, is the love for equality whether it be social, political, or economic equality. Many social movements in these democracies have culminated in making these societies more just and equal such as the Civil Rights Movement in America and the Self-Respect Movement in India. However, these democracies still harbor inequalities along some axes such as income, race, sexual orientation, and religion, among others. The vital strength of these democracies is that these trends do not go unnoticed and stimulate society to present a vocal and forceful response. Just defining equality of opportunity in law does not guarantee its enjoyment by the citizens and they understand this very well. They struggle constantly to realize the Jeffersonian self-evident truths in their lives.

The love for freedom and equality that has been inculcated inside these democratic societies has always been the pillar of their stability. The ideal of Liberty is intertwined with that of Equality. It is not possible to trade one for the other. The two are sisters and attempting to make a choice between them is to lose sight of both. As the words by Charles Caleb Colton that are inscribed on the Indian Parliament House and became a self-fulfilling prophecy remind us: 'Liberty will not descend to a people; a people must raise themselves to liberty; it is a blessing which must be earned before it can be enjoyed.'[113] Without Liberty, it is impossible to realize the ideal of Equality. This is because only by transforming society non-violently through elected leaders and within the boundaries established by democratic institutions is it possible to profess and practice the ideal of Equality (whether be political, economic, or social). Subsequently, it is Equality which by maintaining social stability and thus precluding the rise of anarchic tendencies ensures the propagation of Liberty in the society.

In America, the debate around income inequality dominated the 2016 Presidential Election by far than any other issue and to a large extent featured during the 2020 Presidential Election as well. The "1 percent" has become a euphemism for the phenomenon of income inequality. In the past few years, the Jeffersonian ideal that "all men are created equal" which also signifies the equality of opportunity has come under strain. This is not the first time though when such a huge inequality of wealth has manifested itself in the American Republic. The so-called Gilded Age between the end of the Civil War and the start of the twentieth century had also witnessed the same phenomenon. The second Gilded Age of our times is a product of forces working over the past many decades. Among the major democracies of the developed world, the United States has been at the top in terms of income inequality since 1947. Between four decades from 1972-2012, the average income after adjusting for inflation for most Americans declined by 13 percent while for the top 1 percent it rose by 153 percent.

On top of this, the COVID-19 pandemic and subsequent large-scale unemployment which mostly affected the lower strata of the society have worsened the rampant economic inequality in America as well as India. Those employed in high-earning jobs were usually easily able to switch to working remotely while others who really needed economic support (people employed in hotels, restaurants, theme parks, shopping malls, tourism industry, etc.) were exactly the ones who were most adversely affected. While India had brought millions of individuals out of poverty in the past two decades, COVID-19 has plunged back many of them into poverty in just a few weeks. In both nations, the billionaires have become even richer during the pandemic while those at the bottom of the social strata are witnessing adversities of the kind they had not seen in decades.

These conditions have vindicated John Adams's prophecy regarding the rise of an aristocracy in America distinguished not by titles but rather wealth. Unusually strange at the time but extremely prescient in posterity, Adams's observation about America being no different from other nations has come true in our own times as never before. Even James Madison had by the end of his life predicted the rise of inequality in the American Republic despite a striking characteristic of the early American Republic being equity in the distribution of wealth compared to Europe. In 1829, Madison had prophesized that within a century the mass of Americans would be 'reduced by a competition for employment to wages which would [only] afford them the bare necessities of life.' He thought that as the proportion of citizens without property would increase, the political system would have to be overhauled for representative democracy to survive. 'The institutions and laws of the country must be adapted,' Madison wrote, 'and it will require for the task all the wisdom of the wisest patriots.'[114]

Today, not just the poor but citizens from many social groups in America feel the sentiment that "the system is rigged" against them. The fruits of the Industrial and Scientific Revolutions combined with the effects of globalization intertwined with the government's policies have brought America to a point where its society is under strain as never before. The middle-class is disappearing and the gap between the ends of the wealth spectrum is still widening.[115] Additionally, more than two centuries after Abigail Adams's call for women empowerment, America is still to see a woman president. Though the percentage of women elected to Congress has risen in the past few years, it is still not high enough when compared to other major democracies of the developed world. The same goes for

African Americans and Immigrant communities which still suffer from many handicaps on the path to social equality.

Former United States Secretary of State Henry Kissinger has written about leadership that 'The great statesmen act at the outer limit of that margin [the margin defined by the tradition of a society]. If they fall short, the society stagnates. If they exceed it, they lose the capacity to shape posterity.'[116] The abolition of Zamindars with peacefully carried out land reforms and passage of the provisions of the Hindu Code Bill may act as definitive examples of this statement by Kissinger. To have gone forward too far ahead of the public opinion and interests of the entrenched might have frustrated the passage of the intended legislation. Forceful abolition of Zamindars by using the strong arm of the state rather than the legal route with compensation or endeavoring to get the Hindu Code Bill passed in a single stroke might have ended up either in catastrophe for the society or in failures. Patel's shrewdness in dealing with Zamindars and firm determination gave a clear message to the Constituent Assembly regarding Congress Party's resoluteness to carry out land reforms. Ambedkar's frontal attack on the regressive Hindu social customs sparked a fierce debate on the applicability of ancient religious scriptures to the modern world. Nehru's dogged persistence of the reform in Hindu personal laws for years saw him finally taking it through the door of success despite opposition from within his own party and a significant portion of the general populace.

More than six decades since the passage of those legislations, India still awaits a Uniform Civil Code that was envisioned in the Constitution. Muslim women in India are still subjected to personal law that is based on medieval notions of religion. Additionally, some worrying trends of inequality based on religion have ever manifested in the Republic of India. Even after seven decades of Independence, neither a substantial middle-class nor a robust tradition of progressivism has come up among India's Muslims. Politics of appeasement, as well as communalism, are both responsible for this. Similarly, there is a huge inequality of opportunity and resources based on which geographical part of the country and which community a person belongs to. In general, four categories of citizens continue to face major social, economic, and political inequalities: Women, Muslims, Dalits (broadly those from the lowest castes), and

Tribals. The access to basic amenities such as drinking water, household fuel, sanitation, first aid, healthcare, and education remains highly unequally distributed and especially affects these four social groups. These inequalities of accessibility to resources are further compounded by the inequality in wealth and environmental degradation which are among the worst in the world. Many cities in India have the highest rates of air pollution in the world while soil contamination and reduction in the water table have led to more frequent floods and droughts (amplified by the adverse impact of Global Warming). Those at the bottom of the socio-economic hierarchy suffer the most from these harmful effects.

Yet, there is hope. Madison wrote in *Federalist 51* that 'Justice is the end of government. It is the end of civil society. It ever has been, and ever will be, pursued, until it be obtained...'[117] The long-standing tradition of fighting against injustices stemming from inequalities in society in these two democratic nations continues to push the government and political leaders into taking remedial actions. There might be temporary setbacks on the road to Equality but the history of these two nations shows us that in every single social aspect, the conditions have changed for the better over time. For many of these changes, the founding generations are directly responsible through their actions which showed a way forward to the future generations while indirectly their writings are still quoted by activists on the way to realizing equality. Every single major debate in these nations for any social movement still takes inspiration from the actions of their own founding fathers. Civil society in these democracies remains vocal and plays the watchdog's role against the ruling establishment. As long as there continues to be tolerance for all social groups, an active civil society, and the tradition of constitutionalism, corrective forces will keep playing their part in reducing all kinds of inequalities in these democracies.

---

[1] This thesis has been detailed at length in Danielle Allen, *Our Declaration: A Reading of the Declaration of Independence in Defense of Equality* (New York and London: W. W. Norton & Company, 2014)

[2] Denis James Galligan, *Constitutions and the Classics: Patterns of Constitutional Thought from Fortescue to Bentham* (Oxford University Press, 2014), p. 412

[3] Joseph J. Ellis, *American Dialogue: The Founders and Us* (New York: Alfred A. Knopf, 2018), p. 89

[4] Richard D. Brown, *Self-Evident Truths: Contesting Equal Rights from the Revolution to the Civil War* (New Haven and London: Yale University Press, 2017), p. 68

[5] John Adams, *The Works of John Adams*, Second President of the United States: with a Life of the Author, Notes and Illustrations, by his Grandson Charles Francis Adams (Boston: Little, Brown and Co., 1856). 10 volumes. Vol. 4, p. 381 (Hereafter, referred to as Adams Papers)

[6] Joseph J. Ellis, *American Dialogue: The Founders and Us* (New York: Alfred A. Knopf, 2018), p. 73

[7] David McCullough, *John Adams* (New York: Simon and Schuster, 2001), p. 19

[8] Ron Chernow, *Alexander Hamilton* (Penguin Books, 2004), p. 519

[9] John E. Ferling, *John Adams: A Life* (New York: Henry Holt and Company, 1992), p. 136

[10] David McCullough, *John Adams* (New York: Simon and Schuster, 2001), p. 163

[11] Ibid., p. 119

[12] Ibid., p. 127

[13] Leonard W. Levy, *Seasoned Judgments: The American Constitution, Rights, and History* (New Brunswick and London: Transaction Publishers, 1997), pp. 307-308

[14] David McCullough, *John Adams* (New York: Simon and Schuster, 2001), p. 318

[15] Gordon S. Wood, *Friends Divided: John Adams and Thomas Jefferson* (New York: Penguin Press, 2017), p. 265

[16] David McCullough, *John Adams* (New York: Simon and Schuster, 2001), p. 148

[17] Gordon S. Wood, *Friends Divided: John Adams and Thomas Jefferson* (New York: Penguin Press, 2017), p. 26

[18] Joseph J. Ellis, *Passionate Sage: The Character and Legacy of John Adams* (New York and London: W. W. Norton & Company, 1993), p. 83

[19] Ron Chernow, *Alexander Hamilton* (Penguin Books, 2004), pp. 518-519

[20] David McCullough, *John Adams* (New York: Simon and Schuster, 2001), p. 420

[21] Joseph J. Ellis, *Founding Brothers: The Revolutionary Generation* (New York: Vintage Books, 2002), p. 248

[22] Richard Beeman, *Plain, Honest Men: The Making of the American Constitution* (New York: Random House, 2009), p. 412

[23] Clement Fatovic, *America's Founding and the Struggle over Economic Inequality* (University Press of Kansas, 2015), pp. 17-18

[24] Luke Mayville, *John Adams and the Fear of American Oligarchy* (Princeton and Oxford: Princeton University Press, 2014), p. 26

[25] Ganesh Sitaraman, *The Crisis of the Middle-Class Constitution: Why Economic Inequality Threatens Our Republic* (New York: Vintage Books, 2018), p. 89

[26] Luke Mayville, *John Adams and the Fear of American Oligarchy* (Princeton and Oxford: Princeton University Press, 2014), p. 24

[27] Jay Cost's Introduction to *The Price of Greatness: Alexander Hamilton, James Madison, and the Creation of American Oligarchy* (New York: Basic Books, 2018)

[28] Gordon S. Wood, *Revolutionary Characters: What Made the Founders Different* (Penguin Books, 2006), pp. 179-180
[29] Ganesh Sitaraman, *The Crisis of the Middle-Class Constitution: Why Economic Inequality Threatens Our Republic* (New York: Vintage Books, 2018), pp. 62-67
[30] Ibid., p. 73
[31] Richard B. Freeman and Joseph R. Blasi, *What the Founding Fathers Believed: Stock Ownership for All*, PBS News Hour, 15 Nov 2013
[32] David McCullough, *John Adams* (New York: Simon and Schuster, 2001), p. 373
[33] Gordon S. Wood, *Creation of the American Republic: 1776-1787* (Chapel Hill: University of North Carolina Press, 1969), p. 592
[34] Helen Saltzberg Saltman, *John Adams's Earliest Essays: The Humphrey Ploughjogger Letters*, The William and Mary Quarterly, Vol. 37, No. 1 (Jan., 1980), pp. 125-135
[35] John E. Ferling, *John Adams: A Life* (New York: Henry Holt and Company, 1992), pp. 36-37
[36] Alana Semuels, The Founding Fathers Weren't Concerned With Inequality, *The Atlantic,* 25 April 2016
[37] Ganesh Sitaraman, *The Crisis of the Middle-Class Constitution: Why Economic Inequality Threatens Our Republic* (New York: Vintage Books, 2018), p. 72
[38] David McCullough, *John Adams* (New York: Simon and Schuster, 2001), p. 374
[39] John Adams, Preface to a Defence of the Constitution of the United States of America, Adams Papers, vol. 4, pp. 289-290
[40] John Adams to Thomas Jefferson, 6 December 1787, Adams Papers, vol. 8, p. 464
[41] Luke Mayville, *John Adams and the Fear of American Oligarchy* (Princeton and Oxford: Princeton University Press, 2014), pp. 28, 40
[42] David McCullough, *John Adams* (New York: Simon and Schuster, 2001), p. 379
[43] Gordon S. Wood, *Revolutionary Characters: What Made the Founders Different* (Penguin Books, 2006), p. 194
[44] The Adams Papers, Adams Family Correspondence, vol. 3, April 1778 – September 1780, ed. L. H. Butterfield and Marc Friedlaender. Cambridge, MA: Harvard University Press, 1973, pp. 341–343
[45] Luke Mayville, *John Adams and the Fear of American Oligarchy* (Princeton and Oxford: Princeton University Press, 2014), pp. 43, 46
[46] Gordon S. Wood, *Revolutionary Characters: What Made the Founders Different* (Penguin Books, 2006), p. 184
[47] Alexis de Tocqueville, *Democracy in America: The Complete and Unabridged Volumes I and II* (Bantam Classic Edition, 2000), p. 50
[48] Gordon S. Wood, *Revolutionary Characters: What Made the Founders Different* (Penguin Books, 2006), p. 185
[49] Luke Mayville, *John Adams and the Fear of American Oligarchy* (Princeton and Oxford: Princeton University Press, 2014), p. 28

[50] Joseph J. Ellis, *American Dialogue: The Founders and Us* (New York: Alfred A. Knopf, 2018), pp. 93-98

[51] Thomas G. West, *Vindicating the Founders: Race, Sex, Class, and Justice in the Origins of America* (Rowman & Littlefield Publishers Inc., 1997), pp. 133-135

[52] Thomas Jefferson to James Madison, The Papers of Thomas Jefferson. Edited by Julian P. Boyd et al. Princeton: Princeton University Press, 1950, 28 Oct. 1785, vol. 8, pp. 681-82

[53] Thomas G. West, *Vindicating the Founders: Race, Sex, Class, and Justice in the Origins of America* (Rowman & Littlefield Publishers Inc., 1997), p. 135

[54] The Adams Papers, Adams Family Correspondence, vol. 1, December 1761 – May 1776, ed. Lyman H. Butterfield. Cambridge, MA: Harvard University Press, 1963, pp. 369–371

[55] Ibid., pp. 381–383

[56] Richard D. Brown, *Self-Evident Truths: Contesting Equal Rights from the Revolution to the Civil War* (New Haven and London: Yale University Press, 2017), pp. 168-170

[57] Joseph J. Ellis, *Passionate Sage: The Character and Legacy of John Adams* (New York and London: W. W. Norton & Company, 1993), pp. 185-187

[58] Richard D. Brown, *Self-Evident Truths: Contesting Equal Rights from the Revolution to the Civil War* (New Haven and London: Yale University Press, 2017), p. 175

[59] Richard Hofstadter, *The Founding Fathers: An Age of Realism*, The Moral Foundations of the American republic (Charlottesville: University Press of Virginia, 1986), pp. 62-74

[60] Robert E. Wright, *Hamilton Unbound: Finance and the Creation of the American Republic* (Westport and London: Greenwood Press, 2002), pp. 101-102

[61] Daron Acemoglu and James A. Robinson, *Why Nations Fail* (New York: Crown Business, 2012), pp. 32-33

[62] Ganesh Sitaraman, *The Crisis of the Middle-Class Constitution: Why Economic Inequality Threatens Our Republic* (New York: Vintage Books, 2018), pp. 114-115

[63] Joseph J. Ellis, *Passionate Sage: The Character and Legacy of John Adams* (New York and London: W. W. Norton & Company, 1993), p. 161

[64] The Adams Papers, Papers of John Adams, vol. 3, May 1775 – January 1776, ed. Robert J. Taylor. Cambridge, MA: Harvard University Press, 1979, pp. 397–399

[65] Joseph J. Ellis, *American Dialogue: The Founders and Us* (New York: Alfred A. Knopf, 2018), p. 82

[66] Jawaharlal Nehru, *Nehru's Letters to His Sister* (London: Faber and Faber, 1963), Edited by Krishan Nehru Hutheesing, p. 167

[67] Pattabhi Sitaramayya, *Feathers and Stones: My Study Windows* (Bombay: Padma Publications Ltd., 1946), pp. 46-47

[68] Ibid., p. 116

[69] Ibid., p. 306

[70] Rajmohan Gandhi, *Patel: A Life* (Ahmedabad: Navajivan Publishing House, 2017), pp. 14, 20-21
[71] John Keay, *Midnight's Descendants: A History of South Asia since Partition* (New York: Basic Books, 2014), p. 67
[72] For Patel's detailed role in the unification of India, see V. P. Menon, *Integration of the Indian States* (London: Longmans Green and Co., 1956)
[73] Rajmohan Gandhi, *Understanding the Founding Fathers: An Enquiry into the Indian Republic's Beginnings* (New Delhi: Aleph Book Company, 2016), p. 128
[74] Rajmohan Gandhi, *Patel: A Life* (Ahmedabad: Navajivan Publishing House, 2017), pp. 447-448
[75] Ibid., p. 458
[76] Ramachandra Guha, *India after Gandhi: The History of the World's Largest Democracy* (Picador India, 2008), p. 23
[77] Rajmohan Gandhi, *Patel: A Life* (Ahmedabad: Navajivan Publishing House, 2017), pp. 460, 466-67
[78] Ibid., pp. 470-471
[79] Urvish Kothari, *Seven decades before Statue of Unity, Nehru had unveiled a Sardar Patel statue in Godhra been able to run the state*, ThePrint, 15 December 2018
[80] *Nehru Abhinandan Granth: A Birthday Book* (Allahabad: Law Journal Press, 1949), pp. xxviii-xxix
[81] Ramachandra Guha, *India after Gandhi: The History of the World's Largest Democracy* (Picador India, 2008), pp. 202-203
[82] Granville Austin, *The Indian Constitution: Cornerstone of a Nation* (Oxford: Clarendon Press, 1966), p. 50
[83] Granville Austin, *Working a Democratic Constitution: The Indian Experience* (Oxford University Press, 2000), p. 71
[84] Sardar Vallabhbhai Patel's speech in the Constituent Assembly, 2 May 1947, *Constituent Assembly Debates: Official Report* (reprint New Delhi: Lok Sabha Secretariat, 2014), Vol. III, p. 522
[85] Sardar Vallabhbhai Patel's warning to Jagirdars of Rajasthan to Move with Times, *The Collected Works of Sardar Vallabhbhai Patel* (Konark Publishers Pvt. Ltd., 1999), Vol. XIV, pp. 28-30
[86] Hindol Sengupta, *The Man Who Saved India: Sardar Patel and His Idea of India* (Penguin, 2018), p. 307
[87] Jawaharlal Nehru, *Letters to Chief Ministers 1947-64* (Government of India, 1985), Letter dated 6 December 1948, vol. 1, pp. 243-244
[88] Sanjiv Agarwal, *The Indian Federalist: The Original Will of India's Founding Fathers* (Chennai: Notion Press, 2014), p. 109
[89] Granville Austin, *The Indian Constitution: Cornerstone of a Nation* (Oxford: Clarendon Press, 1966), pp. 97-99

[90] Jawaharlal Nehru's speech in the Constituent Assembly, 10 September 1949, *Constituent Assembly Debates: Official Report* (reprint New Delhi: Lok Sabha Secretariat, 2014), Vol. IX, pp. 1194-1197

[91] Detailed account of the passage of Article 31 has been provided in H. C. L. Merillat, *Land and the Constitution in India* (New York and London: Columbia University Press, 1970)

[92] Granville Austin, *Working a Democratic Constitution: The Indian Experience* (Oxford University Press, 2000), pp. 78-80

[93] Jawaharlal Nehru, *Letters to Chief Ministers 1947-64* (Government of India, 1985), Letter dated 1 February 1951, vol. 2, p. 325

[94] Granville Austin, *Working a Democratic Constitution: The Indian Experience* (Oxford University Press, 2000), pp. 83-84

[95] Ramachandra Guha, *India after Gandhi: The History of the World's Largest Democracy* (Picador India, 2008), p. 220; S. K. Dey, *Power to the People? A Chronicle of India 1947-67* (Orient Longman, 1969), pp. 132-138

[96] A. L. Basham, *The Wonder that was India: A Survey of History and Culture of the Indian Sub-Continent Before the Coming of the Muslims* (Calcutta: Rupa Co., 1986 Reprint), p. 36

[97] Reba Som, *Jawaharlal Nehru and the Hindu Code: A Victory of Symbol over Substance?*, Modern Asian Studies, Vol. 28, No. 1 (Feb., 1994), pp. 165-194

[98] Ramachandra Guha, *India after Gandhi: The History of the World's Largest Democracy* (Picador India, 2008), pp. 228-229

[99] Sardar Vallabhbhai Patel's speech published in *The Hindustan Times* on *24 February 1949*, *The Collected Works of Sardar Vallabhbhai Patel* (Konark Publishers Pvt. Ltd., 1999), Vol. XIV, p. 59

[100] Harold Lewis Levy, *Law & Society Review*, LAWYER-SCHOLARS, LAWYER-POLITICIANS AND THE HINDUCODE BILL, 1921-1956 (Nov., 1968 - Feb., 1969), Vol. 3, No. 2/3, pp. 303- 316

[101] Chitra Sinha, *Debating Patriarchy: The Hindu Code Bill Controversy in India (1941-1956)* (New Delhi: Oxford University Press, 2012), p. 142

[102] Ramachandra Guha, *India after Gandhi: The History of the World's Largest Democracy* (Picador India, 2008), pp. 230-231

[103] Reba Som, *Jawaharlal Nehru and the Hindu Code: A Victory of Symbol over Substance?*, Modern Asian Studies, Vol. 28, No. 1 (Feb., 1994), pp. 165-194

[104] Chitra Sinha, *Debating Patriarchy: The Hindu Code Bill Controversy in India (1941-1956)* (New Delhi: Oxford University Press, 2012), pp. 144-145

[105] Ramachandra Guha, *India after Gandhi: The History of the World's Largest Democracy* (Picador India, 2008), pp. 232-234

[106] Reba Som, *Jawaharlal Nehru and the Hindu Code: A Victory of Symbol over Substance?*, Modern Asian Studies, Vol. 28, No. 1 (Feb., 1994), pp. 165-194

[107] Sarvepalli Gopal, *Jawaharlal Nehru—A Biography* (Oxford University Press, 2015 Edition), Vol. 2, p. 155

[108] Dhananjay Keer, *Dr. Babasaheb Ambedkar: Life and Mission* (Mumbai: Popular Prakashan, Fifth Edition, May 2018 Reprint), p. 434

[109] John A. Banningan, *The Hindu Code Bill, Far Eastern Survey, Vol. 21, No. 17 (Dec. 3, 1952),* pp. 173-176

[110] Ramachandra Guha, *Makers of Modern India* (Penguin Books, 2012), p. 366

[111] Ramachandra Guha, *India after Gandhi: The History of the World's Largest Democracy* (Picador India, 2008), pp. 240-241

[112] Jawaharlal Nehru, *Letters to Chief Ministers 1947-64* (Government of India, 1985), Letter dated 10 May 1956, vol. 4, p. 369

[113] Sunil Khilnani, *The Idea of India* (New York: Farrar Straus Giroux, 1999), p. 122

[114] Ganesh Sitaraman, *Divided We Fall, The New Republic Magazine,* 10 April 2017

[115] Joseph J. Ellis, *American Dialogue: The Founders and Us* (New York: Alfred A. Knopf, 2018), p. 105

[116] Henry Kissinger, *World Order* (New York: Penguin Press, 2014), p. 255

[117] Federalist No. 51: The Structure of the Government Must Furnish the Proper Checks and Balances Between the Different Departments, *The Federalist Papers* (New York: Dover Publications, Dover Thrift Edition, 2014), p. 256

5. NATIONALISM

Perhaps the ten most relevant words which characterize Americanism i.e. the spirit of the American people are Individualism, Diligence, Optimism, Liberty, Dissent, Entrepreneurship, Idealism, Hedonism, Hypocrisy, and Pragmatism. The founding father who embodied all of these features more than any other was Benjamin Franklin. Among the founding fathers, not only was Franklin the living embodiment of what later came to be known as the "American way of life" but was its chief inventor. He has been variously called "the First American," "the Prophet of Tolerance," and "The Patron Saint of Advertising." In the words of his biographer, Gordon Wood, Franklin 'has represented everything Americans like about themselves—their levelheadedness, common sense, pragmatism, ingenuity, and get-up-and-go...He has stood for industry, frugality, thrift, and every materialistic virtue that Americans have valued.'[1] Famous around the world today for his kite-flying experiments with electricity, Franklin was also a 'printer, postmaster, almanac maker, essayist, chemist, orator, tinker, statesman, humorist, philosopher, parlor-man, political economist, professor of housewifery, ambassador, projector, maxim-monger, herb-doctor, wit,' among other roles such as that of an inventor and civic activist that he played from time to time.[2]

Among other things, Franklin was also the inventor of "the American Dream." His pioneering of the spirit of self-help, teaching himself everything from languages to philosophy and business, and establishing many public institutions are a testimony of his passion for betterment. His autobiography is full of amusing maxims and details his rise from being a nobody. It also chronicles his principles of self-help and disseminates free advice to youngsters searching for opportunities for betterment. Perhaps no American work has matched it ever for inspiring the young to work hard and pursue their dreams.[3] Alexis de Tocqueville had noted in the mid-1830s that the 'first thing which strikes a traveller in the United States is the innumerable multitude of those who seek to throw off their original condition.' By the time Tocqueville observed this, Franklin's autobiography had already reprinted almost a hundred times and his life had inspired a multitude of common folk.[4]

Franklin's life story had played a great role in creating the narrative that anybody who worked hard could make it in America. He had written his memoir with the aim of propagating among Americans his ideas about the virtues of personal, fiscal, and social improvement. Another of his contributions was to make natural and ubiquitous the idea that working with the aim to earn money is honorable and that every and any kind of work is respectable.[5] Furthermore, Franklin's autobiography also served to bind Americans by a common heritage around nationalistic feelings arising from perseverance and zeal for hard work. It became a source of inspiration for immigrants migrating from various parts of Europe who then contributed to nation-building while getting gradually dissolved in the American multi-cultural melting pot. Today, more than two hundred years after his death, Franklin still continues to inspire Americans and give them hope in their pursuit of "the American Dream."[6]

This extraordinarily complex man, who is chiefly remembered today as a scientist and promoter of capitalism, regarded public service as being more impactful than his scientific pursuits. He was the only American who signed all four documents that gave birth to the United States of America: the Declaration of Independence (1776), the Treaty of Alliance with France (1778), the Treaty of Paris establishing peace with Great Britain (1783) and the U.S. Constitution (1787). No other leader of the revolutionary generation was so indispensable as Franklin when it came to diplomacy and statecraft. He doggedly persuaded France to enter the Revolutionary War on the American side while securing financial assistance from the French when it was needed the most. However, grouping Franklin in the term "Revolutionary Generation" can be misleading since he was already seventy and the most celebrated and respected American by the time the United States declared Independence.

Before the Revolutionary War commenced, Franklin had already become a member of the Royal Society and had received honorary degrees from universities in America and Britain including Oxford. He was consulted by philosophers around the world on things varying from how to build a fireplace to why oceans were salty. This most famous American was already in the company of the most renowned men in the world. He conversed and dined with kings and counted many lords among his friends and admirers. Thus, he had most to lose—reputation, dignity, wealth—by siding with young naïve inexperienced provincial American leaders like Washington, Adams, and Jefferson, against the most powerful empire in the world. This was the same British Empire to which Franklin had owed allegiance since his birth and under which he had served loyally in multiple roles. In 1776 when Americans declared Independence, Franklin had been deeply committed to the British Empire for many more years than the sum of years that Madison and Hamilton had been alive for. He had already achieved much more than what other American leaders of the time cumulatively aspired to achieve in their lives.[7]

Franklin's transformation from loyalist to revolutionary despite the high stature that he risked to lose is the story of the rise of American Nationalism. Unlike factors like common ancestry, race, religion, or language, American Nationalism was not dependent on social identity. As Historian George Bancroft wrote about America: 'France contributed to its independence, the origin of the language we speak carries us to India; our religion is from Palestine; of the hymns sung in our churches, some were first heard in Italy, some in the deserts of Arabia, some on the banks of the Euphrates; our arts come from Greece; our jurisprudence from Rome.' There was not a single social identity that could distinguish Americans from Europeans. After winning the war with the British, the last thing Americans wanted was to still put up with the label "English." Thus, a new myth needed to be stitched for binding the colonists together in the fabric of nationalism and transform America into a nation-state.[8]

The ideals of pluralism and cosmopolitanism as the pillars of American Nationalism (as conveyed in the above lines by Bancroft) combined with an idea of manifest destiny was weaved by the founding fathers to keep the newborn nation together. This mirrored Franklin's own transformation, ideas, and actions. Franklin was the most British among the founding fathers, having been born a generation before Washington and two generations before Madison and Hamilton. At the same time, he had lived outside America for the bulk of his last thirty-three years, which also contained many instances when it was doubtful that he would ever return back to America or even if he cared much about America.⁹ Yet, Franklin was first among the founding fathers to conceptualize inside himself what America sans its British identity could be and should be. His life was the very embodiment of an America based on pluralism and "the American Dream." He worked more than anybody else on the world stage to make America a reality. After his death, it was the U.S. Constitution that served as the most profound symbol of American Nationalism.

    Writing about Franklin's life is like using a handheld bucket for catching fish swimming downstream in a river. No matter how hard you may try to portray all the colorful perspectives of Franklin's extraordinary life, most of them will still remain out of your reach. The greatest American polymath Benjamin Franklin was born on 17 January 1706 as one of seventeen children to Josiah Franklin. Unable to complete his formal education due to lack of funds, Franklin self-taught himself through voracious reading. At the age of twelve, he started an apprenticeship at his brother's printing shop where he could also continue to read. Among all the founding fathers, Franklin understood the depths and intricacies of human nature the most. On being denied permission to publish a letter in his brother's newspaper, this teenager donned the hat of a middle-aged widow with the pseudonym "Silence Dogood" to publish his writings. During his life, Franklin used hundreds of pseudonyms and assumed a wide array of varied human characters. And so, it is hard to separate the elusive man from the caricatures and fictions he weaved around himself all his life. Unable to work under his brother's apprenticeship for long, Franklin ran away and set out at the age of 17 to make himself in Philadelphia.

    Arriving in Philadelphia as a poor hungry teenager, Franklin started working in a printing house. Soon, he visited London on the advice of the Pennsylvania Governor to acquire the equipment for establishing a newspaper, only to find that the Governor had made empty promises. Arriving back in Philadelphia, Franklin started to work as a clerk and shopkeeper in a merchant Thomas Denham's business. It was at this time that Franklin's interest in self-improvement and the establishment of institutions took a veritable turn. In 1727, Franklin, then 21, created the Junto, a group of like-minded people of which 'The rules I drew up required that every member in his turn should produce one or more queries on any point of morals, politics, or natural philosophy, to be discussed by the company; and once in three months produce and read an essay of his own writing on any subject he pleased.'[10] The Junto was modeled on London coffeehouses while its establishment itself was an innovation in America. Franklin also started a subscription library in which members from the Junto pooled money to buy otherwise-costly books that anybody in the group could read. This reading group later paved the way for the establishment of the city's first public library, today's Library Company of Philadelphia. In 1728, after Denham's death, Franklin established a printing house and started to publish a newspaper, *The Pennsylvania Gazette*. It was also around this time that he started maintaining a "virtue table" to daily mark which among the thirteen virtues that he most admired were followed on any particular day.

In 1733, Franklin started publishing *Poor Richard's Almanack* under the pseudonym Richard Saunders which in the coming years sealed his reputation as the master of quips. Perhaps more of Franklin's quips from the *Almanack, The Way to Wealth,* and other writings are still used in the world than of any other author. "Early to bed and early to rise makes a man healthy, wealthy, and wise," "A penny saved is twopence dear," "Fish and visitors stink in three days," "Love your Enemies, for they tell you your Faults," "No gains without pains," "God helps them that helps themselves," and "Don't throw stones at your neighbors, if your own windows are glass," are just some examples. *Poor Richard's Almanack* made Franklin a household name. Simultaneously, he also went on to lay the foundation of many public institutions in America of which many were firsts: the American Philosophical Society, Pennsylvania Hospital, University of Pennsylvania, and Philadelphia's first fire department, among others.

Making a fortune from the printing business by the time he turned 41, Franklin retired from printing. Then inaugurated Franklin, the scientist, inventor, and public servant. He investigated weather patterns, ocean currents, demographic studies, the origin of mountains, the saltiness of the sea, and everything else that was not a part of established science at the time. His experiments with electricity brought lasting fame to him. He was the first to identify the positive and negative charge and to discover the principle of the conservation of charge. In 1752, Franklin conducted his famous kite experiment in which during a thunderstorm he flew a silk kite and felt an electric shock after touching a knuckle attached to a key on the wet string. He published the account of his experiments as *Experiments and Observations on Electricity* which was translated into Latin, French, German, and Italian. It helped in sealing Franklin's reputation in Europe. He was granted the membership of the English Royal Society and the French Académie des Sciences and received honorary degrees from Harvard, Yale, and Oxford among other universities. Franklin invented the lightning rod which could protect buildings from lightning by drawing it out from them. Among his many other inventions, the prominent ones are bifocals, glass harmonica, Franklin stove, and urinary catheter.

In 1751, Franklin was elected to the Pennsylvania Assembly and a couple of years later, he was made the deputy postmaster-general of British North America. He appealed for the thirteen colonies to unite during the French and Indian War and also organized the Pennsylvania Militia for service in the war. From the mid-1750s to the mid-1770s, Franklin spent much of his time in London. He met many notable people there, furthered his scientific and innovative explorations, and acted as a representative of the American colonies. When the tensions between the American colonies and Britain reached a breaking point, Franklin advocated nationalism among the colonies based on mutual cooperation and pluralism. He published various articles to unite the colonies in the common struggle while forgetting all mutual tensions arising from the diversity of their social identities like religion, sect, and language. "The First American" worked hard to convince Americans that they were a nation in their own right.

'What say you to your friend and brother Philosopher Franklin, who at upwards of seventy years of age, quits the Study of the Laws of Nature, in order to give Laws to new Commonwealth; and has crossed the Atlantick ocean at that time of Life, not to seek repose but to plunge into the midst of the most laborious and most arduous affairs that ever were,' thus wrote Edmund Burke to a French friend.[11] In December 1776, Franklin had sailed for France as the ambassador of the newly inaugurated United States. In France, he played his part to perfection by taking full advantage of the image of a philosopher from the exotic New World which he had cultivated over time. Wearing a fur cap and dressed plainly, exactly opposite to the French elite customs, Franklin became a specimen of awe and curiosity among powdered heads of Paris. He became so famous that he was often addressed as "The Doctor" just like great ancient Greek philosophers. His portraits seemed to appear everywhere from medallions, rings, and hats to wall plaques. When John Adams visited Paris, he was so startled to see Franklin's popularity that he enviously wrote: 'His [Franklin's] name was familiar to government and people, to kings, courtiers, nobility, clergy, and philosophers, as well as plebeians, to such a degree that there was scarcely a peasant or citizen, a *valet de chambre,* coachman or footman, a lady's chambermaid or a scullion in a kitchen, who was not familiar with it, and who did not consider him as a friend of humankind. When they spoke of him, they seemed to think he was to restore the golden age.'[12]

Throughout his life, Franklin also remained a man with many irreconcilable traits. He initially owned as many as seven slaves but in later years became a forceful abolitionist. He published several essays to argue for the abolition of slavery and also established the Pennsylvania Abolitionist Society. As another example, Franklin loved to lecture on morality and virtues (Chastity was one of the virtues in his virtue table) and yet could not contain his passions and frequented dubious quarters of the city—he also had at least one illegitimate son. He did not take care of his wife, Deborah, and did not even hear her plea to return from Europe by her dying bed. He was insensitive to his daughter whom he did not allow to marry the man she loved and later he never forgave his son for siding with the British during the Revolution.

Franklin was instrumental in securing French support in the Revolutionary War, financially and militarily, which ensured American victory. Franklin then served on the committee to negotiate the 1783 Treaty of Paris which ended the War. Having completed his work in France, Franklin returned to America in 1785 to a warm reception. By now, his reputation in America was second only to General Washington. Franklin then served as the President of Pennsylvania and a delegate to the Constitutional Convention. In the

Constitutional Convention, he was instrumental in bringing about the Connecticut Compromise and came out forcefully in support of the freedom of speech. In a fitting case of succession, it so happened that he wrote his last letter to his spiritual heir, Jefferson. Just like his own constitution which slowly changed from being lean and agile in youth to obese and dull in old age, Franklin's character displayed varying changes as his life progressed. His life came a full circle when from owning slaves himself, he transformed and petitioned the newly inaugurated government for the abolition of slavery. Franklin's last years were dominated by prolonged suffering from various ailments and he died in April 1790. Apparently, his last words being another quip: 'A dying man can do nothing easy.'[13] A succinct summary of his extraordinary and peculiar life can be that Franklin's greatest invention was himself.

Franklin's efforts to promote Americanism started long before the establishment of the American nation. For the first half of the eighteenth century, the American colonists had dual identities: one associated with their mother-nation Britain based on ancestral ties and the other with their own colony based on their religion and day-to-day life. There was no sense of a Pan-American identity superseding the colonial identity and so there was minimal collaboration and coordination between the colonies. This led to a policy paralysis when it came to dealing with Native American affairs or with the expanding influence of the French on the North American continent. In 1751, Franklin had recognized this and appealed in a letter for unity among the colonies. He wrote: 'It would be a very strange thing if six nations of ignorant savages [Native American Iroquois Confederacy] should be capable of forming a scheme for such a union, and be able to execute it in such a manner as that it has subsisted for ages, and appears indissoluble; and yet that a like union should be impracticable for ten or a dozen English colonies, to whom it is more necessary, and must be more advantageous.' He further proposed a detailed blueprint of such a union with delegates to be selected from every colony and a governor-general above them to be appointed by the Crown. Franklin believed that 'A voluntary union entered into by the Colonies themselves, I think, would be preferable to one imposed by Parliament.' But nobody listened to him at the time since there was no urgent reason for any colony to let go of its independence and privileges by entering into a common agreement with others.[14]

In May 1754, a 22-year-old soldier named George Washington inadvertently kick-started the French and Indian War (as we read in the first chapter). A conflict with the powerful French Empire meant that for the first time American colonists felt the need for solidarity toward each other to face a common enemy. As the news of Washington's defeat reached Franklin, he wrote an editorial in the *Gazette,* parts of which are reproduced below:

> The Confidence of the French in this Undertaking seems well-grounded on the present disunited State of the British Colonies, and the extreme Difficulty of bringing so many different Governments and Assemblies to agree in any speedy and effectual Measures for our common Defence and Security; while our Enemies have the very great Advantage of being under one Direction, with one Council, and one Purse. Hence, and from the great Distance of Britain, they presume that they may with Impunity violate the most solemn Treaties subsisting between the two Crowns, kill, seize and imprison our Traders, and confiscate their Effects at Pleasure (as they have done for several Years past) murder and scalp our Farmers, with their Wives and Children, and take an easy Possession of such Parts of the British Territory as they find most convenient for them; which if they are permitted to do, must end in the Destruction of the British Interest, Trade and Plantations in America.[15]

Just below this forceful appeal was published a cartoon that has been described as the first and most famous political cartoon in American history. The "Snake Cartoon" showed a dismembered snake divided into eight segments representing the American colonies by their initials printed next to each part. Beneath this captivating visual illustration was the motto "Join or Die." This cartoon and motto were to later become a symbol of American unity during the Revolutionary War.

In June 1754, the Albany Congress was convened which was attended by delegates from seven colonies. Franklin was selected as one of the four representatives from Pennsylvania to participate in the Albany Congress. As he left Philadelphia, Franklin carried a document with a detailed scheme of the union titled *Short Hints towards a Scheme for Uniting the Northern Colonies.* Just like in scientific exploration, Franklin was already ahead of other Americans in envisioning a nation out of the colonies. However, the Albany Congress was destined to be a failure due to apprehensions about the decrease in the power of respective colonies by such a planned union. Furthermore, the most heavyweight colony, Virginia, had boycotted it. Franklin tried hard to convince the other delegates that a union would be in their interests but to no avail. The Albany Plan was rejected by all colonies while London did not support the plan either from the fear of creating a political unity among the different colonies across the Atlantic. One thing which did have a psychological impact on the colonies because of the ongoing war was Franklin's "Join, or Die" illustration. It was circulated far and beyond and gave a sense of distinctiveness and urgency to the colonists.[16] Until now the identity of colonists was attached only with Britain and their own colony, but for the first time, they began to see themselves as North Americans in the geographical sense of the term—separated from their mother-country by an ocean spanning more than three thousand miles—who may have to fend off for themselves.

The next crisis which further developed a sense of unity among the colonies was instigated by the British Parliament. To recuperate from the broken financial crisis triggered by the French and Indian War, the Parliament thought it best to make the colonies pay for the same and passed the Stamp Act of 1765. Everything from legal documents, magazines, playing cards, newspapers, and many other types of paper were taxed by the Parliament. Naturally then, the tax was abhorred by the colonists and it also sparked the debate if the British Parliament has complete sovereignty over the American colonies without providing them voting rights and formal representation in the Parliament. Franklin was at the time in London continuing his struggle against the proprietorship of Pennsylvania by the Penn family, but the passage of the Stamp Act altered his mission. He started canvassing in London for the American colonies by acting as their voice against the Stamp Act. Coming from a background in printing and still heavily invested financially in the same, Franklin also had a personal reason to oppose the new tax as it would have affected most the printing business. There are speculations that he may have been the largest paper dealer in the English-speaking world. Additionally, he was a prolific creditor, almost a bank for personal loans, dealt in land speculation, and owned a good amount of rental property much of which was associated with the printing business in Philadelphia.[17]

However, Franklin's first instinct after the passage of the tax was to make use of it for his own benefit. When London thought that appointing Americans as tax collectors would gain sympathy and streamline the tax collection, Franklin got one of his close associates, John Hughes, appointed as the stamp commissioner for Pennsylvania. This folly of going against the prevailing mood in the colonies where uncontrollable mobs were violently agitating against the tax and assembly leaders were arguing the constitutionality of the British Parliament to tax Americans almost cost Hughes his life and Franklin his reputation. Franklin was accused of being responsible for the passage of the Stamp Act so that he could profit from his monetary assets. Perhaps living in London from years past, Franklin had become disconnected from the colonial world that had led him to take such a politically miscalculated step. Franklin's condoning of the Stamp Tax showed how very little he knew of the public opinion in the colonies where colony after colony, resolutions were being passed in assemblies declaring the tax "unconstitutional." His newly built home in Philadelphia was threatened to be leveled by the unruly mob while Franklin was accused of profiting from the tax that was a scourge on the face of "Americans" who were now questioning their identity as colonists. Fortunately, the incident opened his eyes. Franklin realized that his warm sentiments toward the British were not generally acceptable in America. The only course of action in front of him was to change course or risk losing his reputation in the colonies.[18]

The public opinion in Britain especially among the English (and not the Scots or Irish) was to disregard Americans as a bunch of squealing convicts. Their sense of English distinctiveness had amplified after the victory in the French and Indian War which had made Britain the most powerful empire in the world. As a result, Britain started to view Americans as just another people to be ruled over by not providing them any representation in the parliament. Franklin, still a loyal subject of the Empire, wrote many pieces in 1765-66 to appeal to the British reason and reflection. He tried to convince the Englishmen that Americans were as English and as loyal subjects of His Majesty as they were. Taking to satire, he wrote anonymously as an Englishman: 'The gentle terms of *republican race, mixed rabble of Scotch, Irish and foreign vagabonds, descendants of convicts, ungrateful rebels*, &c., are some of the sweet flowers of English rhetorick, with which our colonists have of late been regaled. Surely, if we are so much their superiors, we should shew the superiority of our breeding by our better manners!'

Going forward with his biting satire, Franklin also wrote in another article under the pseudonym "Pacifus" that Britain should consider burning all American capitals, kill every man, woman, and child and destroy all trade by military force. 'No Man in his Wits, after such terrible Military Execution, will refuse to purchase stamp'd Paper. If any one should hesitate, five or six Hundred Lashes in a cold frosty Morning would soon bring him to Reason,' wrote Franklin scathingly. Such sarcastic pieces apart, he tenaciously worked for the American cause by lobbying parliamentarians and writing serious articles to make the Englishmen aware that they and American colonists had a common interest in the Empire. He wrote presciently that any endeavor by Britain backed by force to bow Americans into accepting the Stamp Tax would have the effect 'by mutual Violences, Excesses and Severities, of creating a deep-rooted Aversion between the two Countries, and laying the Foundation of a future total Separation.' Clearly, Franklin was slowly changing his course to position himself firmly behind the American sentiment.[19]

By now, the newly inaugurated British Whig government was also looking for a way out of the impasse. The British Parliament was able to neither soothe the tempers nor enforce the tax in the face of a violent mob in America that was destroying the tax-collection infrastructure. Thus, it invited the foremost American voice in London, Franklin, to testify before the parliament to understand the Americans' perspective. Though Franklin did not initially represent the true public opinion in America, fortunately, his views regarding the Stamp Act had changed substantially after the initial setbacks he had received. This was Franklin's opportunity to restore his reputation back in America in a single afternoon and he played the part theatrically to perfection. He was asked to answer 174 questions which he did being calm and reposed. He started by explaining that while the colonies had been paying various sorts of taxes for a long time, 'There is not gold and silver enough in the colonies to pay the stamp duty for one year.' Franklin explained that before the new tax was introduced, Americans 'submitted willingly to the government of the Crown, and paid, in all their courts, obedience to the acts of Parliament,' while now their temper had become 'very much altered.' He further expressed that no military force could be applied now to compel the colonists because such a force 'will find nobody in arms…They will not find a rebellion; they may indeed make one.' The finale came when Franklin made it explicitly clear that the colonies would not acknowledge the right of the parliament to tax them and thus made a distinction between external and internal taxes. This was a foreboding of the events to come later.[20]

After the testimony, Franklin emerged as the most effective American spokesman and the unofficial "ambassador" of America in Britain so much so that in addition to Pennsylvania, he was also named as the agent for Georgia, New Jersey, and Massachusetts. Thus, Franklin became the first real American to transcend the boundaries of colonial sectarianism, a full decade before the start of the Revolutionary War. Since in American fiction, especially in Pennsylvania, Franklin was responsible for the imposition of the Stamp Act to profit his business, it served conveniently to now hail Franklin as the chief reason in London for the repeal of the Act. More importantly, the whole saga made Americans realize for the first time that their identity could be more than just being "British," that they could unite against the British Parliament. Franklin's perspective of looking at what in his view was the greatest creation of humankind, the British Empire, had drastically altered. He now started to view the colonial assemblies as parliaments in their own right.

The sense of American Nationalism which had started to develop among American colonies had found its most vocal proponent in Franklin. A nationalistic feeling among the American colonists was brewing by now. While the core substance of this feeling was contempt for the British authority, it was also forging solidarity among the different colonies. Fearing such sentiments, the Parliament soon followed the repeal by a Declaratory Act to affirm its right to legislate for colonies in all cases whatsoever. These events left a sour taste on both sides of the Atlantic. Given its track record towards

American colonists, one could be sure that the British Parliament would make more mistakes in the near future.

Franklin's gradual transformation was soon to make him the most inveterate enemy of the Empire. To retaliate against the colonists and show its full sovereignty over them, the British Parliament passed the Townshend Acts in 1767. These Acts imposed an indirect tax on many commodities, most notably tea, and stationed British army troops in recalcitrant Boston the next year which ultimately led to the Boston Massacre in 1770. Since the British Parliament continued to deny representation to colonists, resentment against Britain kept increasing. When the Tea Act was passed in 1773 to help the precarious East India Company in dumping its tea on the American colonies, the situation reached a breaking point. The Act left American duty on the tea as is while allowing the company to dump its tea by rebating other duties paid by it. Colonists were outraged and at the forefront of the storm was Massachusetts. Since Franklin was serving as its agent in Britain, he was trying to play the role of a conciliator. Until now, he believed that a break between the Crown and the colonies could be avoided. Ironically, his own inadvertent actions escalated the break and his metamorphosis away from the British.

Thomas Hutchinson who was appointed the Governor of Massachusetts in 1770 by the British had written some inflammatory letters reflecting his views on the current tensions between the colonists and the Crown. In the most damning passage, Hutchinson had suggested that 'There must be an abridgment of what are called English liberties…I doubt whether it is possible to project a system of government in which a colony 3000 miles distant from the parent state shall enjoy all the liberty of the parent state.' Franklin had somehow got his hands on several such provoking letters. He calculated that by sending the letters to Massachusetts Assembly members for them to read privately would reconcile the Assembly into believing that the present imbroglio was largely of the making of a few British-appointed officials like Hutchinson. Franklin hoped that the Assembly members would understand that there is no conspiracy from the British side to divest Americans of their liberties but rather malicious propaganda originating from a few characters like

Hutchinson. While Franklin had never wished and had in fact explicitly asked that the letters not be made public, they created such fury among legislators that they were published soon after. The legislators were outraged and the ensuing firestorm engulfed many colonies. The colonists lost any trust that was remaining in the British officials and the distress culminated in the Boston Tea Party[α]. On the other side, Franklin admitted that he had passed on the letters while still hoping to act as a reconciliatory voice among the uproar in England over the leak.[21]

Now came the last phase of Franklin's transformation in which from a loyal supporter of the Empire still hoping for reconciliation, he turned into the most passionate American patriot. As the news of the Boston Tea Party reached London after a month, temperatures soared in London at the peak of winter. The greatest American and the most representative voice of America in the city was accused of being the cause of all that was wrong between Britain and the American colonies. Franklin was being viewed as the symbol of the "treachery" of the colonists. The hearing of the Massachusetts petition to remove Hutchinson from the office became a full-blown courtroom indictment of Franklin.

In an amphitheater aptly named Cockpit, Franklin was surrounded by scores of spectators when the Solicitor General Alexander Wedderburn started to grill him. Wedderburn denounced the Massachusetts Assembly for having gone against Hutchinson by drafting the petition and accused Franklin of orchestrating the whole drama by sending Hutchinson's letters to Massachusetts. Wedderburn went further to accuse Franklin of being an incendiary who set a whole province 'in flame,' of not being a gentleman and instead of being a thief alluding to Franklin's getting hold of those letters in the first place. One of the most famous men in the world, scientist and philosopher, Franklin was shouted on as 'the actor and secret spring...the inventor and the first planner of the whole contrivance.' For over an hour, he stood calmly, betraying any expression of

---

[α] Protestors threw the chests of tea into the Boston Harbor to protest against the Townshend Acts. The event made the British government respond harshly to the protestors and the ensuing chain of events ultimately led to the American Revolution.

emotion on his face as many hostile detractors cheered from the crowd. At the end of the ordeal, the Massachusetts petition was deemed groundless and disposed of. The next day, Franklin was informed that he had been divested of the post of deputy postmaster general of North America.[22] Getting fired was probably the last thing on Franklin's mind right now after the shameful ordeal of the previous day. An apocryphal story says that before Franklin had left the Cockpit the previous day, he had whispered in Wedderburn's ear: 'I will make your master a LITTLE KING for this.'[23]

Franklin stayed for another year in England, mostly lying low, and only meeting few parliamentarians and other well-wishers still desirous of a way out from the imbroglio lest there be a revolution against the Empire. By then, events were moving fast in America and the First Continental Congress had met to affirm its token loyalty to the Crown but not to the Parliament. As a consequence, the House of Lords took no time in rejecting a final ditch reconciliatory proposal that was drafted by Franklin and presented by one of his friends. Hated by now in England as a traitor to the British interests, Franklin left for Philadelphia. He had been the major figure in the efforts to bringing together the colonies under the Empire's protection against the French. He had also played a major role during the Stamp Act crisis by trying to reconcile the difference between the Parliament and the colonies.

But now, Franklin transformed into one of the most loyal supporters of separation from Britain. From British-loyalist turned American patriot to becoming an American revolutionary, such was Franklin's transformation in the past two decades. Franklin's transformation also mirrored that of other nationalists in America who were finally starting to see themselves as being distinct from the citizens of the British Empire. The sense of hurt that Franklin felt in Britain was shared by many in America. This common suffering at the hands of the British—whether originating from Franklin's trial or from the taxes levied by the Parliament—quickly developed a new feeling of common nationalism between the American colonies. History was being shaped by this new sense of nationalism among the colonists with diverse social and economic backgrounds.

Franklin arrived back in Philadelphia in May 1775 after having carried out many experiments regarding the temperature of the ocean water and course of the Gulf Stream during his voyage. By the time he arrived on American soil, military conflict had already initiated between British soldiers and Massachusetts militiamen. However, open talk of Independence was still uncommon. Franklin was received by the ringing of bells in the city to honor him. The next day, he was elected as a member of the Second Continental Congress scheduled to meet soon. Congress soon appointed him as the Postmaster General of the thirteen American colonies (later of the United States) and the postal system established under him continues to this day.

By far the oldest member in Congress, Franklin was also by now one of the most vocal voices against any reconciliation. Many delegates were still in dilemma about Independence or greater autonomy within the Empire by continuing the link with the Crown. Then there was Franklin who had already firmly decided that only Independence was the just course to follow. He had even distanced himself (almost disowned) his son, William, who was the governor of New Jersey and a British Loyalist. Many delegates to Congress were of the view that one last appeal should be made to the King to hold his ministers responsible for the trouble and prevent further conflict. While Congress started to draft the so-called Olive Branch Petition to beseech the King, Franklin almost 70, was doing something unusual. After signing the petition for the sake of consensus, Franklin wrote a letter to his long-time London friend William Strahan and made it public the same day:

> Mr. Strahan,
> You are a Member of Parliament, and one of that Majority which has doomed my country to destruction. You have begun to burn our towns, and murder our people. Look upon your hands! They are stained with the blood of your relations! You and I were long friends: You are now my enemy, and I am, Yours,
> B. Franklin.[24]

After the letter's publication, Franklin was hailed as a passionate American patriot who despite being a loyal British subject for most of his life now stood for nothing but American interests. But the catch was that Franklin never sent this extremely piquant letter! In fact, two days later he wrote and actually sent a very affectionate letter to his dear friend which he did not make public. Clearly, this theatrical act was carefully directed by Franklin to remove any doubts regarding which side he stood by and to further hasten the schism by inciting passions. A full year before the Congress formally declared Independence and at a time when eminent delegates like Washington, Adams, and Jefferson were still not voicing their opinions fervently in the open, Franklin emerged as the most forceful advocate of severing all ties with Britain. What makes this even more fascinating is that Franklin had served Britain in multiple roles more than any other founding father. For Franklin, all diversity between the colonists—such as of religion, language, and economic status—and allegiance to any colony did not matter anymore. Anyone on this side of the Atlantic was an American and ought to struggle for Independence.

In 1774, a young man by the name of Thomas Paine had met Franklin in London. Franklin had recognized Paine's deep aversion to the British Parliament and his sympathies with the American cause. Franklin had subsequently recommended him to move to America and had given him a letter of recommendation. Armed with Franklin's recommendation, Paine secured the editorship of the *Pennsylvania Magazine* after emigrating to America. In January 1776, Paine published the pamphlet *Common Sense* which made him eternal in the American folklore. More than 100,000 copies of his pamphlet were circulated in the colonies in just three months (among only about two million residents). The pamphlet was shown by Paine to Franklin before publication and Franklin had suggested some revisions. Overnight, the mood of the nation changed from confusion to resoluteness.

Perhaps the most far-reaching and incendiary pamphlet in American history, *Common Sense* which remains the all-time best-selling American title, made an impassioned case for Independence in words that citizens from all walks of life could understand. Paine presented the case for a distinctly American political identity by arguing as if giving a Protestant sermon in the pamphlet. The most quotable passages included: 'Why is it that we hesitate? From Britain we can expect nothing but ruin. If she is once admitted to the government of America again, this Continent will not be worth living in,'[25] and 'until an independence is declared, the Continent will feel itself like a man who continues putting off some unpleasant business from day to day, yet knows it must be done, hates to set about it, wishes it over, and is continually haunted with the thoughts of its necessity.' Paine's pamphlet removed any distinction between the King and the Parliament in American minds and ignited a sensational urge for self-rule. Nationalism established on the premise to oppose Britain had taken firm root in the American minds.[26]

As the colonies prepared to declare Independence, the venerable Franklin was, of course, one of the five members of the committee tasked with drafting the declaration. The committee delegated Jefferson to draft the initial document single-handedly. Franklin then made a few changes while editing Jefferson's draft. One of them was small but resounding. "We hold these truths to be sacred and undeniable" was changed by Franklin to "We hold these truths to be self-evident." A legend says that as the declaration was signed by the delegates, the president of Congress John Hancock commented that 'we must all hang together' to which Franklin commented, 'Yes, we must, indeed all hang together, or most assuredly we shall all hang separately.' Franklin was also appointed on the committee with Adams and Jefferson to design the seal for the United States. With his suggestions, the seal was launched with the motto *E Pluribus Unum* with an eye of Providence along with the caption on the back side: "Rebellion to tyrants is obedience to God."[27]

On paper, America had achieved Independence. Now, Franklin set out to make it a reality. He knew that as the most famous American in the world, he must serve his newly born nation in Europe to gather support in the Revolutionary War from Britain's traditional adversary—France. Participation by France in the Revolutionary War on the American side meant that victory was almost surely assured for the United States. No other American was more familiar with the sophisticated manners of the French Court nor was more famous than Franklin. As we read above in this chapter, Franklin's masterful performance in Paris gained him many accolades and he played his role to perfection. Almost single-handedly, Franklin brought France into armed conflict with Britain which ensured America's victory in the Revolutionary War.

The Revolutionary War in America sustained and flourished the common feeling of nationalism between the states. All states understood well that they would all win or lose the war together. Solidarity with each other and aversion to the British were the pillars of American Nationalism during the Revolutionary War. As long as there was a common enemy (Britain) to bind the colonies together in fear, all went well. But, as discussed in Chapter Two, once the Revolutionary War ended, the Articles of Confederation were not enough to keep the Union together. The thirteen states started to drift away and become entangled in disputes over trade and territory. While Franklin held an esteemed position only next to Washington in the American folklore, by now he was too old and infirm to assert himself like his heydays. As soon as Washington arrived in Philadelphia to attend the Constitutional Convention, he paid respect by going to meet Franklin. Franklin served as a delegate to the Convention but only seldom engaged in debates (though he played a crucial role in bringing about the Connecticut Compromise which stipulated the representation that states would have in Senate and House). The Constitutional Convention itself though was of great consequence to America's future.

Historian John Murrin notes that 'American national identity was, in short, an unexpected, impromptu, artificial, and therefore extremely fragile creation of the Revolution.' The dilemma before the founding fathers was how to bring about the confluence of revolutionary principles with the creation of national identity among the thirteen states once the war had ended. They found the solution to this dilemma in the Constitution. Murrin further writes that 'The Constitution seemed to provide an exit from this dilemma, a way of instilling energy in government while showing genuine respect for revolutionary principles…American nationalism is distinct because, for nearly its first century, it was narrowly and peculiarly constitutional. People knew that without the Constitution there would be no America…[But] Americans had erected their constitutional roof before they put up the national walls.'[28] The Constitution was instituted by the founding fathers as a device to which Americans could pay allegiance and serve under it as faithful citizens by deriving their national identity from it. The walls of the newborn nation would be slowly erected.

Singing praise while also being realistic about the Constitution that had just been drafted, Franklin said in the Constitutional Convention that there were 'several parts of this Constitution which I do not at present approve...[Nevertheless] I agree to this Constitution with all its faults, if they are such, because I think a general government necessary for us...I doubt too whether any other Convention we can obtain may be able to make a better Constitution.' During the signing of the Constitution, various delegates made speeches but Franklin had the last word. Observing the half-sunburst carved at the back of the chair on which Washington had sat as President of the Convention throughout that summer, Franklin reflected that 'in the course of the session, and the vicissitudes of my hopes and fears,' he had often gazed at the half-sunburst sign 'without being able to tell whether it [the sun, referring symbolically to the future of America] was rising or setting.' He then added satisfactorily that 'now at length I have the happiness to know that it is a rising and not a setting sun.'[29]

Washington, who had assumed the President's chair took the path of nation-building forward from there. In a symbolic show of the passing of the baton, Franklin drafted in the codicil to his will to bequeath his gold-capped walking stick to Washington and died a year after Washington's inauguration as president. Washington's greatest challenge as the first President of the United States was to instill the loyalty of Americans to the new Constitution. Unlike Britain, there was no precedent of a monarch or parliament going back centuries while unlike other European states, there was a sense of detachment toward English (the native language of England) among the inhabitants of the colonies. As another historian put it: 'It [America] was, rather, an artificial state or series of states, bound together by negotiated agreements and compacts, charters and covenants. It was made by bits of parchment, bred by lawyers.'[30] The Constitution was the only device that could bind Americans for the coming time until shared memory and culture could develop between the states to instill a sense of American Nationalism.

The stakes were high for the just-inaugurated national government. Failure of the Constitution and the government would have ended in chaos while success needed the ability to navigate unchartered stormy waters. Historian Carol Berkin writes: 'The

Federalists needed help to lay the foundation for a strong and enduring central government. They found it in the least expected places: crises of government legitimacy and sovereignty....The central story of the 1790s is how patriotism came to be associated with this support for the Constitution and its government.' Federalists like Washington and Adams faced many financial and diplomatic crises during this time as discussed in the Second and Third Chapters but in many ways, the first crisis that Washington's presidency faced was the most representative of the "anti-national" tendencies that still manifested in the American polity.[31]

When as a part of his financial program, Hamilton introduced a tax on distilled liquor, it sparked a crisis so big that President Washington described it as 'dangerous to the very being of the government.' As we read in the previous chapters, many Antifederalists had not supported the ratification of the Constitution due to the fears of a reduction in states' rights. Even the American Revolution itself had its roots in the issue of non-payment of taxes deemed unconstitutional by Americans. This tendency of going against the government's legislation came to the forefront again when in 1794, more than six thousand men gathered outside Pittsburgh putting violent scenes of resistance. This event triggered what came to be known as the "Whiskey Rebellion." The rebels were getting ready to march on to Philadelphia and terrorize the state legislators. The situation was fraught with deeper consequences since it centered on the fundamental question: Were all Americans capable of being loyal to the Constitution and derive their national identity from it? Historian Carol Berkin writes: 'the refusal to obey a law passed by Congress was, in effect, a denial of the authority and legitimacy of that federal government. To allow rebels a victory would be to concede that other segments of American society could pick and choose which laws to obey and which laws to ignore.'[32]

Drawing inspiration from the French Revolution, the rebels clamored for bringing the guillotine to America to chop off the heads of "tyrants." There was even talk of declaring independence from the United States and joining with Spain or Great Britain. An elaborate flag with six stripes was also prepared which represented the six rebellious counties. Destroying property, burning buildings, and killing a few people, the rebels also tried to get the support of nearby counties in other states to resurrect a truly national uprising. When the rebel commander Major James McFarlane, a Revolutionary War veteran, died in a confrontation with the local militiamen, the countryside was further radicalized. The federal government was getting the dose of the same medicine which those now in power had served to the British as revolutionaries. The only difference was that thankfully, in this case, the rebellion was not at such a large scale that it could not be contained.[33]

Ironically, the rebellion served as a stimulant in furthering the cause of American Nationalism. Washington asked states to raise militiamen and troops were contributed by Virginia, Maryland, New Jersey, and Pennsylvania. The fact that many states happily contributed to the raising of militiamen to crush the rebellion and defend the Constitution strengthened the feeling of solidarity among the states. Washington had first considered military action against the rebels as the last resort but their intransigence left him no choice. The rebels saw themselves as heroes fighting against the same issue of arbitrary taxation that had sparked the American Revolution. Washington understood well that such a tendency of going violently against the decisions of the government would be very harmful to the future of the United States especially when the new national government was still fragile.

Despite raising troops to crush the rebellion, for the sake of appearance, Washington dispatched some commissioners to discuss the possibility of reconciliation with the rebels. Simultaneously, Hamilton worked on solidifying the public opinion behind the government by publishing articles under different pseudonyms in Pennsylvania newspapers. In a disproportionate show of arms, Washington then personally commanded more than 13000 troops to crush the insurrection (it remains the first and only time that a sitting president personally led troops to a battle). Historian Joseph Ellis notes that the confrontation between the rebels and the federal government was '"the spirit of '76" [Revolutionary War] against "the spirit of '87" [American Constitution], one historic embodiment of "the people" against another.' Thankfully, such a resolute show of strength worked, and the rebellion vaporized as soon as the federal troops approached the rebels. Washington justified his decision of commanding an army to Congress by noting that such a heavy-handed response was necessary for national unity and the survival of the union. Under Washington's leadership, a common feeling of nationalism started to strengthen the roots of the newly born United States.[34]

Washington's presidency of eight years helped the most in instilling loyalty for the national government among citizens. His ceremonial tour across all the states of the Union promoted unity. Furthermore, the many disputes between the Hamiltonians and Jeffersonians (discussed in the third chapter) which played out amidst presidential elections but without violent means ensured that the business of the government shall be conducted within the framework of the Constitution. The Anti-federalists had realized that they could only achieve power through the ballot and thus consolidated behind Jefferson as the presidential candidate. As the debates around Hamilton's banking system, Jay's Treaty, XYZ Affair, and Alien and Sedition Acts polarized the nation in the 1790s, a sense of nationhood within the boundaries of the Constitution evolved.

It was this same national spirit owning allegiance to the Constitution that Abraham Lincoln utilized as the argument for unity six decades later during the Civil War. The travails and tragedies of the Civil War forged another national spirit that transcended allegiance to the Constitution. As immigrants from across Europe, Canada, Mexico, and Cuba (Asians were not welcome) came pouring into America during the nineteenth century, Franklin's idea of "the American Dream" helped the most in assimilating them to embark on a collective voyage of self-improvement and nation-building. When America industrialized and took an active part in global affairs by becoming the most powerful nation on the planet, this sense of American Nationalism associated with Franklin's "American Dream" later gave way to American Exceptionalism which equated the nation's interests with those of humanity.[35] What started with colonists looking at themselves as the offshoots of a mother country morphed into the sprouting of a national identity owing allegiance to the Constitution and finally transcended into becoming a way of life to be propagated around the World.

There are broadly two definitions of Indian Nationalism as put forward by academicians. The first celebrates nationalism in India as being pluralistic under which a citizen can successfully and harmoniously cultivate multiple identities. These identities are rooted in loyalty to various social institutions such as religion, caste, linguistic group, etc., and have been encouraged by the Constitution. The second definition of Indian Nationalism advocates that India is an artificial creation. According to this definition, no geographical, cultural, political, or social entity could be construed as India before the British took over the subcontinent. This definition credits the British for politically integrating the Indian subcontinent into a single entity and portrays the present nation as another British legacy. These two definitions are, of course, fundamentally opposed to each other. During the years preceding the Independence, the idea of India as propounded by the first definition was fiercely challenged by the British. The greatest rebuttal to the British came from Subhas Bose and his Indian National Army which fought the British militarily. Soon after Independence, the call for establishing linguistic provinces in India initially seemed to validate the second definition but ultimately transcended it. This chapter is a tale of these two happenings and the fostering of pluralistic Indian Nationalism.

India is a land of dichotomies. It is the land of Buddha and Gandhi—two of the greatest apostles of non-violence. Yet, its most popular epics, Ramayana and Mahabharata, are essentially the stories of war and the necessity of taking up arms to fulfill one's rightful duty. Gandhi did not believe in justifying the means to achieve the ends if the ends could only be achieved through violence. The antithesis of Gandhi was Subhas Bose who gave the British the greatest military challenge in the Indian Subcontinent since the Revolt of 1857. Just like Gandhi's teachings, the legend of Bose does not die. Even after conclusive proof of his death in an airplane crash in 1945 at a young age[36], legends circulated for decades about his escape with the hope of his eventual comeback to lead the nation. Scholars still vigorously debate the enigma regarding what the nation's course would have been had Bose survived that fateful airplane crash. Among the founding fathers, Bose's contributions toward erecting the foundation of the Republic of India are least tangible. Bose did not become a member of the first government of the Republic of India, did not participate in the drafting of the Constitution, was not even in India for years before Independence, but rather had died two years before freedom came to India. Yet, making the case of his legacy most curious, Bose is revered across the nation as a founding father, a synonym of patriotism, and a fierce advocate for pluralistic nationalism. While non-violence was an article of faith to Gandhi, it was 'only a weapon for the other [Bose], to be used or discarded according to the necessities of the situation.'[37] Nevertheless, Indians dichotomously find it perfectly acceptable to revere both Bose and Gandhi—whose mutual relationship had all the shades, simultaneously, from unbounded love to extreme dissent—despite the fact that they took paths at divergent with each other in the common cause of freedom.

After his return from South Africa in 1915, Gandhi had capitalized on the spirit of nationalism that was brewing in India. He had channeled the nationalistic spirit of resistance against the British through his own methods of passive resistance and orchestrated a mass movement against the British-rule which became a major spectacle around the world. While Gandhi gave a concrete shape to the idea of India as being a plural democratic independent nation, Bose materialized the idea in his own way by forming a truly national army and heading the first Indian Government-in-exile. Both of these institutions, Bose's Indian National Army and the first Indian Government-in-exile reflected India's vast diversity. In a dispirited nation which was being governed brutally under the heels of the British for almost two centuries and where armed repression by His Majesty's Government had broken the martial spirit, Bose ignited a new fire that was to spread across the nation as a wave of patriotism, self-confidence, and valor. He capitalized on that section of mass support which had no trust in Gandhi's methods of non-cooperation and demonstrated to the British that the martial spirit had not been extinguished among Indians. Through his actions to free India and his uncompromising attitude toward the inclusion of India's diversity, Bose ignited a new sense of pluralistic nationalism among Indians who had long forgotten what freedom meant.

The achievements of this 'natural leader of men' were more than just military accomplishments.[38] Erect, bespectacled, with a firm look on the face and majestic qualities of leadership, Bose had a magnetic power of influencing others just by his countenance. Such was the effect of his valor on Gandhi that though opposed to his methods, Gandhi described Bose as one whose 'patriotism is second to none…His bravery shines through all his actions…The lesson that Netaji [Bose] and his army brings to us is one of self-sacrifice, unity irrespective of class and community, and discipline.'[39] The Indian National Army formed by Bose became the grand symbol of India's pluralism and nationalism. It was the first time in history that an army marched under the banner of "India" and not under that of a British or an Indian monarch. Various national symbols in today's India are derived from Bose's Indian National Army. These include the national greeting of "Jai Hind" ("Victory to India") and the choice of "Jana Gana Mana" as the national anthem.[40]

Subhas Chandra Bose, 'the Lost Hero' as one of his biographers called him, was the youngest of the founding fathers discussed in this book.[41] He was born in 1897 in Cuttack, Bengal Province as ninth of the fourteen children. Influenced by the works of Swami Vivekananda and Ramakrishna Paramahansa during his teenage years, Bose always maintained a sense of renunciation of materialistic desires and rejoiced in performing social service as a duty to humanity. At the age of 17, he quietly left home and traveled in India with a friend in search of a guru who could give him a purpose in life. Two months later, he came back home dejected and disillusioned from the ascetic way of life.[42] By then, the First World War had broken out and over a million Indian soldiers were taking part in the War overseas. While Indians started to raise their voice for more rights within the Empire, Bose started to channel his inner passions toward nationalism. After being expelled from the Presidency College in Calcutta on the allegation of assaulting a professor who had manhandled some Indian students and iterated anti-India comments, Bose left for England in 1919. Even without much preparation, he secured the fourth rank in the highly selective and coveted Indian Civil Services (ICS) examination which secured for him a life of power and luxury. But there was only one issue. He had appeared in the examination because of his father's desire and personally never wanted to help the British administration by becoming a part of it. Thus, he resigned from the Indian Civil

Services against the wishes of his father. 'Only on the soil of sacrifice and suffering can we raise our national edifice,' wrote Bose to his brother and returned back to India.[43]

As this young lad of twenty-four landed in India at Bombay, he straight went to see Gandhi—by this time the acknowledged leader of the Indian freedom movement—the same day to test if the latter was worthy of being followed as a political mentor. As Bose himself wrote, he went to meet Gandhi to 'get from the leader of the campaign I was about to join, a clear conception of his plan of action...I wanted to study the Mahatma's [Gandhi's] mind and purpose.' He shot three questions at Gandhi about his methods, activities, and aims respectively. 'His reply to the first question satisfied me....The Mahatma's replies to the other two questions were not convincing...What his real expectation was, I was unable to understand...Altogether, his reply to the second question was disappointing and his reply to the third was no better.' Thus, even from their first meeting, Bose could not convince himself about Gandhi's way of resisting the British. 'Depressed and disappointed as I was,' Bose left for Calcutta on Gandhi's advice to report to the Congress leader C. R. Das who became his political mentor until the latter's death in 1925.[44]

Bose spent most of the late 1920s in prison due to his protests and activities against the British. Elected as the general secretary of the Congress party in 1927, he also worked closely with Nehru. Together, the two pushed Gandhi into accepting the demand of Independence rather than Dominion Status within the Empire as the goal of the freedom struggle for the Congress Party. Over the next few years, the two collaborated and disagreed over many issues but the personal relationship triumphed their differences. The two never had a sense of rivalry while Bose continued to consider Nehru as his elder brother.[45] In the mid-1930s, Bose traveled to Europe and observed communism and fascism from close quarters. He also wrote a part of his autobiography, but the book was banned by the British in India due to the fear of encouraging unrest. Bose married Emilie Schenkl, an Austrian who had become his assistant. As the clouds of war started to hover over Europe in the late 1930s, they provided an opportunity for renewing the struggle for the freedom of India and Bose returned back leaving his wife when duty called him. Emerging as a leader of national stature by the time of his return, Bose was elected as the Congress President in 1938.

During his first term as Congress president, many disagreements emerged between him representing the left-wing of the Congress and the old guard led by Patel. Next year, Bose wanted to contest for re-election but Gandhi tried to dissuade him from doing so as he felt that Bose was hot-headed and temperamental, and that his first term had created a wedge in the Congress Party. But Bose did not deter and comfortably won the election for the presidency against Gandhi's chosen candidate, Pattabhi Sitaramayya. Gandhi issued a statement the essence of which was that Sitaramayya's defeat 'was more mine than his.' Gandhi then went into the mode of passive resistance which he knew best—non-cooperation. Taking a cue from Gandhi, most members of the Congress Working Committee—highest decision-making body of the Party—resigned. Thus, Bose was left alone as captain of a ship that had no crew members. A resolution was passed by the Party to force Bose to nominate the Working Committee with Gandhi's wishes. This left Bose in an untenable position since Gandhi refused to nominate the Working Committee and deferred the decision to Bose who could not now nominate his chosen candidates. Hence, in the end, Bose resigned. As Historian Rudrangshu Mukherjee writes, 'Gandhi emerges from this episode at his worst: petty and given to machinations, the archetypal Tammany Hall politician, his moral posturing notwithstanding.'[46]

Ousted from Congress's leadership, Bose formed his own political party within the wider Congress Party's umbrella and his distance from Gandhi and the mainstream Congress kept increasing. Fortunately, their personal relationship survived the public break. Gandhi wrote in 1940: 'So long as Subhas Babu considers a particular course of action to be correct, he has the right, and it is his duty, to pursue it whether the Congress likes it or not…[I]f success attends his effort and India gains her freedom, it will justify his rebellion, and the Congress will not only not condemn his rebellion but welcome him as a savior.'[47]

While Patel was the master organizer within the Congress, he could never go against Gandhi. While Rajaji was Gandhi's prescient pupil who could take a path different than his mentor's path, he always worked within the fold of Gandhi's ideals. While Nehru was

Gandhi's lovable son who often disagreed with his political father in the morning, he could only throw tantrums and write long resentful letters before following Gandhi's path by the evening. Then there was Bose, Gandhi's prodigal and rebellious son, with unmatched organizational capabilities who dared to publicly go against Gandhi and all that Gandhi stood for. At the same time, such was their relationship that even after their break, Bose later hailed Gandhi as the "Father of Our Nation" and was the first to do so.[48] No other leader than Bose could have even dreamt of escaping India from the British custody with the sole aim of getting foreign help to achieve his ends, organizing an army outside India by instigating a rebellion among captured soldiers of the British Indian Army, getting support and formal recognition from Axis powers to establish a national government-in-exile, and launching an attack on the Indian subcontinent to free India from the British rule.

In his book *The Indian Struggle*, Bose had written warmly about armed resistance and had criticized Gandhi's approach to science and non-violence. As Bose's biographer writes, he believed that 'India needed a strong, vigorous, military-type leader—perhaps even himself—not a hesitating, confused, reformist guru.'[49]

The outbreak of the Second World War had provided Bose just such an opportunity. He was thrown into jail by authorities when he organized mass protests in Calcutta against the British. Finding himself incapacitated inside the prison and unable to actively lead the campaign, Bose went on a hunger strike. Bose's popularity was very high among the youth and so the British understood that if Bose died in the prison, mass rioting may start to occur in Bengal. Thus, he was placed under house arrest by the authorities after a week. Then started the most memorable phase of Bose's life for which he is remembered, revered, and respected across India.

From his home, Bose wrote to Gandhi offering his support in any movement that Gandhi would lead in the coming days. At odds with Bose's path, Gandhi replied that 'Till one of us is converted to the other's view, we must sail in different boats, though their destination may appear, only appear, to be the same' and that 'You are irrepressible whether ill or well. Do get well before going in for fireworks.'[50] Unbeknownst to Gandhi, Bose had already started the preparation for fireworks. Bose meticulously planned his escape with his nephew, Sisir, and on the night of 16 January 1941, disguised as a Pathan, he escaped from Calcutta. He traveled to Bihar from where he took a train under disguise to reach Peshawar (now in Pakistan). He planned to reach the Soviet Union and get help to launch an attack on the British. Acting as a deaf and dumb tribesman, Bose assimilated among the frontier tribes and reached Afghanistan, all the while fooling the British spies and patrols. Securing an Italian passport, Bose then again changed his guise to travel to Moscow. In less than three months, he had traversed the world's highest mountain ranges by foot, boat, car, and train while evading the British spies planning to assassinate him. However, Bose who always had a fascination with military men was probably also flirting with the idea of becoming a self-styled dictator. In an interview in Kabul, he declared: 'For a few years at least after the end of British rule in India there must be a dictatorship. No other constitution can flourish in the country. And it is to India's good that she should be ruled by a dictator to begin with.'[51]

Subsequently, from Moscow, Bose controversially flew to the regime of one of the evilest dictators that history has ever witnessed, Adolf Hitler. Reaching Berlin, Bose started to organize armed resistance against the British. With German support, he founded the Indian Legion consisting of more than 4,500 soldiers of the British Indian Army who were prisoners of war. These soldiers had been captured by the Axis forces since they had been fighting on Britain's side. But Hitler's declaration of war on Soviet Russia and his army's retreat later disheartened Bose as Germany was unable to provide a military platform for him to launch an attack on the British Indian Army. After a meeting with Hitler, Bose prepared to reach Southeast Asia since Singapore had fallen to the Japanese who were fast advancing toward India from the East. He discerned that it would be easier to launch an attack on the Indian mainland against the British with Japanese assistance due to the geographical proximity of the latter's captured territory.

Acting as a self-appointed revolutionary plenipotentiary of India, Bose started to carry out propaganda through the Azad Hind Radio which broadcasted news bulletins in English and seven South Asian languages to seek support in the fight for freedom of India. These broadcasts were tuned in regularly by more than 120,000 radio sets in India. Listening to his broadcasts became a clandestine activity sprouting new hopes of freedom in India. To reach out to other sections of the Indian society, Bose also launched two more radio broadcast stations: National Congress Radio and Azad Muslim Radio.[52] However, despite taking support from Germany, in a radio broadcast, he made it clear that he was 'not an apologist of the Tripartite Powers' and that 'My allegiance and my loyalty has ever been and will ever be to India and India alone, no matter in which part of the world I may live at any given time.' Later he also iterated that 'While standing for full collaboration with the Tripartite Powers in the external sphere, I stand for absolute self-determination for India where her national affairs are concerned.'[53]

'Freedom is not given, it is taken,' Bose repeatedly said. Unlike other Congress leaders who were gearing for the Quit India Movement and filling prisons in India, Bose was roaring for unity to fight against the British with military power: 'In India we have many religions and many gods. But here [within his army] everything is Jai Hind [i.e. loyalty only to the nation].'[54] Since taking a flight or a ship voyage to reach Japan was deemed too fraught with danger, a submarine was arranged by the Germans to transport him. Bose left on a German U-boat and was transferred to a Japanese submarine nearby Madagascar. This was the only time in the Second World War when two submarines belonging to two different navies transferred a civilian between them.[55] After a journey of eighteen weeks from his departure in Germany, Bose finally reached Tokyo. Receiving a warm welcome from the Japanese in Tokyo, he reached Singapore and started to coordinate with Indians living in Burma, Siam, and Malaya to help in the war effort. Such was his popularity in India at the moment due to his fearless flight and captivating radio broadcasts that there were talks in Gandhi's own ashram about how Bose could unite the nation if his army would enter India. It seemed to an ashramite that Bose 'was more popular than Nehru, and in certain circumstances had a stronger appeal than Gandhi.'[56]

'We have a grim fight ahead of us—for the enemy is powerful, unscrupulous and ruthless,' Bose roared in Singapore amidst more than 50,000 Indians, 'In this final march to freedom you will have to face hunger, thirst, privation, forced marches and death. Only when you pass this test will freedom be yours.' With the clarion calls of "Chalo Delhi" (March to Delhi) and "Tum Mujhe Khoon Do, Main Tumhein Azadi Dunga" (Give me Blood and I shall give you Freedom), Bose motivated the troops of his Indian National Army (I.N.A.) as recruitment soared to fight shoulder to shoulder with each other against the British. Addressed by his army men as "Netaji" (Revered Leader), Bose naturally assumed the role of a general. With monetary backing from overseas Indians particularly in Southeast Asia and logistical support from the Japanese, Bose's Indian National Army was preparing to witness live action in the war and on the Indian land.[57]

To provide further legitimacy to his efforts and link them with the national movement in India, Bose named three of the four brigades of the I.N.A. after Congress leaders Mohandas Gandhi, Jawaharlal Nehru, and Abul Kalam Azad. The fourth brigade was named after Bose on insistence from the soldiers. On Gandhi's seventy-fourth birthday in 1943, Bose heaped high praise on his estranged political mentor. Bose termed Gandhi's contributions to the freedom struggle as 'unique and unparalleled' and added that 'no single man could have achieved more in one single lifetime under similar circumstances.'

It may seem to us as nothing out of the ordinary but unlike the British custom of having separate mess halls in its military, soldiers from all religions—Hindu, Muslim, Sikh, and Christian—and belonging to all castes dined together in the I.N.A. Soldiers from the majority groups were advised to be generous to the minorities. When the priests of the main Chettiar temple in Singapore objected to their entry into a function due to religious and caste prejudices, Bose decided to forego the program despite Chettiars being one of the major funders of his campaign. Only when they agreed to host a national meeting by sidelining their practices did Bose agree to visit them.[58] Breaking the barriers of religion and caste, Bose also broke another ceiling that was unprecedented at the time. He proposed to train a women's regiment that would fight alongside the Indian men. The regiment was duly formed (and later served in Burma) against the opposition from the Japanese and named after the heroine of the Revolt of 1857, Rani of Jhansi. Reflecting the vision of pluralistic nationalism, a new vision of India breaking all barriers of religion, caste, linguistic groups, and gender was being materialized by Bose in the I.N.A.[59]

While the British military regiments were grouped based on caste and geographical loyalties, thousands of soldiers from every part of the nation belonging to every religion, linguistic group, caste, and both genders (a spectacle at the time as it would be now) fought together with only one identity—Indian. This was a big achievement at the time when the Indian society was divided along multiple social identities (religion, caste, language, etc.) and the British encouraged these divisions through their divide-and-rule policy.

The prominent political scientist Stephen Cohen writes that Bose's 'charismatic leadership alone was undoubtedly sufficient motivation for many Indians to join the I.N.A. He actually managed to put a force into the field and engage in several battles…Without him, it is doubtful whether a force could have been deployed at all….Bose was an individual with enough international prestige to deal with the Japanese and regain some independent status for the I.N.A. officers and men.' Bose's magnetic personality and popularity gravitated Indians from all regions of the nation to fight for the freedom of India. As Stephen Cohen writes further about the new form of pluralistic nationalism that was brewing in the I.N.A.

> [T]o almost all but the Communists, the I.N.A. symbolized a united India struggling against British colonialism. The I.N.A. was a truly non-communal, united nationalist movement, even though it had relied upon Axis aid. That this unity should have arisen from the Indian Army added to its interest, for the army had been the one group most sheltered by the British from nationalist sentiments. The I.N.A. seemed to prove the British wrong who maintained that India was not really a nation, and that Indians could not work together. The theme of unity in Subhas Bose's propaganda war against the British does not seem to have been recognized by the British themselves.[60]

Bose also proclaimed the formation of the Provisional Government of Free India on 21 October 1943. This was a masterstroke of propaganda that had dual objectives. On the one hand, the recognition of Bose's government by the Axis powers brought legitimacy and rattled the British Indian Government while on the other hand, it boosted the morale of the I.N.A. personnel since they now saw themselves as actually fighting under the Indian flag.

However, the biggest handicap during the war—never resolved—for the I.N.A. was supplies. It had to be dependent largely on Japan for replenishment and the supplies did not always arrive smoothly. To gain some financial autonomy, Bose also established the National Bank of Azad Hind and started printing Indian currency along with issuing paper stamps but it was not enough. As I.N.A. fought alongside the Japanese in Burma and India's northeast frontier, it had to battle not only the enemy but also malaria, insufficient amount of medicines, and lack of pack animals in one of the most humid and dense forests in the world. Yet, by March 1944, I.N.A. finally entered the Indian frontier by pushing back the Allied forces. A symbolic victory that it was, it meant that a larger invasion of India could be performed soon after the takeover of Imphal.

The onset of the monsoon slowed the campaign to seize Imphal. From their side, the British maintained complete censorship on the news of I.N.A. inside India so that no mass uprising toward India's northeast frontier could take place. I.N.A. soldiers were fighting bravely and creating dissensions among the British Indian Army to defect to their own side. However, as heavy rains poured in for months and the campaign slowed, pessimism set in and desertions from the I.N.A. started to take place. While a large section of the Officer Corps of the I.N.A. was composed of the officers from the British Indian Army, much of it was made up of men who had undergone little training in the past few months. In bad conditions, this fundamental handicap started to take its toll. The issues of supplying goods to the army and uneasy collaboration with the Japanese also came to the forefront and the campaign had to be halted. As I.N.A. soldiers retreated, many died of starvation and the Allied forces gained footing while chasing them from behind. Many times during this retreat, Bose staked his own life and escaped death by inches while he ensured the safe evacuation of his forces.[61]

The I.N.A. together with the Japanese fought valiantly for the first half of 1945 while retreating across Burma. However, by May, with Hitler's suicide and Germany's surrender, the war in the European theater came to an end. The Japanese too started the discussions of a possible surrender. When atomic bombs were dropped by the United States on Hiroshima (6 August) and Nagasaki (9 August), Japan's surrender became a foregone conclusion. Bose was persuaded by the Japanese to go underground. But his overloaded plane crashed in Japanese-ruled Formosa (now Taiwan) on 18 August 1945. Bose's clothes were soaked in gasoline and while escaping the burning plane, he suffered third-degree burns all over his body. He was still conscious after being admitted to a hospital and for some time thereafter. As per one account, before going into a coma and dying the same night, his last words were: 'I have fought all my life for my country's freedom. I am dying for my country's freedom. Go and tell my countrymen to continue the fight for India's freedom. India will be free, and before long.'[62] Thus ended one of the most illustrious Indian lives of the twentieth century.

Bose had striven for India's freedom and unity among Indian's diverse social groups all his life. As the war ended, with the relaxation of censors by the British and the release of Congress leaders from the prison, Bose's efforts and the stories of I.N.A.'s valor started to circulate and broadcast freely. 'In this mortal world, everything perishes and will perish—but ideas, ideals and dreams do not. One individual may die for an idea but that idea will, after his death, incarnate itself in a thousand lives,' Bose had written in 1940.[63] The most deep-rooted Indian tree that stood against the imperialistic winds of the Empire had fallen down but its tremors were felt across the nation in the following year. As a confidential file of the Government of British India noted: 'S.C. Bose may be dead but much that he did lives still.'[64] Bose was no more to lead the Independence Movement. Yet, the fire of pluralistic nationalism ignited by him was still blazing and other founding fathers utilized it to challenge the British afresh.

For more than three years between 1942-1946, Congress leaders were in jail and brutal suppression of any nationalist sentiment by the British had dampened the spirit of the masses. Now, after Independence, Congress needed something to reinvigorate the nationalistic sentiment among the demoralized people. The British had charged a number of officers of the I.N.A. with treason due to their defection from the British Indian Army. The British held several trials by courts-martial in the historic Red Fort between November 1945 and May 1946. They could not have a chosen worse time or a worse choice of personnel for these trials. These trials came as a godsend for the Congress, and it resolved in September 1945 that it would be 'a tragedy if these officers, men and women, were punished for the offence of having labored, however mistakenly, for the freedom of India.' For the first of these trials, the British had chosen three officers—Shah Nawaz Khan, Gurbaksh Singh Dhillon, and Prem Sahgal. It skipped their minds that they had chosen a Muslim, a Sikh, and a Hindu respectively for this trial, representing India's religious diversity. Congress took full advantage of this fact by calling for mass solidarity and national unity behind these officers while Gandhi gave the example of I.N.A.'s pluralism across the nation.[65] In a speech, Nehru remarked

> The I.N.A. trial has created a mass upheaval. Wherever I went, even in the remotest villages, there have been anxious enquiries about the I.N.A. men. There are profuse sympathies for these brave men and all, irrespective of caste, colour and creed, have liberally contributed to their defence.... The continuance of the trial is sheer madness undermining the position of the British in this country. The trial has taken us many steps forward on our path to freedom. Never before in Indian history had such unified sentiments and feelings been manifested by various divergent sections of the Indian population...[66]

As the sword of death or life imprisonment lay hanging over the heads of I.N.A. men, Congress prepared a defense committee to represent them in the trials. Nehru, who had earlier left his law practice to participate in Gandhi's non-cooperation movement now put on his barrister's gown after twenty-five years as a member of the defense team. He also organized relief work for the I.N.A. soldiers and helped in amassing favorable public opinion toward them. On a visit to Singapore in early 1946, he was asked by Lord Mountbatten, the Supreme Allied Commander, to not visit the I.N.A. memorial and to not preside over a guard of honor by the former I.N.A. soldiers in Singapore. To agree with Mountbatten would have meant forgoing Bose's legacy and delegitimizing the I.N.A.'s achievements which the elder brother could not come to terms with. Thus, Nehru refused to oblige Mountbatten and the British Government, and attended a big function arranged in his honor by the former I.N.A. men. The only concession he made was to visit the I.N.A. memorial privately and unannounced to lay some flowers but of course, this soon became known to the local population and the news spread.[67]

The I.N.A. trials showcased a great lineup of lawyers on both sides with intricate legal arguments. The British Commander-in-Chief Claude Auchinleck found himself in an unenvious position since making an example out of the three accused would have been the British policy but at the same time, it would have degraded the law and order situation in the whole of India considerably. Even the Muslim League which had been the chief opposition party of Congress was standing alongside the latter on this issue. In the end, the court-martial was announced and the three were sentenced to deportation for life but the sentence was never carried out. Intense public pressure and agitation by Congress forced Auchinleck to release the three officers. Nehru also summarized the outcome of the I.N.A. trials in a speech to mark the occasion: 'The trial dramatized and gave visible form to the old contest: England *versus* India. It became in reality not merely a question of law or of forensic eloquence...but rather a trial of strength between the will of the Indian people and will of those who hold power in India. And it was that will of the Indian people that triumphed in the end. Therein lies significance, therein lies the promise of the future.'[68]

After Independence, Nehru appointed many of the capable I.N.A. officers in the diplomatic services and they served as India's ambassadors to other nations. In another speech, he summarized Bose's achievements on the latter's birthday: 'Netaji Subhas has set an example of courage and passionate devotion to the cause of Indian freedom, which will live long in India's history. Equally important is the way in which he has demonstrated how to weld the different communities in a common unity.'[69]

While the trials were undergoing in February 1946, a mutiny broke out in the Royal Indian Navy. It spread rapidly from Karachi to Calcutta and more than 20,000 sailors in 78 ships joined it. These mutineers enthusiastically displayed a fine show of communal harmony among their ranks in their support of the defendants in the I.N.A. trials. Taking inspiration from Bose and the I.N.A., these mutineers started to call themselves as Indian National Navy. The British were dumbstruck, alarmed, and rattled by this show of flouting of their authority by their own navy personnel. The British were so exasperated that they even issued threats to bomb the disaffected ships. For more than a century, the British Indian Army had been the single-most-important institution in holding Indians under the English writ. It had been pampered by the rulers to earn its absolute allegiance and its personnel selected carefully to forestall the emergence of any unity. Now, this same institution was displaying multiple cracks right after the Second World War when the British power was at its lowest. To put it simply: without the absolute and unquestionable allegiance of the British Indian Army to hold down Indian nationalistic sentiments, there would have been no British India in the first place.[70] As General Sir Hastings Ismay wrote to the British prime minister only two months before the mutiny: 'It is clear that nearly everything depends on the reliability and spirit of the Indian Army. Provided they do their duty, armed insurrection in India would not be an insoluble problem. If, however, the Indian Army were to go the other way the picture would be very different.'[71]

As many I.N.A. personnel went back to their villages spread across India, they further instigated unrest in the countryside. A major worry for the British was the families and social groups that had traditionally been "loyal" to them by sending young men to fight in the British Indian Army were now agitating against them. Some confrontations took place between the Royal Indian Navy and the mutineers. The British Government had decided to send a Cabinet Mission weeks before the mutiny to negotiate the future of India with the Congress and the Muslim League. At this stage, both Congress and the Muslim League despite their support of the I.N.A. personnel in the Red Fort trials feared that unorganized violence like the Navy Mutiny could only lead to delay in the transfer of power. Thus, Patel went himself as a peace delegate to talk to the leaders of the mutiny and calm tempers.[72] In any case, the mutineers had not a slight chance of winning as Patel wrote to Nehru from Bombay: 'The overpowering forces, both naval and military gathered here is so strong that [the mutineers] can be exterminated altogether.' In the end, though the mutiny was easily clamped down when the mutineers surrendered, the episode showed that the adamantine edifice of the British Indian Army was now breaking down.[73]

The legacies of Bose's I.N.A. and Royal Navy Mutiny have been contentious. The dichotomy that is the Indians' view toward violence is inescapable here. Bose was regarded by the British and the West as a fascist with dictatorial ambitions who took help from Nazi Germany and thus undeserving of any sympathy. He was labeled by Gandhi and Congress at large as a misguided patriot who made no distinction between the aims and the means. Nonetheless, Indians venerate him as one of the most popular nationalists and unifying leaders who lived and died for the freedom of India. Bose is also remembered for his absolute and unwavering commitment to India's diversity and forging a nationalism that transcended loyalty to one's caste, religion, linguistic group, etc. Scholars still debate the path India would have taken had Bose lived through that fateful plane crash. Could he have saved India from the communal violence and Partition that followed only months after the nation had come together behind the I.N.A. defendants? We would never know the answer to this question.

As prime minister, when Nehru first addressed the nation from the Red Fort after Independence, he lamented: 'I cannot help mentioning Subhas Chandra Bose who left this country and formed the Indian National Army abroad and fought bravely for the freedom of the country. He hoisted this flag in foreign countries and when the day came for hoisting it on the Red Fort, he was not to see his dream fulfilled. This should have been the day of his return, but alas he is no longer in this world.' Bose could not return to breathe in Independent India but by his actions, he had already materialized what Nehru said further in his speech: 'It is wrong to suggest that in this country there would be the rule of a particular religion or sect. All who owe allegiance to the flag will enjoy equal rights of citizenship, irrespective of caste and creed.'[74]

However, as the British left, various communities divided along the three fault lines of caste, religion, and linguistic groups again started to compete for influence. The first and second were fragmented across the geography of the nation while the Constitution had ensured that no distinction could be made based on caste and religion among Indians. The third gave the biggest challenge to the idea of pluralistic nationalism in India. Both Gandhi and Bose were dead and it was on the other founding fathers to face this challenge.

The most contentious issue debated in the Constituent Assembly was that of the national language. Taking inspiration from European nations, many delegates thought that in the long term, a common language would help the most in forging a sense of unity and nationalism among Indians. But, the nation had more than a dozen major languages—each with its own written script—and none of them was the language spoken by the majority. Even Hindustani, a broad amalgam of Hindi, Urdu, Panjabi, and regional dialects from multiple languages was only spoken by about 45% of the total population. For all official purposes, the common language was that of the Imperial power—English. How could one language be given precedence over others by declaring it the national language? And yet, there was an emotional sentiment attached to the idea of a national language. The founding fathers wondered how to adopt a common language between Indians from all regions of the nation. As Nehru worried: 'How shall we promote the unity of India and yet preserve the rich diversity of our inheritance?'[75]

The debate around national language ended at a half-hearted compromise: there was to be no national language. Hindi was recognized as the "official" language and not the "national" language of the Union. It was to be used alongside English for the next fifteen years in all official texts used in inter-province communication. The states could choose their own native language or English for their own affairs. This compromise was seen at the time by the Hindi supporters as a tool to buy time until Hindi could be imposed on the whole nation. But, it did not quash the larger debate over language-based nationalism that was still on.

After his return to India from South Africa, Gandhi had asked the Congress Party to approach people in their native languages. 'It is my humble but firm opinion that unless we give Hindi its national status and the provincial languages their due place in the life of the people, all talk of Swaraj [self-rule] is useless,' Gandhi had said in 1918. Under his leadership, Congress was divided into provincial units not based on the British-defined administrative boundaries but rather linguistic boundaries. This strategy of reaching out to people in their native language had proved highly effective in taking Congress's agendas to the masses.[76]

Just like it functioned through local units based along linguistic boundaries, Congress had also agreed to the formation of states in the Union of India after Independence on the basis of language. Shortly after Independence, Gandhi again expressed the wish: 'I do believe that we should hurry up with the reorganization of linguistic provinces...There may be an illusion for the time being that different languages stand for different cultures, but there is also the possibility that with the establishment of linguistic provinces it may disappear...I am not unaware that a class of people have been saying that linguistic provinces are wrong. In my opinion, this class takes delight in creating obstacles.'[77] Three influential leaders who had previously supported the creation of linguistic provinces but were now opposing it were Gandhi's own chief lieutenants—Nehru, Patel, and Rajaji.

India had just been partitioned on the basis of religion. A war with Pakistan over Kashmir was underway. The process of assimilating princely states into the Union was also ongoing. Millions of refugees were pouring into the country amidst widespread rioting. So much was happening so rapidly that there was a genuine fear of everything falling apart. Thus, Nehru and his colleagues felt that dividing the nation at this point into linguistic provinces will only stimulate the fissiparous tendencies against the nation's unity and degrade the already fragile stability of the Union. Nehru said in the Constituent Assembly that while Congress had earlier promised the creation of linguistic provinces, the nation was presently facing 'a very critical situation resulting from partition. [Now] disruptionist tendencies had come to the fore...The first essential therefore is for India as a whole to be strong and firmly established, confident in her capacity to meet all possible dangers and face and meet all problems. If India lives, all parts of India also live and prosper. If India is enfeebled, all her component elements grow weak.'[78]

Under Patel's direction, a committee of jurists was formed in the Constituent Assembly to tactfully go back on Congress's earlier stated position on the creation of linguistic provinces. This committee concluded that as India is presently facing so many dangers concerning national unity, 'the first and last need of India at the present moment is that it should be made a nation...Everything which helps the growth of nationalism has to go forward and everything which throws obstacles in its way has to be rejected or should stand over. We have applied this test to linguistic province also, and judged by this test, in our opinion [they] cannot be supported.'

But there was wide dissension inside the Congress itself over this committee's report. Among the residents of the Bombay state, Marathi speakers wanted their own state of Maharashtra while

Gujarati speakers expressed the hope to establish their province as well. Kannada, Telugu, Malayalam, Oriya speakers too aspired to establish new provinces for themselves. It was as if like Europe, each group of people speaking a different language wanted a country of their own. Under pressure, Nehru and Patel constituted another committee with themselves as members this time. This committee again reiterated the report of the earlier committee by arguing that 'language was not only a binding force but also a separating one.' Now, when the 'primary consideration must be the security, unity and economic prosperity of India,' 'every separatist and disruptive tendency should be rigorously discouraged.' This report cooled the tempers for a while since the two most powerful men of the nation served on it but the fires started to flare back again soon.[79] Patel knew that the present measures could only delay the creation of linguistic states to buy more time for the national government to assert its authority but not quash the demand. 'Let us have business as usual till separation takes place,' he said in a meeting as late as 1949.[80]

The Sikh community was the first to demand a religion-based Sikh-majority linguistically homogeneous Punjab state. Sikhs had been the greatest victims of the Partition since their homeland of Punjab had been divided while hundreds of thousands had perished in the subsequent rioting. Their demand for a separate linguistic province (they wrote and read Panjabi in the Gurumukhi script) intersected with the divide of religion as well (Sikhism being a distinct religion from traditional Hinduism). A much more passionate agitation for the creation of a separate linguistic state was carried on by the Telugu speakers in Andhra. Telugu was the second most spoken language in the nation after Hindi. Telugu-speaking people had a strong sense of regional identity cultivated by their ancient glory under the Vijayanagar Empire. They felt that they had been discriminated against by the Tamil-speaking community with which they cohabited the Madras presidency.

Surrounded by various problems after Independence, Nehru asked the Telugu leaders to calm down by saying that 'no one who is in a responsible position can, at this present juncture, do anything which might upset a very delicate balance. I should like to have a little peace or the semblance of peace for sometime. After that we can go ahead in many directions.'[81] But, by 1952 the movement to establish a separate Telugu state (by breaking away from the Madras state) had again gained momentum. Rajaji was the chief minister of the Madras between 1952-54. One of his recent biographers writes, 'Rajaji resisted linguistic reorganization, which he called a "tribal idea," and displayed all his cunning in delaying the formation of Andhra, thus earning the reputation of a fox.' In Rajaji's view, the creation of linguistic states would not just have undermined India's unity but also that 'separation would lead to discontent, political or economic unsettlement, and a set-back to the successful development of self-government.' When a man named Potti Sriramulu went on a hunger strike on 19 October 1952 demanding the creation of a separate Andhra State, Rajaji played delay tactics even until the fiftieth day of his fast and did not let his fast be debated in the Madras Assembly.[82]

Even Nehru ignored the fast for the first fifty-five days thinking that the wave will quietly pass under the ship. As he wrote to Rajaji on the forty-sixth day of the fast: 'Some kind of a fast is going on for the Andhra Province and I get frantic telegrams. I am totally unmoved by this and I propose to ignore it completely.'[83] Next week, Nehru became mellower when he wrote to Rajaji about his inclination to concede the demand of a separate Telugu state, or else 'complete frustration will grow among the Andhras, and we will not be able to catch up with it.'[84] However, it was already too late by now since Sriramulu died on the fifty-eighth day and this created great havoc in public order and administration in the Madras State. Several protestors died in the violence that followed while public property worth millions was damaged. Trains were halted and widespread rioting took place. Finally, under pressure, Prime Minister Nehru had to give in and the government announced the creation of an Andhra province. In the next few months, the new state of Andhra was carved out which comprised of Telugu speaking areas of the Madras Province.[85] Cunning Rajaji, the 'staunchest Tamilian tribesman' according to Ambedkar, succeeded in keeping the metropolis of Madras for Tamil Nadu but had to concede the temple town Tirupati to Andhra.[86]

'You will observe that we have disturbed the hornet's nest and I believe most of us are likely to be badly stung,' wrote a worried Nehru to a colleague. By agreeing to the formation of a separate state for the Telugu-speaking people, the government had in principle conceded the demand of linguistic states. Nehru was anxious that the national unity might get buried under the deluge of demands of separate statehoods from all regions of the nation. Feeling hostage in his developmental agendas due to forced public pressure of creating linguistic states, Nehru complained that in such a case, people should get another prime minister: 'I cannot be responsible for taking a step which, I am convinced, means injury to the cause of India and to something which I have cherished and worked for.' To look at the issue in a more holistic and detached manner, Nehru instituted a States Reorganization Commission (SRC) in December 1953. This Commission was tasked with touring the country, interviewing and receiving feedback from people of all regions, and compile a report to advise the government about the reorganization of states. Since the issue could have possibly led to the "Balkanization" of India, Nehru stressed that the issue should be viewed in a non-partisan manner and with the goodwill of all concerned or else 'all attention and resources would have been taken up by this and we would have had to say a long goodbye to planning and economic progress.'[87]

The SRC report was a 267-page document compiled within a period of almost two years during which the Commission's members traveled over 38,000 miles, interviewed 9,000 persons, and examined about 2,000 memoranda.[88] The report recommended the establishment of Karnataka and Kerala as separate provinces while continuing Bombay as a bilingual one—including people who spoke Gujarati and Marathi. This led to another upsurge in the passions. 'One might almost think from reading reports of speeches etc. that we were on the verge of civil war in some parts of India,' wrote Nehru. In the Bombay province, Marathi-speakers wanted their own province instead of being cobbled with Gujarati-speakers in a bilingual one. Even if their demand was to be met, the city of Bombay, the hub of India's financial and industrial activity and its most cosmopolitan metropolis, had an influential and powerful community of Gujarati speakers while almost half of the city consisted of Marathi-speakers. The big issue that agitated Marathi speakers was the question if Bombay should be merged with their Maharashtra province or it should remain as a separate city-state. As the violence grew, Nehru's first instinct was to refuse the demand of Maharashtra unless violent agitation would stop: 'Obviously no Government can be coerced by such methods. Indeed the Government will cease to function if it tolerated such methods and the success of this behavior would lead to its being followed in many other places. Our country would be reduced not only to chaos but to chaos of the lowest and most vulgar type.'[89]

But, as protests intensified against Nehru himself, the situation worsened. In 1956, while visiting Bombay he was met with black flags while stones were thrown at the Congress Party's meeting in which many members were injured. Congress leaders of Maharashtra were themselves divided over the future status of Bombay. Personally, Nehru still wanted Bombay to become a city-state but there was intense pressure from the Marathi-speaking community and thus he kept vacillating. To his embarrassment, his colleague and Union Finance Minister C. D. Deshmukh resigned from the government to protest against Nehru's predilection to not merge Bombay with Maharashtra. In the end, Nehru had to relent once more. On 1 November 1956, new states of Gujarat and Maharashtra based on language came into being with Bombay becoming a part of the latter. Nehru had been forced from being one of the staunchest opponents of linguistic states to helplessly becoming the orchestrator of their genesis.

The founding fathers had tried their best to stop the creation of states based on social identities like language and religion. Language proved to be a stronger social identity for people than the founding fathers predicted. However, the creation of linguistic states due to popular will and against the wishes of the founding fathers proved very beneficial for the nation. The founding fathers could not anticipate that such linguistic states would help in flourishing regional arts and culture, and strengthening native languages rather than undermining India's unity. As Historian Ramachandra Guha has concluded in his magisterial history of post-Independent India: 'In retrospect, however, linguistic reorganization seems rather to have consolidated the unity of India....[It] has acted as a largely constructive channel for provincial pride. It has proved quite feasible to be peaceably Kannadiga—or Tamil, or Oriya—as well as contentedly Indian.'[90] At the same time, the founding fathers' decision to not provide the status of national language to any helped in consolidating the feeling of linguistic equality. There are twenty-two scheduled languages today in the Republic of India. Apart from English and Hindi, fifteen more languages are printed on every single currency note in the country. The history of India of the past seven decades has shown that India has become a successful outlier in following a model of nationalism where people have cultivated multiple identities based on their caste, religion, and language, all of them superseded by the identity of being an Indian.

> We are a nation of many nationalities, many races, many religions—bound together by a single unity, the unity of freedom and equality. Whoever seeks to set one nationality against another, seeks to degrade all nationalities. Whoever seeks to set one race against another seeks to enslave all races. Whoever seeks to set one religion against another, seeks to destroy all religion.
> -Franklin Delano Roosevelt

> I do not want that our loyalty as Indians should be in the slightest way affected by any competitive loyalty whether that loyalty arises out of our religion, out of our culture or out of our language. I want all people to be Indians first, Indians last and nothing else but Indians.
> -B. R. Ambedkar

What is a nation? As we read in the Preface, both America and India do not conform to the Oxford English Dictionary's definition of being *A community of people of mainly common descent, history, language, etc., forming a state or inhabiting a territory.* It is natural to ask then that how did these two unorthodox nations come into being? The colonists had declared America to be a nation by drafting the United States Declaration of Independence in 1776. The Declaration started with the proclamation: "When in the Course of human events it becomes necessary for one people to dissolve the political bands which have connected them with another, and to assume among the powers of the earth, the separate and equal station to which the Laws of Nature and of Nature's God entitle them, a decent respect to the opinions of mankind requires that they should declare the causes which impel them to the separation." Justifying the colonists' grievances in this manner, the Declaration went further to declare the independence of thirteen colonies from the mother country of Britain and established them as sovereign states in their own right.

On the other hand, India is an ancient civilization in which the coming and going of the British was only a fleeting epoch. Yet, the contemporary Republic of India and the concept of India being a politically integrated nation-state is a modern one. Just like in America and taking inspiration from it, *Purna Swaraj*, the Indian Declaration of Independence in 1930 had announced the creation of a new political order in India by declaring the aim of the freedom struggle to be the achievement of complete independence from the British rule.[91] It had done so by pronouncing in a similar vein: "We believe that it is the inalienable right of the Indian people, as of any other people, to have freedom and to enjoy the fruits of their toil and have the necessities of life, so that they may have full opportunities of growth. We believe also that if any government deprives a people of these rights and oppresses them the people have a further right to alter it or to abolish it."

In these ways, America and India had declared the intent of establishing a new sociopolitical entity called "nation." I say intent here since, at the times of the declaration of their independence respectively, these nations were actually engaged in the struggle for freedom from the British. In America, it took thirteen years for Americans to inaugurate a national government as per the Constitution from the time of the declaration. In India, it took two decades. Thus, just the Declaration of Independence did not in any way overnight transform these two societies into nations. Something more went into the forging of these two nations. Nationalism evolves only when a common feeling of shared identity and unity develops among the inhabitants of a territory. For a nation to remain united, this feeling of nationalism should be independent of a state-enforced system i.e. it should come from among the citizens.[92]

In America, the sense of nationalism came gradually. It began with the identification by the colonists as being distinct from the inhabitants of mainland Europe during the French and Indian War.

The colonies discovered during this war that they may have to fend off for themselves and so wisdom led them on the path toward unity. The sense of being British too worked at this time to foster togetherness between the thirteen colonies. However, with time animosity towards the British developed in the colonies due to the taxation policies instituted by the Parliament without providing representation to the Americans. This led to the stoking of the feeling that the colonists were different from the British which ultimately led to the breakout of the Revolutionary War. More than other founding fathers, Franklin's transformation from being the most loyal Britisher in America to the most vigorous opponent of ties with the British reflected the sense of nationalism that transformed American society between 1750-1780.

Once the Revolutionary War was won by Americans, the founding fathers orchestrated sort of a coup by designing a new constitution behind closed doors through legislators not directly chosen by the citizens. It was only after the Constitution was drafted that it was taken to the general public for ratification. Washington's inauguration as president and the paraphernalia attached to the new national government such as the symbols of a national anthem, seal, currency, flag, etc. helped in fostering a sense of common allegiance to the Constitution. When anti-national tendencies (such as during the Whiskey Rebellion) tried to challenge the government, its response was swift and overwhelming. Slowly, cohabiting the nation within the frame of the Constitution, inhabitants of North America descending from different European cultures, belonging to various Christian sects (and Jews), and speaking multiple European languages assimilated together to become Americans. In the following decades, captivated by the lure of pursuing Franklin's version of "the American Dream," more immigrants came to America. These immigrants then assimilated within the boiling cauldron of American society by pledging their allegiance to the American Constitution.

In India, the arrival of the British as conquerors preceded the concept of the nation-state. India had had a distinct cultural consciousness permeating its fabric across the subcontinent at least since the ninth century when the Hindu sage and philosopher Adi Shankaracharya had established four Mathas (monasteries) in the four corners of the present Indian nation.[93] India's division into many kingdoms of varying sizes (even in their heyday in the seventeenth century, the Mughals did not control Southern India) meant that the cultural consciousness pervading the Indian subcontinent could not transform into becoming a politically unifying force. As resistance to the British rule grew in India, the Western concept of nation-state started to pervade the Indian mindset. Gandhi capitalized the most on this feeling to emerge as India's most venerated leader in the struggle against the British rule. Among the many objectives that Gandhi had for India's future, the topmost was the existence of all religious and linguistic groups in complete harmony. While Gandhi's methods of the struggle consisted of non-violent methods such as non-cooperation and civil disobedience, Bose tried to free India using the brute force of arms.

Bose's Indian National Army became a symbol of pluralistic nationalism amidst the fraught times of the Second World War when Congress's leadership was in prison. Its product, the Red Fort Trials, again infused a sense of pluralistic nationalism among the masses. However, this was not enough. With India's partition, communal hatred and anti-nationalist tendencies came to the fore. While Prime Minister Nehru served as a unifying force in his own right to keep the nation together while ensuring fair play to all its diverse groups, he had to face a strong challenge in the form of the desire to establish linguistic provinces. Thankfully, the bond of common nationalism that had been forged between various linguistic groups of the nation while struggling against the British rule was strong enough to keep them in the Union. In the end, the establishment of these linguistic provinces entrenched nationalism even further by cultivating the concept of a dual identity—being Tamil, Kannadiga or Malayali was superseded by being an Indian. The cultivation of distinct linguistic identities by states, while they collaborated with each other and with the Central Government on broader issues, helped in strengthening India's federal structure of governance.

'Nationalism is good in its place, but it is an unreliable friend and an unsafe historian. It blinds us to many happenings, and sometimes distorts the truth, especially when it concerns us or our country,' wrote Nehru to his daughter from prison in 1932.[94] Nationalism is a double-edged sword. It helps in fostering a unifying identity among the inhabitants of a territory but at the same time, its interpretation is subjective and varies with time. For example, in America during the Cold War, the sense of nationalism once associated with living "the American Dream" sometimes gave way to identification with Capitalism and xenophobia toward communists. Similarly, the meaning of being an American is constantly being debated today in the context of Immigration. In a sense, the debate today has veered from how to more peacefully and easily assimilate immigrants to how to keep them away. The broken political dialogue between the two main political parties is further fueling these fissiparous tendencies. Much of this xenophobia has been caused by the unintended effects of globalization and income inequality in America. This is as far from Franklin's vision of American Nationalism founded on "the American Dream" as it can get.

There are still some forces in India, beyond those discussed in this chapter, which challenge the idea of pluralistic Indian Nationalism. The chauvinistic forces of the Hindu right want to establish a state with one dominant language (Hindi) and one religion (Hinduism). Furthermore, Hindu-Muslim tensions frequently collide with the secular view of nationalism since there is a historical sense among a section of Hindus that they have been wronged against by Muslim conquerors in the past many centuries. This interpretation today challenges the very basic structure of pluralistic and secular nationalism erected by the founding fathers of India. There are other fault lines too that come up from time to time in India. Northeast Indians face discrimination (and are often called by the derogative term, "Chinki") in other parts of the nation where they migrate for educational and employment opportunities. Similarly, except as tourists, there is still a very harmful tendency between North and South Indians to look at each other with xenophobic tendencies. Many North Indians still phlegmatically refer to all Southerners as "Madarasis" as if a city defines the mindboggling diversity of the whole of South India. More than seven decades after Ambedkar proposed and Gandhi agreed that the end of casteism can only happen with inter-caste marriages (one may also add that the end of regional jingoism can only come with inter-cultural marriages), the bonds associated with caste are still very strong. What is the use of paying respect to the National Flag if one cannot accept that all others saluting the same flag are your fellow brethren, socially equal to you in all aspects, and engaged in the development of the same nation?

In both nations, the nation was held together by one iconic personality (Washington and Nehru respectively) after the establishment of the national government. In America, the lure of living "the American Dream" meant that immigrants kept coming in from Europe for decades and peacefully got assimilated into the nation while in Europe they would have been treated as foreigners outside their own homelands. Adherence and allegiance to the Constitution were alone taken as the symbols of being American. The political theorist Bhikhu Parekh writes that 'For him [Nehru] "modernization" was India's national philosophy and involved seven national goals—national unity, parliamentary democracy, industrialisation, socialism, scientific temper, secularism and non-alignment.'[95] India could make progress due to the peaceful existence of its many diverse population groups. 'The Indian Constitution,' writes Rochana Bajpai 'despite its flaws, remains a key source of inclusion in the polity. It endures and continues to elicit a high level of support from across the political spectrum, including from critics seeking political change.'[96]

In both nations, as we saw in this chapter, faith in Pluralism i.e. the acceptance of diversity became the bedrock of nationalism. This pluralistic nationalism makes it perfectly acceptable to be a German-speaking Jewish Pennsylvanian and be an American just like it is absolutely easy to be a Punjabi-speaking Sikh Rajasthani and be an Indian at the same time. In India, as in America, History teaches us that Pluralism that has been erected on constitutional principles has been the single biggest source of nationalism that has kept the nation united. It must be treasured and nurtured.

---

[1] Gordon S. Wood, *The Americanization of Benjamin Franklin* (New York: The Penguin Press, 2004), p. 3

[2] Quoted in Ibid., p. 6

[3] Jim Powell, *Benjamin Franklin: The Man Who Invented the American Dream*, Foundation for Economic Education, 1 April 1997

[4] Alexis de Tocqueville, *Democracy in America: The Complete and Unabridged Volumes I and II* (Bantam Classic Edition, 2000), p. 785

[5] Nian-Sheng Huang and Carla Mulford, *Benjamin Franklin and the American Dream*, The Cambridge Companion to Benjamin Franklin (Cambridge University Press), 2009, pp 145-158

[6] Gerardo del Guercio, *How Benjamin Franklin's Dream Came True: The Origins of the American Dream in His Autobiography*, Early America Review, Dec 2009, Vol. 9 Issue 3

[7] Gordon S. Wood, *The Americanization of Benjamin Franklin* (New York: The Penguin Press, 2004), p. 11

[8] Jill Lepore, *These Truths: A History of the United States* (New York and London: W. W. Norton & Company, 2018), pp. 9-10

[9] Gordon S. Wood, *Revolutionary Characters: What Made Founders Different* (Penguin Books, 2006), p. 68

[10] Benjamin Franklin, *The Autobiography of Benjamin Franklin* (New York: Barnes and Noble, 1994), p. 81

[11] Jim Powell, *Benjamin Franklin: The Man Who Invented the American Dream*, Foundation for Economic Education, 1 April 1997

[12] David McCullough, *John Adams* (New York: Simon and Schuster, 2001), p. 193

[13] H. W. Brands, *The First American: The Life and Times of Benjamin Franklin* (New York: Anchor Books, 2000), p. 711

[14] Ibid., pp. 232-233

[15] From Benjamin Franklin to Richard Partridge, 8 May 1754, The Papers of Benjamin Franklin, vol. 5, July 1, 1753, through March 31, 1755, ed. Leonard W. Labaree. New Haven: Yale University Press, 1962, pp. 272–275

[16] Walter Isaacson, *Benjamin Franklin: An American Life* (New York: Simon and Schuster Paperbacks, 2004), pp. 159-161

[17] Gordon S. Wood, *Revolutionary Characters: What Made Founders Different* (Penguin Books, 2006), p. 76

[18] Gordon S. Wood, *The Americanization of Benjamin Franklin* (New York: The Penguin Press, 2004), pp. 108-111

[19] Ibid., pp. 114-117

[20] Walter Isaacson, *Benjamin Franklin: An American Life* (New York: Simon and Schuster Paperbacks, 2004), pp. 229-231

[21] H. W. Brands, *The First American: The Life and Times of Benjamin Franklin* (New York: Anchor Books, 2000), pp. 453-454

[22] Carl Van Doren, *Benjamin Franklin* (New York: The Viking Press, 1938), pp. 471-473

[23] Quoted in P. M. Zall, *Ben Franklin Laughing: Anecdotes from Original Sources by and About Benjamin Franklin* (Berkeley: University of California Press, 1980), p. 77

[24] Walter Isaacson, *Benjamin Franklin: An American Life* (New York: Simon and Schuster Paperbacks, 2004), pp. 295-296

[25] Thomas Paine, *Common Sense* (Mineola: Dover Publications, Dover Thrift Edition, 1997), p. 39

[26] Ibid., p. 44
[27] Carl Van Doren, *Benjamin Franklin* (New York: The Viking Press, 1938), pp. 550-551, 553
[28] John M. Murrin, *A Roof without Walls: The Dilemma of American National Identity* essay, from *Beyond Confederation: Origins of the Constitution and American Identity* by Richard Beeman, Stephen Botein, Edward C. Carter II (Chapel Hill: University of North Carolina Press, 1987), pp. 333-348
[29] Richard Beeman, *Plain, Honest Men: The Making of the American Constitution* (New York: Random House, 2009), pp. 360-361, 367-368
[30] Paul Johnson, *A History of the American People* (Harper Perennial, 1997), p. 423
[31] Carol Berkin, *A Sovereign People: The Crises of the 1790s and the Birth of American Nationalism* (New York: Basic Books, 2017), p. 3
[32] Ibid., pp. 8-9
[33] Wythe Holt, The Whiskey Rebellion of 1794: A Democratic Working-Class Insurrection, Paper presented at The Georgia Workshop in Early American History and Culture, 2004
[34] Joseph J. Ellis, *His Excellency: George Washington* (New York: Vintage Books, 2004), pp. 224-225
[35] Jonathan Monten, *The Roots of the Bush Doctrine: Power, Nationalism, and Democracy Promotion in U.S. Strategy, International Security*, vol. 29, pp. 112-156, 2005
[36] Detailed discussion about the circumstances related to Bose's death has been done by his grandson and biographer in Sugata Bose, *His Majesty's Opponent: Subhas Chandra Bose and India's Struggle Against Empire* (Penguin Books, 2013),
[37] B. Shiva Rao, *India's Freedom Movement: Some Notable Figures* (Orient Longman, 1972), pp. 150-151
[38] J. B. Kripalani, *My Times: An Autobiography* (New Delhi: Rupa co., 2004), p. 361
[39] *The Collected Works of Mahatma Gandhi (CWMG)*, Vol. 83: January 20, 1946 – April 13, 1946, How to Canalize Hatred, 15 February 1946, p. 135
[40] Meghnad Desai, *The Rediscovery of India* (New Delhi: Allen Lane, 2009), p. 236
[41] Mihir Bose, *The Lost Hero: A Biography of Subhas Bose* (London: Quartet Books, 1982)
[42] Sugata Bose, *His Majesty's Opponent: Subhas Chandra Bose and India's Struggle Against Empire* (Penguin Books, 2013), p. 27
[43] Ibid., p. 41
[44] Subhas Chandra Bose, *The Indian Struggle 1920-42*, Edited by Sisir K. Bose and Sugata Bose (New Delhi: Oxford University Press, 1997), pp. 57-59
[45] The relationship between Subhas and Nehru is described in detail in Rudrangshu Mukherjee, *Nehru & Bose: Parallel Lives* (New Delhi: Penguin Books, 2014)
[46] Rudrangshu Mukherjee, *Nehru & Bose: Parallel Lives* (New Delhi: Penguin Books, 2014), pp. 181, 198

[47] *The Collected Works of Mahatma Gandhi (CWMG)*, Vol. 72: 16 April, 1940 – 11 September, 1940, Subhas Babu, 9 July 1940, p. 260
[48] Sugata Bose, *His Majesty's Opponent: Subhas Chandra Bose and India's Struggle Against Empire* (Penguin Books, 2013), p. 1
[49] Ramachandra Guha, *Gandhi: The Years that Changed the World 1914-1948* (Penguin Random House, 2018), p. 573
[50] *The Collected Works of Mahatma Gandhi (CWMG)*, Vol. 73: 12 September 1940 – 15 April 1941, Letter to Subhas Chandra Bose, 29 December 1940, p. 264
[51] Hugh Toye, *Subhash Chandra Bose: The Springing Tiger* (Bombay: Jaico Publishing House, 1970), p. 66
[52] Sugata Bose, *His Majesty's Opponent: Subhas Chandra Bose and India's Struggle Against Empire* (Penguin Books, 2013), p. 225
[53] Ibid., pp. 218-222
[54] Hugh Toye, *Subhash Chandra Bose: The Springing Tiger* (Bombay: Jaico Publishing House, 1970), pp. 80-81
[55] Ranjan Borra, *Subhas Chandra Bose, The Indian National Army, and The War of India's Liberation*, The Journal of Historical Review, Winter 1982 (Vol. 3, No. 4), pp. 407-439
[56] Louis Fischer, *A Week with Gandhi* (New York: Duell, Sloan and Pearce, 1942), pp. 28-29
[57] Hugh Toye, *Subhash Chandra Bose: The Springing Tiger* (Bombay: Jaico Publishing House, 1970), pp. 89-90
[58] Sugata Bose, *His Majesty's Opponent: Subhas Chandra Bose and India's Struggle Against Empire* (Penguin Books, 2013), pp. 252, 256-257
[59] Leonard A. Gordon, *Brothers Against the Raj: A Biography* (Abridged and Revised Edition, New Delhi: Rupa Publications, 2015), pp. 305-306
[60] Stephen P. Cohen, *The Indian Army: Its Contribution to the Development of a Nation* (New Delhi: Oxford University Press, 2001), pp. 154, 160-161
[61] Hugh Toye, *Subhash Chandra Bose: The Springing Tiger* (Bombay: Jaico Publishing House, 1970), Ch. 6
[62] Leonard A. Gordon, *Brothers Against the Raj: A Biography* (Abridged and Revised Edition, New Delhi: Rupa Publications, 2015), p. 337
[63] Subhas Chandra Bose, *The Alternative Leadership: Speeches, Articles, Statements and Letters,* Edited by Sisir Kumar Bose and Sugata Bose (New Delhi: Permanent Black, 2004), p. 197
[64] Leonard A. Gordon, *Brothers Against the Raj: A Biography* (Abridged and Revised Edition, New Delhi: Rupa Publications, 2015), p. 343
[65] Sugata Bose, *The Nation as Mother and Other Visions of Nationhood* (Penguin Random House, 2017), pp. 129-131
[66] Jawaharlal Nehru, *Selected Works of Jawaharlal Nehru*, Volume 14, Speech on Jayaprakash Narayan, pp. 279-280

[67] Sarvepalli Gopal, *Jawaharlal Nehru—A Biography* (Oxford University Press, 2015 Edition), Vol. 1, pp. 309-310

[68] Jawaharlal Nehru, *Selected Works of Jawaharlal Nehru*, Volume 14, The Triumph of the Indian People, p. 372

[69] Ibid., The Example of Subhas Bose, p. 371

[70] John Keay, *India: A History* (New York: Grove Press, 2000), p. 505

[71] Ronald Specter, *The Royal Indian Navy Strike of 1946: A Study of Cohesion and Disintegration in Colonial Armed Forces*, Armed Forces & Society, Vol. 7, Issue 2, 1981, pp. 271-284

[72] Bipin Chandra and others, *India's Struggle for Independence 1857-1947* (New Delhi: Penguin Books, 1989), pp. 478-484

[73] Ronald Specter, *The Royal Indian Navy Strike of 1946: A Study of Cohesion and Disintegration in Colonial Armed Forces*, Armed Forces & Society, Vol. 7, Issue 2, 1981, pp. 271-284

[74] Jawaharlal Nehru, *Selected Works of Jawaharlal Nehru*, Second Series, Volume 4, The Honour of the Flag, 16 August 1947, p. 2

[75] Granville Austin, *The Indian Constitution: Cornerstone of a Nation* (Oxford: Clarendon Press, 1966), p. 265

[76] Ibid., pp. 270-271

[77] *The Collected Works of Mahatma Gandhi (CWMG)*, Vol. 89: 1 August 1947 – 10 November 1947, Letter to D. B. Kalelkar, 10/11 October 1947, p. 316

[78] Quoted in Robert D. King, *Nehru and the Language Politics of India* (Delhi: Oxford University Press, 1997), p. 102

[79] Quoted in Ramachandra Guha, *India after Gandhi: The History of the World's Largest Democracy* (Picador India, 2008), p. 183

[80] *The Collected Works of Sardar Vallabhbhai Patel* (Konark Publishers Pvt. Ltd., 1999), Vol. XIV, p. 56

[81] Jawaharlal Nehru, *Selected Works of Jawaharlal Nehru*, Second Series, Volume 9, Letter to T. Prakasam, p. 137

[82] Vasanthi Srinivasan, *Gandhi's Conscience Keeper: C. Rajagopalachari and Indian Politics* (Permanent Black, 2018 edition; First published in 2009), pp. 146-148

[83] Jawaharlal Nehru, *Selected Works of Jawaharlal Nehru*, Second Series, Volume 20, Letter to C. Rajagopalachari, p. 235

[84] Ibid., Letter to C. Rajagopalachari, p. 245

[85] Ramachandra Guha, *India after Gandhi: The History of the World's Largest Democracy* (Picador India, 2008), pp. 188-189

[86] Vasanthi Srinivasan, *Gandhi's Conscience Keeper: C. Rajagopalachari and Indian Politics* (Permanent Black, 2018 edition; First published in 2009), p. 149

[87] Sarvepalli Gopal, *Jawaharlal Nehru—A Biography* (Oxford University Press, 2015 Edition), Vol. 2, pp. 259-261

[88] Marshall Windmiller, *The Politics of States Reorganization in India: The Case of Bombay*, Far Eastern Survey, Vol. XXV, No. 9, September 1956

[89] Sarvepalli Gopal, *Jawaharlal Nehru—A Biography* (Oxford University Press, 2015 Edition), Vol. 2, pp. 261-263

[90] Ramachandra Guha, *India after Gandhi: The History of the World's Largest Democracy* (Picador India, 2008), pp. 196-200

[91] Danielle Allen, *Our Declaration: A Reading of the Declaration of Independence in Defense of Equality* (New York and London: W. W. Norton & Company, 2014), p. 100

[92] For discussion of Nations and Nationalism see E. J. Hobsbawm, *Nations and Nationalism since 1780: Programme, Myth, Reality* (Cambridge: Cambridge University Press, 2000)

[93] For more information about Adi Shankaracharya, among other works see Pavan K. Varma, *Adi Shankaracharya: Hinduism's Greatest Thinker* (Chennai: Tranquebar Press)

[94] Jawaharlal Nehru, *Glimpses of World History* (Penguin Books Edition, 2004), p. 514

[95] Bhikhu Parekh, *Nehru and the National Philosophy of India*, Economic and Political Weekly, Vol. 26, No. 1/2, 1991

[96] Rochana Bajpai, *Why Did India Choose Pluralism? Lessons from a Postcolonial State,* 2017

6. COMPROMISES

Most books on the history of the American people start with the account of the fateful journey made by Christopher Columbus in 1492. It is as if the Americas, north and south, were barren pieces of land that were suddenly populated by Europeans and thus commenced the story of Americans. In fact, to the contrary, about seventy-five million Native Americans (I will use this term for referring to the aboriginal people of the Americas instead of the pejorative and spurious "Indians") lived in the Americas in 1492. In contrast, the population of Europe at the time was only about sixty million. The lives of Native Americans before 1492 with their rich culture, languages, arts, religions, calendars, foods, and pretty much everything else have been consigned to the dustbin of history—to be cursorily mentioned and forgotten. In this sense, Columbus's journey was really fateful i.e. it had far-reaching and disastrous consequences not only because it discovered the "New World" but also because it radically re-defined the meaning of being American.

Columbus's voyage transformed Europe as well. Europe had been suffering from scarcity and famine until 1492 but suddenly found its condition thoroughly transformed for the better due to the vast wealth it acquired from the Americas in the coming centuries. However, this extraction of wealth had disastrous consequences not just for Native Americans who in due course of time were vanished from their own homelands. It also brought misery for Africans whose forced labor became the pedestal on which were erected the monuments of prosperity, pleasure, and pride in Europe. The stimulus provided by the newly-acquired wealth unleashed the cannibalistic European Imperialism around the world. The foundation of this European expansion was built over the displacement of Native Americans and the drudgery of the Africans undergoing the travails of slavery. Almost three centuries after Columbus's voyage i.e. during the founding fathers' time, Native Americans and Africans inhabiting the Americas were still considered something less than Americans, less than civilized, less than humans.[1]

In the three centuries between 1500 and 1800, as many as fifty million Native Americans perished from diseases and violence. Millions of Native Americans died from diseases against which, unlike Europeans, they had no acquired immunity due to their isolation: smallpox, measles, diphtheria, chickenpox, malaria, yellow fever, influenza, etc. The extraction of land and other natural resources in the Americas was possible either through reconciliation and entering into treaties with Native Americans to peacefully conduct trade and commerce or by divesting them of these resources and their lives. Europeans preferred the latter option, sometimes deliberately, often unknowingly by transmitting diseases.

Once Europeans owned the natural resources in the Americas, the problem of the lack of human capital dawned over them. The hot climate and the lack of immunity against various pests meant that the Europeans could not utilize the natural resources in many regions (such as in the Southern United States). This was solved by the advent of the slave trade. In those same three centuries between 1500 and 1800, about two and a half million Europeans transmigrated across the Atlantic to the Americas and forcefully "shipped" twelve million Africans as slaves. These slaves were transported under inhumane conditions and underwent all sorts of torments and violence on the plantations in America. Europe witnessed rapid growth following this unbounded extraction of wealth from the large American continents through slavery. Historian Jill Lepore writes that the flow of wealth from the Americas to Europe 'ended famine and led to four centuries of economic growth, growth without precedent, growth many Europeans understood as evidence of the grace of God....The European extraction of the wealth of the Americas made possible the rise of capitalism: new forms of trade, investment, and profit. Between 1500 and 1600 alone, Europeans recorded carrying back to Europe from the Americas nearly two hundred tons of gold and sixteen thousand tons of silver; much more traveled as contraband.'[2]

The politics of the founding fathers toward Native Americans and African Americans involved many compromises. These compromises are the greatest failures of the American founding generation and we discuss them in this chapter.

Founding fathers' response to the atrocities against these two "non-American" peoples i.e. Native Americans and African Americans varied from black to white encompassing all shades of grey in between. As we shall see in this chapter, the founding fathers' perception of Native Americans varied from being "savages" to "noble warriors." Native Americans emerged as the 'biggest losers' of the "American" Revolution since those who had supported the British were exiled from their ancestral homes while the newly-found United States repeatedly violated its treaties with them. They continued to be treated as "foreign" nations rather than American citizens. As "foreign" nations and possessing separate administrative units, Native Americans became a fair game for the American government to be in continuous armed conflict with.[3]

Furthermore, slavery to the founding fathers was "abhorrent" as well as an "undesired necessity," while their opinion of African Americans ranged from being "brutes unworthy of cohabiting with Whites," to being "equal beings." While many founding fathers like Franklin, Adams, and Jefferson advocated for the abolition of slavery, the emancipation of African Americans into American society remained beyond their imagination. The ideal and self-evident truth, "All men are created equal," so much propagated by the founding fathers, holistically excluded this group of Americans from its purview. In this sense, the founding of America was a paradoxical event midwifed by the founding fathers who declared liberty and equality for all "Americans" amidst the cries of violence, hypocrisy, inequality, racism, and xenophobia.

The Declaration of Independence which is today most remembered for the part about "Life, Liberty and the pursuit of Happiness" itself provides a succinct summary of the founders' troubled relationship with Native Americans and African Americans. It noted that the British king 'has excited domestic insurrections amongst us, and has endeavoured to bring on the inhabitants of our frontiers, the merciless Indian Savages, whose known rule of warfare, is an undistinguished destruction of all ages, sexes and conditions.' Thus, by the stroke of a single pen, "Americans" declared Independence from Britain while designating Native Americans as "merciless Indian Savages" to be ideally kept away from the new nation's frontiers.[4]

The Declaration was also based on the unstated compromise between the founding fathers that no mention of similar liberation of slaves should be made while declaring Independence from Britain. The document as originally drafted by Jefferson (not the later one revised by the Congress during the editing process) had this to say about slaves: by promoting the slave trade, the British king 'has waged cruel war against human nature itself, violating it's most sacred rights of life & liberty in the persons of a distant people who never offended him, captivating & carrying them into slavery in another hemisphere, or to incur miserable death in their transportation thither.' Jefferson had absurdly planned to blame the British king for that very institution of slavery which he and many of his fellow "Americans" had used to prosper. Thus, diabolically, the founding fathers were content to blame the British king for their own compromises and prejudices. No matter that this was the same king who until a few months earlier had been the revered protector of their Life and Liberty when the slave trade was flourishing under his rule.[5]

'[N]othing is more certainly written in the book of fate than that these people [slaves] are to be free, nor is it less certain that the two races, equally free, cannot live in the same government. Nature, habit, opinion has drawn indelible lines of distinction between them,' wrote Jefferson in his autobiography in 1821. This, in three short sentences, summarizes the views of most of the founding fathers toward slavery and slaves. They desired the end of slavery and many among them also took active steps in that direction. But they could not imagine coexisting with the former slaves in the same nation. As another example of this sentiment (shared by other founding fathers especially southerners), Jefferson had earlier written in *Notes on the States of Virginia,* the only book he ever published, that 'I tremble for my country when I reflect that God is just…justice cannot sleep for ever: that considering numbers, nature and natural means only, a revolution of the wheel of fortune, an exchange of situation, is among possible events: that it may become probable by supernatural interference!' The freedom of slaves was sure to come whether by the consent of their owners or by the 'extirpation' of their masters. So far so good. But, in the same book, Jefferson also elaborated on his racist sentiments by writing that blacks 'are inferior to the whites in the endowments both of body and mind.'[6]

Yet, this was the same Jefferson under whose leadership, the Virginia legislature had banned the importation of slaves within its borders making it one among the first colonies to do so in 1778. Jefferson had also drafted the Ordinance of 1784 which stipulated that all new states that would be added into the Union should have no slavery by the year 1800. When this Bill was defeated in the legislature by one vote, Jefferson had lamented that 'the fate of millions unborn [was] hanging on the tongue of one man, and Heaven was silent in that awful moment!' These conflicting opinions toward slavery and African Americans that Jefferson naturally contained in his character were reflected not just in his own writings but also in the founding documents of the nation.[7]

The founding fathers' arguments against cohabitation with African Americans combined with another hysteria from the Revolutionary War to complicate the emancipation of slaves. Since the British had incentivized the slaves for joining them in the Revolutionary War by promising to free them, it added another grudge for the revolutionaries. Almost without exception, newspapers during the Revolutionary War had shown slaves to be in collusion with the British and fighting for them. It led to the notion propagated in America even by the founders that while white Americans were fighting for freedom and risking their lives, the African Americans were deserting them and thus were unworthy of the same freedom. African Americans could never recover from this portrayal and were rendered unworthy of being granted citizenship. Slaveholders started attacking any abolitionist as being pro-British and enemy of the American Revolution.

The mass frenzy of war with Britain in the mid-1790s (as we saw in the third chapter) made sure that Americans pursued the policy of national unity at the expense of discussing slavery which had the potential of breaking the Union. The Naturalization Act of 1790 had stipulated that "a person of good character" who supported "the Constitution of the United States" could become an American citizen. There was no need to specify any exception for Native Americans or Slaves or Free Blacks because it was automatically understood that these people did not belong to the category of persons "of good character." Those thousands of Blacks who had been freed in New England and other northern states thus remained "inhabitants" and not "citizens" of America.[8]

The founding document which most characterizes this dilemma at the heart of the founding generation is the Constitution. Through the drafting of a Constitution, the founding fathers were giving the new nation a rulebook of governance. It was an unprecedented opportunity to ban the slave trade, make provisions against slavery, and free the present slaves within the boundaries of the whole nation with the stroke of a pen. Only about twenty-five of the fifty-five delegates to the Constitutional Convention in 1787 owned slaves and so, there was a realistic chance to pass such legislation. But the sectarian tensions along the north-south dimension of the nation made it harder to clinch this opportunity. At the time about twenty percent of the nation's population consisted of slaves and was mostly concentrated in the southern states. Only the state of Massachusetts (in the north) had abolished slavery by the year 1787. Due to the nature of the political economy of the south based on large plantations, the relative population of slaves varied from being less than half percent in northern New England states to being over forty percent in the southern state of South Carolina. In such a climate of sectarian strife, before studying the Constitution's view on slavery, let us first briefly look at the views on slavery of the four founding fathers who were attending the Constitutional Convention in 1787 at Philadelphia (John Adams and Thomas Jefferson were serving in Europe at the time).[9]

The president of the Convention and its most respected delegate, George Washington, remained silent about everything throughout the proceedings which included not raising any voice against slavery. One reason for this silence was that Washington owned more than a hundred slaves at the time and had never before publicly advocated the abolition of slavery. Only after demitting from the office of the president did Washington freed his slaves in his will, to be executed after his and his wife's death. On the same subject, Washington's protégé Alexander Hamilton sat squarely at the other side of the aisle. Hamilton never owned a slave in his life and in 1785 had become a founding member of the New York Society for Promoting the Manumission of Slaves. He had proposed an elaborate plan to free slaves, end the slave trade in New York, and petitioned the state legislature thereby declaring the slave trade to be 'repugnant to humanity' and 'so inconsistent with the liberality and justice which should distinguish a free and enlightened people.' While Hamilton often publicly came out as an abolitionist on his own, he followed Washington and maintained calculated silence in the Convention to achieve a compromise of interests between north and south.[10]

One highly-distinguished delegate to the Constitutional Convention (and its oldest delegate), Benjamin Franklin, had assumed the post of the president of the Pennsylvania Society for the Abolition of Slavery in 1787. The most famous American in the world and the foremost public figure in Philadelphia, Franklin, had also earlier freed his one remaining slave. Toward the end of his life, Franklin had come to believe that slavery was 'an atrocious debasement of human nature.' He was being persuaded by the members of the Pennsylvania Society to petition the Convention for abolishing slavery in the Constitution. But, when the time came to speak against slavery in the Convention, Franklin remained silent so that the north and south could arrive at a compromise on the issue. Hanging together of the two parts of the nation took precedence over his convictions. Franklin also believed that the sudden abolition of slavery would mean that American society would not remain safe either for the Free Blacks or the Whites. He was convinced that both races would feel insecure from each other since there was no history of their peaceful co-existence in America. However, as soon as the Constitution was drafted and ratified, Franklin found his lost voice and became outspoken against slavery by petitioning Congress in 1790. Franklin wrote eloquently: 'Mankind are all formed by the same Almighty Being, alike objects of his care, and equally designed for the enjoyment of happiness,' which made it the duty of Congress to secure 'the blessings of liberty to the People of the United States…without distinction of color…[Congress should grant] liberty to those unhappy men who alone in this land of freedom are degraded into perpetual bondage.' However, by then, it was too little too late. Nobody was willing to discuss a matter they believed had been laid to rest in the Constitutional Convention and so Franklin received no serious audience to his plea.[11]

James Madison, later known as the "Father of the Constitution," just like Franklin had a deeper connection with the city of Philadelphia where the Constitutional Convention was taking place. Earlier in the decade, Madison had served in the Continental Congress in Philadelphia. When in 1783 he was embarking back to Virginia, Madison had to free his slave Billey against his wishes. This was because living in the company of free blacks in Philadelphia for more than four years, Billey had tasted the sweet syrup of freedom. This had made Madison uncomfortable since, in his view, Billey had become 'too thoroughly tainted to be a fit companion for fellow slaves in Virginia.' Concluding that Billey's presence among his slaves in Virginia would make them non-compliant, Madison sold Billey for a seven-year term of service. He grumbled that he would be unable to get compensated for Billey's "worth" but had no other choice. To justify selling Billey, Madison wrote asking if Billey should be punished 'merely for coveting that liberty for which we have paid the price of so much blood, and have proclaimed so often to be right, and worth the pursuit, of every human being?'[12] Madison owned a large number of slaves himself. In the Constitutional Convention, just like Washington and Franklin, Madison also gave precedence to arriving at a compromise between north and south over the abolition of the slave trade. Neither did he propose the end of slavery nor did he push for putting an immediate end to the slave trade. Thus, Madison helped in erecting a document that protected slavery while he kept criticizing the very institution feebly from time to time. This apostle of religious freedom who worked hard to protect religious minorities (as we saw in the first chapter) could not muster enough strength to extend the principle of safeguarding minorities to African Americans.

The product of the Constitutional Convention was thus a document with no denunciation or even mention of the word "slavery." It was a peculiar patchwork of compromises between north and south. The Constitution began with the lofty words: 'We the People of the United States, in Order to form a more perfect Union, establish Justice, insure domestic Tranquility, provide for the common defence, promote the general Welfare, and secure the Blessings of Liberty to ourselves and our Posterity, do ordain and establish this Constitution for the United States of America.' In this way, the Constitution bestowed the ideals of Justice, Welfare, and

Liberty on the citizens of the United States. But on whom exactly? For the Native Americans and Blacks, the Constitution had this to say: 'Representatives and direct Taxes shall be apportioned among the several States which may be included within this Union, according to their respective Numbers, which shall be determined by adding to the whole Number of free Persons, including those bound to Service for a Term of Years, and excluding Indians not taxed, three fifths of all other Persons.'[13] These "all other Persons" were nobody but slaves. Instead of freedom, African Americans were rewarded with the inhumane three-fifths principle. This three-fifths compromise between the north and south stipulated that instead of the power to vote, slaves would be counted as three-fifths of free men for legislative representation and taxation purposes for each state. Such was the blatant hypocrisy of the Constitution that without writing explicitly about the practice of slavery as being beneath human dignity, the slaves were quietly assigned a position of being counted as three-fifths of "normal" human beings i.e. the White citizens of the nation. This was akin to proclaiming into law the common feeling about them being lesser than human beings.

The other mention of slavery without writing the dreaded word in the Constitution was in Article 1, Section 9 which read: 'The Migration or Importation of such Persons as any of the States now existing shall think proper to admit, shall not be prohibited by the Congress prior to the Year one thousand eight hundred and eight.' Thus, instead of making a provision to end the slave trade in the coming years, the Constitution instead explicitly stated that the slave trade could not be banned until 1808! This was because just like for the three-fifths compromise, the southern delegates in the Convention only agreed to endorse the document when their demands to continue the slave trade were met.[14] The cessation of slavery would have been economically disastrous for the southern states whose plantations were totally dependent on slave labor. Northerners had to compromise in the face of opposition from southerners. Thus, on the one hand, the Constitution emerged as a visionary document that had the strength to bind the states together in a Union and forge nationalism among the citizens. It has survived very well for more than 230 years now. But, on the other hand, its original definition of being an American citizen was deeply flawed.

This sanctioning of continuing the slave trade for two decades had dire consequences for the nation. Between 1788 and 1808, more than two hundred thousand slaves were imported into the United States, 'only about fifty thousand fewer than the total number of slaves imported to America in the preceding 170 years.' With an increase in the population of slaves, the three-fifths provision gave a hefty electoral weight to the southern states over the northern ones. This was one of the chief factors leading to Jefferson's victory over Adams in the presidential elections of 1800 and the dominance of presidents from the South (Jefferson, Madison, and Monroe) for 24 years. This made any political resolution to the issue of slavery much more difficult to achieve. Compromises between the north and south saved the Union in 1787 but took the nation on the road to the bloody American Civil War. If the founding fathers had not compromised their ideals and had shown enough strength to push for legislation to ban the slave trade in due course of time, it may have averted the bloodbath of the Civil War. Historian Richard Beeman notes: 'If there is a villain in this story it is the collective *indifference* of the Founding Fathers to the inhumanity of the institution [slavery] to which they gave sanction. It was an indifference born both of their sense of innate superiority over African Americans and of their preoccupation with protecting *property rights,* even if that meant accommodating themselves to a "necessary evil."' [emphasis original][15]

The central reason why in 1787 the founding fathers did not stand up to the moral stature they had earlier shown for the protection of religious minorities was that they could not imagine a multi-racial society. It was inconceivable for them to imagine that Whites and Blacks could live together peacefully in the nation whose foundation they were erecting. Below, we see the expression of this sentiment through the writings of the founding fathers. This sentiment reflects the inner compromises that the founding fathers made between their ideals and actions.

As early as 1751, Franklin had fully expressed in writing what he thought at the time—a sentiment shared by other Americans as well—that America should be settled only by White peoples:

> That the Number of purely white People in the World is proportionably very small. All Africa is black or tawny. Asia chiefly tawny. America (exclusive of the new Comers) wholly so. And in Europe,

the Spaniards, Italians, French, Russians and Swedes, are generally of what we call a swarthy Complexion; as are the Germans also, the Saxons only excepted, who with the English, make the principal Body of White People on the Face of the Earth. I could wish their Numbers were increased.[16]

In the founding fathers' view, there was an unbridgeable gap between the two races which made it impossible for them to exist together. Similar views as Franklin were expressed by John Adams. Adams, who belonged to New England (i.e. in the north) had no fondness for slavery or the slave trade. He unequivocally and vituperatively denounced slavery all his life. Yet, he could also not look forward to a time when the two races could comingle. While replying to two abolitionists who had sent him an anti-slavery pamphlet, Adams wrote in 1801 after demitting office that his opinion against slavery 'has always been known, and my practice has been so conformable to my sentiments that I have always employed freeman, both as domestics and laborers, and never in my life did I own a slave.' He then added that how the 'abolition of slavery must be gradual, and accomplished with much caution and circumspection.' Denunciation of slavery was habitual for Adams, cohabiting with erstwhile slaves was anathema. Circuitously, he then mourned how a 'general relaxation of education and government' and 'pestilential philosophical principles' spreading in Jefferson's America were 'more serious and threatening evils than even the slavery of the blacks, hateful as that is.' Somehow hearing from sources the details of which he did not provide in his correspondence, Adams also concluded that 'the condition of the common sort of white people in some of the Southern States, particularly Virginia, is more oppressed, degraded and miserable, than that of the negroes.' Thus, Adams's detestation of Jefferson's presidency was perhaps even more than his abhorrence toward the miseries of slavery and he had no qualms about playing politics on this absurdity.[17]

Washington had written in 1786 i.e. before becoming the president: it should not be conceived that 'it is my wish to hold the unhappy people who are the subject of this letter [slaves], in slavery. I can only say that there is not a man living who wishes more sincerely than I do, to see a plan adopted for the abolition of it [slavery]—but there is only one proper and effectual mode by which it can be accomplished, & that is by Legislative authority: and this, as far as my suffrage will go, shall never be wanting.'[18] Three years later, Washington was inaugurated as the president. At no point in his eight-year-long presidency did he again so thoroughly express his sentiments against slavery, let alone bring legislation for abolishing it. In 1793, President Washington signed the Fugitive Slave Act which gave the power to slaveowners for tracking down and recapture runaway slaves across state borders. He utilized this Act in 1795 when one of his own slaves ran away while advising his associate that 'I would not have my name appear in any advertisement, or other measure, leading to it.' Washington was worried that his association with the search for the runaway slave will tarnish his reputation. When he published his Farewell Address in 1795 advising Americans on all sorts of themes like separation of powers between the arms of government, maintaining neutrality in foreign relations, and warning against political factions, he conspicuously omitted any mention of slavery in the document. The "foundingest" founding father of all had nothing to advise his fellow Americans on this vexed issue since he himself could not imagine his nation as a multi-racial society.[19]

Another president, Madison, maintained the same calculated silence as Washington. Slavery never attained a position of importance in his scheme of things as an influential legislator. In his view, due to the 'existing and probably unalterable prejudices in the United States,' the only practical way to solve the problem of dealing with Blacks after the abolition of slavery at some point in the future was that they 'be permanently removed beyond the region occupied by, or allotted to, a white population.' According to Madison, '[p]hysical and lasting peculiarities' of the Blacks would ensure that they could not be incorporated into the White society because such a measure would lead to 'a change only from one to another species of oppression.' Ingrained prejudices against Blacks were so strong inside Madison that he proposed to transport free Blacks to sparsely populated areas of Western Africa. This plan which was economically and logistically impractical was given serious consideration by him with the view that Blacks could only develop their human potential to the fullest strength on another continent (read away from the Whites).[20]

The most detailed and lucid expression of this sentiment against cohabitation with Blacks came (like it was so often the case for most ideological discussions) from Jefferson. Jefferson looked to the problem of slavery defined by racial identities in terms of separate nations. "Indelible lines" had made distinctions between the two races. For Jefferson, the African Americans' presence in North America had to be viewed just like the Native Americans' presence—an aberration in the European scheme of things. He did not buy the arguments of those abolitionists who insisted that the end of slavery and the emancipation of the slaves would usher America toward prosperity. In his view, it was not so easy to transform African Americans into American citizens like Whites to assimilate them. Thus, he posed the scenario: 'It will probably be asked, Why not retain and incorporate the blacks into the state, and thus save the expence of supplying, by importation of white settlers, the vacancies they will leave?' In theory, this looked like an attractive proposition where Blacks could take the place of White settlers as peasants and slowly be assimilated into the American society. But as one of Jefferson's biographer writes while quoting him:

> Jefferson insisted that such a rational accommodation was impossible: whites and blacks would continue to see each other in racial or national terms; indeed, awareness of national distinctions would become much more acute—and dangerous—as the institution of slavery ceased to define and secure them. The end of slavery would inaugurate the state of war that the institution had held in suspense, making whites more conscious of, and prone to act on, their "deep rooted prejudices" and giving blacks a radically empowering sense of their own history—"ten thousand recollections...of the injuries they have sustained"—that slavery had suppressed. If history was not enough to provoke violence, the reciprocal awareness of racial difference that it promoted would inevitably give rise to "new provocations," so "divid[ing] us into parties, and produc[ing] convulsions which will probably never end but in the extermination of the one or the other race."[21]

Hence, Jefferson arrived at the same solution (sort of a "two-nation theory") of separating the two races as did Madison: expatriate the Blacks to a different location, ideally in Africa. Blacks being the members of a different "nation" could only secure independence and become the masters of their destiny in a newly colonized land. He continued to propagate this idea in his correspondence until his death. The greatest tragedy was that Jefferson's ideas belied his own actions. As Historian Paul Johnson notices: 'Jefferson's fundamental difficulty can be simply explained: he was a passionate idealist, to some extent indeed an intellectual puritan, but at the same time a sybarite, an art-lover, and a fastidious devotee of all life's luxuries. From claret to concubinage, there was no delight he did not sample, or rather indulge in habitually.'[22]

Since it was almost self-evident to Jefferson that 'blacks are inferior to whites in the endowments of both mind and body,' he concluded that any sexual relationship between these two races could only produce an inferior race. This led him to propose that 'when freed they [blacks] must be removed beyond the reach of mixture.' But miscegenation is exactly what he pursued! From the late 1780s, Jefferson established a secret sexual relationship with one of his slaves, Sally Hemings. He promised her that he will free all her children upon adulthood and the relationship between them continued for thirty-six years, until his death in 1826.[23] As many historians have pointed out, it is notable that she became pregnant only when Jefferson stayed with her and not when he was away in the national capital for extended periods of time. The exact nature of their relationship—love, forced sex, or something else—has never been known. Irrespectively, DNA analysis has proved beyond doubt the veracity of rumors that circulated for almost two centuries (as early as 1804 a cartoon had appeared in Massachusetts depicting Jefferson as a preening rooster and Hemings as a hen with the title "A Philosophic Cock"). The author of the American Declaration of Independence could not even live up to his own words and displayed blatant hypocrisy.

It was perhaps providential that due to Jefferson's relationship with the institution of slavery being the most complex among all founding fathers, he was provided an opportunity by circumstances to abolish slavery. 'Should an occasion ever occur in which I can interpose with decisive effect, I shall certainly know and do my duty with promptitude and zeal,' President Jefferson had written himself in 1805 to an abolitionist with assurance. In fact, fate had provided him an occasion at this very time but tragically (as it was the case so very often with Jefferson) it was missed. Jefferson had famously envisioned and propagated the idea of an "Empire of Liberty" that would expand westward over the American continent and start a new glorious chapter in human history.

At the rate of fewer than three cents per acre, for the meager sum of $15 million (about $270 million today), America bought more than 530 million acres and effectively doubled its size. The Louisiana Purchase of 1803 expanded the nation's boundaries from the Gulf of Mexico to Canada. This territory was sparsely controlled by France while most of it was settled by Native Americans. Amidst the ongoing war with Britain and mired in financial troubles, the French dictator Napoleon Bonaparte had in desperation sold the territory to Americans. As a result, the United States materialized an opportunity to expand its borders up to the Pacific in the coming time. Despite always being a fierce opponent of a strong Executive, Jefferson went all the way in this case against his own principles so as to not miss a providential opportunity of doubling the nation's size. Subsequently, due to the quasi-monarchical nature of the purchase being solely controlled by the Executive, President Jefferson received unlimited authority to set federal policy in the new territory.

Historian Joseph Ellis writes that 'Suddenly, in one dramatic and wholly unpredictable set of circumstances, the conditions for resolving the slavery dilemma had converged, creating the providential opportunity to take decisive action that Jefferson, with utter sincerity, claimed he was waiting for.' Here was a chance to use his executive power to ban slavery in the newly acquired western territory and thus hammer a death nail on its expansion. He could have at the same time used the money from the sale of these lands to compensate slave owners while freeing all the slaves in the nation. Finally, these new lands could have been used to settle the slaves and their descendants as he had proposed earlier. But, again Jefferson's limitations of unable to accept a biracial American society surfaced. He made one change in the Treaty's language while approving the purchase. He added the word "white" before "inhabitants of the ceded territory" for referring to those who would enjoy the rights in the new territory. One word made all the difference in the world. With this word ended any hopes of peaceful emancipation of the slaves. More than 600,000 Americans died in the bloodiest war of the nation—the American Civil War—six decades later to settle the ideal of "All Men are Created Equal" that Jefferson had proposed in the Declaration of Independence but could not live up to himself.[24]

"The Empire of Liberty" that Jefferson envisioned and materialized by the Louisiana Purchase not only paved the way for the Civil War by losing the last realistic opportunity to end slavery, it also had another huge and disastrous consequence. The Louisiana Purchase sounded the final death knell in the story of the glorious Native American culture. But, before discussing it, let us chronologically approach the founding fathers' views toward the Native Americans.

Perhaps no other founding father understood (or was willing to acknowledge) as much as the venerable Doctor Franklin the sophisticated form of governance that had been established by the Native Americans long before Europeans first encountered them. 'It would be a very strange thing if Six Nations of Ignorant Savages should be capable of forming a Scheme for such an Union,' wrote Franklin as early as 1751, 'and be able to execute it in such a manner, as that it has subsisted Ages, and appears indissoluble, and yet a like union should be impracticable for ten or a dozen English colonies.' Franklin was thus giving the example of the Native American Iroquois Confederacy more than two decades before the American Revolution to unite the American colonies. He drew inspiration from the Iroquois Confederacy and coined the term "Join, or Die" for his own countrymen and proposed the Albany Plan to unite the colonies (as we saw in the fifth chapter). Even in the Confederation Congress, Franklin proposed a "federalist" structure between the different states (former colonies) that was motivated by the relations between the constituents of the Iroquois Confederacy.[25]

However, contrarily, Franklin wrote in his autobiography two decades later about Native Americans that 'if it be the design of Providence to extirpate these savages in order to make room for the cultivators of the earth, it seems not impossible that rum may be the appointed means. It has already annihilated all the tribes who formerly inhabited the sea-coast.' Franklin had thus placed the blame of the Native Americans' extirpation on alcoholism rather than accepting the role played by White settlers.[26] Just like his contradictory views on slavery, on the other hand, Franklin had later also come out in support of the Native Americans while defying the prejudices against them: 'Savages we call them, because their manners differ from ours, which we think the Perfection of Civility; they think the same of theirs….Perhaps if we could examine the manners of different Nations with Impartiality, we should find no People so rude as to be without Rules of Politeness; nor any so polite as not to have some remains of Rudeness.' Expressions of praise for Native Americans especially for their valor and "nobility" were expressed by the founding fathers but what they could not come to terms with—just like for African Americans—was co-existence with them. It was as if for both of these races, the founders had made compromises with their own ideals, indeed with themselves.[27]

The Declaration of Independence in 1776 had described Native Americans as "merciless Indian savages." However, in the same year, General Washington had sought their assistance and had sealed a formal alliance with the Delaware Nation of Native Americans for securing food and supplies. This collaboration had culminated in 1778 when the newly-created United States entered its first Native American treaty to get the latter's support in the Revolutionary War.[28] By this treaty, Native Americans were formally acknowledged as foreign nations and had no locus standi in the functioning of the American Republic. And, they were treated like that. Those Native Americans who sided with Americans during the Revolutionary War were temporarily given respite while others were eliminated. Furthermore, in the same period, the diabolical nature of the American administration continued.

'Nothing will reduce those wretches so soon as pushing the war into the heart of their country. But I would not stop there. I would never cease pursuing them while one of them remained on this side [of] the Mississippi,' wrote Jefferson to the lieutenant governor of Virginia during the Revolutionary War. The author of the Declaration of Independence was not content with this declaration. When a Native American force attacked the revolutionaries, Jefferson demanded the removal of all Native Americans from the continent: 'So unprovoked an attack and so treacherous one should never be forgiven while one of them remains near enough to do us injury.' Truly, in the Jeffersonian scheme of things, there was no space for a biracial society.[29]

After the Revolutionary War ended in 1783, even those Native Americans who had sided with the United States faced the brunt of American expansion. Oneida, Stockbridge, and Tuscarora Indians who had been reliable friends during the American Revolution started to suffer heavy losses of their homeland and livelihood almost as soon as the war ended. An Oneida leader lamented that he 'did not then expect' that they will be 'reduced to our present situation' by the United States administration. They lamented years later again to President Madison by which time they had already been reduced to a miserable state: 'We fought. We bled. We conquered by the side of our American Brethren, and our bone with thiers [sic] whiten the fields where British tyranny yielded to the prowess of the American Arms. We are the same people still.' For their valuable service in the Revolutionary War, the gifts Native Americans received in return were homelessness, removal, and extinction.[30]

In the same year i.e. 1783, while sending his last circular letter to the states, General Washington had written about his expansive view of the American Republic:

> The Citizens of America, placed on the most enviable conditions, as the Sole Lords and Proprietors of a vast tract of Continent, Comprehending all the various Soils, and climates of the World, and abounding with all the necessaries and conveniences of life, are now by the late satisfactory pacification, acknowledged to be possessed of absolute freedom and Independency. They are, from this period, to be considered as Actors on a most conspicuous Theatre, which seems to be designed by Providence for the display of human greatness and felicity.

This usage of the expression "Sole Lords and Proprietors" was not coincidental. Washington was acutely aware that Native Americans inhabited those lands but he, of course, could not imagine them as a part of being the American citizenry. Washington's worldview for the expanding American Republic was undoubtedly toward the western territories where he had bought large sections of land. Native Americans could either assimilate peacefully in that worldview or face extermination.

This attitude of the founding fathers was also reflected in the American Constitution which declared that Congress shall have the power "To regulate Commerce with foreign Nations, and among the several States, and with the Indian Tribes."[31] As foreign nations,

Native Americans were ineligible to enjoy the same rights and freedoms as the "American" people. Thus, as the Constitution was being drafted and the founding fathers were safeguarding religious freedom for Whites (as we saw in the first chapter), this enlightened notion of Equality, unfortunately, did not extend to the Native Americans. Native American religions were abhorred by the founding fathers. Jefferson's writings from a later time throw light on why nobody stood up for the Native Americans. In his words, it was because their religions were seen as nothing 'more than pagan ignorance at best, and nefarious devil worship at worst.' The apostle of religious freedom, Jefferson, further wrote that 'the last step of the process [for a] plan of civilizing the Indians' should be carried out in the form of instructions from 'religious missionaries…Habits of industry, easy subsistence, attachment to property, are necessary to prepare their minds for the first elements of science, and afterwards for moral and religious instruction.'[32]

In 1789, Washington was inaugurated as the first president of the United States. By the time he assumed office, President Washington had already dealt in land speculation for most of his life. Through his life, Washington accumulated more than 45,000 acres of land estate in the western territories. This act had by default meant that he did not visualize Native Americans as the sole proprietors of those lands. During his presidency, a large portion of the federal budget went into fighting wars with the Native Americans while his policies divested them of their homelands. At the same time, Washington made sure to not make public his dealings in land speculation and deliberately avoided any mentioning of the same. Clearly, he never wanted that his duplicitous behavior should be known to posterity—his paramour.[33]

Even during Washington's (and subsequently in Adams's) presidency, federal funds were appropriated to "civilize" the Native Americans by "promoting Christianity" among them. The founding fathers' beliefs of civilization associated with Christianity were enforced on the Native Americans through numerous treaties. This was despite the fact that the separation of state and religion was enshrined by the founding fathers as a central feature of the American Republic (as we read in the first chapter).[34] Treating Native Americans as "separate nations," Washington did try once to establish peace with them in his own capacity as the president. Though critics can point out with strong arguments that Washington only sued for a temporary peace so that the American Republic could become strong enough to deal with Native Americans from a stronger position in the future.[35]

As Americans were pouring without inhibition in the western territories and displacing Native Americans, Washington was cautioned by the Secretary of War Henry Knox: 'Indians being the prior occupants possess the right of the soil, so to dispossess them would be a gross violation of the fundamental Laws of Nature and the distributive justice which is the glory of our nation.' Knox was pointing out to the president that such policies of the American administration were against the principles on which the American Republic was founded.

Knox continued to press on Washington about the change in policy: 'It would reflect honor on the new government were a declarative Law to be passed that the Indian tribes possess the right of the soil of all lands…and that they are not to be divested thereof but in consequence of fair and bona fide purchases, made under the authority, or with the express approbation of the United States.' His pleas did have an effect on Washington who made Native American policy the single most important foreign policy issue in the first year of his presidency. Washington worked closely with Knox to lay out a policy which necessitated that Native Americans could not be forcefully displaced in their homelands. Washington envisioned the establishment of secluded conclaves in the West where white settlers could not forcibly displace Native Americans while any such attempt would be foiled by the federal troops.[36]

It was decided that to try this new approach, the Washington administration would approach Alexander McGillivray, the chief of the Creek Nation tribe which was a powerful and populous Native American tribe. After a comical episode in the Senate where Washington had gone to ask for approval of his new policy and had to stand exasperated while senators debated the proposal, a meeting was set up between him and McGillivray. But it was not so easy to convince (or deceive) McGillivray who was well versed in classics, fluent in English and Spanish, and had the first-hand experience of dealing with Whites since he had sided with the British during the

Revolutionary War. McGillivray had earlier denounced the Treaty of Paris which had established American sovereignty on a lot of Native American lands in the following fashion:

> We…do hereby in the most solemn manner protest against any title claim or demand the American Congress may set up for or against our lands, Settlements, and hunting Grounds in Consequence of the Said treaty of peace between the King of Great Britain and the States of America, declaring that we were not partys…it being a Notorious fact known to the Americans, known to any person who is in any ways conversant in, or acquainted with American affairs, that his Britiannick Majesty was never possessed either by session, purchase or by right of Conquest of our Territorys and which the Said treaty gives away.

The Creek Nation being very powerful and its constituents being absolutely subservient to McGillivray, he was initially in no hurry to enter into a treaty with Americans. Nevertheless, in July 1790, he came to New York and was treated with lavish dinners, parades, and ceremonies equaling and probably exceeding those offered to European diplomatic missions. After much fanfare, the Treaty of New York was signed between the two sovereign heads of state. This Treaty bestowed sovereign control to the Creek Nation over a vast amount of land. Washington was relieved. He believed that this new strategy of respectfully dealing with the Native Americans will prove to be a noble beginning.

'But the ink was hardly dry on the Treaty,' when bad news started to trickle in. The settlers at the Georgia frontier started to pour across the border by thousands into the same tract of land that had been given to the Creek Nation by the treaty. They were totally oblivious to what had transpired in New York. Washington was infuriated. He wanted to stop this illegal flow of Americans but was handicapped by the resources he possessed because of a weak and overstretched military at the time. Remember that this was a time when a large standing army was looked to with suspicion and militias had to be raised for any law enforcement expeditions. The Federal Government was still newborn, weak, and economically broke after the Revolutionary War. It did not possess the authority to secure its territory in the far west reaches of the nation.

Washington had made a promise to McGillivray which he now found that he could not keep. He lamented: 'Until we can restrain the turbulence and disorderly conduct of our own borders, it will be in vain I fear to expect peace with the Indians—or that they will govern their people better than we do ours.' This was the most tragic part of the whole Native American confrontation story. The most respected American statesman had tried to avert the removal and extinction of Native Americans but had failed miserably because of the limits of his own power. Washington died with the lament that he could not do enough for these war-like honorable people.[37]

Washington was succeeded as president by the piquantly brilliant John Adams who had mastered ancient Greek and Latin could give lectures on almost everything—Philosophy, Religion, Science. Yet, Adams confessed himself about not taking much note of the Native Americans and their culture. His administration continued the disastrous policies from the previous administration while maintaining silence—a calculated compromise—over the issue. It was only after demitting office that he wrote that Native Americans had 'a Right to Life Liberty and Property in common with all Men.' However, Adams also reservedly questioned whether 'a few handful of Scattering Tribes of Savages have a right of Dominion or Property over a quarter of the Globe capable of nourishing hundreds of Millions of happy human Beings?' The answer in his own words was a resounding negative. The land acquired by Whites through the displacement of Native Americans belonged to Whites only in his view.[38]

Having read the views and actions of individual founding fathers toward Native Americans, let us revisit the Louisiana Purchase. After Adams was succeeded as president by Jefferson, the Louisiana Purchase being negotiated between Americans and French had presented another opportunity to freshly look at the Native American dilemma. However, the purchase was finalized as if the large territory exchanging hands was an unpopulated area of vegetation. No side approached the multitude of Native Americans who had lived there for centuries for bilateral diplomatic negotiations or even to provide them any compensation. Once the Treaty went through, Jefferson wished to designate a large part of the new territory as a huge Native American reservation for the foreseeable future, where Whites could not relocate. This was not a scheme motivated by morality or generosity. In fact, it was a ploy to deposit the Native American tribes of the Ohio Valley further westward to clear the way for the White settlers in this area without confrontation. European immigrants were flowing in at ever-increasing numbers and prosperity after the consolidation of the national government was ensuring rapid growth in the population. The new territory came as a boon for the White settlers and provided a chance to also "terminate" the Native American "problem" which was hindering their westward expansion.

The Louisiana Purchase Treaty before Jefferson's insertion of the word "white" before "inhabitants" had optimistically stipulated that "the inhabitants of the ceded territory shall be incorporated in the Union of the United States, and admitted as soon as possible, according to the principles of the federal Constitution, to the enjoyment of all these rights, advantages, and immunities of citizens of the United States, and in the meantime they shall be maintained and protected in the free enjoyment of their liberty, property, and the Religion which they profess." This clause committed the American government to ultimate but not immediate admission of the inhabitants as American citizens. It was a clever ploy to satisfy Congress into ratifying the purchase and eventually came to mean nothing for Native Americans. Again, one word made all the difference in the world.[39]

The removal of Native Americans from the areas of confrontation had been earlier thought about but there was no way to materialize it since there was no additional territory to the west owned by the United States. When the Louisiana Purchase fundamentally altered this situation, President Jefferson elaborately planned how to drive Native Americans 'into debt in order to accelerate the pace of their impoverishment and desperation, thereby speeding their extinction or removal.' As he instructed to officials: 'Should any tribe be foolhardy enough to take up the hatchet, [their behavior should be deemed worthy of seizing] the whole country of the tribe, driving them across the Mississippi as an example to others, and a furtherance of our final consolidation.'[40]

Looking back from the shore of hindsight, it is self-evident that "by our final consolidation," Jefferson meant the expansion of the White population in the western territories. In the next four decades, many court decisions helped in this "consolidation" by removing tribes to the east of the Mississippi and finally culminating in the Trail of Tears. Native Americans died by thousands while being forcefully removed to the West because of the official policy of the American government.

Such were the tragedies of Native Americans. Years later in the mid-1830s, Alexis de Tocqueville succinctly and sarcastically summarized the Native American policy of various American governments which deserves to be quoted at length: 'The Spaniards were unable to exterminate the Indian race by those unparalleled atrocities which brand them with indelible shame, nor did they even succeed in wholly depriving it of its rights; but the Americans of the United States have accomplished this twofold purpose with singular felicity; tranquilly, legally, philanthropically, without shedding blood, and without violating a single great principle of morality in the eyes of the world. It is impossible to destroy men with more respect for the laws of humanity.' No democratic government in the world could have thought about inflicting such misery duplicitously on its own people. But, then, here was the catch. Native Americans were always treated as foreign people. They constituted foreign nations. They were un-American. They, just like African Americans, were casualties of the compromises made by the founding fathers.[41]

President Washington had once written about Native Americans that 'They, poor wretches, have no Press thro' which their grievances are related; and it is well known that when one side only of a story is heard, and often repeated, the human mind becomes impressed with it, insensibly.' Posterity did not belie his expectations in this regard either.[42]

Assessing the shortcomings of the Indian founding fathers is like trying to balance on tumultuous waters because of what may be called the "Nehru Era Skewness." Bose, Gandhi, and Patel died either before India became independent or not long afterward while Ambedkar and Rajaji never assumed a position of authority in the central government for an extended period of time. Thus, in a way, Nehru who headed the government continuously for seventeen years after Independence appears to bear the responsibility for the shortcomings of postcolonial India more than any other founding father. After all, power in one's life is often followed by woe in posterity. Hence, while India transformed so much under Nehru's leadership that the doyen of contemporary historians of modern India, Ramachandra Guha, has concluded that 'more progress had probably been made in the first seventeen years of Indian independence than in the previous seventeen hundred,'[43] Nehru also receives much blame what all has gone wrong in modern India. Regardless, we shall discuss here the shortcomings and compromises of the collective founding generation, despite the fact that many of these manifested themselves explicitly during Nehru's tenure as the prime minister.

The single most defining event of the twentieth century in the Indian subcontinent was the Partition of India into two nation-states (India and Pakistan) in 1947. Perhaps, it was the greatest political compromise in human history. The repercussions of Partition are still widely felt throughout the subcontinent. The event had triggered the largest migration in human history and led to devastation for millions who lost their lives or livelihood. Scholars have worked for more than seven decades to understand the causes and impact of this momentous event. As Historian John Keay summarizes Partition: 'Most Indian Muslims had come around to the idea of a Muslim homeland of their own, most Indian nationalists were insisting on a successor state that was strong enough to resist such demands, and the British were desperate for a fast-track exit. Adopted only as a last-minute expedient, Partition was widely regretted at the time. And it has been rued ever since by all who hold life, livelihood, and peace to be dear.' Millions of Hindus migrated to India while an equally large number of Muslims migrated to Pakistan (today's Pakistan and Bangladesh). Such were the seeds of communal poison that were sowed by Partition in the subcontinent that John Keay further writes, 'Immediately after the Great Partition of 1947, people who crossed the border were known as "refugees." In the 1960s they became "evacuees," in the 1970s either "optees" or "oustees," in the 1980s "illegal immigrants," and now "potential terrorists."'[44]

Relations between Hindus and Muslims in India had never been entirely peaceful. There had been localized spurts of violence between the two communities from time to time. But, by and large, Hindus and Muslims had co-existed peacefully in the subcontinent. During the freedom struggle, paranoia was bred by the demands for a separate nation by Muslim League over the so-called "two-nation theory." This theory claimed that Hindus and Muslims constituted two separate irreconcilable nations due to the differences in their way of life. This tragedy was compounded by the fact that Hinduism does not make any distinction between religions based on a set of specific beliefs or practices. Hinduism has no single authoritative text, prophet, or sacred site. There are a variety of cultural and doctrinal differences among Hindus who consider the followers of Buddhism, Jainism, and Sikhism as their brethren. The chief criterion for the exclusion of Muslims and Christians from the point of view of Hindu extremists (because by and large most Hindus never accepted this ideology) was that Islam and Christianity were not originated in India and are thus foreign. The saga of various atrocities committed by Islamic rulers on a largely Hindu population over centuries too had its generational memory breeding animosity between the two groups.[45]

In fact, the founding fathers were never able to fully eliminate the animosity between Hindus and Muslims. The history of the Congress Party between 1900-1947 showed phases of waxing and waning of Muslim support while Gandhi kept trying repeatedly to win their trust. But, even by 1937 when Congress was pitched against the Muslim League in provincial elections under the British, its membership was 97 percent Hindu. This was a failure of the founding fathers. While Congress swept elections throughout the nation, it could not even win a single Muslim seat (since Muslims had separate electoral representation) in the political heartland of United Provinces. Gandhi had repeatedly tried to bring Muslims at large under the Congress umbrella but had only enjoyed transient success in the endeavor. And so Congress's base remained largely Hindu-centric.[46]

The distrust between the two communities culminated in the calls for a separate nation-state for Muslims. Muhammad Ali Jinnah, the leader of the Muslim League, used every trick in the playbook of politics to establish this Muslim-exclusive separate nation by partitioning India. Instead of actively engaging with the demand for a separate nation based on the "two-nation theory," Nehru categorically rejected it: 'Politically, the idea [of a separate Muslim nation] is absurd, economically it is fantastic; it is hardly worth considering…[the] idea of a Moslem nation is a figment of a few imaginations only, and even if many people believed in it, it would still vanish at the touch of reality.' Instead of debunking and discrediting the "two-nation theory" at its inception, Nehru looked the other way when the Muslim League was arguing that Muslim and Hindu civilizations are incompatible and argued: 'The real struggle today in India is not between Hindu culture and Moslem culture but between these two and the conquering scientific culture of modern civilization.' This was akin to running away from the problem by fantasizing that the wave will calmly pass under the ship. But, it did not and when the Partition came, the Congress leadership found itself unprepared.[47]

Rajaji was the only leader with the audacity to differ from the official line of the Congress Party. Rajaji recommended making a deal with the Muslim League. He put forward a proposal (known as the Rajaji formula) to peacefully divide the Muslim-majority provinces of Bengal and Punjab for the creation of Pakistan. This would have served as a starting point of talks between the Congress and the Muslim League. Everybody in Congress was outraged to hear this scheme. Nobody was prepared to accept India's partition nor were they ready to start talks with the Muslim League. Like Nehru's disregard for the Muslim League's influence on Muslims, Gandhi and others were sure of their hold on India's Muslims. Thus, Nehru accused Rajaji of 'splitting the Congress over Pakistan,' while Patel was so furious that he sought Rajaji's resignation from the Assembly. Gandhi, who was the last person to accept India's division based on religion, went further by recommending to Rajaji to sever all connections with the Congress: 'It will be most becoming for you to sever your connection with the Congress and then carry on your campaign with all the zeal and ability you are capable of.' The result was that Rajaji left the Congress Party.[48]

The "two-nation theory" had become anathema to Congress by 1942 and it caused chaos among its leadership. Nobody wanted to touch this vexed and complicated issue amidst the opposition to the

British as the Second World War was underway. No acknowledgment came forward from the Congress leadership of the fact that they did not represent the majority of Indian Muslims (thus no talks were initiated with the Muslim League) and consequently, Partition was rapidly becoming a reality which they were not accepting. They did not realize that the eventual compromise would inflict untold misery in the subcontinent. By the time Gandhi came round to Rajaji's view in 1944 and initiated talks with Jinnah on the basis of the Rajaji Plan, it was too late. By then, in the absence of Congress leaders from the political arena (Congress leaders who had been jailed by the British in August 1942 were still in prison), Jinnah and the Muslim League had grown in stature and popularity among Indian Muslims.

Only Ambedkar (who was outside of the Congress fold) among the founding fathers, dealt head-on with Partition but alas in the support of the Muslim League's scheme. Around the same time as Nehru was dismissing the "two-nation theory" advocated by the Muslim League, Ambedkar published his book, what Ambedkar's principal biographer calls his *magnum opus,* "Thoughts on Pakistan." Ambedkar took a completely different view of Partition by arguing that Muslims should be accepted as being a separate nation. He further went on to advise that since Pakistan would be much smaller and geographically weaker than India, Hindus should not fear the prospect of Partition. Making a distinction between "loyal" and "disloyal" Muslims, Ambedkar assured that Hindus need not worry since it would be better to coexist with "loyal" Muslims than "disloyal" ones. In a way, Ambedkar was speaking Muslim League's language by also proposing a complete exchange of population based on religion between the two future nations. The book then went further to antagonize Muslims by castigating their religious dogmas and criticizing their politics.[49] Ambedkar had become so convinced of the inevitability and importance of Partition even before the prospect had been taken seriously by Congress that he wrote: 'If by reason of some superior force the dissolution does not take place, one thing is sure to happen to India—namely, that this continued union will go on sapping her vitality, loosening its cohesion, weakening its hold on the love and faith of her people and preventing the use, if not retarding the growth, of its moral and material resources. India will be an anaemic and sickly state, ineffective, a living corpse, dead though not buried.'[50]

When the Partition was underway, some unfortunate statements made by Patel like Muslims who are not loyal to India should go to Pakistan while adding that he suspected a majority of them to be disloyal further increased the tensions.[51] An example of Patel's words would suffice:

> I am a true friend of Muslims although I am dubbed as their greatest enemy. I believe in plain speaking. I do not know how to mince matters. I want to tell them frankly that mere declarations of loyalty to the Indian Union will not help them at this critical juncture. They must give practicable proofs of their declarations. To Indian Muslims, I want to ask only one question. In the recent All India Muslim Conference why did they not open their mouth on the Kashmir issue? Why did you not condemn the action of Pakistan? These things create doubts in the minds of people.[52]

Patel was the frankest and most direct among the founding fathers. He neither had any ill will toward Muslims nor did he discriminate against them as the Home Minister in the government. As he himself also iterated: 'Ours is a secular state. We cannot fashion our policies or shape our conduct in the way Pakistan does it. We must see that our secular ideals are equally realized in practice....Here every Muslim should feel that he is an Indian citizen and has equal rights as an Indian. If we cannot make him feel like this, we shall not be worthy of our heritage and of our country.'[53] But the way some statements came out from his agitated and pained mouth and were played up by the press, they did not create a friendly environment for Muslims. This is because the ensuing communal rioting had made their position precarious since they were the minority community in India.

The founding fathers bear part of the responsibility of the inability to peacefully bringing together Hindus and Muslims vis-à-vis Partition. The disastrous result of their failure in doing so, was that Indians who looked the same, wore the same clothes, spoke the same language, ate the same food, and listened to the same music, were divided solely based on which gods they prayed to.

When Nehru was at the helm of the nation for seventeen years, not a single major Hindu-Muslim riot broke out in the country. This is a testimony of his secular credentials and the bond of trust he was able to cultivate among Indian Muslims. Kashmir was another matter though. It remained a dagger in India's heart. The history of the Kashmir dispute is too long and complex to be summarized here. Nehru tried to handle it in multiple ways right until his death in May 1964 but failed. Furthermore, during the same time, for the fear of antagonizing Muslims he did not take any step toward implementing a Uniform Civil Code. The Uniform Civil Code had been documented in the Directive Principles of the Constitution to mandate the replacement of personal laws for each major religion by a common set of rules for every Indian citizen. While drafting the Constitution, the founding fathers believed that introducing Uniform Civil Code at the time would have made the minority Muslim community nervous and it was left for future governments to implement it as societal conditions change.[54]

'I must confess to you,' Nehru had himself written once to Mohammad Ali Jinnah, 'that in this matter [dealing with Muslim minority] I have lost confidence in myself, though I am not usually given that way... And so, though I have given much thought to the problem and understand most of its implications, I feel as if I was an outsider and alien in spirit.'[55] While the Hindu Code Bill (which we discussed in the fourth chapter) steered by Nehru as its most vigorous proponent helped in transforming the conditions of Hindu women, Muslim women and the Muslim community at large continued to be administered by oppressive personal laws. Where, on the one hand, insistence on monogamy was restricted only to Hindu men, on the other hand, Muslim women did not even get the right to divorce and inheritance.

This became an anomaly in the ideal of equality before the law. Nehru remained the most popular figure in national politics while heading the government but chose not to push the Uniform Civil Code through the Parliament. Even today, Nehru's compromise manifests itself in the flourishing Indian democracy. Behind the garb of following culture, religious tenets, and preserving a particular way of life, the nation's laws are progressive for a section of the society and reactionary for another. Unable to separate religion from the law has led to religion miring further into the nation's politics. This was another failure that the founding fathers were conscious of but still could not avoid from happening.

In the end, the Partition had a big effect on the mass psyche on both sides of the border. While Hindus have been actively persecuted in both Pakistan and Bangladesh over many decades which has led to the declining Hindu population in both of these countries, India has fared decidedly well with a flourishing and largely well-assimilated Muslim population.[56] However, this does not mean that Indian Muslims enjoy the same quality of life as their Hindu brethren or that there are no tensions between the two communities today. Founding fathers' compromises have led to certain unsaid compromises between the two communities that fuel hatred between them from time to time.

While the Indian founding fathers were quick to express their opinions and work for the betterment of the erstwhile Untouchables (as we read in the first chapter), their voluminous writings seem to be singularly absent of consideration toward Tribals. Here and there, one finds bits and pieces about their views on this depressed community in the writings of the founding fathers. It is as if there is an unspoken compromise to not talk about the Tribals since they did not matter much in the national politics of the time. The Tribals or *Adivasis* (original inhabitants) are the indigenous people of the Indian subcontinent. Today, they number more than 100 million (about 8.4% of India's total population) and a large number of them still live either as foragers or in tribal settlements in areas of dense forest cover. These Tribals, constituting a population more than most nations on the planet, mostly never came under an organized religion. Empires have risen and fallen, invaders have come and gone, religions have soared and ebbed, but Tribals have remained how they were across millennia. Their way of life has been minimally influenced while their beliefs have been touched none at all. This may not be unambiguously a bad thing but in the 21st century, Tribals remain the most educationally backward community in India and face economic exploitation as by no other community.[57] Living mostly in the forested and hilly regions of the nation and practicing foraging and subsistence agriculture, they have often fallen prey to a vicious circle of economic exploitation, ecological disturbance, and armed insurgencies. No leader of the stature of Gandhi, Nehru, or Ambedkar has risen among them while these same founding fathers failed in becoming their representatives. Tribals remain among the most downtrodden Indians even by the abysmal standards of the caste system.

For Gandhi and the Congress, the struggle for freedom from the British Empire was a joint venture in which all Indians could play significant roles. Gandhi did everything he felt was necessary to put a united front against the British comprising of Indians from all religions, caste groups, and linguistic communities. However, since Tribals living in their traditional homelands and secluded from the outside world were mostly unaffected by the British rule or were politically uneducated, Gandhi's copious amount of writings dedicate comparatively very few passages to them. This was despite the fact that Gandhi knew very well about the problems facing the Tribals. In 1942, he had written: 'The Adivasis are the original inhabitants whose material position is perhaps no better than that of Harijans [Untouchables] and who have long been victims of neglect on the part of the so-called high classes...no one who hopes to construct Swaraj [self-rule] on the foundation on non-violence can afford to neglect even the least of India's sons. Adivasis are too numerous to be counted among the least.'[58]

However, the conception of India as a nation and a civilization for Gandhi and Congressmen was surely different from the notion of a homeland for the Tribals. The singular difference between Tribals and other inhabitants of the Indian subcontinent was that while the latter had to be united together for the struggle against the British, the former had to be made "Indians" first. At the same time, a debate was ongoing between Gandhi and his followers who worked among the Tribals (chief among whom was A. V. Thakkar). Many of them proposed the idea of "Sarvodaya [good for all]" and suggested "assimilation" of Tribals into the rest of Indian society while activists like Verrier Elwin were advocating for autonomous regions for the Tribals. Gandhi's followers performed social service in villages and tribal settlements. The socio-economic betterment of the Tribals through such peaceful assimilation remained a goal for Gandhi. However, this was never fully achieved.[59]

It is a tragedy that through his writings, the greatest emancipator of the so-called Untouchables, Ambedkar, comes out as indifferent and spiteful of the Tribals. He drove a wedge between the two depressed communities, Untouchables and Tribals, by making an implicit distinction between the "civilized" and "uncivilized." This distinction was absurd since, on almost all social indicators of progress, the conditions of Tribals were no better than that of Untouchables. While in later life, Ambedkar had favored Universal Adult Franchise as a means of political empowerment for all, especially those at the bottom of the social strata, in 1929 he had expressed that this may exclude the Tribals. 'The aboriginal tribes have not as yet developed a political sense to make the best use of their political opportunities,' communicated Ambedkar, 'and they may easily become mere instruments in the hands of either of a majority or a minority and thereby disturb the balance without doing any good to themselves.' This could have as well been true for his own community of Untouchables due to the low level of education and economic development. But the "uncivilized" ways of Tribals were what was at the heart of Ambedkar's argument for not extending voting rights to them. He did not ask the question that how without voting rights will Tribals become politically empowered when he was struggling to provide the same rights to his own community.[60] Ambedkar's views come out as even more outdated when he wrote in his book *Annihilation of Caste*: 'Physically speaking, the Hindus are a C^3 people. They are a race of pygmies and dwarfs, stunted in stature and wanting in stamina,' thus clearly validating the then-prevalent Western notions of racial discrimination.[61]

The Constitution of India whose drafting was headed by Ambedkar made no distinction between Indians based on ethnicity, religion, language, or caste. Tribals were in a different league though. It was due to the efforts of Tribal leaders such as Jaipal Singh (a prolific writer, politician, and a great hockey player) that delegates of the Constituent Assembly were sensitized to the "tribal predicament." When during deliberations in the subcommittees of the Constituent Assembly, the reservation in government jobs and legislature was provided only to the Untouchables (the cause being spearheaded by Ambedkar), Jaipal Singh was exasperated. '[T]he most needy, the most deserving group of adibasis [tribals] has been completely left out of the picture,' he cried. In an eloquent speech, Jaipal Singh expressed:

> I am not expected to understand the legal intricacies of the Resolution. But my common sense tells me that every one of us should march in that road to freedom and fight together. Sir, if there is any group of Indian people that has been shabbily treated it is my people. They have been disgracefully treated, neglected for the last 6,000 years. The history of the Indus Valley civilization, a child of which I am, shows quite clearly that it is the newcomers – most of you here are intruders as far as I am concerned – it is the newcomers who have driven away my people from the Indus Valley to the jungle fastness...The whole history of my people is one of continuous exploitation and dispossession by the non-aboriginals of India punctuated by rebellions and disorder, and yet I take Pandit Jawahar Lal Nehru at his word. I take you all at your word that now we are going to start a new chapter, a new chapter of independent India where there is equality of opportunity, where no one would be neglected.[62]

In the coming days, the Constituent Assembly acceded to the request and extended reservations to the Tribals as well. But, by continuing the British policy of land ownership, it empowered the government to become the custodian of Tribal homelands—a move that made them squatters in their own forests. Jaipal Singh had warned against destroying the tribal way of life: 'You cannot teach democracy to the tribal people; you have to learn democratic ways from them. They are the most democratic people on earth…We do not ask for any special protection. We want to be treated like every other Indian.'[63]

However, the largest democracy in the world consistently failed in learning from the democratic ways of the Tribals and consigned them to the periphery of the governmental institutions. Jaipal Singh had placed his trust in Nehru's word of providing adequate safeguards to his people and he paid dearly for this. Nehru differed from Gandhi in many ways regarding the approach to modernity. Nehru's approach to development was built on science, industrialization, and modernity. A significant part of this approach consisted of the construction of big dams, which Nehru fondly called the temples of modern India. The development of these dams was highly beneficial to many but they also became a source of sorrow and suffering for Tribals whose traditional homelands were submerged by them. Nehru had outlined his policy toward Tribals as the so-called *Panchsheel* or "Five Pillars of Tribal Development." In principle, this policy provided autonomy to the Tribals in the flourishment of their arts and culture along with respecting their rights of the land. Nehru had himself asked the government officials to respect Tribals' rights and way of life and not force them to become mere imitations of other Indians. As he iterated: 'In the tribal people, I have found many qualities which I miss in the people of plains, cities and other parts of India. It was these very qualities that attracted me.'

Nehru could also be diabolical. On the one hand, he idolized the Tribals: 'The need, today, is to understand these people [Tribals], make them understand us and thus create a bond of affection and understanding.' However, on the other hand, during the inauguration ceremony of one of the dams, he addressed the displaced people (mostly Tribals) by saying: 'If you are to suffer, you should suffer in the interest of the country.' This was akin to applying butter after dismembering their limbs. It is because of this attitude that one critic has accused Nehru, the architect of Modern India, as 'the architect of *Adivasi* misery. Today, it seems, millions of *Adivasis* are struggling for survival because of the policies of Nehru and his Congress Party.' One project after the other, unsustainable strategies were followed by his government which led to the ruination of Tribals. Hirakud Dam Project displaced more than 20,000 people from 249 villages and could only rehabilitate 300 out of 1,636 displaced families, Bhakra Nangal Dam project could resettle only 33 percent of the displaced families till 1978, the Tungabhadra project displaced 55,000 people belonging to 12,000 families, the Damodar Valley Project displaced 93,874 persons and the list goes on in every corner of India. Tribals were the most affected group among the displaced. The rapid development of the nation through industrialization was no doubt necessary but equally important was the need to resettle the displaced and dispossessed, and the government failed miserably in this.[64]

A forgotten episode in this saga is Nehru's plan of resettling refugees from Bengal after the Partition in the tribal heartland of Dandakaranya. More than 3.5 million refugees came into India through West Bengal in the decade succeeding Partition. It was the government's responsibility to clothe, feed, and provide shelter to them. Nehru planned to re-settle them around Dandakaranya so that Tribals living in the area may become "civilized" through close contact with these refugees and pursue the fruits of development in the same way as other Indians. The government planned to carve out 80,000 square miles for this project by clearing the land and resettling the refugees. Nehru promised that '...apart from the protection of the adivasi interests the first priority in Dandakaranya is the rehabilitation in camps. Later as the scheme develops others may also come in. Indeed long after the problem of displaced persons has settled the Dandakaranya scheme will be progressing and developing.'

Of course, this was not to be. As the land was cleared without consent from the Tribals, they continued to shift toward denser forests. They had been asked by the government to make compromises for others and lose their livelihood in the process. The refugees were allotted the lands and they kept on expanding into the tribal territory through illegal means. Forests were cut down to illegally sell timber while the Tribal economy and its means of sustenance were destroyed. The resulting violence continues even today. Steps have been taken in the past few years to correct the wrongs done to Tribals such as the creation of Jharkhand as a separate state—a demand since Independence. But, much damage has already been done. Recklessly designed industrial and mining projects have contributed to making Tribals the largest displaced community in India today with meager access to schools and healthcare facilities. Because of their views toward the Tribals, the founding fathers had inadvertently become complicit in the system of economic exploitation—similar to the colonial system that they had fought against all their lives for all other Indians. Unlike the British, now the exploiters were the citizens of the same nation whose inhabitants were being exploited.[65]

Just like it was a collective failure of the Indian founding fathers that they were unable to prevent Partition and forge Hindu-Muslim unity, another failure exhibited by them, unwillingly, was the absence of a collective novel vision to develop Independent India. Historian Rajmohan Gandhi writes, 'Where did these founding figures fall short? From today's perspective, it may be said that they did not recognize the master-servant relationship between rulers and the people, an equation bequeathed by the [British] Raj, as the great problem that it was and is.'[66] In many ways, India's governance ushered on a similar path after Independence that had earlier been the hallmark of British rule—a heavy-handed state with highly centralized administration. This was the idea practicalized in his administration by Nehru. Another constitutional expert writes candidly that 'India inherited the British system of government and administration in its original form. The framers of the new Constitution could not think of an altogether new system.'[67]

Or, maybe the circumstances were such that they could not. Partition, the unification of princely states, Hindu-Muslim riots, refugee crisis, and vigorous debate over national language and linguistic provinces, all occurring simultaneously during the framing of the Constitution meant that the founders became naturally suspect of a weak central government. Untold compromises were made through legislation by the founders to nullify the same ideals that they had vigorously propagated before Independence.

Article 19(1)(a) in the Constitution had originally guaranteed the fundamental right to freedom of speech and expression subject to some qualifiers like on any matter 'which undermines the security of or tends to overthrow, the State.' After the Constitution came into effect, Nehru's government brought in amendment after amendment to change the Constitution for curbing civil liberties on lines of the British model. Not only this, but his government also revised laws to preclude judicial review so that they could not be struck down by the judiciary. These steps were taken in the name of protecting India from threats arising from Communism. For example, when in 1950 the judiciary came to the rescue of a communist journal *Crossroads* which had been banned by the Madras government, Home Minister Patel was furious. All founding fathers at the moment agreed that the press had to be "regulated" or else the precarious national unity may be broken into shatters. In Patel's view, freedom of expression was not sacrosanct and the judiciary's decision had knocked 'the bottom out of most of our penal laws for the control and regulation of the press.'[68]

In a hurry, Patel prodded Prime Minister Nehru to write to the Law Minister Ambedkar for drafting amendments to the Constitution. Ambedkar replied that he was in the favor of adding further restrictions about undermining the security of the state to the clause guaranteeing the freedom of speech and that this amendment would be exempted from the purview of the judiciary. As news spread of what the government was trying to do, the press vocally excoriated the planned move. *Hindustan Times* published that the changes 'animated...by a desire to conserve and consolidate the power and patronage of the executive...Particularly dangerous is the attempt to qualify freedom of speech.' President Rajendra Prasad too advised the government against amending the Constitution like this. But, Nehru was adamant and was receiving full support from his colleagues in the endeavor. He showed contempt toward the press journals by asking in the Parliament if they were 'some two-page news-sheet...full of vulgarity, indecency and falsehood?' To create more hysteria among people, Nehru also played the fear card by saying the 'international situation is delicate' and the amendment was important to maintain friendly relations with other nations. In what the *Times of India* noted as the other great oration of the day, the leader of the Bharatiya Jana Sangh, Shyama Prasad Mookerjee, questioned Nehru by asking that who is to decide about what is good or bad for the nation in terms of foreign policy and why the present laws are not sufficient to curb any misuse of the freedom of expression.[69]

Nehru remained unmoved and expressed that the standards of the newspapers have deranged to a level of vulgarity: 'The other day I was looking through a large number of cuttings from the Urdu and Hindi press. I cannot tell you how thoroughly ashamed I felt; I blushed with shame to read that such things should be printed day after day, cartoons and letterpress and the rest. I could not imagine anything more disgusting and obscene and vile.' Nehru's personal views were coloring his political judgment. It was as if he wanted to control what an obscene editor in a corner of India was publishing against the government.[70]

There was a lot of criticism and opposition that Nehru faced over this amendment curbing the freedom of expression. But, because of his sheer stature within the Congress Party which had a majority in the parliament, the bill was passed. The only concession that Nehru gave to the opposition was the addition of the word "reasonable" so that the judiciary could judge if the case was actually a violation of the freedom of expression. Sadly, the First Amendment to the Constitution received the dubious distinction of being an attack on the freedom of expression and speech. It was passed by the same government whose head, Nehru, had also eloquently spoken multiple times about the freedom of the press: 'For my part, I do think that basically it is dangerous to suppress thought and the expression of thought in any way, because this may, besides suppressing a particular good thing, produce many kinds of evil which stunt the growth of a social group.'[71] A precedent when established is often repeated again, especially when it is a bad one. A bad idea was made worse as time passed. Successive governments over the years utilized this law for curbing individual freedom. Sadly, this was not all. Another remarkable law enacted by the government shared close features with the British colonial state.

Anybody in British India who agitated against the administration during the freedom movement could be subjected to preventive detention by the government. A mere voice against the government could land the protestor in prison with all judicial niceties being done later—a gross violation of life and liberty. Congress Party had protested against these laws for years before the Independence. Now while drafting the Constitution, Patel himself advocated for strong powers of detention and 'in a nice irony, the article was included among the Fundamental Rights.' When in 1950 a bill was introduced to strengthen the powers of the government for preventive detention, both Nehru and Patel pulled their weight behind it while expressing regret. Their argument was that India was in danger of breakup due to Communists' mischief and communal passions that plan to overthrow the newborn government. Thus, while introducing the Bill, Nehru showed 'contrition' because it was 'repugnant to the ideal of a free and democratic government.' Patel talked about sleepless nights because of his conscience that was against Bill's passage. Yet, Patel added that the bill was necessary since 'where the very basis of law is sought to be undermined and attempts are made to create a state of affairs in which…"men would not be men and law would not be law."' He emphasized that the Bill was not against any particular ideology but against anarchists who do not let the government function. As he put it unequivocally that the 'liberties of the millions of persons' were threatened by those 'individuals whose liberties we have curtailed…We want to protect and defend civil liberties, but I hate criminal liberties.' With both Nehru's and Patel's backing, it goes without saying that the Bill was passed unanimously. It gave the government enormous power to curb civil liberties on vague and all-encompassing phrases like "maintenance of public order" and "security of the State."[72]

Next year, the Parliament extended the powers of this legislation for another year. Rajaji who had become the Home Minister now after Patel's death backed the law even more aggressively and vocally than his predecessor. 'Stern and ruthless' action was needed, Rajaji said, against 'mischievous and violent elements, fanatical' communists and communalists. While he admitted that preventive detention would be 'certainly an infringement of what may be called a normal principle of criminal justice,' he justified the move by saying that 'we cannot have the same amount of concreteness in evidence as we can demand when a prosecutor alleges overt acts in providing an attempt or an abetment of a specific crime.' The founding fathers were introducing and supporting the same oppressive legislation against which they had protested on the streets and filled prisons in the British era. More Preventive Detention Acts were passed in 1952, 1954, 1957, and 1960 i.e. during Nehru's tenure. These were blots on the face of democracy. There was a lot of criticism in the Indian and foreign press but Nehru persisted. He justified these acts—which he would have opposed by going to jail in the British era—in the name of social welfare and combating anti-social forces. In the coming years, the succeeding governments only strengthened such laws and misused them time and again.[73]

Many of these torment the nation's citizens even today. Instead of being temporary expedients, such laws have, for the foreseeable future, become a permanent part of the Indian democracy. A scholar wrote in 1962 what is equally true for the present times: 'Communalism, religious fanacticism [sic], language rivalry, provincial separatism, and caste recrimination have not disappeared. They have shown an unlooked for hardihood and, as a consequence, the legal weapon which has been forged to cope with their harmful effects has been extended time and again. The Preventive Detention Act is a symbol of India's permanent emergency.'[74]

Nehru's heavily centralized administration served as the foundation for his socialist economic policies (about which we read in the third chapter). Thus, it may not be a bad idea to ask here if there was another vision of India laid out by the founding fathers? The answer is yes. Could there have been a compromise between the two visions? Maybe not, since that other vision was as extreme in the opposite direction as the one adopted later by Nehru.

Right from the time of his return from South Africa, Gandhi had advocated the establishment of village republics, economic self-reliance, and the development of village industries. He had an instinctive dislike for machine-made goods and promoted the manufacturing of hand-spun textile goods. As early as 1909, Gandhi had written that 'Machinery has begun to desolate Europe. Ruination is now knocking at the English gates. Machinery is the chief symbol of modern civilisation; it represents a great sin.' Gandhi held so vehement views against machine-made goods that he remarked 'As long as we cannot make pins without machinery, so long will we do without them.'[75] Riding on this wave of anti-machinery ideas, single-handedly, Gandhi had made the renunciation of wearing foreign machine-made cloth and burning them as symbols of the freedom movement. His walks in the Indian villages had left such a deep impression on him that he had come to view villages with a romanticized version of life—simple, non-violent, and truthful.

It may be interesting here to contrast the images of rural India among Gandhi, Ambedkar, and Nehru. In a nation where about three-fourths of the population lived in rural settlements, the three leaders differed in the role that villages should play in post-Independent India. Gandhi idealized village life and fantasized about self-sufficient village republics across India. Ambedkar who had faced oppression for being an Untouchable all his life and was the only leader among the three to have actually been raised in a village had poignantly remarked in the Constituent Assembly: 'The love of the intellectual Indians for the village community is of course infinite if not pathetic....I hold that these village republics have been the ruination of India. I am therefore surprised that those who condemn Provincialism and communalism should come forward as champions of the village. What is the village but a sink of localism, a den of ignorance, narrow-mindedness and communalism?'[76]

Gandhi's perception of cities was inconsonant with "modern" ideas: 'To me the rise of cities like Calcutta and Bombay is a matter of sorrow rather than congratulation. India has lost in having broken up a part of her village system.' In contrast, Nehru saw no virtues in the traditional social order represented by villages. He was against both the class and caste distinctions manifest in rural life and favored the industrialization of India as the remedy to create a new social order. Unlike Gandhi, Nehru also favored the introduction of modern scientific technology in agriculture. He criticized the cultivators for 'using outdated methods' and for being 'content with whatever little they produced.' Nor did Nehru favor the establishment of village republics. Rather, he viewed villages as electoral units, 'each such unit functioning as a self-governing community within the larger political framework.'[77]

These ideas of self-reliance also colored Gandhi's views about economic development after Independence. Once asked about his vision of post-Independent India, Gandhi said: 'Independence must begin at the bottom. Thus, every village will be a republic or panchayat having full powers. It follows, therefore, that every village has to be self-sustained and capable of managing its affairs even to the extent of defending itself against the whole world....In this there is no room for machines that would displace human labour and that would concentrate power in a few hands. Labour has its unique place in a cultured human family. Every machine that helps every individual has a place.'[78]

This extraordinarily idealistic vision of a decentralized nation composed of self-sufficient villages could not, of course, build a strong and modern nation-state of the twentieth century. A decentralized and unindustrialized nation of India's size and diversity could neither have effectively governed itself nor would it have been strong enough to face external threats. Yet, Gandhi criticized Nehru whose ideas about industrialization did not intersect with those of Gandhi's: 'Pandit Nehru wants industrialization because he thinks that, if it is socialized, it would be free from the evils of capitalism. My own view is that evils are inherent in industrialism, and no amount of socialization can eradicate them.'[79] Gandhi insisted that 'India's salvation consists in unlearning what she learnt during the last fifty years. The railways, telegraphs, hospitals, lawyers, doctors, and suchlike have all to go,' but Nehru sharply differed with him: 'All this seems to me utterly wrong and harmful doctrine, and impossible of achievement. Behind it lies Gandhiji's love and praise of poverty and suffering and the ascetic life.' It was not just Nehru who differed with Gandhi but his other recalcitrant and prodigal son, Bose, too disagreed with him.[80]

In 1938, as president of the Congress Party, Bose had formed the National Planning Committee. He firmly believed in the industrialization of the nation along the lines of the West. Bose believed that the goal of the Congress Party should be that 'everybody—man, woman, and child, is better clothed, better educated and has sufficient leisure for recreation and for cultural activity. [India had] resources similar to those of the United States of America,' what was needed was to utilize them for the nation. 'You cannot imagine,' Bose wrote to Nehru, 'how I have missed you all these months,' when the latter was away in Europe. Nehru was the closest among Congress leaders to Bose's view on industrialization and so Bose nominated Nehru as the head of the Planning Committee while saying 'you must [assume the role] if it is to be a success.' Most of the members of this committee were scientists, economists, and politicians who believed in rapid industrialization and the development of a modern state. Both of Gandhi's political sons differed with him conclusively on what post-Independent India would look like.[81]

The conflict in the views of the founding fathers had a direct consequence on the development of India in the coming decades with Nehru's administration propagating centralization and modernity while Gandhian activists and social reformers uniting for more freedom.

After Patel's death in 1950, any other vision of India's development was meaningless since Nehru's influence over the Congress Party was uncontested from now on. After Rajaji's exit from the Congress Party not much later, there was nobody of Nehru's stature or half as popular in the Congress Party to put checks and balances over Nehru's ideas and powers. Nehru's primary preoccupation was with industrializing and modernizing India through a socialist structure. While Gandhi's vision was of total decentralization of power to villages motivated by dislike for industrialization, Nehru believed in a centralized government whose main aim was to promote industrialization at any cost. Nehru had been a committed socialist since the early 1930s though he had not been doctrinaire.[82] However, Nehru's socialist views combined with a push for rapid and deep industrialization led to another failure—the creation of an omnipotent, omnipresent, and omniscient bureaucracy.

When he was heading the government, Nehru's policies dictated that reform programs were to be initiated, controlled, monitored, implemented, and evaluated from the top echelons of the government. Five-year plans inaugurated by the government took India toward blind industrialization without the provisions to evaluate the government's policies in the long term. Nehru and his government took people as merely 'objects of the development process' whose progress could be managed through decisions taken by bureaucrats. 'Every advance of this rhetoricized bureaucracy in the control of social life was celebrated as a further step towards a mystical socialistic pattern of society…' Everything from buying land for agriculture to opening a new business firm came under the government's scrutiny and one needed to make his/her way through the bureaucratic labyrinth to get work done. The effects of this ubiquity of the state are felt even today when railways, postal system, communication, education, healthcare, among other sectors are heavily bureaucratized and do not work efficiently.[83]

In effect, Nehru planned to bring industrialization to India in one go under a socialist economic architecture instead of letting the market forces and private entrepreneurship take over. This meant that the nascent Indian state had to be made stronger to deal with challenges emanating from economic backwardness and social unrest while it industrialized at a feverish pace. This could only be done by concentrating greater power in the hands of the central government and its bureaucrats. Too much devolution of power to states may have led to delays and Nehru was in a hurry. He wanted to irrevocably place India on the route to modernity. Historian Sudipta Kaviraj writes that 'The most serious consequence of this, of course, was that the state became omnipresent, since it was performing functions left to the institutions of civil society, and it was impossible to abjure transaction with this state. At the same time, it could work only through the techniques of an unreconstructed colonialist bureaucratic style, wholly monological, criminally wasteful, utterly irresponsible and unresponsive to public sensitivity.'[84]

Rajaji vehemently disagreed with Nehru's economic policies on centralized control and was at the forefront of the opposition (as we read in the third chapter). Rajaji wrote a biting critique to oppose the policies of the Congress Party:

> It is remarkable that in this scientific and rationalistic age, centralized economic planning by the State has been raised to the pedestal of a holy cult. The dominant theme in India for some years past has been the economic uplift of the masses, and centralized all-out planning has been resorted to as the means of promoting that object. And this, in spite of reiterated lip-service to decentralization. The major fault of centralized, comprehensive planning is that it imposes a monolithic burden on a people composed of diverse elements at all levels and in all occupations. The achievements that it might show in a few selected areas are bought at the cost of the freedom and enterprise of the individual. The individual and his creative ability are smothered by a proliferating bureaucracy and innumerable rules and regulations.[85]

When Rajaji saw no improvement in the situation despite his appeals to Nehru, he planned to actively contest elections against the Congress Party (again, as we read in the third chapter). In another article, Rajaji wrote: 'Centralization is growing apace and should be halted. "The rush of blood to the head is bad for the country." Socialism and collective planning have led to an unmistakable drift to the totalitarian State. This must be resisted. The power of the State must no doubt be used to protect the weak, to prevent exploitation, and to better the condition of the people. There is no dispute over this. But the dispute is over the extent of State interference that is consistent with democracy.'[86]

The plain truth was that long years in the British prisons and the animosity toward the rulers had cultivated in founding fathers an abhorrence for the British capitalistic economic system. If something in the economic domain was British or originated in one of the Imperialistic Western powers, it was looked at with suspicion. This was ironic in the sense that the founding fathers had willingly adopted and propagated parliamentary democracy from the British and heavy-handed state control from the colonial era. But in the economic domain, the sudden rise of Soviet-style Socialism on the world stage presented itself as an alternative to the founding fathers. They also gravitated toward this new economic philosophy since the British

Imperialism they abhorred had its roots in laissez-faire capitalism. To many founding fathers, the vast intellectual breadth of Marxists at the time combined with the gaining foothold of Socialism around the world pointed to a pause in history—henceforth the world was a playing ground between Capitalism and Socialism. Nehru, especially, tried to bring the best of both worlds in India but in many aspects, an uneasy compromise between these economic systems gifted India the worst of both worlds.

Gandhi himself never became so much dogmatic when it came to Socialism or Capitalism as the economic system that India should adopt after Independence but remained skeptical of the applicability of free-market economics in the Indian context. Other leaders like Nehru and Bose had become self-styled socialists in their youth. This had happened as a gradual transformation over the years when they read Marxist literature while serving long sentences in British prisons. In his presidential address to the Congress Party in 1936, Nehru had declared: 'I am convinced that the only key to the solution of world's problem and of India's problems lies in socialism...I see no way of ending poverty, the vast unemployment, the degradation and the subjection of the Indian people except through socialism. That involves vast and revolutionary changes in our political and social structure....Socialism is thus for me not merely an economic doctrine which I favour; it is a vital creed which I hold with all my head and heart.'[87]

After Independence, there was much self-righteousness about the socialistic path that India was taking, backed by the heavy centralization of state power within a democratic structure of government. It did give fast results in starting with rapid industrialization in the 1950s but with time the approach stifled India's growth. Not until 1991 did India's economy really took off when the old ideologies were set aside after the fall of the Soviet Union and a grave economic crisis. It was a shortcoming of the founding fathers that they were unable to coherently visualize a future that borrowed from the West without the prejudices inculcated in them due to colonialization.

> Had the directors of these movements [founding fathers] subsequently proved wanting in the art of reconstructing the fabric of society; had the issue been anarchy, and decline in civilization, refinement, and whatever goes to make the human family happy, intelligent, moral, and religious, the failure would have reacted upon the past...To posterity, all those who boldly commence, only to fail at last, appear heavily responsible for the vast amount of misery which their attempt necessarily entails upon their fellow-men.
> -Charles Francis Adams

> It is really the architects of this generation and the next we [framers of the Indian Constitution] are going to put this Constitution into working, on whom will depend a great deal, its success or its failure. It is not for us to say whether we have come our job well or badly. It is only posterity that can really judge of us.
> -Renuka Ray

We went over some achievements of the founding fathers of the United States and India in the previous five chapters. Oppression against minorities (particularly against African Americans, Native Americans, and Immigrants in the United States and Scheduled Castes, Scheduled Tribes, and Muslims in India); misuse of power by political leaders; putting partisanship over national interest by the opposition; social, gender, and economic inequality; and equating a particular ideology as the sole custodian of nationalism are issues that still inflict these two (world's largest) democracies. In both nations, despite the best of intentions, the founding fathers did not succeed in uprooting all sources of friction. They could not. Perfection is a constant endeavor. The democratic experiments launched by the two founding generations in these two pluralistic nations are thus works in progress. The compromises made by the two founding generations are still reflected in the society of these two nations. As a result, the founding fathers have ever been so indispensable to the nation's narrative that history is often twisted so that they can be quoted and misquoted to support one's own position. Below are some examples.

American founding fathers' abhorrence of co-existing with African Americans on the same continent was codified by different means into the founding documents of the nation. More than two centuries later, the African American community still feels alienated from the government and the affluent section of society. Yet, social movements in the United States, as a general rule, invoke the words and actions of the "failed" founding fathers. It took almost eight decades after the Constitutional Convention to free the slaves from bondage after a deadly civil war. When President Abraham Lincoln delivered the iconic Gettysburg Address, he used the words written by the founding father who had the most intimate and diabolical relationship with slavery. By declaring America as being dedicated to the proposition, "All Men Are Created Equal," coined by Jefferson, Lincoln harked back to the nation's founding to justify the moral high ground that he had been taking during the war. It then took another century of struggle for the African American community to gain equal rights of democratic participation. It is interesting to note that to justify his actions and the moral ground taken by him, Lincoln quoted the most eloquent founding father of the nation. It is also interesting to mark as a side note that Gandhi too had praised Lincoln for his actions by writing in his journal *Indian Opinion* in 1905: 'It is believed that the greatest and noblest man of the last century was Abraham Lincoln.'[88]

When Martin Luther King Jr. gave his momentous "I Have a Dream" speech from the steps of the Lincoln Memorial exactly a century after Lincoln's Gettysburg Address, he declared that he had come to collect the "promissory note" that Jefferson and other founding fathers had promised to all Americans. 'In a sense,' declared King, 'we've come to our nation's capital to cash a check. When the architects of our republic wrote the magnificent words of the Constitution and the Declaration of Independence, they were signing a promissory note to which every American was to fall heir. This note was a promise that all men, yes, black men as well as white men, would be guaranteed the unalienable rights of life, liberty, and the pursuit of happiness. It is obvious today that America has defaulted on this promissory note insofar as her citizens of color are concerned.'[89]

Just like Lincoln before him, King found it necessary to connect the dots between the civil rights movement and the founding of the United States by invoking the founding fathers. In both cases, the leaders (Lincoln and King) re-interpreted (some would say turned upside down) the words and deeds of the founding fathers to justify their own actions. The compromise made by the founding fathers in their inability to assimilate the African Americans into society was re-interpreted as a promise to the future generations. Today, in Washington D.C., King's Memorial stands nearby Lincoln's Memorial and opposite the Jefferson Memorial which is separated from these by a body of water (Tidal Basin). It may not be so farfetched to see the unfolding before our eyes of the moral standings of these three historical figures in the positioning of these three memorials. The struggle for equality for African Americans is still underway and may yet require more social movements connecting the present with the founding of the nation.

The contempt shown by American founding fathers toward Native Americans by designating them as foreign nations in some ways reflects America's contemporary attitude toward them as well as its overseas military engagements. Repeated assaults on the Native Americans and their culture in the nineteenth century resulted in their ghettoization in many pockets of the nation. Once better off than the colonialists, they are today neither fully assimilated in the American society nor do they enjoy the same levels of healthcare and education in their own settlements. Counted as citizens of the United States, they still constitute "foreign nations" in the eyes of most Americans and many times are visited as such—out of curiosity and for trade. There is also an unmistakable pattern between the treatment of Native Americans by the founding fathers as "foreign nations" and America's overseas engagements as a superpower. Historian Joseph Ellis writes that 'the creedal conviction that American values are transplantable to all regions of the world is highly suspect and likely to draw the United States into nation-building projects beyond its will or capacity to complete.' Sounds familiar? Two centuries ago, the route taken by the founding fathers of conveniently neglecting the Native Americans for the larger picture of gaining political and economic resources bears striking resemblance to the nation's actions today in many volatile regions of the world.[90]

In the foothills of the Himalayas, something remarkable happened in the 1970s. The so-called Chipko Movement was launched by the peasants to protest against rapid deforestation and the resulting loss of livelihood. Without fearing for their lives, villagers (both men and women) hugged the trees en masse to prevent them from being cut down by authorities. This non-violent form of protest, indeed a kind of Satyagraha, closely matched Gandhi's methods of passive resistance against the British. Many leaders of the movement were indeed Gandhian in the true sense of the term. In the ensuing years, this movement became an inspiration for many environmental movements around the world. It also brought into focus the ecological issues faced by tribal and other marginalized people in India. Though Adivasis were marginalized by the founding fathers, Gandhi's methods of passive resistance still empowered them through such social movements. On the eve of India's Independence, Nehru had expressed in his *Tryst with Destiny* speech that 'The ambition of the greatest man of our generation [Gandhi] has been to wipe every tear from every eye. That may be beyond us but [so] long as there are tears and suffering, so long our work will not be over.' Decades after Gandhi's death, his ideas and ideals are still helping the marginalized in India in realizing his life's ambition. In the same way, Ambedkar is today idolized by the Dalit (broadly erstwhile Untouchables) community which takes inspiration from him for its own empowerment.[91]

When the Babri Mosque was unlawfully demolished by a Hindu mob in December 1992, many in India saw it as the end of Secularism instituted by Gandhi and Nehru. While both of them had failed in precluding Partition, they had nonetheless promised a safe and prosperous future to India's Muslims. They promised equality in all respects to Muslims alongside their Hindu brethren. The breaking of that promise and India's thread of Secularism was expressed by many akin to the feeling that Gandhi had been assassinated once again. Subsequently, in various movements organized by Muslims for demanding equal rights or opposing the ruling government's policies (such as happened in December 2019 to oppose the Citizenship Amendment Act), the Preamble of the Indian Constitution and the portraits of Gandhi and Ambedkar have ever been a common sight.

Every government in India invokes Gandhi's legacy when it launches a scheme for the poor and oppressed of the society or for the decentralization of state power. If the government's policy instead deals with India's unification (such as the abrogation of Article 370 in August 2019 to integrate the state of Jammu and Kashmir with the Union of India by ending its special powers), Patel becomes the favorite founding father of the government. Since the political party currently in power, the Bharatiya Janata Party, has the Congress Party as its chief rival, it conveniently forgets that the laws of preventive detention it is utilizing for hammering the insurgencies or those for curbing the freedom of speech were actually initially introduced by Nehru's government. Thus, it is a curious case of history where Nehru—who is otherwise vilified by many for every ill in India—is not receiving backlash for his failure because those oppressive laws are being used openly today. The political narrative shifts when the Congress Party is in power with Nehru taking the center stage other founding fathers are assigned to the background. Thus, the founding fathers' compromises are up for grabs too just like their achievements are.

We saw in this chapter how the founding fathers in both nations compromised on several accounts. The shortcomings arising from these compromises are not an exhaustive list but rather highlighted some glaring shortcomings that have a deep impact on these nations' contemporary fault lines. Just like it is impossible to praise the Constitution or the political history without crediting the founding fathers for the republic's founding, it is impossible to discuss the nation's shortcomings without making them share a part of the blame. The positioning of this chapter as the last in the book was done not to amplify the role of the founding fathers' successes but rather to place them in perspective as mere human beings. While the founding fathers are often idolized as demigods, their unfortunate compromises give us a moment to reflect on their legacy. But, how to holistically evaluate the legacy of the founding fathers?

Nobel Laureate Amartya Sen insists that 'any evaluative judgment has to be, in some sense, comparative.'[92] The question then arises is if we should compare the two founding generations discussed in this book with each other or should we look for such precedents from ancient history or should we wait for the future to show us more such examples of a remarkable generation founding a nation? This seems like a never-ending debate. But, perhaps we do not need to debate it at all and leave it to the wisdom of posterity (since they have become immortal in posterity's arena). It may well be that in posterity's report card, the founding fathers would receive many A+ grades followed by a few Ds. They were all too human after all.

---

[1] Jill Lepore, *These Truths: A History of the United States* (New York and London: W. W. Norton & Company, 2018), pp. 8-9

[2] Ibid., pp. 16-19

[3] R. B. Bernstein, *The Founding Fathers Reconsidered* (Oxford: Oxford University Press, 2009), pp. 22-24

[4] Mark Anthony Rolo, *Founding Fathers saw native people as 'savages,'* Great Falls Tribune, 8 July 2016

[5] Peter S. Onuf, *Jefferson's Empire: The Language of American Nationhood* (Charlottesville and London: University Press of Virginia, 2000), pp. 155-156

[6] Ibid., pp. 147-151

[7] Joseph J. Ellis, *American Sphinx: The Character of Thomas Jefferson* (New York: Vintage Books, 1998), pp. 79-80

[8] Robert G. Parkinson, *The Common Cause: Creating Race and Nation in the American Revolution* (Chapel Hill: University of North Carolina Press, 2016), pp. 637-639

[9] Richard Beeman, *Plain, Honest Men: The Making of the American Constitution* (New York: Random House, 2009), pp. 309-310

[10] Ron Chernow, *Alexander Hamilton* (Penguin Books, 2004), pp. 214-216

[11] Walter Isaacson, *Benjamin Franklin: An American Life* (New York: Simon and Schuster Paperbacks, 2004), pp. 464-466

[12] Ralph Ketcham, *James Madison: A Biography* (University of Virginia Press, 1990), p. 148

[13] Joseph J. Ellis, *The Quartet: Orchestrating the Second American Revolution 1783-1789* (New York: Alfred A. Knopf, 2015), p. 233

[14] Joseph J. Ellis, *Founding Brothers: The Revolutionary Generation* (New York: Vintage Books, 2002), p. 82

[15] Richard Beeman, *Plain, Honest Men: The Making of the American Constitution* (New York: Random House, 2009), pp. 333-334

[16] The Papers of Benjamin Franklin, vol. 4, July 1, 1750, through June 30, 1753, ed. Leonard W. Labaree. New Haven: Yale University Press, 1961, pp. 225–234

[17] John Adams, *The Works of John Adams*, Second President of the United States: with a Life of the Author, Notes and Illustrations, by his Grandson Charles Francis Adams (Boston: Little, Brown and Co., 1856). 10 volumes. Vol. 9, pp. 92-93

[18] The Papers of George Washington, Confederation Series, vol. 4, 2 April 1786 – 31 January 1787, ed. W. W. Abbot. Charlottesville: University Press of Virginia, 1995, pp. 15–17.
[19] Ron Chernow, *Washington: A Life* (New York: The Penguin Press, 2010), p. 758
[20] Ralph Ketcham, *James Madison: A Biography* (University of Virginia Press, 1990), pp. 625-626
[21] Peter S. Onuf, *Jefferson's Empire: The Language of American Nationhood* (Charlottesville and London: University Press of Virginia, 2000), pp. 148-150
[22] Paul Johnson, *A History of the American People* (Harper Perennial, 1997), p. 242
[23] Joseph J. Ellis, *American Dialogue: The Founders and Us* (New York: Alfred A. Knopf, 2018), pp. 26-29
[24] Joseph J. Ellis, *American Dialogue: The Founders and Us* (New York: Alfred A. Knopf, 2018), pp. 33-35
[25] Mike Lee, *Written Out of History: The Forgotten Founders Who Fought Big Government* (New York: Sentinel, 2017), pp. 68-70
[26] Benjamin Franklin, *The Autobiography of Benjamin Franklin* (New York: Barnes and Noble, 1994), p. 158
[27] The Papers of Benjamin Franklin, vol. 41, September 16, 1783, through February 29, 1784, ed. Ellen R. Cohn. New Haven and London: Yale University Press, 2014, pp. 412–423
[28] Mark Van Norman, *Founding Fathers Knew Indian Nations Are Sovereign,* Indian Country Today, 1 November 2014
[29] Robert G. Parkinson, *The Common Cause: Creating Race and Nation in the American Revolution* (Chapel Hill: University of North Carolina Press, 2016), pp. 271-272
[30] Ibid., pp. 658-659
[31] Joseph J. Ellis, *The Quartet: Orchestrating the Second American Revolution 1783-1789* (New York: Alfred A. Knopf, 2015), p. 237
[32] Michael I. Meyerson, *Endowed by Our Creator: The Birth of Religious Freedom in America* (New Haven and London: Yale University Press, 2012), p. 220
[33] Colin G. Calloway, *The Indian World of George Washington: The First President, The First Americans, And The Birth of the Nation* (New York: Oxford University Press, 2018), p. 7
[34] Mark Douglas McGarvie, *One Nation Under Law: America's Early National Struggles to Separate Church and State* (Northern Illinois University Press, 2004), pp. 59-60
[35] Joseph J. Ellis, *American Dialogue: The Founders and Us* (New York: Alfred A. Knopf, 2018), pp. 176-177
[36] Joseph J. Ellis, *American Dialogue: The Founders and Us* (New York: Alfred A. Knopf, 2018), pp. 185-186
[37] Ibid., pp. 188-191

[38] Gordon S. Wood, *Friends Divided: John Adams and Thomas Jefferson* (New York: Penguin Press, 2017), p. 370

[39] THE LOUISIANA PURCHASE TRANSCRIPTIONS TREATY BETWEEN THE UNITED STATES OF AMERICA AND THE FRENCH REPUBLIC, National Archives and Records Administration

[40] Joseph J. Ellis, *American Creation* (New York: Vintage Books, 2007), pp. 232-233

[41] Alexis de Tocqueville, *Democracy in America: The Complete and Unabridged Volumes I and II* (Bantam Classic Edition, 2000), p. 410

[42] Joseph J. Ellis, *American Dialogue: The Founders and Us* (New York: Alfred A. Knopf, 2018), p. 191

[43] Ramachandra Guha, *India after Gandhi: The History of the World's Largest Democracy* (Picador India, 2008), p. 384

[44] John Keay, *Midnight's Descendants: A History of South Asia since Partition* (New York: Basic Books, 2014), p. xvii

[45] Partha Chatterjee, *The Nation and its Fragments: Colonial and Postcolonial Histories* (New Jersey, Princeton University Press, 1993), p. 110

[46] Perry Anderson, *The Indian Ideology* (Gurgaon: Three Essays Collective, 2012), p. 56

[47] Hafeez Malik, *Moslem Nationalism in India and Pakistan* (Washington D. C.: Public Affairs Press, 1963), p. 288

[48] Rajmohan Gandhi, *Rajaji: A Life* (Penguin Books, 1997), pp. 239-240

[49] Dhananjay Keer, *Dr. Babasaheb Ambedkar: Life and Mission* (Popular Prakashan, Reprint May 2018), pp. 333-334

[50] B. R. Ambedkar, *Pakistan or Partition of India* (Bombay: Thacker and Company Limited, 1945), p. 335

[51] Rajmohan Gandhi, *Patel: A Life* (Ahmedabad: Navajivan Publishing House, 2017), p. 431

[52] Neerja Singh, *Patel, Prasad and Rajaji: Myth of the Indian Right* (New Delhi: Sage Publications, 2015), p. 86

[53] Ibid., p. 78

[54] Granville Austin, *The Indian Constitution: Cornerstone of a Nation* (Oxford: Clarendon Press, 1966), pp. 80-81

[55] S. Gopal, *Nehru and Minorities,* Economic and Political Weekly, vol. 23, No. 45/47, Nov 1988, pp. 2463+1465-2466

[56] Anand Ranganathan, *The Vanishing Hindus of Pakistan—a Demographic Study,* Newslaundry, 9 Jan 2015

[57] T. Brahmanandam and T. BosuBabu, *Educational status among the scheduled tribes: Issues and challenges,* Journal of Politics and Governance, 5(3), 2016, pp. 57-66

[58] *The Collected Works of Mahatma Gandhi (CWMG),* Vol. 75: October 11, 1941 – March 31, 1942, Notes on Adivasis, 9 Jan 1942, pp. 210-211

[59] Bina Kumari Sengar, *Gandhian Approach to Tribals,* Proceedings of the Indian History Congress, Vol. 62, 2001, pp. 627-636

[60] Vishal Pratap Singh Deo, *Ambedkar on Adivasis and Gandhi on Dalits,* Forward Press, 1 June 2017

[61] *Encyclopedia of Dalits in India* (Delhi: Kalpaz Publications, 2002), edited by Sanjay Paswan and Paramanshi Jaideva, vol. 3, p. 232

[62] Ramachandra Guha, *India after Gandhi: The History of the World's Largest Democracy* (Picador India, 2008), pp. 115-116

[63] Jaipal Singh's speech in the Constituent Assembly, 19 Dec 1946, *Constituent Assembly Debates: Official Report* (reprint New Delhi: Lok Sabha Secretariat, 2014), Vol. I, p. 143

[64] Debasree De, *Nehruvian Vision of Sustainable Development for Tribals in India: A Critique,* South Asia Research, 34(1), 1–18, 2014

[65] Ibid.

[66] Rajmohan Gandhi, *Understanding the Founding Fathers* (New Delhi: Aleph Book Company, 2016), p. 129

[67] M. V. Pylee, *Constitutional History of India, 1600-1950* (Bombay: Asia, 1967), p. v

[68] Granville Austin, *Working a Democratic Constitution: The Indian Experience* (Oxford University Press, 2000), pp. 40-42

[69] Ibid., pp. 43-47

[70] Donald Eugene Smith, *Nehru and Democracy: The Political Thought of an Asian Democrat* (Orient Longman, 1958), p. 88

[71] Ibid., p. 85

[72] Granville Austin, *Working a Democratic Constitution: The Indian Experience* (Oxford University Press, 2000), pp. 55-57

[73] Ibid., pp. 60-61

[74] David H. Bayley, *The Indian Experience with Preventive Detention,* Pacific Affairs, Vol. 35, No. 2, 1962, pp. 99-115

[75] M. K. Gandhi, *Hind Swaraj or Indian Home Rule* (Madras: G. A. Natesan & Co., 1921), pp. 95-97

[76] B. R. Ambedkar's speech in the Constituent Assembly, 4 Nov 1948, *Constituent Assembly Debates: Official Report* (reprint New Delhi: Lok Sabha Secretariat, 2014), Vol. VII, p. 39

[77] Surinder S. Jodhka, *Nation and Village: Images of Rural India in Gandhi, Nehru and Ambedkar,* Economic and Political Weekly, Vol. 37, No. 32, 2002, pp. 3343-3353

[78] *The Collected Works of Mahatma Gandhi (CWMG),* Vol. 85: July 16, 1946 – October 20, 1946, Independence, 21 July 1946, pp. 32-34

[79] *The Collected Works of Mahatma Gandhi (CWMG),* Vol. 73: September 12, 1940 - April 15, 1941, Interview to Francis G. Hickman, 17 September 1940, pp. 29-30

[80] Jawaharlal Nehru, *An Autobiography* (Gurgaon: Penguin Random House, 2004), p. 527

[81] Sugata Bose, *His Majesty's Opponent: Subhas Chandra Bose and India's Struggle Against Empire* (Penguin Books, 2013), pp. 145-146

[82] Ranajit Guha, *The Small Voice of History: Collected Essays* (Ranikhet: Permanent Black, 2009), p. 505

[83] Sudipta Kaviraj, *The Trajectories of the Indian State: Politics and Ideas* (Ranikhet: Permanent Black, Fifth Impression, 2017), pp. 116-117

[84] Sudipta Kaviraj, *The Imaginary Institution of India: Politics and Ideas* (New York: Columbia University Press, 2010), p. 25

[85] C. Rajagopalachari, *Rajaji Reader: Selections from Writings of C. Rajagopalachari* (Madras: Vyasa Publications, 1980), p. 105

[86] C. Rajagopalachari, published in *Swarajya* on 13 Feb 1960, *Satyam Eva Jayate* (Madras: Bharatan Publications), vol. 1, p. 502

[87] Jawaharlal Nehru, *Selected Works of Jawaharlal Nehru*, Volume 7, The Presidential Address, pp. 180-181

[88] Rajmohan Gandhi, *A Tale of Two Revolts: India's Mutiny and the American Civil War* (London: Haus Publishing, 2011), p. 306

[89] Excerpt taken from American National Archives, 1963

[90] Joseph J. Ellis, *American Dialogue: The Founders and Us* (New York: Alfred A. Knopf, 2018), p. 216

[91] Jawaharlal Nehru, *Selected Works of Jawaharlal Nehru*, Second Series - 3, A Tryst with Destiny, p. 136

[92] Amartya Sen, *Indian Development: Lessons and Non-Lessons*, Daedalus, Vol. 118, No. 4, Another India (Fall, 1989), p. 371

EPILOGUE

The Russian revolutionary Vladimir Lenin once remarked that there are decades where nothing happens, and there are weeks where decades happen. The ongoing epidemiological pandemic, COVID-19, has already emerged as an apt example of the latter part of Lenin's remark. In the past few weeks, nations across the world have witnessed alarming levels of unemployment (exacerbating economic inequality), political upheavals, social unrest, and policy paralysis. On top of all these, the COVID-19 pandemic has effectively caused the severest economic recession since the Great Depression (1929-33). In normal times, such disruptions may have happened in years but not so during the COVID-19 pandemic. Even the acceptance of various technologies like online learning, remote collaboration platforms, biomarkers-based surveillance, online shopping, etc. has increased manifold just in the past few weeks. In this sense, the COVID-19 pandemic is surely a catalyst for many social, technological, and political changes in the world.

The globalized, industrialized, and incessantly-driven economic world that we inhabit is similar to an amateur riding a bicycle. The moment she bears a shock, there is a genuine fear of her halting down and falling off the ridge. The COVID-19 pandemic is fast-emerging as the greatest shock of our times to the world economy. The unemployment rate in America until recently was the highest since the Great Depression while the pandemic has pushed back millions into poverty in India. The economic progress of the past many years has been wiped out in a matter of a few weeks. As of writing this, America and India respectively have the largest number of coronavirus positive cases in the whole world while the rate of deaths per million in America is among the highest in the world. Socioeconomic unrest that is evident in these nations because of the pandemic will shape these democracies in unimaginable ways. A stringent test awaits the various democratic institutions—originally established by the founding generations for their times—in these nations.

Take, for example, the 2020 United States presidential election. After everything we have read in this book, it is not difficult to visualize how the legacy of the American founding generation connects with the election. This is even without stating the obvious fact that the election was held under the auspices of the same constitution that was drafted by the American founding generation during the summer of 1787 in Philadelphia. First, the debates around economic and income inequality with the focus on the so-called "1 percent" surfaced at various times during the election especially because of the economic recession caused by the COVID-19 pandemic. Each candidate debated various policies to tackle this issue such as proportionally taxing the rich, breaking up multi-billion-dollar conglomerates, increasing the federal minimum wage, and instituting new social benefits schemes for the poor. These debates are just the 21st-century version of the debate between Adams and Jefferson about how to preclude the emergence of an American aristocracy as we saw in the Equality chapter. Adams's fear that an aristocracy would arise in America which unlike Europe would distinguish itself not by titles but by wealth has come true in our own "Second Gilded Age."

Second, another issue that dominated the election was the Black Lives Matter movement which gained a renewed vigor when the killing of George Floyd in May 2020 triggered widespread protests across the nation. Except in a few places where the protests turned violent, the protestors came out peacefully in large numbers to demand the realization of Jefferson's self-evident truth that all men are created equal. While they blamed the other party for fomenting the troubles, each side in the election affirmed that America was founded on this Jeffersonian principle and that if elected, they would carry out reforms like retraining police officers, reducing the wealth gap between the communities, and protecting ethnic minorities by instituting new laws. All of this bears a striking resemblance to the debate in the Minorities chapter of this book.

Third, President Donald Trump did not officially concede the election until mid-November 2020 (as of writing this) despite all independent institutions calling the election in the favor of Joe Biden.

Contrast this prevarication with the actions of the first president of the United States, George Washington, who had graciously chosen retirement after two terms in office (as we read in the Power chapter) and the second president, John Adams, who had conceded defeat in a very polarized election (as we read in the Opposition chapter) which led to the first peaceful transition of power in American democracy.

Fourth, the debate around what it means to be an American (as we read in the Nationalism chapter) resurfaced during the election around the immigration policy of the nation. The debate around whom to admit into the nation and whom not, who should be provided asylum, and who should be deported revolves around particular nationalities and religious groups today while during the founding era, these debates revolved around various ethnic, religious, and linguistic groups. The availability of Franklin's "American Dream" to prospective immigrants has always been debated but these polarizing times have seen it becoming a central issue in the presidential election.

Fifth, America's role in the international arena and especially its relationship with China in the post-COVID world naturally figured in the election debate. President Trump was a fierce advocate of American Isolationism. He withdrew America from the Paris Agreement on climate change and had moved to withdraw the U.S. from the World Health Organization (WHO). On the other hand, President-elect Joe Biden has pledged for a larger American presence in world affairs. This wrangling may seem to be new to us but the founding fathers were already debating the same during the war between Britain and France in the 1790s (as we read in the Opposition chapter). For more than a century after the founding era, until the Second World War, America followed the policy of isolationism propounded by Washington during his presidency and in his Farewell Address. In the globalized world of ours, the debate between Trump and Biden seems to be between Washington's vision of American exceptionalism established on isolationism and Franklin Roosevelt's American exceptionalism built on interventionism. Editorials in newspapers from both sides of the argument bear a striking resemblance with the pieces that were published by Hamilton and Madison during the furor caused by the Jay's Treaty.

Henry Kissinger has written in his book *World Order* that '[L]ike America's Founding Fathers, India's early leaders equated the national interest with moral rectitude....India presented the vindication of its own national interest as a uniquely enlightened enterprise—much as America had nearly two centuries earlier.'[1] As we have seen in this book, there are so many parallels in the trajectories followed by the two nations that one can scarcely exhaust the examples. To draw parallels in our present times, just like we did above through the example of the 2020 United States Presidential Election, let us briefly look at two recent events in India. These events fomented debates with motivation and roots in the founding era.

First, on August 5, 2019, the Government of India revoked the special status provided to the state of Jammu and Kashmir under Article 370 of the Indian Constitution. The causes, effects, and geopolitics behind this move are out of the scope of this book but what is interesting to mention here is how the ruling party and the opposition both cited the founding fathers to justify their own position. The Home Minister of India, Amit Shah, proclaimed that the government's move 'fulfilled Sardar Patel's incomplete dream.'[2] From the other side, parliamentarian Kapil Sibal had charged at the government saying: 'Sardar Patel introduced Article 370 and when discussions were happening, he was willing to let Kashmir go to Pakistan [rather than become a part of India in the first place].'[3] Clearly, the two statements are fundamentally contradictory and as is usually the case, the truth was rather complex. Yet, many historians with various ideological persuasions wrote scores of articles to support or criticize either side, bringing Patel, Nehru, and Ambedkar into the debates. More than seven decades after Independence, validation from the founding fathers is still very necessary to bolster one's ideological position.

Second, in December 2019, the Government of India passed the Citizenship Amendment Act (CAA) that triggered widespread protests across the nation. By enacting the new law, the government provided citizenship to all those persecuted in the neighboring nations except Muslims. This provoked many groups into expressing the sentiment that since the Indian Constitution does not distinguish between different religions, the law is discriminating on the basis of religion. The protestors widely used Gandhi's and Ambedkar's portraits along with copies of the Indian Constitution as symbols of their dissent. While Gandhi's portraits signified the Hindu-Muslim unity for which he gave up his life, Ambedkar's portraits symbolized the secular ethos of the Indian Constitution since he was the chief draftsman of the same. The government rebutted with claims like had Patel been elected as the first prime minister of India rather than Nehru, many of the problems India is facing today within the nation and in its neighborhood would not have arisen. Clearly, no major debate takes place in India even on the policy issues of our times without referring to the successes and failings of the founding fathers.

Nonetheless, it is important to mention here that the lessons from the founding times cannot be directly applied to today since we live in a world that the founding fathers could not ever have imagined. The laws and conventions of those times cannot be transplanted to ours. Nor is it possible for any generation to institute universal laws that would apply to all future generations since society's norms change with time. As Jefferson once evocatively wrote, 'we may consider each generation as a distinct nation with a right, by the will of it's majority, to bind themselves, but none to bind the succeeding generation, more than the inhabitants of another country.'[4] During the drafting of the Indian Constitution, Ambedkar endorsed Jefferson's above remark and admitted 'that what Jefferson has said is not merely true, but is absolutely true.'[5] Despite this caveat, understanding the origins of our present democratic institutions and the debates from the founding era are crucial for appreciating how we reached where we stand today.

The journey that we undertook in this book took us through two different historical eras during which we traveled to two plural democratic nations situated at the opposite ends of the globe. In our expedition, we met twelve historical figures and witnessed many key events that shaped these two democracies. To end this journey, let us ponder over a single question: what is that one chief characteristic of the two founding generations that made them so successful in their times and their legacy so impactful in ours? The answer to this question may be our greatest learning from the thoughts and actions of the two founding generations. Perhaps utilizing the answer to this question, we will also be able to concentrate better on our efforts as citizens toward bolstering the foundations of our democratic institutions.

The answer to the above question may be different for each one of us. For me, the answer lies in a thought that I often had while writing this book—that the book's title should be "Investigating the Debates between the Founding Fathers." I believe that the various debates that the members of the two founding generations conducted amongst each other were the supreme source of the success of the two great democratic experiments—America and India. In my view, constant disagreements and the will to resolve them by debating made each founding generation much more than the sum of its constituent founding fathers.

More than two millennia ago, the Greek philosopher Heraclitus of Ephesus wrote 'Opposition brings concord: Out of discord comes the fairest harmony.'[6] It is easy to see how the many debates between the founding fathers that we read about in this book led to the establishment of robust democratic institutions and practices. Had Jefferson and Madison not debated with each other about how best to protect the religious minorities, the Virginia Statute for Religious Freedom and the Bill of Rights would not have come into existence as we know them. Had Ambedkar and Gandhi not disagreed and fiercely debated with each other, it would not have been possible to mobilize the Untouchables from the bottom and reform the Hindu society from above. Had Jefferson and Hamilton not debated the economic and foreign policies within the structure of the U.S. Constitution, the emergence of political parties and a democratic opposition would not have happened. The same goes for the debates between Nehru and Rajaji in India.

The founding fathers could also debate by their actions and not just by words. Washington showed his unwavering belief in the primacy of civilian rule over authoritarianism by resigning after the Revolutionary War ended when Americans were wondering if he should be installed as the king. Similarly, Gandhi utilized all his moral power and gave up his life for Hindu-Muslim unity to achieve peace in the subcontinent when these two communities were displaying by rioting that they really constituted two nations. Franklin and other founding fathers transformed themselves to visualize the inhabitants of all colonies as Americans rather than subjects of the British Empire divided by various religious denominations. This led to the creation of a Pan-American nationalism. Similarly, through his Indian National Army, Bose realized the vision of a plural India in which Indians belonging to all religious, caste, and linguistic groups shared a common idea of Indian Nationalism subsuming their individual (often) conflicting sociological identities.

The flip side of this coin is that the absence of debates between the American founding fathers on the issues of slavery and peaceful assimilation of the Native Americans led to unsaid compromises. These compromises proved highly detrimental not just for African Americans and Native Americans but also for the democratic fiber of the American society. In the same vein, the absence of debates among the Indian founding fathers about Partition, Tribals, and post-Independence economic policies led to a lot of misery whose effects are still manifest in the Indian society. We read about these in detail in the Compromises chapter.

A necessary condition for the peaceful resolution of debates is that both parties should have an accommodative spirit. This democratic spirit of accommodation cannot be enforced by force on people. As Gandhi had once remarked, 'The spirit of democracy cannot be imposed from without. It has to come from within.'[7] This spirit was repeatedly displayed by Washington as president by not ruthlessly crushing the Jeffersonians (which he was very capable of doing) or treating any political group harshly like his European counterparts did. Similarly, Nehru exercised this democratic spirit as prime minister by stimulating and promoting debates in the parliament. He made it a point to regularly attend the parliament and answer the opposition's questions no matter how low was the electoral strength of the political parties opposed to him.

Washington, Gandhi, Jefferson, Nehru, Franklin, Rajaji, and others are like the central characters of a great novel whose story is continually unfolding at opposite sides of the world. That the story of this novel will soon come to an abrupt end has ever been predicted by scholars. This novel may have some unpleasant twists and turns, but if anything, it has become even more engaging with time i.e. these democracies have thrived. The story that the present protagonists of the novel—us—write on the world stage is still dictated by the rules set by the central characters of the novel. Despite being dead for long, the two founding generations cast a long shadow over our thinking and style, poetry and prose, ideas and ideals.

America and India remain the two largest and most plural democracies of the world. Various geopolitical considerations are today bringing them together as never before in the pursuit of freedom and liberty. These democracies thrive on loud (sometimes too loud) debates between various diverse sociological groups. The peaceful co-existence of many diverse groups with socioeconomic advancement is a "Promise of Pluralism" each generation makes to the next in these democracies. The founding generations of America and India were the first to codify this promise in the constitutions of these nations. These constitutions have evolved from just being parchment records to become living embodiments of the mindboggling diversities of these two democracies.

At the start of this book, we noted how these democracies do not fit into the traditional definition of the word *nation*. The COVID-19 pandemic is another test of the democratic institutions of these "anomalous" nations and of the "Promise of Pluralism" manifest in their democratic institutions. The success of these democracies in combating the various detrimental effects of the COVID-19 pandemic will predominantly depend on the peaceful resolution of disagreements between affected groups. As long as the "Promise of Pluralism" will remain accessible to every citizen and debates will continue with an accommodating spirit, these democracies will prosper. The 18th century Urdu poet Mohammad Ibrahim "Zauq" who was a contemporary of that other great Urdu poet "Ghalib" has written:

> Gul hain rang rang se hai raunaq-e-chaman
> Ae 'zauq' is chaman ko hai zeb ikhtilāf se
> [Flowers of diverse colors form the garden's splendor
> This garden's beauty springs from such disagreements]

---

[1] Henry Kissinger, *World Order: Reflections on the Character of Nations and the Course of History* (New York: Penguin Books, 2014), Ch. 5

[2] Amit Shah: Article 370 move fulfilled Sardar Vallabhbhai Patel's dream, *Indian Express*, November 1, 2019

[3] Sardar Patel Wanted Kashmir to Go to Pakistan, Says Congress MP Kapil Sibal, *News18,* August 5, 2019
[4] From Thomas Jefferson to John Wayles Eppes, 24 June 1813, *The Papers of Thomas Jefferson, Retirement Series*, vol. 6, 11 March to 27 November 1813, ed. J. Jefferson Looney. Princeton: Princeton University Press, 2009, pp. 220–226
[5] Ambedkar in the Constituent Assembly, 25 November 1949, *Constituent Assembly Debates: Official Report* (reprint New Delhi: Lok Sabha Secretariat, 2014), Vol. XI, p. 976
[6] Paul Hague, *Revealing the Hidden Harmony,* 2015
[7] *The Collected Works of Mahatma Gandhi (CWMG)*, Vol. 59: September 16, 1934 – December 15, 1934, Statement to the Press, 17 September 1934, p. 13

ACKNOWLEDGMENTS

To thoroughly study the complete works of all twelve political leaders portrayed in this book would have taken many years. Unfortunately, being enrolled as a full-time doctoral student in an absolutely different research field did not provide me the luxury of doing so. Consequently, to study the two founding generations and their times, I chiefly relied on the books and research papers published by various scholars. Nevertheless, I delved deep into the personal writings of the two founding generations for a selected set of themes relevant to the book. Standing on the shoulders of giants, foremost I am thankful to the authors of the cited works and the many editors of the founding generations' personal writings, without whose hard work this book would not have been written in the first place.

This book would not have come to its present form without the hard work and perseverance of my editor Sumedha Kshirsagar. Her illuminating insights, perceptive feedback, and positive attitude refined the original manuscript in innumerable ways. Draft after draft, she provided valuable comments that helped me in making the manuscript readable for a wide range of audiences. Performing the role of an editor to perfection, she constantly provided me suggestions about everything from arranging the material, replacing archaic words, and re-thinking about chapters' themes to footnotes, indexing, and cover design.

Conducting research for this book provided me the valuable opportunity of meeting and conversing with many historians, authors, and academicians. Their feedback helped me in re-thinking different aspects of the book from the chapters' themes to particular sentences. Foremost, I am thankful to Sugata Bose and Ramachandra Guha for their time, encouragement, and positive criticism. It is a testament to their generosity that they encouraged a young scholar like me despite the fact that History is not my formal area of research. Similarly, I am also indebted to Nico Slate, Rajmohan Gandhi, Sunil Khilnani, Vikram Raghavan, Ashok Swain, and Steven Cassedy for motivating me, directing me to various references, and providing comments on the manuscript. This book would not have seen the light of day if not for these wonderful scholars whose words of encouragement renewed my will and confidence in myself. Additionally, I am grateful to Rohit De, Kamala Visweswaran, and V. K. Jain for pointing me to many useful references.

I am also very thankful to Roger Bingham for continuously showing trust in me and supporting my endeavors in many ways. His magnanimity, resourcefulness, and kindness are testified by everyone who has ever come in contact with him and I was thus very fortunate to continuously have his staunch support. I am also grateful to my dear friend, Sabareesh Ramachandran, who not only provided detailed and highly beneficial feedback on the manuscript but who also enlightened me many times during our conversations.

Last but not the least, I am heavily indebted to Reshma Shinde who showed remarkable ingenuity and creativity in designing the book's cover. Iteration after iteration, I witnessed her visionary ideas which kept on making the cover more appealing in every way imaginable.

This book could not have been written while pursuing doctoral studies in engineering (albeit during the daytime) without the support of my doctoral advisers—Tzyy-Ping Jung, Terry Sejnowski, and Mohan Trivedi. I thank them for reposing faith in my abilities despite this book being unrelated to my doctoral research. Short of money as a graduate student, I also thank the University of California San Diego Geisel Library, University of Washington Suzallo and Allen Libraries, and Nehru Memorial Museum and Library for freely providing me many resources required to work on the manuscript. Additionally, I extend my gratitude to those two wonderful used books' websites—AbeBooks and ThriftBooks—without which I would not have ever conceived of writing a book.

Lest I forget to mention, above people and institutions deserve all the praise that the book may gather while any faults and errors are entirely mine.

ABOUT THE AUTHOR

Siddharth is a Seattle-based writer and this is his first book. He is presently working as a User Research Specialist in the Human Factors Engineering Lab at Microsoft USA. He obtained his Ph.D. from the University of California San Diego (UC San Diego) in June 2020 majoring in Intelligent Systems, Robotics, and Control.

At UC San Diego, Siddharth served as the Graduate Fellow Editor of the Prospect Journal of International Affairs and a Graduate Student Member of the South Asia Initiative. A long-term goal of his reading and writing is to understand the factors leading to the rise and fall of various human institutions like Nations, Religions, Companies, etc.

Apart from his formal research in engineering, Siddharth took out time during his doctoral studies to conduct research on the parallels in the origins of American and Indian democracies. The choice of this book's theme was motivated by his reading and personal experiences in America and India. He intends to write more on related topics in the future.

 @SidSapien

 ssiddharth@ucsd.edu

 https://ssiddharth.in

www.ingramcontent.com/pod-product-compliance
Lightning Source LLC
Chambersburg PA
CBHW070045080526
44586CB00013B/913